MIXING RACE, MIXING CULTURE

MIXING RACE,
MIXING CULTURE

Inter-American
Literary Dialogues

Edited by Monika Kaup and Debra J. Rosenthal

UNIVERSITY OF TEXAS PRESS, AUSTIN

Chapter 2 previously appeared in *Proceed with Caution* by Doris Summer (Cambridge, Mass: Harvard University Press, copyright 1999 by the President and Fellows of Harvard College). Reprinted with permission.

Portions of Chapter 4 first appeared in *Emergences: Journal for the Study of Media and Composite Cultures* (May 2000). Reprinted with permission.

Chapter 9 previously appeared in *American Literature*, 70:1 (March 1998): 153–176. Copyright 1998, Duke University Press. All rights reserved. Reprinted with permission.

The quoted material on pages 171–173 is from the poem *Scene from the Movie Giant*, copyright 1993 by Tino Villanueva. Reprinted with permission of Curbstone Press. Distributed by Consortium.

The poem "Crow" first appeared in *Emplumada* by Lorna Dee Cervantes, copyright 1981. Reprinted with permission of the University of Pennsylvania Press.

Library of Congress Cataloging-in-Publication Data

Mixing race, mixing culture : inter-American literary dialogues / edited by Monika Kaup and Debra J. Rosenthal.
    p.   cm.
Includes bibliographical references and index.
ISBN 0-292-74346-7 — ISBN 0-292-74348-3 (pbk.)
1. American literature—20th century—History and criticism.
2. Miscegenation in literature. 3. Latin American literature—20th century—History and criticism. 4. Literature, Comparative—American and Latin American. 5. Literature, Comparative—Latin American and American. 6. America—Literatures—History and criticism. 7. Pluralism (Social sciences) in literature. 8. Intercultural communication in literature. 9. Racially mixed people in literature. 10. Passing (Identity) in literature. I. Kaup, Monika. II. Rosenthal, Debra J., 1964–
PS228.M57 M59 2002
810.9'355—dc21   2002000646

CONTENTS

Illustrations

Acknowledgments

One of the pleasures of working on a multi-authored project is that we have the opportunity to acknowledge the beneficence of many people. Early inspiration and encouragement, critical for the existence of this volume, came from Linda Hutcheon and Mario Valdés, who believed in the importance of such a collection.

Much of the work on this volume was made possible by the generosity of John Carroll University and the College of William and Mary. John Carroll University provided two summer research fellowships, as well as personal and intellectual encouragement from Jeanne Colleran, Anna Hocevar, Maryclaire Moroney, and Brenda Wirkus. The College of William and Mary generously provided support through a summer research grant.

Ideas in the essays and ideas for the essays in this volume benefited from discussions with Martha Cutter, Susan Gillman, Carolyn Sorisio, Glenn Starkman, and Robert Mugerauer.

We are extremely grateful to Theresa May, Rachel Chance, and Lynne Chapman for their patience and enthusiasm during the publication process.

INTRODUCTION

Monika Kaup and Debra J. Rosenthal

This collection takes up the challenge of transforming American literary and cultural studies into a comparative discipline by examining the
dynamics of racial and cultural mixture and its opposite tendency, racial
and cultural disjunction, in literatures of the Americas. Our project addresses a pervasive theme in New World literature, the issue of "miscegenation," attendant fears and hopes concerning the mixing of races,
and the legacy of cultural hybridization and fusion. Our theme is framed
within the method of hemispheric New World Studies, which compares
the treatment of racial and cultural mixture in distinct regional, ethnic, and
national literatures of the Americas. Our hope is to make visible the intricate processes of cultural and racial interaction in racial consciousness and
identity in the Americas, which have been obscured by the dominant oppositional thinking that undergirds both ethnic studies and the nationalist
frameworks of American and Latin American Studies. Further, in break-
ing down the walls between American and Latin American Studies and by
building bridges between disciplines isolated by their nationalist focus, our
transnational method complements its transcultural object of study.

From their various angles, the essays in this collection[1] together chart
an alternative map of the Americas which undoes the dominant linear genealogies of racial and national purity, displaying a decentered web of lines
and crossings, points of encounter and fusion across boundaries. *Mixing
Race, Mixing Culture: Inter-American Literary Dialogues* remaps the Americas as a multicultural and multiracial hemisphere, constituted through hybrid narrative geographies. It charts a transracial Other America, in José
Martí's sense, from between the cracks of the dominant cultural map of the
Americas. By focusing on racial and cultural mixture, the essays also show
that the Other America can be Other than nation, Other than national
literature, Other than regionalism, Other than regional literature. The
Americas can be rezoned as a hemispheric entity, challenging conceptions
of national and regional identity, with a common history of colonialism,

slavery, racism, and, most important to this volume, racial and cultural hybridity.

This collection also fills an absence—to date, there is no publication that examines race mixture in a hemispheric context. While many scholars have published studies about race in the U.S. or the Americas, this is the first collection to focus extensively on the mixing of races.[2] At the same time, it joins efforts to construct alternative plural studies of American literatures that emerged in the late 1980s and have been gathering force ever since.[3] While we understand that there is no calcified pan-American aesthetic and that it would be naïve to claim a unified hemispheric identity, the essays nonetheless demonstrate the commonality of racial hybridity to the North and South.

Why study race mixture and cultural crossings in the literature of the Americas and devote a whole book to it? The experience of "miscegenation," as Earl Fitz points out in his contribution to this volume, lies "at the heart of the entire American experience" (Fitz 244). Race mixture, Fitz continues, long interpreted too narrowly as a question of biology, is a process that extends into the realm of culture, where it has had its most powerful impacts, affecting all areas of human lives and worlds. The cultural repercussions of race mixture require us to examine this theme: that cultural meanings, metaphors, and negative and positive charges attributed to the union of races, rather than "race mixture" taken as a question in human biology, constitute our real subject.

In his study, *Hybrid Cultures: Strategies for Entering and Leaving Modernity*, an investigation of hybridity in the Latin American context, Néstor García Canclini makes a point of this need to advance analysis "from blood to culture." According to García Canclini, race mixture in Latin America needs to appear in the larger context of cultural and "multitemporal heterogeneity" (García Canclini 3), for the mixture of the indigenous and the European is inseparable from parallel contacts between tradition and modernity and popular and elite culture.[4] "In Latin America, where traditions have not yet disappeared and modernity has not completely arrived," writes García Canclini, and "the cultured, the popular, and the mass-based are not where we are used to finding [them, it] is necessary to deconstruct that division and verify [its] *hybridization*" (García Canclini 1, 2). García Canclini's investigation of Latin American hybridity as a question of uneven "development" or modernization is an important contribution to hemispheric New World Studies, precisely because it would be helpful for similar analyses in the North American context where academics typically overlook such features. According to García Canclini, to limit the question of hybridity to human biology of "blood" is to bypass Latin America's "intercultural hybridization" (207) at the level of a postmodern heterogeneity of modern and premodern cultural forms. García Canclini's idea of mapping Latin America's hybrid cultures by way of "entering" and "leaving" its heterogeneous network at multiple points (rather than constructing a linear narrative of beginning, middle, and end) is very similar to the way this collection is conceived—as probing distinct clusters of problematics that interconnect in multiple ways.

Multiculturalism is crucial to the Americas. The cultural identity of migrants to the Americas is not so much defined by their unique place of origin as it is by multiculturalism. Constituted by (im)migration and the transplantation and superimposition of European, African, and Asian cultures onto indigenous American cultures, culture is as hybrid in the Americas as anywhere else in the world. Previous literary and cultural studies of the Americas, working within the national framework, have tended to understand migrant lineage in the Americas in terms of the need to trace the American scion back to the European, African, or Asian root. Yet in the attempt to understand American identity through a return to an ancestral "elsewhere"—to the native land, to transoceanic origins—a unique pattern of culture in the Americas has been overlooked. The mixing of races and meeting of cultures in the New World represents a new beginning, constituted in this second birth in the here and now of a new place. As Pérez Firmat notes in his introduction to the collection *Do the Americas Have a Common Literature?*, "the Americas' cultural indebtedness to Europe is but one feature that the literatures of the New World have in common. And not enough has been said about this commonality, about the intersections and tangencies among diverse literatures of the New World considered apart from their extrahemispheric antecedents and analogues" (Pérez Firmat 2–3). To trace American cultures back to their transoceanic sources is to ignore their new beginnings, their mestizo, mulatto, or métis rebirths in the American hemisphere.

Mixing Race, Mixing Culture: Inter-American Literary Dialogues marks the transition from tracing singular lineages between the American cultures as offspring of one particular extrahemispheric parent to seeing what emerges in the encounter and clash of cultures once they have arrived. To take New World studies seriously, we need to recognize and study a problem unique to the Americas—the multicultural and multiracial mixture of distinct extrahemispheric lineages. It entails delegitimizing the au-

thority of pure cultural origins and legitimizing the bastard syncretic cre-
ations born of American interbreeding. For the Caribbean in particular,
as Michael Dash points out in his study, *The Other America: Caribbean
Literature in a New World Context*, the focus on hybridity and cultural
interchanges is essential (Dash 3–5). The Caribbean is paradigmatically
syncretic; transculturation is what the Caribbean is all about—for the purposes of this collection, Caribbean hybridity is a miniature prototype of
the mixed-race Americas.

The shift from immigrant origins to cultural crossroads, from pure-
blood lineage to mixed-blood Americas parallels another critical reorienta-
tion central to this volume. In North America, as elsewhere in the Americas, national literature and nationalist criticism has pursued the question
of how European immigrants become Americans or Canadians. How to
claim legitimacy as "native" Americans in a nation of immigrants? How
can a nation of settlers become native to its national territory? As Leslie
Fiedler, Terry Goldie, and others have pointed out, a strong link exists
between cultural and literary nationalism and the figure of the indigene,
the Native. Idealized portrayals of Indians are a staple of white nationalist writing in the Americas, as the essays by Priscilla Archibald and Debra
Rosenthal show. The important question hinges on telling what kind of
kinship is constructed between Native and white. Is it a relation of blood,
a relation of love, biological family kinship, or spiritual friendship? Indeed, the encounter between indigenous peoples and white immigrants
and settlers represents one of the main cultural stages of interracial encounters and cultural crossbreeding in the Americas. The Indian-white
contact zone is one of the major field sites in the geography of a transracial Other America, which this collection aims to chart and which is the
focal subject of the section entitled "Indigenization, Miscegenation, and
Nationalism."

The setting of the meeting-ground between Indian and white could
not be anywhere but America. Its cultural interactions are sedimented in
identity changes (or hybridization) on the part of both partners in the exchange. Importantly, though, this dialogic contamination is asymmetrical, not parallel. In the white literary imagination, the encounter between
idealized Native and white is constructed so as to enable the European immigrant to become native—to become an American, Canadian, Peruvian
like the Indian. The whole point, in other words, is cultural appropriation of indigenous identity by whites. As both Archibald and Rosenthal
show, that is why in nationalist literature we find that, paradoxically, the

symptom of the "Vanishing American" accompanies the process of "Becoming American." Real Natives are donors of native identity whose recipient is the nationalist constituency, the "new" native Americans. Real Indians disappear so that immigrants can adopt their cultural heritage as "native" Americans. So far, this is a familiar story, canonized in American Studies. Witness, for instance, Leslie Fiedler's discussion of the American Western in *The Return of the Vanishing American:*

> The Western story ... is ... a fiction dealing with the confrontation in the wilderness of a transplanted WASP and a racially alien other, an Indian— leading either to a metamorphosis of the WASP into something neither White nor Red (sometimes by adoption, sometimes by sheer emulation, but *never* by actual miscegenation), or else to the annihilation of the Indian .... [T]he ultimate Westerner ceases to be White at all and turns back into the Indian, his boots becoming moccasins, ... he has fallen ... out of the Europeanized West, into an aboriginal and archaic America (Fiedler 24–25).

In *Fear and Temptation: The Image of the Indigene in Canadian, Australian, and New Zealand Literatures,* Terry Goldie discusses the representation of indigenous peoples by white settlers as "indigenization": "In their need to become 'native,' to belong here, whites in Canada, New Zealand, and Australia have adopted a process which I have termed 'indigenization'" (Goldie 13). The difference between Fiedler's classic analysis and Goldie's ideological critique of Indian mythology in white fiction is that Goldie identifies the reality of semiotic colonialism underneath the mythical metamorphosis of whites into "aboriginal" Americans described by Fiedler. Yet both Fiedler's classic American Studies approach and Goldie's postcolonial critique of this position remain caught within a binary mode (white vs. Indian), which cannot adequately recognize a third dynamic, the process of hybrid crossing. To view the imaginary kinship of whites with Natives merely in terms of appropriation, as Goldie would have it, is to overlook that the process of imaginary projection as native American is more than semiotic kidnapping to empower Euro-Americans (whom Goldie assumes remain essentially unchanged).

The goal of this collection is to remind readers that the mythological transformation of immigrants into native Americans is more than the transplantation of a changeless Eurocentric culture from one place to another. If the white nationalist imagination appropriates indigenous identity, the conquest also cuts both ways: "indigenization" hybridizes the European agent. Tellingly, Fiedler's comments are rife with the language

of "breeding": speaking of Cooper's Natty Bumppo, Fiedler calls him the
"first . . . of those Americans reborn in their encounter with the Indian
on his own home grounds, which is to say, born again out of a union between men. Though he has, as he likes to boast over and over, 'no cross in
my blood,' no taint of miscegenation in his begetting, he is neither a white
man nor a Red, but something new under the sun . . ." (Fiedler 117–118).
The object of this collection is to reread Fiedler's comments not through
the lens of a postcolonial analysis of power and resistance, but as a description of a moment in the genesis of the Other America, the transcultural, hybrid America. Both alluding to and rejecting the idea of a biological union between Indian and white, Fiedler invokes the discourse of
"unnatural" breeding—between the races, without taint of blood, and yet
without doubt "fertile" (a "begetting") in its lasting transformation of the
identity of the white counterpart in crossing with the indigene. The figure
of a newborn American, brainchild of the white nationalist imagination,
neither can be reduced to a Eurocentric figure nor is it a pure-blood descendant of Europe's mythological lineage. We hope that this collection
can show that, in indigenizing the white settler who wants to belong to the
land like a native, the nationalist imaginary breeds a hybrid identity.

Nationalist indigenization, a cross-cultural formation, is indigenous to
the Americas *in another way:*[5] indigenous not in the biological sense in
which indigenous peoples have aboriginal ancestry (to assert this would
be in bad faith; it would also be to essentialize, literalize, and naturalize
what, as Fiedler playfully suggests, is artifice, an unnatural signification on
aboriginality). Hybrid culturally, white nationalist nativism is indigenous
to the Americas because that is where it is "begotten," as a cross-cultural
formation whose semiotic emergence nationalist writing conveys in the
language of biology to stress the authority that it should rightfully carry,
founding, as it does, a new origin and a new cultural inheritance of belonging to the Americas.

Generalizing from what has just been said, and taking up our initial
comment on the comparativist methodology of this book, it is clear that
our theme of cultural "miscegenation" goes beyond nationalist concepts
of culture that underlie the traditional framework of American and Latin
American studies. Hybridization suggests a nonexclusive, plural, dialogic,
or multicultural model of culture. As with the example of imaginary indigenization we have just discussed in detail, the essays in this collection do
not address themselves to distinctions between authenticity and contamination, purity and appropriation. Instead, our goal is to show how transna-

tional and transcultural currents generate new multicultural formations, whose legitimacy as American cultures derives not from any transplantation of a pure extrahemispheric lineage, but from (ongoing) dynamics of cultural creation.

Any collection on "miscegenation" and cultural hybridity needs to address the question of terminology. Among the wide variety of terms used in essays in this collection—hybridity, miscegenation, race mixture, amalgamation, cultural fusion, transculturation, creolization, *métissage, mestizaje,* mixedblood, etc.—the most important distinction is that between "blood" and culture, or "crossbreeding" in a biological and a cultural sense. Some terms, like mixedblood, miscegenation, or amalgamation, evoke the biological union of different races; others, like creolization, *métissage* and *mestizaje,* hybridity, and transculturation, are used to refer to the mixing of cultures in cross-cultural formations. While other scholars pay a great deal of attention to the social constitution of these concepts, our interest in this collection is not in the etymological and scientific history of these terms. Rather, following what Robert Young points out, we want to acknowledge that even those terms that today we take to evoke cultural formations, such as hybridity, are deeply embroiled in nineteenth-century racial ideology. A nineteenth-century word whose origins in the essentializing biology of human races has been forgotten in late twentieth-century cultural criticism, "[h]ybridity in particular," Young reminds us, "shows the connections between the racial categories of the past and contemporary cultural discourse" (Young 27).

Because the issues Young raises have both historical and epistemological dimensions, this collection leads off with an essay by Werner Sollors entitled, "Can Rabbits Have Interracial Sex?" Perhaps the most important historical point (we discuss the epistemological issue later in the introduction) is seen in Sollors' rejoinder to Young about the forgotten roots of hybridity in nineteenth-century debates about race in terms of biological "species." If, as the racist position argued, whites and blacks belonged to different human species (the polygenists' position), then intermarriage could legitimately be prohibited as "unnatural mongrelization." If on the other hand all humans, regardless of race, constitute a single species, then interracial crossings and amalgamation would lose their stigma (the monogenists' position).[6] Sollors' essay discusses a controversy over "miscegenation" that erupted in the U.S. South in 1958 after the publication of Garth Williams' *The Rabbits' Wedding,* a children's book and an innocuous animal fable about a black and a white rabbit who get married and start a family. "*The Rabbits' Wedding*," reports Sollors, "was thus publicly themed as a dangerous text promoting racial integration" (Sollors 59). That segregationists made a connection between rabbits and humans with respect to "breeding" serves as a pertinent reminder that "the racial categories of the past," as Young points out, remain residual in "contemporary cultural discourse" (Young 27).

Given the close links between race and culture, however, readers need not be reminded that historical differences exist between the way the Hispanophone and Francophone Americas on the one hand and Anglophone America on the other have treated other races and their cultures. U.S. removal and exclusionary practices in relation to Amerindians and blacks are in stark contrast to Latin America's subordinate inclusion of non-European races.[7] Consequently, our project of re-visioning the Americas through the lens of its multicultural formations imports an analytical and social pattern to U.S. studies that is more native to Latin America and the Caribbean than to the U.S. Indeed, a main purpose of our hemispheric comparativism is to affirm cultural realities that also are prevalent in the U.S. Our goal is to bring to light the hidden mixed-race history of the U.S. and help create a public discourse about race mixture and multiculturalism that ends its denial as an all-American reality.

As noted at the outset, this collection situates itself among other hemispheric and comparative studies of literature of the Americas. The collection thus asks about shared cultural and literary patterns in the New World. The real question, however, is what kind of kinships, continuities, or dialogues (established by which agents) exist among the diverse literatures of North America, Latin America, and the Caribbean. In his introduction to the sophisticated collection *Do the Americas Have a Common Literature?*, Gustavo Pérez Firmat lists four kinds of comparative methods, "which can be labeled *generic, genetic, appositional,* and *mediative*" (Pérez Firmat 3). The connections range among extreme looseness and existing trans-American literary genealogies, from the "appositional" method of side-by-side juxtaposition of texts to tracing "genetic" connection (that is, of documented influence) between authors and texts.

The need to construct bridges through creative criticism, given the scarcity of documented kinships, shows us how much inter-American comparisons remain a discipline-in-progress. To a large extent, its object becomes visible through gradual and imaginative formulations of its methods. At the same time, our theme, race and cultural mixture, belongs to Pérez Firmat's first category (the generic), defined as transnational concepts of "wide applicability" in the hemispheric context (3).[8] Race mixture is an all-American phenomenon, but its discrete regional and national instances do not stem from one single origin. Thus, our theme is situated between the "appositional" and the "genetic," or halfway between constituting a set of concepts that belong to the same literary/cultural inter-American "blood" family and a dialogue between foreign languages. In short, in inter-American criticism, race and cultural mixture occupies a hybrid position between difference and sameness—indeed, a mirror image of itself.

In contrast to José David Saldívar's terminological choice in *The Dialectics of Our America*, we prefer the notion of "dialogics" to "dialectics" as a methodological umbrella term for our multicultural and pan-American project. Dialectics stresses the antithetical posture of countering, or, as Saldívar writes, "redirects the Eurocentric focus of earlier scholarship in American Studies and identifies a distinctive postcolonial, pan-American consciousness" (Saldívar xi). Saldívar's dialectical method emphasizes the opposition between what he calls "our distinctive *mestizo* American culture—a culture of hybrid Americans, ethnic and cultural descendants of aborigines, Africans, and Europeans" (xii) and the Eurocentric America which has been the traditional subject of American and Latin American Studies. Are race mixture and multiculturalism better understood as conflict or fusion? We believe that the answer is neither oppositionality nor obliteration of differences, while we also need to distinguish between two separate dimensions: on the one hand, the actual racial and cultural exchanges, and, on the other, the two opposed modes of affirming (on the part of Martí's mixed-race America) and negating (on the part of Eurocentric America) multicultural dynamics in the Americas, which, to oversimplify, are generally parallel to the geographical divide between South and North, Latin and Anglo America.[9]

Thinking about how to emphasize continuities and conflicts opens up the question about the relationship between counterdiscourse and hybridity, taken up in Section II, "*Métissage* and Counterdiscourse." As Françoise Lionnet advocates, *métissage* is "more complex than a 'double consciousness'" or "standard postcolonial counter-discourse" (Lionnet 78, 81). Discussing the feminist vision in the work of French Caribbean writer Maryse Condé, Lionnet points out that her novel, *Windward Heights*, is "not simply a reaction against the misrepresentations that inform an earlier European text" (74). Rather, the "novel forces the re-visioning of counter-discursive practices in light of feminist ones" (78). Hence, Lionnet suggests viewing *métissage* as a "braiding of traditions" (86, n. 4), what she calls a "*trans*colonial" mode of responding in a plural, inclusionary rather than reductive, exclusionary manner. Once more than one set of conflicts enters the equation, Lionnet argues, and if we want to understand the compounded intersections of race, gender, and other differences, we need to shift to models of triangulation, as with her example of the crossroads of feminism and racial hybridity. To extrapolate from Lionnet's premise, in three-way and other, even more complex crossings, dialogic interweaving overwhelms dialectical antithesis.

In her essay, "Créolité or Ambiguity?", Michèle Praeger argues that the Martiniquan Creolists, Jean Bernabé, Patrick Chamoiseau, and Raphaël Confiant, authors of *Eloge de la Creolité,* have reached an "aporia" because as they try to reject Western universalist identity, they are still complicit with it. Like Lionnet, Praeger explores the complexities and internal contradictions of creolist counterdiscourse to Metropolitan French culture. While the better-known *Eloge de la Creolité* affirms a unified counteridentity by repetitive negation of Western identity ("Neither European, nor African, nor Asian, we proclaim ourselves *créoles*"), Praeger argues, creole identity should be viewed as identity-in-progress, one that is also embroiled in the Western "web of illusions and exoticisms" (Praeger 99). Thus, "Suzanne Césaire, and contemporary critics, emphasize . . . that French Caribbean identity is yet to be born" (99).

This collection is subtitled *Inter-American Literary Dialogues.* Pointing out the potential of dialogics, and, specifically, Bakhtinian dialogic discourse as a model of literary criticism, Don Bialostosky writes,

> To read others dialogically, then, would be to read for an opening in the discussion or a provocation to further discourse, and if such reading errs, it would not be likely to do so in the same ways as dialectical or rhetorical readings do. Dialogic reading would not generally reduce others to consistent dialectical counterparts, or dwell on the inconsistencies in their positions, or transcend them in higher syntheses. Nor would it minimize others as rhetorical opponents by attempting to discredit them. Instead, dialogic reading would assume the right to represent others in terms they might not have anticipated or acknowledged (Bialostosky 790).

In agreement with Bialostosky, we believe that dialogics' openness to otherness, rather than the antithetical pattern of dialectics (with its drive toward synthesis and identity), creates the necessary unstructured space for a pluralistic cross-cultural exchange to take place, as well as for criticism to explain the mixing of cultures. At the same time, in order not to take an extreme position, we admit that multiculturalism is both dialectical and dialogical, as it tends towards contestation and confluence. Thus, the approaches taken by essays in this collection range between both models of two-way and three-way comparisons, where two-way comparisons, as Debra J. Rosenthal's contribution shows, need not be dialectical, but they can also be dialogic (Rosenthal uses Pérez Firmat's term, "appositional").

If we select and isolate single dualistic scenarios, such as "miscegenation" between black and white, or white and Indian,[10] cross-breeding cultures fits the dialectical structure of the encounter and clash of two distinct counterparts. Yet if we open the focus to larger-scale comparisons, and especially if we depart from the dominant U.S. tradition of pitting opposites against each other, as in this hemispheric collection that encompasses multiple arenas of cultural encounter with numerous agents, the pattern of their meeting needs to be understood as polydirectional and multivocal — thus, like the unpredictable and chaotic rhythm of an ongoing dialogue. While dialectics assumes that the encounter will proceed along set lines (thesis, antithesis, synthesis), dialogics never predicts future turns of the process: as Bialostosky points out, new voices joining the dialogue "may not offer an antithesis to a given thesis or an answer to a proposed question but may introduce another way of talking that challenges the very language of the present interlocutors" (790).

In his discussion of the socio-historical origins of the concept of hybridity, Robert Young identifies two "models of cultural interaction, language and sex" (Young 6). Bakhtin's concept of hybridity, which appears as a component of his theory of dialogic discourse in *The Dialogic Imagination*, constitutes Young's case for the former model of cultural exchange, "linguistic hybridity" (Young 20ff.). It is while discussing Bakhtin that Young offers his pertinent idea that "Hybridity is . . . itself a hybrid concept" (Young 21). As Young explains, Bakhtin distinguishes two types of linguistic hybridity: the first type, "an organic hybridity, which will tend towards fusion, [is] in conflict with [a second type,] intentional hybridity, which enables a contestatory activity, a politicized setting of cultural differences against each other dialogically" (Young 22). In the essay "Discourse in the Novel," the source of all of Young's comments, Bakhtin explains this subtle difference constituting what Young calls a "double form" of hybridity: all languages, in all times and cultures, display organic hybridity, a living heteroglossia. For as long as they remain living languages, they evolve by hybridization, by adopting and incorporating alien voices and elements and expelling others, always existing as a mixed conglomerate of socially heterogeneous components. Social heteroglossia (and heteroglossia would include multiculturalism) defines any living language; for, ever since Adam's mythical first word naming a "yet verbally unqualified world" (Bakhtin 279), the linguistic condition has been a border zone, where new discourse must encounter a Borgesian universe already spoken and written about by others. Because Bakhtin views language as inseparable from spoken utterance in the real world, his theory of dialogic discourse (unlike formalist linguistics) lends itself to theories of cross-cultural exchanges and texts as socially symbolic forms. According to Bakhtin, novelistic discourse takes this organic, unintentional hybridity of language (where "the mixture remains mute and opaque, never making use of conscious contrasts and oppositions" [Bakhtin 360]) and reconfigures it as an artistic, conscious, intentional hybridity. Thus, in the intentional hybrid (of novelistic discourse), heteroglossia becomes "internally dialogic," by which Bakhtin means that the oppositional voices are set against each other and "consciously fight it out on the territory of the utterance" (Bakhtin 360). "Double-accented," "double-voiced," and "double-languaged," intentional (literary) hybridity enables one voice to unmask and ironize another, such that it generates a conversation between mixed but competing voices whose point is not fusion or resolution but the ongoing mutual illumination of their differences.

In sum, Bakhtin posits that stylized hybridization in the dialogic discourse of the novel is grounded in the universal organic ur-hybridity of *language itself*, whose dialogism is yet unconscious and mute. *Literature* (for Bakhtin, principally novelistic prose) only brings this pre-existing hybridity of language to its fruition as a self-conscious principle. Young comments that "Bakhtin's doubled form of hybridity therefore offers a particularly significant dialectical model for cultural interaction" (Young 22). We agree that Bakhtin's unique understanding of the relation of *language and literature as grounded in a common principle—socially symbolic hybridization*—whose organic manifestation in language "tends towards fusion" (Young 22), while its stylized manifestation in literature displays the dialogic potential of hybridity as an art of the border zone, is a significant contribution for hemispheric American Studies as a discipline-in-progress and the subject of this collection in particular. The idea of dialogic discourse as mutual illumination of social heteroglossia takes us beyond the nationalist model of literature, where texts are framed as univocal utterances of "imagined communities" speaking in a single voice. Bakhtin's theory not only lends itself to the discussion of transnational and cross-border literature, but also uncovers the heteroglossia of *métissage* and *mestizaje* within "American" and "Latin American" literature. Finally, because organic hybridity of language results in amalgamation, while intentional hybridity of literature maintains the dialectical conflict and separation between voices, Bakhtin points out (as Bialostosky notes) a new way of representing conflicts in an open and non-reductive manner. It seems that dialectics opens out to dialogics, while dialogics narrows down to dialectics—both are interwoven.

To move on to the discussion of the collection's organization, while Section II, "*Métissage* and Counterdiscourse," debates the notion of Caribbean *métissage* as counterdiscourse to European discourse, Section IV, "Hybrid Hybridity," explores more directly the multiplicity of hybridity and juxtaposes competing versions of hybridity. For Francophone Caribbean discourse, Lionnet's and Praeger's essays both showed the limits of the Manichean model of "pure" counterdiscourse (which only perpetuates the rigid binaries of colonial discourse), making the case for a plural and dialogic model of contestation.

Thus, Pérez-Torres' and Kaup's essays both reinforce Lionnet's and Praeger's case for *métissage* understood as relational interweaving of contending discourses (Lionnet), thus exemplifying Young's comment that hybridity itself is hybrid. Discussing hybridity in Chicano literature, Pérez-Torres speaks of *mestizaje*'s "over-determination" (Pérez-Torres 180). Setting out with the white suppression of the Chicano Other, as evidenced in the 1956 Texas film *Giant*, which doubly marginalizes the mestizo by devaluing his/her brown body and silencing his/her voice, Pérez-Torres' argument traces the emergence of Chicano subjectivity out of the void and toward a public affirmation of the mestiza/o voice and a "reclamation" (175) of the dark body. Chicano self-definition "resurrect[s]" (176ff.) the mestizo from his/her marginalization in Eurocentric discourse. At the same time, Pérez-Torres insists that mestizo self-definition is not univocal, but "enacts that self-definition in multiple ways" (181). Kaup takes up the story where Pérez-Torres leaves off, examining the assumption that, under the current "euphoria about hybridity and liminality," the "'new peoples' of North America, too, are finally emerging from their long public invisibility" (Kaup 186). Looking at Mexican American and Métis Canadian discourse, her argument shows that their hybridity is hybrid. Repeated cycles of conquest in the North American West interrupted the unfolding process of *métissage* and *mestizaje*, causing it to be overwhelmed by the discourse of nationalism, and hybridity to be split by the battle between dominant discourse and ethnic counterdiscourse.

The question concerning how knowledge about mixed-race identity and the crossing of cultures is constituted is posed in Section I, "Mixed-Blood Epistemologies." Who can be a "knower"? Is there a mixed-blood standpoint that outsiders, too, can or need to assume to generate mixed-blood discourse? Should mixed-blood discourse be founded on the authority of experience? As with women and other minorities, traditional epistemology has excluded the possibility that "half-breeds" and "mulattos," as lesser humans (mulatto derives from "mule"), can be agents of knowledge. At the same time, unlike women or, say, blacks, some mixed-race people can "pass," and thus assume authority under a false guise. Thus, mixed-race people share with lesbians and gays the experience of passing, and double lives that can pass back and forth between hidden private selves and public masks. What Eve Kosofsky Sedgwick calls "the epistemology of the closet," the crisscrossing of the line between closeted selves and public disclosure also characterizes the lives of mixed-blood people. Werner Sollors explores this epistemological uncertainty by questioning whether we can tell that "miscegenation" is indeed the theme of a text. If Garth Williams' *The Rabbits' Wedding* is about the marriage between a black and a white rabbit, how could Southern conservative audiences in the pre–Civil Rights era "know," and tell for certain, that the book was really about dreaded miscegenation and racial amalgamation? Discussing Cuban Cirilo Villaverde's novel *Cecilia Valdés*, Doris Sommer shows how Villaverde artfully translates the mixed-blood epistemology of the closet into a narrative strategy of playful concealment and disclosure. The truth about protagonist Cecilia's racial background is known to the black slaves, while the white and mulatto masters are and want to remain ignorant. Clare Kendry, the mulatto woman at the center of Nella Larsen's *Passing*, discussed by Zita Nunes, is a trickster figure who conceals her black descent to assimilate into whiteness. Clare embodies epistemological uncertainty about racial identity, and her passing as white represents an act of crossing racial thresholds that breaks down the order of things, undermining U.S. racial segregation. Nunes' essay further traces hemispheric connections between the U.S. and Brazil, showing how Brazil functioned as a utopia of racial hybridity and racial democracy in the African American imagination in the early twentieth century. Representative of the African American construction of what Nunes calls a "phantasmatic Brazil," Larsen's *Passing* juxtaposes the U.S. model of racial purity to a utopian image of Brazilian racial integration, an image to which Afro-Brazilian writers would object, pointing out that it is a black North American dream rather than a South American reality.

The treatment of miscegenation and interracial love in nationalist novels of nineteenth- and twentieth-century U.S. and Andean literature is discussed in Section III, "Indigenization, Miscegenation, and Nationalism." Without repeating the relevant argument treated earlier in this introduction, nationalism idealizes and essentializes Amerindians while rejecting *mestizaje* and the mestizo as illegitimate and unnatural. Why the striking clash between discursive approval of pure-blood Indians and disapproval of mixed-blood unions and offspring? Both Archibald and Rosenthal show that national literature wants to appropriate Amerindian claims to belonging to the homeland, and therefore must exclude mixedbloods as agents who blur the purity of Native lineage. As Debra J. Rosenthal points out, "miscegenation" is the usage appropriate to this section on national literature, where cross-racial unions are viewed negatively (Rosenthal 136, n. 2). Archibald and Rosenthal both show that *Indigenismo* revindicates Indian cultures but does so while constructing them in a romantic and ahistorical image. Archibald's essay critiques the Andean version of indigenization through the lens of gender. Like Lionnet in her discussion of *métissage*, Archibald examines *mestizaje* through a feminist lens. The indigenous mother is blamed for breeding mestizo children, which shows that the Native male is the idealized object of the mirror relationship between the fraternal nation and its elective Native "kin." Rosenthal's essay applies two Andean literary critical categories, *Indianismo* and *Indigenismo*, to nineteenth-century U.S. novels about Indians. Rosenthal's side-by-side comparison of two Andean novels (*Cumandá, Aves sin nido*) with two U.S. novels (*The Last of the Mohicans, Ramona*) shows surprising similarities and differences. On the one hand, Andean and U.S. national literature are in agreement in the distinction between romantic (*Indianismo*) and politically engaged (*Indigenismo*) novels about Indians. On the other hand, unlike the U.S. texts, the Andean novels mix relations of love and "blood," miscegenation and incest. The Latin American disclosure that miscegenous love would be incest, because the interracial lovers turn out to be brother and sister, speaks volumes about differences between Anglo and Latin American treatment of racial Others as inside or outside the same nation-family.

In her essay "The Squatter, the Don, and the Grandissimes in Our America," Susan Gillman reads interracial politics via José Martí to question late nineteenth-century interest in race and ethnicity. As the translator of Helen Hunt Jackson's *Ramona*, Martí views *Ramona* as another *Uncle Tom's Cabin*, for both tried to vindicate an oppressed minority. Gillman establishes these two novels and the black-Indian connection reinforced by Martí's twinning of Jackson-Stowe as a base from which to explore the ways local color and regionalism construct a hemispheric tenor. She performs a Martíean reading of María Amparo Ruiz de Burton's *The Squatter and the Don* and George Washington Cable's *The Grandissimes* to conjoin the Spanish Borderlands with the black Atlantic. These authors, Gillman argues, "have thus reshaped the dominant national cultural icons of Americanization at their time, from the romance of reunion to nostalgia for the passing of the Southern, Mission and Indian (fantasy) pasts, into tools of critical internationalism and types of imagined international communities" (Gillman 157). Gillman's essay thus explores the themes of the indigenous, race mixture, and nationalism, generic to the Americas, from a "mediative" perspective à la Pérez Firmat as discussed above: Burton's and Cable's novels embed an inter-American perspective, a "critical internationalism of the kind best identified with Martí" (150) that is internal to the texts themselves.

Chicano writer Rolando Hinojosa-Smith and Native American critic Louis Owens recount memories of growing up mixedblood in Section V, "Sites of Memory in Mixed-Race Autobiography." Both use an external physical object or place, a site of memory, to unfold the meanings of their cross-cultural identity. Hinojosa-Smith shows how a river, the Rio Grande, embodies the memories of a single culture in the Rio Grande Valley that united what are now Mexico and South Texas. The river represents the bridge uniting both sides of the bicultural and biracial Mexican American heritage. Owens takes a 1913 photograph of his great-grandfather's family, exploring the problem of "telling" his indigenous ancestors by their looks. Owens questions whether photographs can "tell" Indians, let alone provide visual evidence to distinguish mixedbloods and fullbloods. Owens thus reminds us of the epistemological question about how one "knows" about, and who knows about, mixed-blood identity, and of continuities between authenticity and simulation. Further, according to Owens, the mixedblood possesses trickster-like qualities of being slippery and undefinable.

The book closes with Earl Fitz' essay, a survey of eight mixed-race texts from across the hemisphere. As his survey shows, treatments of "miscegenation" have gradually yielded to images of race mixture as multiculturalism. Formerly exoticized portrayals of interracial crossings are being replaced by representations of race mixture through ordinary people and worlds. As Fitz writes, "these works typify what we may justifiably consider a new and more culturally honest late twentieth-century response to our old blood-based preoccupation with the issue of miscegenation and its various socio-cultural ramifications" (Fitz 245).

The multiple "entries" that this collection makes into the territory of hemispheric American literature and the subject of hybridity are intended as representative openings, which follow the strategies of García Canclini. In the following characteristic passage, García Canclini remaps Latin America in a manner that breaks with dominant models of linear genealogies of racial and national purity:

> There can be no future for our past while we waver between the reactive fundamentalisms against the modernity achieved, and the abstract modernisms that resist problematizing our "deficient" capacity to be modern. To leave behind this "western," the maniacal pendulum, it is not enough to be interested in how traditions are reproduced and transformed. The postmodern contribution is useful for escaping from the impasse insofar as it reveals the constructed and staged character of all tradition, including that of modernity: it refutes the originary quality of traditions and the originality of innovations. At the same time, it offers the opportunity to rethink the modern as a project that is relative, doubtable, not antagonistic to traditions nor destined to overcome them by some unverifiable evolutionary law. It serves, in short, to make us simultaneously take charge of the impure itinerary of traditions and of the disjointed, heterodox achievement of modernity (García Canclini 143–144).

García Canclini's notion of the "impurity" of major cultural formations in the Americas corresponds to the critical framework that this collection has used in its pan-American comparative inquiries. Culture and literature in the Americas reveal themselves, to echo Bakhtin, as hybrid in the sense of their internal dialogism. The literature about race and cultural mixture the contributors have examined, and the critical strategies brought to bear on this literature, accent and reconfigure existing cultural oppositions and syntheses—the organic hybridity of pan-American cultures—and display them as intentional hybridity, as a conscious socio-semiotic exchange which enables previously unrealized or muted conversations between contending cultures-in-contact.

As has hopefully come across to the reader, since "exiting" (following García Canclini) is a kind of opening up, the categories examined in the five sections of this collection are not intended to limit investigations, but rather to invite further reflection. Our central concern has been to convince readers that there is substantial common ground across the many national, cultural, and historical divisions in the Americas that warrants a fresh, non-traditional dialogic investigation of its hybrid cultures. Even the tallest walls, the historical and cultural barriers dividing the Northern and Southern, or the "Anglo" and "Hispanic" regions of the hemisphere, can be torn down and reconstructed as bridges in the traces of previously unrealized (but presently multiplying) currents of North-South exchanges. For more than a century, Latin American intellectuals, including José Martí, Rubén Darío, José Vasconcelos, and Roberto Fernández Retamar, have sounded the theme of "Nuestra América," the idea of a Latinized, Catholic, mestizo America contending with the "Other America," the Anglo, Protestant, racially homogeneous, imperial colossus to the North. Latin Americanism has been "invented," as a transnational cultural tradition, as a self-conscious alternative to the self-confident and expanding America of the North. For our project, the uncovering of North America's "hidden mestizo histories" and the unmasking of the fictions of racial, cultural, and national purity everywhere across the continent, Latin Americanism's heritage of a multicultural, hybrid América can act as a catalyst to help bring about a paradigm change.

Notes

1. In this introduction, we discuss essays and sections not in the sequence of their appearance in the book, but in a way that makes clearest to our readers the major themes that complexly interweave through the essays.

2. Readers may note the scarcity or absence of "hard data" on race mixture in our collection. We are, in fact, familiar with key historical and sociological publications that present such facts and figures, such as the excellent collection, *The Idea of Race in Latin America, 1870–1949*, edited by Richard Graham, which contains pertinent historical and cultural analyses on issues of race and race mixture in Brazil, Cuba and Argentina, and Mexico. While such historical analyses informed our thinking in the planning stage of the collection, we decided the best editorial strategy would be to keep the focus strictly on the literary side of the issue because the purpose of our collection, as our subtitle indicates, is "Inter-American *Literary* Dialogues."

3. The 1990s have seen a burst in publications of hemispheric studies of American literatures: Fitz' *Rediscovering the New World;* Saldivar's *The Dialectics of Our America;* Pérez Firmat's *Do the Americas Have a Common Literature?;* Gale Chevigny and Laguardia's *Reinventing the Americas;* Belnap and Fernandez' *José Martí's "Our America": From National to Hemispheric Cultural Studies;* Zamora's *The Usable Past;* Spillers' *Comparative American Identities.*

4. García Canclini clarifies his terminology as follows: "Occasional mention will be made of the terms *syncretism, mestizaje,* and others used to designate processes of *hybridization.* I

prefer the last term because it includes diverse intercultural mixture—not only the racial ones to which *mestizaje* tends to be limited—and because it permits the inclusion of the modern forms of hybridization better than does 'syncretism,' a term that almost always refers to religious fusions or traditional symbolic movements" (11, n. 1).

5. Readers interested in a postmodern collage-style review of representations of the mythical indigene and of miscegenation in U.S. film should look at David Avalos and Deborah Small's video, "The Birth of Mis-ce-ge-Nation." (The script for the video is published in *Discourse* 18.1–2 [1995–1996].) The video script focuses on the Ramona pageant in California and documents a series of cross-racial couples in Hollywood film, exposing the fetishization of racial difference and strategies of simulation that produce imaginary Indians and mixedbloods and their tragic demise.

6. See Robert Young, *Colonial Desire: Hybridity in Theory, Culture and Race,* pp. 6–19, where Young discusses the development of Victorian debates on the human species and hybridity, fertility, amalgamation, miscegenation, and related terms.

7. Detailed discussion of intra-hemispheric differences in racial practices such as inclusion and segregation can be found in Bell Gale Chevigny and Gari Laguardia's "Introduction" to the collection *Reinventing the Americas* (1986).

8. The fourth and "mediative" approach, Pérez Firmat explains, "concentrates on texts that already embed an inter-American or comparative dimension. In this case the cross-country or cross-cultural appositions are internal to the works themselves" (4). Texts under this category, truly transnational writings (examples listed are the writings of Cubans José Martí and José Lezama Lima), would constitute the "natural" core lineage of hemispheric American literature.

9. Latin America, like Anglo America, has a strong Eurocentric discourse of its own, as Roberto González Echevarría explains in his studies *The Voice of the Masters: Writing and Authority in Latin American Literature* and *Myth and Archive: A Theory of Latin American Literature.* Parallel to his North American counterparts, Echevarría seeks the key to Latin American writing in genealogical continuities with Hispanic and Western European culture. Restating his resistance to postcolonial readings of Latin American literature in the recent pan-American collection *Poetics of the Americas: Race, Founding, and Textuality,* Echevarría writes: "The effort in recent years to align Latin American literature with that of the so-called Third World has been a fiasco. . . . The burden of Latin American culture is a Western culture that reaches back to the Middle Ages, when the foundations of the Spanish Empire in the New World were set. Ours was from the beginning a culture of ostentatious viceregal capitals, surpassing in splendor cities of the Old World . . ." ("Latin American and Comparative Literatures," 50–51).

10. Such preselected dualistic foci characterize much of the previous literature on miscegenation and race mixture. See, for instance, Joel Williamson's *New People: Miscegenation and Mulattoes in the United States;* Judith Berzon's *Neither White Nor Black;* and Daniel Aaron's "The 'Inky Curse': Miscegenation in the White Literary Imagination."

MIXED-BLOOD
EPISTEMOLOGIES

CHAPTER I

CAN RABBITS HAVE INTERRACIAL SEX?

Werner Sollors

For those readers who are pressed for time but dying to find the question settled that the title of my essay promises to address, here is the abstract, so to speak. One answer is, "apparently, yes." And not by marrying goats or horses, either, but just by allying themselves with other rabbits! Another answer is that perhaps they shouldn't—or if they do it anyway, that at least nobody should be told about it. But all of this may become clear by the end of the essay, which, if it had a subtitle, would also promise something like, "Garth Williams' *The Rabbits' Wedding* and Racial Integration." It is an essay connected with the theme of founding a family, and with that of certain families as anathema; and the time is (mostly) from the 1950s to the present. I would like to start with a family as anathema in 1989.

The "family of man" (as it used to be called), or more precisely the family of *fraternité*—now known as siblinghood—was celebrated on a stamp issued by the U.S. Postal Service to commemorate the two-hundredth anniversary of one of the three principles of the French Revolution. There is at first glance nothing much exciting about this stamp, which portrays (on the right panel) a matrifocal family with two silvery children, siblings, under the cloak of Mother Republicanism. How could such an innocent stamp start a controversy? And yet it did. For example, it was said that the woman's nipple seemed removed from the stamp. Where was the image from anyway? Was the nipple there in the original?

This essay is based on the introduction to my book, *Neither Black Nor White Yet Both: Thematic Explorations of Interracial Literature* (New York: Oxford University Press, 1997; pb. Cambridge: Harvard University Press, 1999). Used by permission of Oxford University Press, Inc., and the author.

One of the images close to the one by which the stamp was inspired is
an allegorical representation from 1792, out of the Musée Carnavalet in
Paris, and it does, indeed, represent the mother's breast more explicitly.
Could the removal of the nipple from the picture on the stamp, an action
of the U.S. Postmaster General, be unmasked as a sign of prudishness? Yet
there is another noticeable difference between the two images of brotherhood: the children are more different-looking in the French image than in
the U.S. adaptation. The European version of *fraternité* shows one black
and one white sibling; in the great American melting pot they have become metallic-looking twins or clones. Why did the Postmaster General
prefer to represent the two children embracing each other as the allegory
of "fraternity" in an identical silvery color rather than follow the original?
Voices were raised that there was a race problem in the air. But Ms. Kim
Parks of the Postal Service stamp support branch stated reassuringly that
the figures were "redrawn in bas-relief to resemble statues, and in silver to
stand out against the colored panels." She emphasized this aesthetic motivation also by explicitly stating that silver is "not white" and that the
change had been undertaken "without any thought of race." Was there
perhaps a problem with indicating color difference on so small a format?
The French post office managed to show one black and one white child
on a similar-sized stamp, obviously taken from the same source. Question: Could there be a problem in imagining different colors in the same
brotherhood-family?

By now you must have already guessed that the approach I have chosen
here is "thematic."[1] I assume that aesthetic works are also "about" something—and I am focusing less on form (e.g., the inversion of the French tricolor on the stamp) than on "themes" that may unite texts, images, stamps,
or sculptures.[2] But how do we know that a work of art is about *x* and not
about *y*? Not all works are allegories of the *fraternité* type. So how do we
know that a certain work is about, say, family—and not about itself, a tension between metaphor and metonymy, about undecidability, or about any
of a thousand other topics than the one we have chosen to be our "theme"?
What do we do when we look for "themes" in literature—a process that has
been called "theming" by Gerald Prince? Are themes simply self-evident
and objectively manifested in texts?

Claude Bremond reminded readers that "there is no 'in-and-of-itself'
in the theme,"[3] and even a single uncomplicated sentence can be *absolutely*
or *relatively* "about" something, as Menachem Brinker illustrated:

The sentence "the book is on the table" is absolutely about the book, the table, and the fact that the book is on the table. Yet relative to the information received this morning, according to which "if Peter buys the book he will leave it on the table," the first sentence . . . is also about Peter and about the fact that he bought the book and left it on the table. By implication it may also be about the fact that Peter keeps his promises, that the book has arrived in Israel, and so on and so forth.[4]

If this is true for a simple statement of fact, how much more complicated must it be to say what the theme of a literary work may be? A variety of mixed-up, often unconscious interests may guide the process of theming — for example, aesthetic, logical, statistical, political, moral, genealogical, psychoanalytical, structuralist, nationalistic, or autobiographical motives.[5] Thomas Pavel made a distinction between a text that explicitly makes readers *care* about a theme (lesbianism in Balzac's *Girl with Golden Eyes*) and a text that requires a critic's special (even forced) effort to perceive a theme ("lesbianism" in *Twelfth Night*). How do we arrive at such distinctions? For Pavel the Berkeleyan maxim of undeclared thematics is: "For a theme to be perceived is to be." And David Perkins, who has so marvelously and convincingly challenged the genre of literary history, would seem to agree: ". . . with themes we are free. Individual creativity is much more active in writing literary history than most people suppose, and it riots in thematic literary history."[6] Could we possibly expect any form of general agreement as to what is explicit, what is implicit, in texts? Perhaps the contexts, and, especially, the debates about legitimate and unpredictable contexts, ultimately confer plausibility to what will be considered the themes of a given work; and the contexts surrounding certain themes may be particularly strong in this respect.

The church fathers Boethius, Meletius, Athanasius, and Augustine, who used the word "species" in its original sense of "external aspect, appearance," and who viewed a horse's color as an *accidental* quality that does nothing to the horse's essential horseness, would have been surprised by the modern period.[7] Now "black" and "white" could serve as such forceful agents that they have had the power to eclipse, or racialize, their object; and the metaphoric significance of color could be more important than the subject that was ostensibly represented. Just as black and white could be themed *away* in the case of *fraternité*, so an interracial theme could also be inserted *into* texts that were hardly "absolutely about" this topic. For example, a postcard, probably from the early part of the century, portrayed

two cats, a black one in a man's bathing suit and a white one in a dress, dancing in the shallow ocean waters on the edge of a beach, and other cats are
visible in and near beach tents in the background. The card was titillatingly
entitled "Mixed Bathing." The cats' colors and costumes—or, put differently, the way in which they were coded by race and gender—are the only
aspects that could conceivably make the subject risqué, while the postcard
manufacturer's heading may also represent an attempt to turn potential
tension into humor.[8] In this instance, we do not know why the manufacturer chose that title over such other possibilities as "Cats By the Seaside,"
"Wet Quadrille," "Le Cha(t) Cha(t)," "Hip Cats," "The New Beach Ap-
parel," "Family Vacation" (which would make it suitable for this occasion)
or "Summer"—not to mention such possibilities as "Composition 18" or
(my Macintosh favorite) "Untitled." In each case, however, it would be the
title, a *text*, that would give the central theme to the image: the image would
seem to be "about" different things, dependent on the heading it received.
For example, if we took the theme to be "family" we might wish to connect
the cats in the background and those in the foreground in a generational
story, or distinguish a "clan" from an incipient "nuclear family," and so
forth. In any case, this postcard was not enmeshed in a theming controversy such as the one that emerged in the Alabama Public Library system,
discussed below, that will shortly take us to (or at least, near) the promised
topic of my essay.

   In the last years of legalized racial segregation in the United States, animal fables that were applied to the human situation flourished, as is evidenced, for example, by Zora Neale Hurston's little-studied conservative
essays of the period, in which she denounced the fight for legal desegregation—with her rejection of the supposedly integrationist fable of mules
running after a white mare—as a communist plot for interracial marriage.[9]
Hurston's "Court Order Can't Make Races Mix" was an open letter, published 11 August 1955 in the *Orlando Sentinel*, an anti-integrationist daily
with, at that time, a circulation of approximately 100,000.[10] It is written
flippantly in a way Hurston herself calls "thinking out loud"; and the center of it is taken by an amplification of what Hurston, the author of *Mules
and Men* (1935)—calls "the doctrine of the white mare." She explains:

> Those familiar with the habits of mules are aware that any mule, if not re-
> strained, will automatically follow a white mare. Dishonest mule-traders
> made money out of this knowledge in the old days. Lead a white mare along
> a country road and slyly open the gate and the mules in the lot would run

out and follow this mare. This [Supreme Court] ruling [of Brown v. Board of Education] is being conceived and brought forth in a sly political medium with eyes on [the election of] '56, and brought forth in the same spirit and for the same purpose. It is clear that they have taken the old notion to heart and acted upon it. It is a cunning opening of the barnyard gate with the white mare ambling past. We are expected to hasten pell-mell after her.

The story was illustrated, apparently by the *Orlando Sentinel*, with a little cartoon depicting a white mare with a question mark over her head and a sign reading "desegregation," while across the fence a black mule is thinking, "I just want my own pasture improved." Hurston goes back to the story later in the essay and confesses that, personally, she is "not persuaded and elevated by the white mare technique." The worst periods in the quick history she drafts are "the days of the never-to-be-sufficiently-deplored Reconstruction" (when the belief that Negroes want nothing more than to associate with whites was also current) and the New Deal (when only the "stubborn South and the Midwest kept this nation from being dragged farther to the left than it was"). She seems to consider seriously that the desegregation decision was only a trial balloon and precedent designed to keep Southerners busy while more serious attacks on the political system could be launched: "What if it is contemplated to do away with the two-party system and arrive at Govt. by decree?" What she senses behind such deceptive maneuvering is communism. Hurston, in 1955, specifically warns the readers against attempting integration at a time

when the nation is exerting itself to shake the evils of Communist penetration. It is to be recalled that Moscow, being made aware of this folk belief, made it the main plank in their campaign to win the American Negro from the 1920s on. It was the come-on stuff. Join the party and get yourself a white wife or husband.

This allusion to a communist conspiracy to foment interracial marriages probably found some resonance in the McCarthyist period to which Hurston here explicitly alludes. She concludes the essay with the statement: "That old white mare business can go racking on down the road for all I care."

Hurston had used the white mare fable also in "Why the Negro Won't Buy Communism" (1951) and told readers of *The American Legion Magazine* that Communists, in order to "mount their world rule on Black American backs," had taken for a blueprint "an ancient and long-discarded folk piece. The analogy of the 'white mare.' It got to be said during the Reconstruction that the highest ambition of every Negro man was to have a white woman." She concluded the parable with the interpretation that analogies are dangerous, since it is "possible, and even probable that we might not be mules" though "the reds evidently thought so." Hurston also found in what she bluntly terms the party's "'pig-meat' crusade"—when Harlem "swarmed with party-sent white women"—an explanation for the frequency of mixed couples in party councils, and suspected that it was by "such whoopdedoo" that the Lincoln Brigade was "recruited to go to Spain in a vain attempt to place the Russian Bear at Gibraltar" (57). Hurston's essays of the 1950s suggest the strength of the opposition to interracial plotlines—even among modern, widely celebrated and taught writers.

A more popular animal fable was Walt Disney's animated film, *The Fox and the Hound*, and though it was released only in 1981 it still evokes the ambience of a quarter of a century earlier. It is also a work that resonates for Faulkner readers with a description from *Flags in the Dust* that has a strong undertone of human allegory:

> No two of them looked alike, and none of them looked like any other living creature—neither fox nor hound, partaking of both, yet neither; and despite their soft infancy there was about them something monstrous and contradictory and obscene, here a fox's keen, cruel muzzle between the melting, sad eyes of a hound and its mild ears, there limp ears tried valiantly to stand erect and failed ignobly in flopping points; and limp, brief tails brushed over with a faint golden fuzz like the inside of chestnut burrs. As regards color, they ranged from reddish brown through an indiscriminate brindle to pure ticked beneath a faint dun cast, and one of them had, feature for feature, old General's face in comical miniature, even to his expression of sad and dignified disillusion.[11]

For the critic Gene Bluestein this was a thinly veiled comment on an interracial family. By contrast, Disney made the fable of integration center on the friendship of two males (perhaps the studio was familiar with Leslie Fiedler's well-known thesis in *Love and Death in the American Novel*), the little fox Tod (who receives cow's milk from the farmer's wife who adopts him) and the little hound Copper. The effect is that the "natural boundaries," of which Pearl Bailey as Owl sings, remain intact; in other words, the "species"—now in the modern sense of an essentially different kind—

remain separate even though their representatives may befriend each other at a tender age.

> When you're the best of friends,
> Having so much fun together.
> You're not even aware
> You're such a funny pair
> You're the best of friends
> Life's a happy game
> You could clown around forever
> Neither one of you sees
> Your natural boundaries.
> Life's one happy game.
> If only the world wouldn't get in the way
> If only *people* [12] would just let you play
> They say that you'll both be fools
> You're breaking all the rules
> They can't understand
> the magic of your wanderings [?].
> When you're the best of friends. . . .
> Oh I hope, I hope it never ends,
> For you're the best of friends.

The video cassette box identifies as the themes of *The Fox and the Hound* "such timeless values as love, courage, and respect for life." The utopia of fox and hound is that they do manage to overcome their instinctual animosity—hound even rescues fox at the dramatic climax—but they both end up happy, each in his own separate intraspecies alliance or set. They can "clown around," but they must also recognize that they would make "a funny pair." Growing up means recognizing that life is not just a game, that there are "natural boundaries." They are the best of "friends forever," but they are not the same "family." If Faulkner's fox and hound could be themed as "melting pot," then Disney's version might be read as "pluralism."

Characteristic of the mood of the period of desegregation was the small crisis generated by a children's book published in 1958. The book was *The Rabbits' Wedding*, written and illustrated by Garth Williams (who may be best known for his visual work in E. B. White's novel, *Charlotte's Web*). It is the story of two little rabbits who live in a forest and happily play with each other, hopping, skipping, and jumping around. Their happiness is only interrupted by one of the rabbits' recurring moods of pensiveness, brought on by his wish that he could always be with the other one. The other rabbit says that if he really wishes that, she will be his forever; then they pick flowers together and put them in each other's ears. They get married in a wedding circle of all the other rabbits, and the animals of the forest come to watch the wedding dance. The married rabbits live happily ever after. The book was pitched for an audience of three- to seven-year-olds (though the author later lowered the targeted age group to two to five years), and the well-balanced *New York Times* reviewer felt that children would hug the book tightly, "if only for the bold pictures of frisky, fluffy bunnies romping in the forest. The tale of this bashful suitor and his lady fair, however, is too low-keyed for many readings." And the *Christian Science Monitor* praised the "misty, dreamy brush" that has "painted the two little rabbits . . . with all the soft, defenseless charm of babyhood" and applauded the "brief text, kept simple and happy" and the "heart-stealing water-color illustrations" that "are spread generously over giant pages."[13]

The Rabbits' Wedding seems thematically unrelated to the topic of race. Yet the brief reference to "lady fair" contains the important clue: as in the case of Hurston's mules and mares and that of the cat postcard, it was the *color* of the animals that suggested the context of human difference: As one has discovered from the picture on the cover of the book, the male rabbit was black, the female was white.

In the world of the U.S. South in the 1950s, divided by the issue of racial integration, this was sufficient evidence to invite some people to read the book as a contribution to interracial literature, readings that turned the book virtually into a manual for founding a family where there should be no family ties, where there were "natural boundaries." The presence of the categories black/male and white/female helped to override the species difference between the book's subjects and its readers, and *The Rabbits' Wedding* could thus be themed as *really* about an interracial marriage, an alliance that, at the time of the book's publication, was still illegal in more than half of the United States, among them all Southern states, many of which had provisions in their constitutions prohibiting what was called (since 1863) "miscegenation." The book also appeared three years after the Virginia Supreme Court, in *Naim v. Naim*, had sustained the miscegenation statute and ruled that the state's legislative purpose was "to preserve the racial integrity of its citizens" and to prevent "the corruption of blood," "the obliteration of racial pride," and the creation of "a mongrel breed of citizens."[14] *The Rabbits' Wedding* became controversial 29 years after the state of Mississippi had enacted a criminal statute that made punishable "publishing, printing, or circulating any literature in favor of or urging interracial marriage or social equality."[15] It also was published 29 years *before* the state of Mississippi found enough votes in the State House to overrule the constitutional provision banning interracial marriage.[16] Contexts, contexts. . . .

Once it was themed "interracial," pictures and text of a children's book could appear different from what they seemed, not harmless and joyful but positively dangerous; the representation of the hopping, romping characters could now be deemed taboo, and the images of their physical closeness suggestive of the corruption of (more than rabbit) blood and hence inappropriate for children. The Alabama Citizens' Council (which, despite its post-revolutionary name promising a fraternity of *citoyens,* was an association limited to white male members) used its organ, the weekly *Montgomery Home News,* for a sharp, front-page critique of the book, criticizing it for promoting integration, spelling out the group's fears and the book's method of theming in the headline: "What's Good Enough for Rabbits Should Do for Mere Humans."[17] The book was thus thought not just to *represent* a certain course of action but to *"recommend"* it to human readers. It could not be taken as a "family values" role model that taught the young ones to associate continuous physical pleasure with the "clean" institution of a collectively sanctioned heterosexual marriage; it also could not reassure segregationists that the rabbits were—unlike Faulkner's fox and hound—clearly of the same *species.* The rabbits' color difference overruled all other considerations. The columnist Henry Balch followed the lead of the Alabama Citizens' Council and, in an exhortative piece entitled "Hush Puppies," condemned *The Rabbits' Wedding* in the *Orlando Sentinel*—the same paper that had carried Hurston's white-mare attack on integration four years earlier—as "propaganda" for mixing races and as the "most amazing evidence of brainwashing":

> As soon as you pick up the book and open its pages you realize these rabbits are integrated.
> One of the techniques of brainwashing is conditioning minds to accept what the brainwashers want accepted.
> Where better to start than with youngsters in the formative years in the South?[18]

Balch presented a full quotation of the text of the book as self-evident support of his contention. His phrasing suggests the danger that the very term "integrated" must have contained. The fear of brainwashing, popular in the 1950s, made the children's book look as if it were part of a plot to weaken the defensive potential of the next generation. In "Rabbit Story Called Brazen," a reader's forum in the *Orlando Sentinel*, three critical respondents to Balch's column picked up the term "brainwashing." The opening letter by E. R. Ensey was strongly supportive of Balch, however, and expressed the opinion that without editorials recommending segregation, "the road will be wide open to mongrelization and none of us can fight back." And to some of the critical letters the editor added comments such as, "Thanks for your opinion and for Mr. Balch's."

The peril was all the more momentous since Balch saw the book in the children's section of one of the Florida public libraries in Orlando, where the dangerous work had been checked out so many times since its arrival that a waiting list had been opened for those other young clients who were still interested in reading the book.[19] The segregationist Alabama State Senator E. O. Eddins of Marengo County continued Balch's attack on the book with a focus on public libraries and declared aggressively that "this book and many others should be taken off the shelves and burned," specifying that he meant books "of the same nature" (presumably integrationist) and those that "are communistic."[20] The Cold War lineup of all things that could be called "dirty"—integrationism, communism, and sex—that were also noticeable in Hurston, suggests perhaps a sexually motivated fear of the ideology the representatives of which Ralph Ellison's *Invisible Man* had portrayed as "Brotherhood" a few years earlier.

The Rabbits' Wedding was thus publicly themed as a dangerous text promoting racial integration, and the fact that it did not represent humans at all could make it seem all the more subversive for spreading its illegal message surreptitiously—and to minors, too, who moreover would have access to it through taxpayer-financed public libraries. As we have already seen, it is very difficult to say with any degree of certainty that a given text is not, at least *relatively*, about a particular theme, and the Southern context simply suggested that this was one way in which the book would be read by many others, now that it had been read as an interracial marriage tale—anathema!!—by anti-integrationists. Looked at in legal terms, this theming made it possible to regard the book as an incitement to minors to break *the* law (and not just *a* law.) As *Time* magazine put it: "Indeed, by the very fact of having bought copies of *The Rabbits' Wedding* . . . the Alabama library service had become 'controversial.'"[21] This situation put political pressure on the Alabama library system, and Emily Wheelock Reed, the director of the State Public Library Service (which provided books for local libraries), was personally questioned by the Demopolis Senator Eddins, to whom she also had to make budget requests in the legislature. She now risked losing fiscal appropriations for her library system. Pointing out that the book had not been banned by any court of law and that it had been "purchased on the basis of favorable reviews," she came up with the Solomonic decision to not leave *The Rabbits' Wedding* in the agency's normal open shelves, nor take it completely out of circulation, but to put it on a special, closed shelf "for works on integration or those considered scatological."[22] I imagine this shelf relatively high up in the library's bookcases, out of reach of children, for sure. The effect was that local librarians were permitted to take *The Rabbits' Wedding* to their branches only upon special request. (Libraries that already had their own copies of the book were not affected and could keep them on the shelves, high or low.) In the line of fire for the possible accusation of making available dangerous literature, Reed had chosen the diplomatic course of not prohibiting "circulating the book to anyone, but then again . . . not peddling it." She acknowledged that she had been under indirect pressure and that her action was taken "in view of the troubled times in which we live." She accompanied her directive with a tart statement: "We were surprised that such a motive (integration) could be read into what appears to be a simple animal story using black and white illustrations to differentiate characters."[23] Yet her disclaimer notwithstanding, Reed's action had the effect of further sanctioning the interracial theming of *The Rabbits' Wedding*. This was so much the case that Alabama legislators who privately opposed the restriction, or even ridiculed it, "declined to be quoted by name because they said their position might be misconstrued as pro-integration" if they criticized in the press Reed's measure or Eddins' theming of the book.[24] The thematic interpretation of the Citizens' Council had no doubt prevailed if public opposition to the restricted access to a children's book about rabbits—surely a curtailment of citizens' liberty—could become associated with the offense of promoting racial integration.

All of this brought national attention to the case and generated broad, often overtly humorous coverage of the relatively minor near-suppression. The *New York Times* reported the scandal under the title, "Children's Book Stirs Alabama: White Rabbit Weds Black Rabbit," and *Time* opened its article, "Of Rabbits & Races"—which was placed under the general heading "THE SOUTH"—with excerpts from the book and the statement: "It seems incredible that any sober adult could scent in this fuzzy cottontale

for children the overtones of Karl Marx or even of Martin Luther King."
Time also ironically captioned the reproduction of part of the cover illustration of the book, with an allusion to Balch, "Anyone can see they're
integrated."[25] And some readers similarly went for the humor in the situation. Picking up on the communist theme, one reader of the *Orlando Sen-*
tinel suggested ironically that *The Rabbits' Wedding* could be made safe for
children with the help of crayons: "Color each white rabbit yellow and each
black rabbit green—thus leaving no tinge of red." Another reader wrote
sarcastically that Balch should also worry about such children's classics as
Black Beauty, in which "many fair skinned horses . . . want to nuzzle up to
that black horse," or *Heidi*, in which, this reader claimed, there "is a brown
goat that gets a yen for a white goat," and that Balch should therefore form
a "committee of one to ferret out all this diabolical trash and to see that
from now on the only literature allowed in our public library is about 100
pct. white animals who wouldn't spit on the best part of a darker one."
Finally, one letter-writer invoked a children's book about a marmalade-
colored cat "named of all things, Orlando," that celebrates his wedding
anniversary with his white wife.[26] Garth Williams, the book's author, also
commented on what *Time* called "the nonsense of it all" and, like Reed, he
invoked and defended color differentiation as an aesthetic principle, free
of human, racial, or political referentiality:

> *The Rabbits' Wedding* has no political significance. I was completely unaware
> that animals with white fur, such as white polar bears and white dogs and
> white rabbits, were considered blood relations of white human beings. I was
> only aware that a white horse next to a black horse looks very picturesque—
> and my rabbits were inspired by early Chinese paintings of black and white
> horses in misty landscapes.
>
>   It was written for children from two to five [the newly lowered age] who
> will understand it perfectly. It was not written for adults, who will not under-
> stand it because it is only about a soft furry love and has no hidden message
> of hate.[27]

Without directly invoking the early Christian thinkers and church fathers,
Garth Williams echoed their argument that color was an "accidental" and
not an "essential" quality.
    This episode in the cultural history of racial segregation reads like a ver-
sion of "The Emperor's New Clothes," in which our "normal," common-
sense perception of rabbit reality is restored through the voice of an honest
child that is still free of adult scheming. In a letter to the *Orlando Sen-*

tinel, high school senior Mason D. Kelsey made a similar point when he asked, "How could a child read into this story the problems of our sick society which the child has never run up against?"[28] We might paraphrase this line of argument as "any similarity with living colors is purely accidental and the result of a biased adult imagination." We may, however, be merely laughing off the problem of theming, which is not settled even in this seemingly easy case.

For, upon closer scrutiny, we must admit that there is no safe intellectual ground on which we could offer a *principled* objection to a reading of *The Rabbits' Wedding* as an allegory for a human story. Obviously, animal stories have been read for a very long time, from Aesop's fables to Uncle Remus' Brer Rabbit, as allegories for human tales. If the short text of the book—cited by both sides (*New York Times* and *Orlando Sentinel*) as if it were a self-evident exhibit—has often been seen as proof *against* the segregationists' reading, it also contains clues *for* it:

> Two little rabbits, a white rabbit and a black rabbit, lived in a large forest. . . .
> They loved to spend all day playing together.
> "Let's play Hop Skip And Jump Me," said the little white rabbit.
> "Oh, let's!" said the little black rabbit, and with a hop, skip, and a jump, he sailed right over the little white rabbit's back. . . .
> After a while the little black rabbit stopped eating and sat down and looked very sad.
> "What's the matter?" asked the little white rabbit. . . .
> "I wish you were all mine!" said the little black rabbit.

This scene is repeated in variations: the black rabbit looks sad, and when the white rabbit asks him why, the black rabbit speaks of his wish to be with the white rabbit "forever and always." And so, the white rabbit gives her consent; and the scene that gives the book its title follows.

> All the other little rabbits came out to see how happy they both were, and they danced in a wedding circle around the little black rabbit and the little white rabbit.
> The other animals of the forest came to watch the wedding dance and they too danced all night in the moonlight.
> And so the two little rabbits were wed and lived together happily in the big forest, eating dandelions, playing Jump The Daisies, Run Through The Clover and Find The Acorn all day long.
> And the little black rabbit never looked sad again.

"Hop Skip and Jump Me" could be read as an affirmative answer to the question I have here posed, or as the rabbits' failure to recognize "natural boundaries" or seeing that they "make a funny pair." The text might be said, in Pavel's sense, to make readers "care about" the boundary that the book's context was so strongly bent on upholding.

Garth Williams' rabbits are also quite explicitly anthropomorphic: they talk, decorate themselves with dandelions, and get married, with a big wedding party. They would seem to resemble human beings more than Chinese horses, even though the water-color inspiration is noticeable in Williams' style. More than that, the little black rabbit is repeatedly saddened by the thought (the reasons for which are not explained in the text, but make sense in the context of *Brown v. Board of Education*) that he might not always be with the white rabbit. Interestingly, a similar worry does not seem to cloud the white rabbit's *joie de vivre*, though she is ready to marry the black one if that will dispel his sadness. The missing motivation within the text may be precisely what inspires the referential theming to click in. Theming "race" thus may have gone for an absence, a lacuna in the tale, that it filled. Was the Citizens' Council reading for the gap? Also, by contrast with Garth Williams' *The Rabbits' Wedding*, his roughly contemporary, similar-looking rabbits in *Baby Farm Animals* (1959) and his illustrations for Margaret Wise Brown's *Home for a Bunny* (1961) do not show another black-white contrast in the bunny section of the animal kingdom.

In attempting to refute the "human" reading, Reed had to speak about "a simple animal story" (as if that excluded the possibility of a complex human allegory), and she offered the same explanation as Garth Williams, that black and white were used merely to differentiate characters, following a Chinese tradition. *Time*'s glibly cosmopolitan ridiculing and the author's attempt to make absurd the human theming of the book drew on the impact of invoking animal varieties (horse, dog, and rabbit) and features ("fuzzy" or "fur") to build up contrasts between human:animal, adult:child, and hate:love—all of which actually ended up as an oblique critique of segregation in the same breath in which political motive and significance were denied. Better to have the "soft furry love" of this "cottontale" (an effective pun, as it alludes to Beatrix Potter's famous *Peter Rabbit* and unites storytelling and animal feature) than the hard segregationist logic of columnists and politicians that makes "whites" out of polar bears, dogs, and rabbits. It may thus have been the "fit" between ideology and representation that permitted liberals to laugh at the segregationists' paranoia. In fact, we could generalize that the segregationists' "unmasking" of the children's book also revealed their desire to read rabbits' tales for interracial sex. The very desire to see interracial sex in any rabbit patch was obviously connected with the fear of any representation of it—for it would "brainwash" readers, weakening the young citizens' defenses. Hence representation was logically the same as advocacy, and therefore it had to be stopped. This was also the core of the segregationist fear that resulted in such institutions as exclusive beaches (and that the "Mixed Bathing" cat postcard perhaps also obliquely criticized).

In his book *Race Orthodoxy in the South* (1914), Thomas Pearce Bailey, a professor of psychology and the dean of the Department of Education at the University of Mississippi, expressed his belief that one reaches the "the real *crux* of the question" when one asks, "May not all the equalities be ultimately based on potential social equality,[29] and that in turn on intermarriage?" Bailey was therefore discouraged to discover that "even the high-souled Tennyson, in 'Locksley Hall,' draws a picture of the reckless, disappointed youth who has an impulse to wed a dusky maiden and rear a dusky brood."[30] Simply by representing this theme, Tennyson seems to have made the task of Bailey's educational program more difficult.

> It is just because primary race feeling is *not* deeply based in human instinct, whereas the mating instinct is so based, that a secondary racial feeling, race-pride, comes in from a more developed reflective consciousness to minimize the natural instinct for amalgamation.

Bailey is honest enough not to claim a "race instinct"[31] but, on the contrary, a mating instinct that knows no racial boundaries. And Tennyson's poem of 1842 does, indeed—in its uncut version[32]—contain the lines spoken by the lover who, spurned by his cousin Amy, dreams of an escape from the West of technology and book-learning to an Oriental island paradise:

> There methinks would be enjoyment more than in this march of mind,
> In the steamship, in the railway, in the thoughts that shake mankind.

> There the passions cramped no longer shall have scope and breathing space;
> I will take some savage woman, she shall rear my dusky race.

> Iron jointed, supple-sinew'd, they shall dive, and they shall run,
> Catch the wild goat by the hair, and hurl their lances in the sun;

> Whistle back the parrot's call, and leap the rainbows of the brooks,
> Not with blinded eyesight poring over miserable books—(697–698).

Bailey disapproved of these lines in Tennyson's poem, and they reminded the educator of the need to curb certain instincts—implicitly, by restricting access to certain racially discouraging works of literature. Otherwise, readers were likely to forget "natural boundaries" in their mating instinct. But back to the debate about *The Rabbits' Wedding*. The liberals, by playing literal readers, emphasized the difference between humans and rabbits, and did everything they could to make the segregationist position appear silly. Ingeniously, while denying that animals should ever be mistaken for human beings, they actually scored points against racial segregation as a system that may logically lead to the "banning" of children's books. Needless to say, the slightly exaggerated story of the "ban" appears to have had a wide circulation in the North.

It probably would have constituted a breach of faith, but it certainly would have made the segregationists seem less ridiculous if their opponents had spelled out and conceded the potential for human dimensions of the book. While the journalists seem to have been firm on this point, citizens who wrote letters were more open. Jane Merchant in her letter, "An Explanation," to the *Orlando Sentinel* made a remarkable move in this direction when she wittily gave "segregation-minded mommies" the following advice: "You can safely read The Little White Rabbit and [The] Little Black Rabbit to the kiddies because first you explain all little bunnies are pink and harmless when born. Then they grow hair, white, black, brown just like blonde little Suzie or dark-haired little Bobbie!" Merchant thus connected the discussion of *The Rabbits' Wedding* with the debate about the origins of racial difference.[33]

In this controversy there does not seem to have been a single ardent segregationist who would have supported the circulation of literature representing intermarriage (whether as an animal allegory or in human form) on the principle of free speech. And there was no criticism of the notion that the representation of certain themes *eo ipso* constituted a "promoting" or "recommending" of what was represented. All of these points may be the effects of a politicized discussion; and there is little need to replicate it now. Instead, we might draw the conclusion from the incident that it is hard to predict in which contexts themes will be discovered in texts that are not overtly (though they may be at least relatively, if not perhaps absolutely) "about" these themes.[34] It is also interesting that one obvious theming— that the book's color differentiation was imitative of the outerwear favored by human bridegrooms (black) and brides (white) on their wedding days— was not mentioned in the debate. In the case of *The Rabbits' Wedding*, a book that has stayed in print from its first publication to the writing of these pages, one could identify such themes as love and marriage, the animal kingdom, or sadness and happiness, but it would be hard to categorically *exclude* the interracial theme on the grounds that this is simply an animal tale, and that "animals with white fur" cannot be "blood relations of white humans."

This is not to say that theming is a random process. The method of using an absurdly chosen theme in order to mark the limits of theming is a good one—though it was more convincing on ideological grounds than on intellectual ones in this case. Nilli Diengott once took the effective example of Ezra Pound's "In a Station of the Metro" (remember: "The apparition of these faces in the crowd; /Petals on a wet, black bough"[35]) as a poem that may *not* be said to be about the maxim that we should drink milk regularly. More modestly, Erwin Panofsky observed that the ceiling of the Sistine Chapel can be understood better if we recognize that Michelangelo represents the fall and not a "déjeuner sur l'herbe."[36] Yet the social pressure exerted by the milk industry on the interpretation of imagism (or by Manet scholars on the iconography of Renaissance art) is undoubtedly less forceful than the political context that has surrounded the interracial theme, and has repeatedly denied its legitimacy and its very existence. One could, of course, try to imagine a situation in which Pound could symbolize milk-drinking: for example, in a hypothetical society that banned both Pound's poetry and lactic nutrition, a resistance movement might be provoked to use "In a Station of the Metro" as a toast-in-code before surreptitiously defiant social milk-drinking. (Though not popular at present, politically motivated milk-drinking rituals did take place during the French Revolution, when right on the ruins of the Bastille a statue much like the figure on the stamp that we saw at the beginning of this essay provided nourishment from her breast, thus creating among the diverse drinkers a sense of citizenship as siblinghood, of *fraternité*.[37]) Yet even if we invoked this context it might be hard to argue that Pound's poem was actually "about" the maxim that we should drink milk regularly, though in our hypothetical situation a person reciting "In a Station of the Metro" might be charged with "urging" his audience to drink milk. Absurdly random public theming is by no means uncommon. The German march *Alte Kameraden*, for example, considered so inherently militaristic that it was banned in Germany both after World War I and World War II, became, according to Reginald Rudorf, the club song of the Finnish amateur photographers, apparently because the word "Kameraden" (comrades) was mistranslated as "camera men." In the United States, the entertaining song of a northern Yankee minstrel show was rethemed as a serious tune that became something close to a sectional anthem: "Dixie."[38]

Still, the process of theming is negotiated by debate and, in order to be justifiable, the result should probably also appear plausible *in the work* and not just in the power generated by public contexts, be they advanced by governments, citizens, ideologues, legislators, journalists, librarians, or literary critics. Theming is thus most convincing if the work at hand is plausibly shown to make the reader "care about" that theme. Random theming may lead to tyranny.

Notes

1. For a more detailed survey of the field, see the collection, *The Return of Thematic Criticism*, ed. Werner Sollors. I shall make repeated reference to various parts of it without each time giving a more detailed citation.

2. The original also inspired Charles Cordier's *Aimez-vous les uns les autres ou Fraternité* (1867), reproduced in *The Image of the Black in Western Art*, vol. IV.1 (dist. Cambridge: Harvard University Press, 1989), ill. 159. For the U.S. stamp, see Barth Healey, "Stamp for Bastille Day Reverses the Tricolor," *New York Times*, 5 June 1989, A4.

3. Bremond, *Return*, 58.

4. Brinker, *Return*, 31.

5. Bremond, *Return*, 54.

6. Perkins, *Return*, 120.

7. Boethius, Meletius, Athanasius, and Augustine argue, as the classicist Lloyd A. Thompson summarized, that "although a black horse and an *Aethiops* both share the same 'accidental' quality of blackness, the removal of this blackness leaves the horse still a horse, but entirely eliminates the quality of the *Aethiops* from the *Aethiops*, who thereby becomes 'a white man like other men.'" See Lloyd A. Thompson, *Romans and Blacks*, 77–78. See, by contrast, José Antonio Villareal, *Pocho*, 123, with the account of a racialized socialization that suggests "a white horse is the best horse there is."

8. The card was reproduced in *Katzen lassen grüßen: Ein Postkarten-Bilderbuch . . . aus der Sammlung Stefan Moses*, n.p.

9. Hurston's essay in *The American Legion Magazine* (June 1951, pp. 14–15, 55–60) is a startling contribution that features photographs of communists like Paul Robeson, W. E. B. Du Bois, Langston Hughes, and Howard Fast that resemble most-wanted posters. See also my essay, "Of Mules and Mares in a Land of Difference; or, Quadrupeds All?"

10. Quoted from a microfilm copy provided by R. B. Murray in the Orange County Library System.

11. First published under the title *Sartoris*, 327. Cited in Gene Bluestein, "Faulkner and Miscegenation," 154.

12. Such "people" are embodied in the cartoon as the cracker farmer who looks like Huck Finn's Pa.

13. George A. Woods, "Pictures for Fun, Fact and Fancy," *New York Times Book Review*, 8 June 1958, 42; also cited in "The Rabbits' Wedding," *New York Times*, 24 May 1959, IV:2, and Rod Nordell, "Pictures to Read," *Christian Science Monitor*, 8 May 1958, 15.

14. Va. 80, 87 S.E.2d 749.

15. Charles S. Mangum, Jr., *The Legal Status of the Negro*, 237, referring to *Mississippi Code Ann.* (par. 1103 [1930]).

16. On 4 December 1987, the Mississippi Secretary of State proclaimed that section 263 of the 1890 Constitution, prohibiting interracial marriage, is deleted based upon House Concurrent Resolution #13 and ratification by the electorate on 3 November 1987 (*Mississippi Code* 1990, 198).

17. Cited in "'Rabbits' Wedding' Banned: Black Bunny Marries White," *Atlanta Constitution*, 22 May 1959, 12.

18. "Hush Puppies," *Orlando Sentinel*, 18 May 1959, B8, partly cited in "The Rabbits' Wedding," *New York Times*, 24 May 1959, IV:2, and in "Of Rabbits & Races," *Time*, 1 June 1959, 19.

19. "Rabbit Story Called Brazen," *Orlando Sentinel*, 25 May 1959, A9, published a few days *after* the story had made the *New York Times;* two of the three redirected the charge against the columnist.

20. Cited in "'The Rabbits' Wedding' Should Be Burned," *Birmingham Post-Herald*, 23 May 1959, 1.

21. "Of Rabbits & Races," *Time*, 1 June 1959, 19.

22. "Of Rabbits & Races," *Time*, 1 June 1959, 19.

23. "'Rabbits' Wedding' Banned: Black Bunny Marries White," *Atlanta Constitution*, 22 May 1959, 12. In "White Rabbit Married Black One—Book Banned From Open Shelves," *Birmingham Post-Herald*, 22 May 1959, 26, Reed is quoted as saying, "We have not lost our integrity," and defending her decision to "stop peddling the book" by referring to the charge of the Montgomery *Home News* that Williams' book was "promoting integration."

24. *Birmingham Post-Herald*, 23 May 1959, 1. See also "'Rabbit' Book Burning Urged," *Orlando Sentinel*, 23 May 1959, A3.

25. *New York Times*, 22 May 1959, 29; *Time*, 1 June 1959, 19. See also Morton Zabel in Doris Y. Wilkinson, *Black Male/White Female: Perspectives on Interracial Marriage and Courtship*, 123.

26. Rita Levy, "All About Rabbits" (Letter), *Orlando Sentinel*, 25 May 1959, A9.

27. The press release has been reconstructed here from the excerpts published in the *New York Times*, 22 May 1959, 29; *Time*, 1 June 1959, 19; and the *Orlando Sentinel*, 23 May 1959, A3. Garth Williams, his publisher, and the Alabama Library system did not respond to inquiries.

28. *Orlando Sentinel*, 25 May 1959, A9.

29. This is, of course, the telling code word that qualifies the ideal of *fraternité*. "Social equality" is the term Ellison's innocent young protagonist in *Invisible Man* articulates by mistake, and the concept that the Mississippi legislature prohibited citizens to propagate. As Gunnar Myrdal explained in *An American Dilemma* (New York: Harper, 1944), 586, "the very lack of precision allows the notion of 'no social equality' to rationalize the rather illogical and wavering system of color caste in America." He also stated that the doctrine of "no social equality" was understood as a precaution to hinder miscegenation and "particularly intermarriage" (588), and he mentioned that the Communist Party was exceptional in giving

Negroes full social equality (508). See the perceptive discussion by Milton Mayer, "The Issue is Miscegenation," in *White Racism*, eds. Schwartz and Disch, 207–217.

30. New York: Neale Publishing Co., 1914.

31. This is unlike, for example, Henry W. Grady, who claimed an "ineradicable and positive" instinct "that will keep the races apart" in his attack on George Washington Cable, "In Plain Black and White," *Century* 29.7 (1885): 909–917; here 912.

32. *The Poems of Tennyson*, ed. Christopher Ricks (London: Longmans, 1969), 688–699. *Selections from Tennyson* (London: Leopold B. Hill, n.d.), however, omits all the lines cited below from its only slightly abridged rendition of "Locksley Hall."

33. *Orlando Sentinel*, 25 May 1959, A9.

34. It would be interesting to compare *The Rabbits' Wedding* with, say, the film *Guess Who's Coming to Dinner* (1967) in order to reflect on the difference.

35. From *Selected Poems*, ed. and introd. T. S. Eliot (London: Faber and Faber, n.d.; orig. ed. 1928), 113.

36. Nilli Diengott, "Thematics: Generating or Theming a Text?" *Orbis Litterarum* 43 (1988): 95–107; Panofsky in Kaemmerling, ed., *Ikonographie und Ikonologie: Theorien, Entwicklung, Probleme*, 188.

37. See Marc Shell, *Children of the Earth: Literature, Politics, and Nationhood*, 142–143, for historical examples of revolutionary milk-drinking rituals designed to create a sense of siblinghood. "During the decade of the 1790s—when medical ideologists debated whether children who drank milk from extrafamilial nurse-mothers thereby became essentially bastards, and whether children who drank the milk of extraspecies animals thereby became essentially animals—the idea of national regeneration through common lactation, already a theme in American politics, was literalized at national milk-drinking rituals like the 'Festival of the Unity and Indivisibility of the Republic' (an elaborate ceremony of 10 August 1793, orchestrated by Robespièrre's associate, the painter Jacques-Louis David. A commemorative medal struck for the festival entitled, 'Régéneration française,' depicts milk or water spilling from the breasts of a statuesque alma mater, raised on the ruins of the Bastille and inscribed, 'Ce sont tous mes enfants' ['They are all my children']."

38. See Hans Nathan, "Dixie," *Encyclopedia of Southern Culture*, eds. Reagan Wilson and Ferris, 1052.

CHAPTER 2

WHO CAN TELL?

The Blanks in Villaverde

Doris Sommer

How clever readers feel holding *Cecilia Valdés* (Cuba, 1882), certainly as clever as Cirilo Villaverde's narrator, who doesn't make the obvious connections about the heroine's obscure background. Readers have always understood them and probably have felt flattered by their competence. Clearly, the light-skinned beauty who tries, with some success, to pass for white was born in 1812 to a mulatta who went mad after her white lover sent to an orphanage the shameful evidence of their affair. We know that his cruelty abates too late for the mother, but baby Cecilia is returned to her maternal grandmother's house, where she is taught that any white husband is better than a black one, and to the street where she falls in love with Leonardo Gamboa, the spoiled son of Don Cándido Gamboa, a Spanish sugar planter who—horrors!—happens to be her father, too. The lovers don't know that their attachment is incestuous, or that their conflicting expectations—erotic play for him, marriage for her—will clash violently. Real deceit is the problem. This is not Garcilaso de la Vega's flaunting of insider information in order to command respect, nor Rigoberta Menchú's decorous claims to cultural secrets, nor Sethe's reluctance (in Toni Morrison's *Beloved*) to repeat a damaging story that everyone knows. Were it not for secrecy's perverse effects here, incest could have been avoided. Lukewarm Leonardo would have abstained had he known who was who, as he abstains with his sister Adela, described as Cecilia's double: if they "were not flesh and blood siblings," the narrator volunteers, "they would have been lovers . . ." (57).

The other woman in Leonardo's life is Isabel Ilincheta, elegant, correct, a fitting counterpart to independent and candid Cecilia. Isabel seems

too good to be a standard heroine, although her combination of rational and romantic virtues was standard in the foundational fictions written elsewhere in Latin America. She is practically a hero, modeled perhaps
after Villaverde's wife, a political activist working for Cuba's independence
from Spain.[1] It is Isabel who runs her father's coffee plantation, which is
less labor-intensive than sugar; and her womanly charm doesn't interfere
with a markedly virile appeal.[2] Leonardo's schizophrenic destiny of desire
dooms the match; he can profess love for both women: for his incestuous
and finally narcissistic copy of himself, as well as for the ideal fiscal relationship between Isabel's coffee and his father's sugar, even boasting that
many more women have room in his heart.[3] The campaigns of amorous
conquest, the intrigues and jealousies, the doubts that Isabel feels about
joining a smug and brutal slaveholding family, are all set on a detailed backdrop of a society that denies human rights to blacks and makes monsters
of their masters.

The tragedy comes to a circular climax when Cecilia and her lover set
up house together and have a baby girl, but separate, once bored Leonardo
feels ready to marry Isabel. Cecilia complains about the betrayal to her des-
perate mulatto admirer, a tailor's apprentice by day and musician by night,
which doubles him as a creator of autonomous Cuban style and hints at
the generally mulatto tone of national style.[4] The tailor had been waiting
for a chance to cut out the traitor Leonardo, and his murderous race to
the church ceremony—where Cecilia hoped the bride would die, not the
groom—leaves the mistress as mad as her mother was. And it leaves her
baby quite helplessly orphaned.

Long before that climax, though, the reader has been building toward it
with the pleasure of interpretive control. No one but the reader, it seems,
can predict the nefarious finale from the first pages on. Don Cándido
Gamboa has been careful to keep his illicit affairs secret, even to the point
of sending the baby Cecilia to an orphanage and controlling possible informants. "Not everything is meant to be said" (112), he once winked to
his wife in a conversation about new slave imports after slavery was outlawed in 1817. But everyone knew about the violations of the trade ban that
England forced on Spain, just as everyone knew that rich white men were
having their way with poor mulattas. When his jealous wife and legitimate
daughters call pretty Cecilia into their house, neither she nor they succeed
in learning the girl's parentage. All they know is that she has an uncanny
resemblance to Adela, which is probably why Leonardo finds Cecilia so
alluring. But the reader knows. We know who the father is from the very

beginning of this long four-part novel about Cuba in the 1820s; and we know that incest will be a figure for the social dangers in a slave society, just as we sense that the plotlines of secrecy and intrigue will cross one another to tangle even the legitimate stories of family and nation. All this is obvious, as I say, and it must have been blatant to Cubans when the novel was published, between the wars of independence, when blacks and whites distrusted each other with good reason.

Yet the educated and articulate narrator never spells out the connections between Don Cándido and Cecilia, between her lover and the father they share. For some reason, Cándido's habit of stalking and inquiring after the girl, her resemblance to Adela, and Leonardo's taste for sisters don't come together in a narration that is nevertheless intrigued by these details. The storyteller punctuates the tale with one revealing point after another, but doesn't connect the dots. Why is this so? The connections are plain and the pattern is sadly predictable in a cynical slave society where white privilege acknowledges decent norms only by controlling indecent information. Incest—as a synecdoche for the vice that follows from deceitful relations—was already a compelling theme in Latin American literature (think of Ecuador's *Cumandá*, Peru's *Aves sin nido*), and it would continue to be. What is noteworthy in this 1882 novel is the narrator's apparent nescience. Villaverde is calling attention to discretion that hides nothing, before unreliable narrators became standard in modern fiction. No one could be stupid enough to miss Cuba's obviously perverse social relationships, unless, of course, the narrator and his equally discreet protagonists were acting dumb for some unsaid reason.

Framed

To overlook the white narrator's reluctance to say the obvious misses the point of his narrative style. The bumbling narrator performs a hesitation to assimilate information, while competent readers find it easy. They congratulate themselves for the good job of filling in blanks and tying up loose ends. With the text neatly knotted, readers have rested comfortably, confident of their command. But the rest will be disturbed if readers admit that they don't need it, because the book was too easy and the minimal effort exerted never earned the right to satisfaction. In that state of disturbed inactivity a doubt may gnaw at the hastily tied knots until the texture of a competent reading loosens and frays into a web of worries.

Who, finally, conquered whom? Did readers adeptly process unconnected information? Or was the story studiously disconnected in order to lure readers into weaving so carelessly that they were bound to feel a snag? The problem is precisely the apparent lack of problems for interpretation. The conquest is so ridiculously easy that the conquerors may find themselves as the butt of a textual joke. They feel smart for no reason at all.

Competent readers fill in a story that is purposefully laconic. It makes a spectacle of discretion to show how dangerous it is to be candid. On the very first page, where a gentleman is hiding under a broad-brimmed hat, behind the thick curtain of a carriage that stops at Cecilia's house, the narrator does not identify the obvious. About the gentleman, he says only that "all the precaution seemed superfluous, since there was not a living soul on the street" (1). The narrator might have been describing himself. The same superfluous precaution repeats in his pretense of mystery. It is transparent, practically luminous, as a backdrop for the stark information he supplies. The narrative veil hides nothing, but serves as a figure for the social constraints against *telling* that the narrator locates around himself.

He theatricalizes the limits of communication without creating suspense, as Sethe dramatizes the danger of telling a story everyone knows in *Beloved*. If Villaverde were writing a mystery, he would not supply all of the relevant information long before we have heard the story told straight out. Like *Beloved*, this novel hesitates and stutters at the obstacles that get in the way of knowing and telling. At points, the narrator even thematizes the trouble that positionality makes for understanding, as when he comments on the punishment of a slave by his master. "It is difficult to explain, for those who have been neither one nor the other, and impossible to understand in all its force for those who have never lived in a slave country" (103). Then, the epigraph of Part Three, Chapter Six, reads, "About blacks . . . Oh! my tongue holds back/ From forming the name of their misfortunes!" (210). Each time the narrator underlines his own incompetence, he suggests ours too. And the insistence makes the incompetence of privilege into a thesis of the book, while it puts off—more and more mechanically— those who could tell. It suspends the story every time a character decides to white out the black marks that make up the writing here. Cecilia's grandmother, for example, is relieved when she can stop telling the girl more about her parents than was prudent, though Cecilia has probably guessed more than she wants to know for sure. The novel calls her *maliciosa*, which means astutely suspicious.[5]

Nothing more opportune could have happened than the interruption that came with the friend's visit. The old woman had said more than prudence allowed, and the young one was afraid to find out the intimate meaning of her grandmother's last words. What did she know? Why was her language so veiled? Did she have well-founded suspicions or was she just trying to intimidate her?

The truth is that, during the dispute, with their consciences alarmed and with some facts at hand, both of them had advanced onto a slippery terrain previously hidden from their sight. The first to step in would have to gather an enormous harvest of pain and remorse. For her part, Grandma Josefa didn't think the moment had come to let Cecilia in on the real facts of her life (139).

For related reasons, Don Cándido prefers not to say what he knows. He refuses to discuss either his personal past with his suspicious wife or his political present as a contraband slave dealer.[6] In response to Doña Rosa's curiosity, her husband is discreet, as always. Discretion and double-dealing repeat throughout the book as the origin of intrigue and misunderstanding. "Are you with me?" Cándido asks Rosa, in a scene that echoes back and forth in the book. "Not everything is meant to be said" (112). The cagey reader may be winking back, apparently wise to Cándido and to the rest of the characters who refuse to be candid with one another. Who besides the reader realizes so much about Cecilia's unidentified parents and about her romance with Leonardo? Who else has figured out that the men in her life are already intimately related? Hardly anyone in the novel seems to know what is going on: not the mulatta, not her white lover, and certainly not the apparently benighted narrator.

But there are characters in the novel who can and do tell the story straight to those who will hear it.[7] They are the black slave informants, Dionisio, the lonely cook in the Havana house, and his wife María de Regla, the wet nurse (a figure for the jet-black universal mother *Yemayá*) who is banished to the plantation because she knows too much.[8] Each time a pale protagonist (or reader) turns a deaf ear to the slaves' stories, Villaverde exposes the inability to listen as a dissembled gesture of control that keeps the text of Cecilia's life conveniently blank, that is, white. The gesture is one of those defensive denials that end self-destructively. To defend the privilege that comes with whiting out her history, Cecilia and other presumptively white characters must ignore the details that make her so compromisingly colorful, so available for the final tragedy of misfired affairs.

And to protect the privilege of our expert reading, readers are also tempted to ignore colorful competitors. Rather than defer too soon to the authority of black narrators, readers ignore them for a while and flatter themselves as collaboraters of the prudent white one who frames the novel.

Who suspected that he is framing us, too? Readers to date have not suspected Villaverde of double-dealing, but a suspicion may wedge itself in, as I already suggested, if we notice that the paradoxical interpretive problem here is that it is no problem at all. We win less than a Pyrrhic victory; it is actually delusion. The point of making a spectacle of the narrator's reluctance, I am saying, is to show how difficult it is to say anything in a society based on deceit, especially if (like the narrator and his white readers) deceit is one's guarantee of privilege. Practically the only characters who do not profit from it are the black slaves. If we would listen, they would defy restrictions and tell freely.

Defiance is risky by definition. Not everyone is prepared to listen appropriately, and telling freely can compound the injustices that these stories would tell. "I'm afraid of many things, of everything. Blacks have to be careful about what they say," says María de Regla.[9] To the slave's caution, her young mistress Adela incautiously declares, "Your fear is unfounded," as if an enlightened sense of universal justice were not obscenely out of place in a slave society.[10] "But, my lady," María instructs her, "you seem to forget that a slave always stands to lose when she suspects her masters" (239).

Pierre Menard's Lesson

Over a century of admiring readers of *Cecilia Valdés* have been as forgetful as Adela about the importance of positionality in the circulation of knowledge. The narrator's unconnected story line might have been a constant reminder, long before this late scene when María reminds her mistress that danger is asymmetrical. Readers don't remark on the narrator's stuttering; maybe they excuse it as a tired convention of intrigue. Instead, they have engaged the book's complex realism and enjoyed the satisfactions of piecing together spotty accounts of local customs, psychological complexity, economic and political analyses, its general attention to the details of history.[11] If now I can notice, with you, that the narrator's disconnectedness is conspicuous, theatrical, it is because history makes a difference in reading literature, not only in writing it.[12] Borges gave that lesson in "Pierre Menard, Author of Don Quijote," where Cervantes' classic novel had entirely changed its meanings and allusions from the time it was first published to the time Menard rewrote parts of it, word for word, three centuries later. Barely more than a century has passed since Villaverde published his enduring novel. He described it then as realistic, meaning that it was true to the characters he knew, down to their styles of dress and speech (their "hairs and warts," as the common expression goes). As a realistic novel, it avoided the formulae of romance popularized in Latin America through *Atala* and *Paul et Virginie*.[13] Commentators have generally followed his instructions for reading the book, downplaying the romance, focusing on the sociological information so intimately detailed that it verges on self-ethnography.

Our postmodern moment is suspicious of objectivity and realism; it notices that storytelling is unavoidably partial, in both senses of limited and interested. Questions follow fast about who gives information, for what purpose, inside which interpretive frame. And we can stop to notice that the primary source of information plays the fool in *Cecilia Valdés*. Surely this means something. It certainly means a dysfunction in the tradition of omniscient narrator, which was still viable in contemporary foundational romances, like *Cumandá* (Ecuador, 1879) and *Enriquillo* (Dominican Republic, 1882), written in countries slow to consolidate modern projects. Cuba hadn't achieved political or economic modernity, even at this late date. The opportunities festered in an anachronistic but lucrative slave economy, and in a racist colonial administration. No wonder the white narrator is purposefully underdeveloped.

Postmoderns may be quick to notice that Villaverde's narrator is a joke on master narratives in general. Will we also notice the joke on the reader, whose early textual conquest mocks us later on, after black slaves put the story together more ably than we possibly could? Readers should be "growing wary of the hermeneutic circularity," in George Steiner's words, that assumes a text to be continuous with the reader's cultural assumptions.[14] The old habits have a way of violating the messages moved from one social and cultural context to another, while interpreters are loathe to acknowledge the remainder lost in asymmetrical translation (let us say in the transaction between a Cuban slave and her mistress). That remainder, though, is what Villaverde features; it is the difference between master-slave experience and white reporting, between free love and aristocratic secrecy, between Cuba's cultural autonomy and Spain's colonial accounting for it. Readers disappear that remainder if they force Villaverde's multi-voiced Cuban novel into conventional formulae for reading. They don't get the point if they get it too easily; that is, if the book leaves them thinking that the only character playing the fool here is a white narrator.

Cuban Stories in Black and White

By 1882 Villaverde must have thought that his first version of *Cecilia Valdés* (1839) sounded hopelessly monotone.[15] His narrator had no competitors, no slave storytellers who face the facts that whites won't tell. This narrator is discreet without sounding silly, and engaging enough to let readers *maliciar* the rest. He leaves loose ends for the female readers he addresses directly; and they surely tie things up, along with Leonardo's sisters who immediately see themselves, their brother, and their father in Cecilia's face.[16] The daring feature of the story was its celebration of interracial love, during the repressive colonial regime that outlawed "unequal" marriages, though the Church would have allowed them to avert more bastard births.[17] At the novel's end, Leonardo vows that nothing can keep him from his "santa mulata," neither Isabel's feelings nor earthly treasures.[18] Daring as this is, it was evidently inoffensive enough to appear in Cuba and then in Spain at the same time that Spanish censors were proscribing abolitionist novels like *Francisco* by Anselmo Suárez y Romero (finally published in 1880), and confiscating others, like *Sab* (1841) by Gertrudis Gómez de Avellaneda. The second *Cecilia Valdés* (1882) would be more probing. The title names two different novels, and Villaverde himself is two distinct authors. A lot of history intervened.

Villaverde had written the 1839 novel at the urging of Domingo del Monte, the abolitionist editor and journalist who hosted a famous *tertulia* in Havana where intellectuals read from works that del Monte himself would commission for supporters who would gather to listen. The works might be sent to England as part of the 1838 *dossier* that del Monte was preparing for Richard Madden, the British representative to the International Tribunal of Justice that oversaw the ban on slave trading and the protection of freedmen. The purpose of del Monte's circle of liberal planters and professionals was to embarrass Spain into granting abolition and other reforms to Cuba, including representation in the Spanish *cortes*. Representation had been granted, briefly, before absolute rule returned in the 1830s. And it would be reinstituted in 1879 as a thin formality, after ten years of Cuba's struggle for independence convinced Spain that a measure of Cuban autonomy was the empire's best bet; but the sham soon discouraged the Cuban delegates.[19] Anselmo Suárez y Romero read from *Fran-*

cisco in del Monte's salon. (Gómez de Avellaneda didn't; she lived in the less industrialized province of Oriente and never warmed to the English, who played the opportunists in her *Sab.*) And the slave poet Juan Francisco Manzano read from his *Autobiography*, after which enough money was collected from the audience for the author to buy his freedom.[20] Until recently, Manzano's was considered the only slave narrative in Spanish, but thanks to Sonia Labrador-Rodríguez we know that others had been published before abolition and that they continue to be hidden, or discounted, as if the tradition of a black intelligentsia were still too threatening or embarrassing for a Cuban national culture.[21]

Villaverde was neither a slave nor a planter. If he were, abolition would have been a clear priority.[22] For the slave it meant freedom; and for the modern planter it meant rational reform in an increasingly mechanized sugar industry. The thirty-five-year-old writer was a self-supporting lawyer and journalist. The sixth of ten children born in 1812 (the same year as Cecilia) to a plantation doctor, Villaverde had grown up between the field and the infirmary, where bodies were wrecked and then repaired for more abuse. His parents sent him to the capital for a decent education, which he got after presenting proof of "purity of blood" for admission to the university law school.[23] His proof was probably straightforward; but certificates could often be bought for a price, a corrupt practice that helped to "democratize" the professions in Cuba.[24] Perhaps for these and other personal historical reasons, Villaverde lost patience with reformists who thought they could negotiate Cuba's relative autonomy with the racist, corrupt empire. So he began to conspire against Spain in favor of Cuba's separation. Villaverde left del Monte to his elegant gatherings and joined Narciso López, an early advocate of armed resistance. Their conspiracy was betrayed, however, and Villaverde spent sixth months in jail, from late 1848 until early 1849, when he escaped to Florida and continued to New York City where López was renewing his efforts.

Until his death in 1894, just before the definitive War of Independence, Villaverde was a major figure in the important New York wing of Cuban revolutionary politics. History books have downplayed his leadership in the New York Junta and in spin-off organizations and have almost forgotten his influential journalism in exile, but a closer look is bringing him into the center of that scene.[25] Political historians are more likely to remember his independentist wife Emilia Casanova, an unconventionally outspoken woman memorialized by Villaverde in *Apuntes biográficos de la ilustre cubana Emilia C. de Villaverde* (1874). His reputation as a writer of fiction has evidently overwhelmed his political accomplishments, as he sensed it would by compatriots who dismiss creativity as dreaming or entertainment. In self-defense he explains in the 1879 Prologue to the second *Cecilia Valdés* that politics and fiction didn't mix, that he hadn't so much as read a novel in thirty years. (Is this true? Could he have avoided the ubiquitous *Uncle Tom's Cabin* during the Civil War, for example, or the slave narratives that were being published in the 1850s and 1860s? These would have played in provocative counterpoint—for the future novelist of competing voices—to Stowe's standard sentimental tone.) Lest the reader imagine that Villaverde had frivolously occupied himself with the novel that he was presenting, he adds that it was written in a short period of time. His anxiety about not being taken seriously sounds familiar among Caribbean literati-leaders of the period, although an earlier, more confident moment in already established Latin American republics had made the statesman-novelist into a viable national hero. Like Villaverde, Puerto Rican Eugenio María de Hostos was protesting that his novel *Las peregrinaciones de Bayoán* (1863) had been a distraction from his patriotic responsibilities (though his protest appears, ironically, in the preface to an 1873 second edition of the novel);[26] and José Martí would punish himself, in beautiful poems and other literary genres, for losing time and emotional energy to the seductions of creative writing.[27]

Thirty years in New York is a long time. Forty, between one *Cecilia* and another, is even longer. Villaverde began those New York years as a militant separatist, an ally and secretary to Narciso López. But he was no independentist. That came much later. From the late 1840s through the 1850s, independence seemed impractical to most white Cuban dissidents, for whom the prudent alternatives were either autonomist reforms or separation from Spain with a friendly connection to the United States. (Prudence, you may remember, was the justification Cecilia's grandmother used for keeping the girl's background an explosive secret.) The political options seemed limited to reform or annexation because the vicarious experience of Latin American independent republics was a warning as much as an inspiration. Successful revolutions had typically led to a generation of civil wars that left the new countries poor and mortgaged to neo-colonial powers. Furthermore, and even more troubling, Cubans still had nightmares about revolution in Haiti, where slaves took revenge on their masters. On an island like Cuba, with as many blacks as whites, with enough incentive for vengeance to turn a political struggle into a race war and a disciplined military tradition among blacks and mulattos in Spanish regiments that secured the island against invasion (England managed to capture Havana in 1762), most whites were afraid of independence.[28] The rash of uprisings in Cuba that ended with the slave conspiracy (*La Escalera*) of 1844 worried the white creoles as much as it did the Spanish government. In reprisal, the colonial authorities executed many illustrious mulatto artisans of Havana, whether or not they were guilty of sedition.[29] Villaverde commemorates them in the detailed guest list at the formal "dance for colored people" (Part II, Chap. xvii). Stability mattered for a future country that faced anarchy and bloodletting, not to mention the nuisance of lost property and privilege. Along with separation from Spain, therefore, many Cubans favored annexation to the stable, modern, and prosperous United States.

Why not? White Dominicans were making the same calculations, some in favor of the United States, others in favor of re-annexation to Spain. (The pro-Spanish party won in 1861, but the opposition drove Spain out by 1865. Anything seemed better to the precarious white leadership of the Dominican Republic, recently liberated from Haiti, than a new invasion by the "Africans.") So why not? There was support in the U.S. for expansion to Cuba, notably southern slave-holding support. But black and mulatto insurrectionists would know why not: Because Cubans couldn't trust either self-serving empire, Spain or the U.S. But López was confident that the U.S. would give its tacit blessing to his planned invasion, and that annexed Cuba would maintain its cultural distinctiveness, its language and customs, ready for the next step towards complete independence. Reformist José Antonio Saco thought López was deluded; he warned that annexation would mean the end of Cuba as it had meant the end of autonomy for Texas and California, because the U.S. could not tolerate cultural differences.[30] A generation later, José Martí repeated the warning about Anglo intolerance, and he dismissed the step-by-step approach to independence: "Once the United States is in Cuba, who will drive it out?"[31]

Saco had been exiled from Cuba for daring to object to the illicit slave trade. Exiled in the United States, he continued to argue for Spanish reform and Cuban autonomy. Villaverde fired back a series of polemical editorials in 1852 through New York's *La Verdad*, an émigré newspaper established jointly by the Cuban Junta and U.S. expansionists, including John O'Sullivan who coined the term "Manifest Destiny."[32] Villaverde denounced Saco's impractical abolitionism and his irresponsible refusal of the U.S. connection. Worse, he accused Saco of working in the interest of the few sugar-rich families that would profit from wage slavery in Cuba.

"Mr. Saco, who apparently dedicated himself to the cause of Cuban liberty and independence at the beginning of his political career, later turned all his attention and talents to the cause of one race of Cubans, the blacks. And today he serves the interests of one class . . . that of a few Cuban families."[33] Annexation for Villaverde was a self-preserving calculation, the only prudent move to start the process of gradual emancipation for blacks and for Cuba.

But after the mysterious betrayal of Narciso López in 1851, when Spain was informed of his armed expedition to Cuba so that it could intercept López and execute him, annexationists lost confidence in the host country. The United States was holding out for a diplomatic resolution with Spain and was actively discouraging Cuban insurgency. By 1855 two things were clear: the U.S. would support only a negotiated settlement with Spain; *and* negotiation was impossible because Spain would never sell the island. A letter of a Spanish consul retrieved from Havana mocked McKinley for taking a possible deal seriously.[34] Disappointed dissidents went home to their plantations or to artisanal and professional careers. Villaverde and his family went back for a short while, until Emilia's irrepressible politics made staying in the colony too dangerous. They returned to New York, the provisional home for the most militant separatists. In 1865 they formed the *Sociedad Republicana de Cuba y Puerto Rico*. By then the exiles understood that their alliance with the slave states had hurt the cause. And their policy changed dramatically to uncompromising support for immediate abolition (elite Cubans on the island were still reluctant), probably because by then, ending slavery was a pre-requisite for joining the Union. At the same time, the New York leadership was responding to popular pressure to give up the separatist campaign for U.S. diplomatic support in favor of a military campaign for independentist insurrection.[35]

Villaverde had evidently caught himself in the major blind spot of his political life. As late as 1863, he was telling history with a slaveholding bias, by translating and publishing Edward Pollard's *History of the First Year of the Southern War*.[36] And Villaverde's polemic against Saco's abolitionism was notorious. Cubans still remember it with embarrassment, even Villaverde's official fans who excuse the polemic as a sign of the ideologically immature times.[37] That there was more than one option at the time is obvious from Saco's impassioned anti-slavery campaign and from the reformist platform in general. In 1855 the New York newspaper *El Pueblo* went so far as to include slaves in the call for a separatist revolt. It took nothing less

than the U.S. Civil War to produce Villaverde's about-face on the importance of slavery. He turned completely around from punishing Saco as a
narrow abolitionist, in a newspaper funded by Southern money, to concluding that immediate freedom for slaves was the first and most important
step to Cuba's liberation. Gradually, a broad-based, multi-racial revolution became the nation's only real option. And Villaverde became its most
important and ardent defender.

He had caught himself in another blind spot, an effect of underesti-
mating abolition. Villaverde had thought that annexation was at least prudent, if not ideal; now he admitted that it was corrupt. While white Cubans
were negotiating their continued privilege under one empire or another,
black and mulatto compatriots were mounting a struggle for independence. Whites, including Villaverde and his stubbornly discreet narrator,
tried for a long time not to acknowledge that it was the only way to win
freedom for Cuba. They told themselves one unbelievable story after another: first about annexation bringing gradual freedom; when that made
no sense, some retrieved the equally unconvincing story about autonomy
and Spanish reform. Neither story was politically convincing, but each
kept white privilege at the center. Meanwhile blacks were telling an obvious counter-history (as they would in the novel): that the U.S. couldn't be
trusted, which supported Saco and other reformists, *and* that Spain was a
losing proposition as well, which supported annexationists. The conclusion was that both imperious partners were bad for Cuba. Independence
was the only and obvious route for development. The only thing lost in
this story was white privilege. Cubans of color argued and acted on this
clarity; and the white leaders (along with Villaverde's narrator) continued
to act as if they couldn't put the picture together.

By 1869, shortly after the Ten Years' War (1868–1878) had begun under
the leadership of mulatto General Antonio Maceo and Dominican exile
Máximo Gómez, Villaverde demanded that the New York Junta get behind
its own decree to destroy the island's sugar wealth as part of the insurrection against Spain. He was sure that the junta was sabotaging its own
declared public policy, as sure as his reader will be that Leonardo Gamboa is playing on the mulatta's loyalty to his own advantage. Villaverde accused the junta of opportunism, and now, vehemently anti-annexationist,
he helped to found the pro-independence *Sociedad de Artesanos Cubanos.*
History was telling a story of self-determined Cuban independence, and
Villaverde listened. A year after the frustrated Ten Years' War had left most

white Cubans exhausted and resigned, the Little War (*la Guerra Chiquita*, 1879–1880) was launched by uncompromising black and mulatto forces. And it was denounced by whites as a prelude to race war.

Racial fears for whites and resentments for blacks had apparently put an end to the independence movement by 1880. But then José Martí began an ambitious coalition among the multi-racial Cuban tobacco workers in Florida and the white émigré elite in New York, in order to prepare for the definitive war of 1895–1898. Villaverde was ready to respond.[38] In fact, his 1860s radicalism was probably one of Martí's inspirations for insisting that the insurrection begin inside Cuba, to make military expeditions to the island welcome and useful.[39] Martí succeeded in mitigating some white anxiety by eliminating race as an organizing principle of the war: "Everything that divides men, everything that separates or herds men together in categories is a sin against humanity . . . there can be no racial animosity because there are no races."[40] Other white leaders were erasing the category from their speeches, from the records of armies and hospitals. But black insurgents didn't give up the link between independence and racial liberation. And they resented rich whites who joined the movement late enough to know it would succeed and got army commissions that outranked the black leaders. Villaverde had apparently been hearing the objections to whiting out the difference during preparations for war, to judge from the indelibly colored lines of information he writes into his novel. It is true that all the lines come from one white author, and it is possible that the dialogic tension he creates is too neatly resolved under his control. But even this skeptical reading is testimony to the skepticism and self-doubt that competent readers learn from his novel.[41]

Villaverde died in New York before the definitive war began. He could not have known, but might have suspected, that the white leadership— always afraid of black rule—was negotiating behind Martí's back for a U.S. intervention once the Cubans got control of the island. Secret dealing and sabotage by privileged whites had been the targets of Villaverde's militancy since the 1860s and into the Ten Years' War. Nationalists were sure that the junta was double-dealing: negotiating for U.S. support with Secretary Fish, who always held out for a diplomatic deal with Spain, and saying that the negotiations included U.S. recognition of Cuban independence. "The facts regarding these intrigues are difficult to establish," writes historian Gerald Poyo, "but the nationalists believed that during 1874 and 1875 the junta orchestrated a major effort to find a compromise with the Spanish and terminate the war."[42] (One oppositional response, from the radicalized eastern province of Cuba, was a secret society literally called *Los hermanos del silencio*.)[43] Double-dealing would also be the uncontrollable motor of Villaverde's tragic novel.

Not Meant to Be Said

Is Villaverde's narrator a victim of compatriots' deceit as well as of his own prudence? I don't think so. He knows too much. Prudence is the main problem. The narrator delays transparently, with the studied and stubborn clumsiness of New York leaders who refused to give up privilege, to produce an effect that is more self-critical than denunciatory. Why won't the narrator listen to the black informants that Villaverde supplies? This question may occur to some readers, at least in passing. Forcing it is probably Villaverde's most pointed political effort in the novel. But the answer is depressingly evident, after all the double-dealing and secrecy that had been delaying independence. Whites don't listen to blacks, not even apparently well-meaning whites, like our narrator who tells tragic stories about Cuba, or like those who form separatist juntas in New York. Blacks are the ideal informants here, as they were in Gertrudis Gómez de Avellaneda's abolitionist novel, *Sab* (Cuba, 1841). But white listeners are no longer prepared to hear them.

Before the slave insurrections of the early 1840s, and the baffled cross-racial alliances that finally broke over the *Guerra Chiquita* in 1879, Avellaneda could portray her slave protagonist as an unproblematic hero. Sab was more than an idealized sentimental lover; he was practically the author of his own novel, a figure for the culturally shackled woman who wrote it. *Sab c'est moi*, she could have said. He is omniscient, sensitive, controlling, and then revealing in the posthumous letter that sets all the records straight. When his passion and frustration pitch, when he complains to free-thinking white Teresa (who fearlessly agreed to meet him at midnight) of love's torment in a slave society that makes blacks scream for white blood, readers are poised to listen. They listen to incendiary Sab, afraid for their safety, perhaps, but sure that he is right.[44]

Hardly anyone listens to slaves in *Cecilia Valdés*. One unhappy difference brought by the intervening forty years of white control (and treachery) over black and mulatto initiative is the evidence that whites have not been listening. Their reluctance shows up in Cuba's frustrating history, and it determines Villaverde's Cuban tragedy. Hundreds of pages pass before the slaves can tell about Cecilia, secretly nursed by María de Regla who thereby knows too much. So María is sent to the sugar fields where she nurses the tortured slaves and then knows even more of Don Cándido's indelicate secrets. She is eager to talk, an ideal but unbidden informant, like her husband Dionisio who stays in Havana for a dozen lonely years before anyone can hear him.

The black informants cannot be dismissed as uncivilized or inarticulate in this novel. They speak in a superior register of Spanish that could itself be a promise of social coherence, as it had been in *Sab*.[45] Minor characters of color do keep their linguistic distance, while those newcomers or social marginals who refuse to collaborate in standard spoken Cuban either give Villaverde the opportunity for innovative writing in local slang or they stop the interaction through suicidal muteness.[46] No one, for example, damns slavery louder than the recently imported field hand who literally swallowed his tongue instead of learning to speak like a slave. These ideal informants are black, as I said, unmistakably distinct from their white masters. They are no longer light-skinned like Sab, who passed for white as easily as does Villaverde's deluded heroine. In 1839, Sab's racially indefinite color was a promise of freedom. It had no old world name to confine or to control it. Not white or black or Indian, or even mulatto, Sab was a new world original, a Cuban whose local color could soon recognize itself as a nationality. By 1882, though, a distinctly Cuban coloring was making the whites nervous about losing the privileges that came with color coding. So color lines mattered more than the revolutionary leadership could say. Cecilia's light skin is a mirage of national color. It encourages her to pass; but it also makes the whites defensive, duplicitous, and bent on stopping her.[47] More dangerous than the blacks was the conclusion about mulattos in the Crown's 1844 "Report on the Promotion of White Population in the Island of Cuba." The colonial administration openly warned against the population boom in the mixed races, because it was believed they were notorious social climbers and imitators of whites.[48]

Sab's skin had been an invitation to recognize a composite and common Cuban color, "a yellowish white with a dark tinge."[49] But Cecilia's identical and indefinite color focuses the narrator's inquisitorial eye:

> To what race, then, did this girl belong? It was hard to say. Nevertheless, to a trained eye, the red lips could not hide their dark border, nor could the light on her face fail to show the shadow at the hairline. Her blood was not pure, and you might be sure that somewhere back in the third or fourth generation it was mixed with Ethiopians' (7).[50]

Cecilia can't tell to which generation she belongs, but black Dionisio can tell a lot. He is an educated slave who knows how to read and write (104), which means he knows too much. The poet Manzano had already told us autobiographical stories of being beaten when his masters caught him writing.[51] At least as credible and certainly more Cuban than his coarse slave-smuggling Spanish master, Dionisio has an "aristocratic mien, [is] well-spoken and rational" (103). And his wife, María de Regla, impresses her white listeners with "the precision and clarity of her words . . . along with her crystalline pronunciation." The problem for a slave society that legitimates inequality through color-coded grades of intelligence is precisely how well these slaves speak, and how informed they are.

> "That black woman knows how to talk," said Cocco to Don Cándido as they left the (plantation) infirmary.
> "You have no idea how well," replied Don Cándido in a lowered voice. "That is the very source of her many misfortunes" (222).

Given the opportunity, María de Regla promises the information requested about the suicidal silence of the captured field slave, and she delivers. The text reports her preamble and repeats it: "I will tell my master what has happened," to insist that, at last, we have a trustworthy teller. But other, more personal information that she commands remains unrequired for a long time. Finally, at the end of Part Three, Chapter viii, she is invited to connect the dots in what had remained a spotty story.

Adela Gamboa asks María to talk; she ushers her former nurse into the ladies' bedroom during the family's visit to the sugar plantation, because the young mistress is determined to find out why María was exiled to the fields. She and the others get more than they ask for. As the nurse who provided Adela Gamboa and Cecilia Valdés with mother's milk, María de Regla also knows who fathered both. She was the one who never got the chance to nurse the field slave who swallows his tongue to make his forced silence felt; the one who now keeps the ladies of the house listening for hours about the sinister effects of slavery that separates black families and sells them off in pieces; the Hegelian slave whose storytelling power over the enchanted mistresses comes from having done the work that only she was fit to do.

Although the ladies demand to be told, the intelligence is dismissed with an authoritarian gesture that dramatizes—again—the crisis of legitimacy when the authorities (and authors) resist knowing enough to be responsible. María de Regla fills pages with a long report that ties up the story lines left purposefully hanging by the narrator. She tells about having been rented out to a doctor in order to nurse a baby girl whose origins were kept scrupulously secret, about a mother driven mad and a suspiciously discreet grandmother, about a gentleman hidden behind his cloak but nevertheless familiar . . .

— "Who was the gentleman on the street corner?" Adela and Carmen asked together, as if in a single voice.
— "I'm not really sure, my noble ladies," stammered the old nurse. "I wouldn't dare vow that the doctor said: Don Cán . . ."
— "Aha!" Carmen exclaimed. "If you're not sure who it was, that means at least you have someone in mind. What did you think his name was?"
— "I don't think anything at all, mistress Carmita," María de Regla answered, much disturbed. "I wouldn't even dare to say my own name at this point . . . ."
— "Your fear is unfounded," Adela interceded.
— "But, my lady, you seem to forget that a slave always stands to lose when she suspects her masters."
— "What! How can you?!" interrupted Carmen, visibly angered. . . . You act dumb when it suits you and then you think you know more than we do" (239–240).

Of course she knows more, a chastened reader is saying. The figure for the good reader here is not Carmen, who refuses to listen and rushes to interpret away whatever the slave could tell her. The ideal reader is Isabel Ilincheta, who stays quiet and listens; the hard-working coffee-grower is on a visit to the Gamboa plantation as Leonardo's fiancée.

Once María's invitation to the ladies' bedroom frees the novel's flow of information, the reader who identifies with honest Isabel may feel an uncomfortable twinge of self-reproach in retrospect. The feeling has nothing to do with the incestuous mystery plot that María lays out and that had unfolded from the very beginning of the novel. Any reader can enjoy the satisfaction of getting the point long before the punchline. The self-reproach or self-doubt would be an effect of remembering a scene of refusing to hear the same information María de Regla has just authorized, just as Carmen refuses, because the information comes from a questionable source. It comes from the kind of man that white people, especially white women, have been taught to ignore: María's husband, Dionisio.

Much earlier (in Part II, chapter xvii), the lonely and bitter man, separated from his wife for twelve years, had crashed a formal dance restricted to free "colored" artisans (whose fame survives *La escalera* in this commemorative chapter). At the dance, Dionisio invites Cecilia to be his partner and she rebuffs him. Enraged, he blurts out what we partially know and she suspects: that she and Leonardo are already too intimately related to be lovers, that her nursemaid was banished to the sugar plantation where Gamboa Sr. would be safe from the nurse's knowledge. In short, that because of this haughty and thoughtless mulatta who was about to consummate her own disaster, Dionisio and his wife were leading disastrously lonely and humiliating lives.

It's not the badly guarded information that is troubling, especially not when the same facts are repeated by a non-threatening female slave in the ladies' bedroom, the conventional space for reading sentimental novels. It is the refusal to know, Cecilia's refusal, that of her admiring companions and, perhaps, of her readers. Villaverde sets the trap of racially restricted listening by keeping Dionisio anonymous for a while, yet crafting him as an aging, too-black man dressed in ill-fitting finery who forces himself on the Cuban Venus. Borrowing standards of good taste—and whole pages[52]—from his society articles for *La Moda*, Villaverde's novel counts on conventions of etiquette that would censure the aggressive outsider for inappropriately coveting the lightly bronzed object of everyone's desire. Arguably, fashion news was meant to customize a particular national style in Cuba, as it did in Juan Bautista Alberdi's Argentine journal of the same title. Surely the free men documented by their invitations to the ball, and by the references to their fashionable professions, are more worthy of her attention.

Isn't Cecilia's caution, even her disdain, understandable? Who was this easily aroused, unsolicited suitor? What possible significance could Dionisio's string of recriminations have for her? She worries about this for a little while, at least until the next dance. But then she forgets, as we may also forget. María de Regla's story can remind the reader to worry again, about why Dionisio, a good source of information and appropriate storyteller ("well-spoken and rational"), cannot be appropriately heard. Shouldn't the setting have enabled more communication? Dances were the occasion for cross-racial contacts and romance. But there was an obvious difference between this *baile de etiqueta* (where free mulatto artisans emulate the aristocracy) and the *bailes de cuna* that brought Cecilia and Leonardo together and provided the main setting for *Cecilia* in 1839.[53] They were open to everyone, as functions of religious fairs (called "Babel, scandal," in the early novel).[54]

Cuban readers just after the Ten Years' War might have appreciated the political potential of the dance scene, as the black man advanced and the light girl retreated, because dances in the revolutionary camps turned out to be testing grounds for a nascent democratic culture. Campaign diaries recently collected by Ada Ferrer are telling:

> Two similar incidents, one in 1876 during the first war and the other in 1895 during the final war, reveal the uses to which that language [to attack racist behaviors] could be put by the end of the independence period. One night in 1876 at a gathering in a rebel camp, a white woman rejected the overtures of an officer of color. The officer became furious, insisting that she refused him only because of his color. In anger, he then threatened her and anyone who dared to court her in the future. Twenty years and two wars later, at a dance at another rebel camp, another black officer tried to court a white woman. He asked her to dance, and when she refused the black officer again became angry and confronted the woman with an accusation similar to the one made in 1876. "You won't dance with me," he said, "because I am black." In this instance, however, the officer made no threats. Instead he gave a long speech on valor, patriotism, and equality, and he condemned her refusal as anti-patriotic. Now, to be racist was to be anti-Cuban.[55]

We won't dance with Dionisio, not Villaverde's heroine nor his readers. By the time we realize that he was a fine leading partner, the opportunity has gone. If this pessimistic novel shares with *Sab* a contrast between slaves who know how to lead and masters who don't, the difference is that Avellaneda's slaveholders seem innocently inept compared with Villaverde's disingenuous whites and almost whites. To keep that bad faith in focus, Villaverde does not confuse his authorial self with an omniscient informant, as Avellaneda had done. Her narrator and the slave protagonist shared information so equally that the colored line between them blurred enough to have Sab sign his name at the end of her book. Villaverde plays at the same game, but perversely. His signature appears at the beginning, on the initial page, through his own initials (and credentials?): C. V., which are also the initials of his heroine, Cecilia Valdés.[56]

He is Cecilia, born in the same year, deluded like her, unwilling but obliged to divorce desire from destiny, more white than black, but as Leonardo Gamboa remarks about his own privileged color, it is definitely Cuban in its indefinite origins. "My mother really is a Creole, and I can't vouch for her purity of blood" (38). The confusion doesn't produce the new autochthonous archetype of *Sab*, but an impossibly precarious hierarchy in which the mulatta's desire to move up tragically meets her white lover's taste for slumming. Compared to Avellaneda's bold abolitionist pronouncements, the politics in *Cecilia Valdés* are insidious, because color coding has become so constitutive of Cuban culture that the lovers never unlearn it. Instead, one yearns for racial privilege while the other plays on it.

Conscious of his complicity with privileged compatriots, Villaverde repeats their defensive deafness and blindness in his narrator. They refuse to hear or see the population of blacks, emboldened after the liberalizing Moret Law of 1870 and just over the brink of abolition (it finally came in 1880).[57] The whites simply decline legitimate intercourse with blacks. And Villaverde's text keeps pointing to the white narrator who draws blanks in order to preserve the color-fast fabric of slave society. Gesticulating at the limits of information, Cirilo Villaverde apparently invites white compatriots to notice that they have been reading Cuba inside the claustrophobic constraints of a colonial society. Maybe they will notice that the exits are marked by black guides.

Talk Cuban

This is a novel about impossible relationships, not because blacks and whites should not love one another, but because slavery makes it impossible. As Havana's frustrated district magistrate (*alcalde mayor*) puts it, "In a country with slaves . . . morals tend . . . towards laxity and the strangest, most monstrous and perverse ideas reign" (279).[58] Unlike the foundational fictions of other Latin American countries, where passion together with patriotism produced model citizens, Villaverde's Cuban novel cannot make romance and convenience coincide.[59] Cuba was not quite American, or even a country yet. It was too closely bonded with aristocratic, hierarchical Europe. We know that Gamboa Sr. married his wife for money and then looked elsewhere for love (she probably accepted him because he was European and unquestionably white), and that Leonardo admired Isabel for her useful virtues but lusted after sexy Cecilia. Both men undercut—or overextend—their affections because archaic privilege exceeds the individual bourgeois self. Father and son are seduced as much by the absolute power of their racial and sexual advantage as by their partners' charms. This is no modern and rational free market of feeling where unprotected desire could produce social growth,[60] but a bastion of colonial custom where erotic protectionism doesn't give local (re)production a legitimate chance.

The novel, then, poses the problem of racial exploitation whose other face is self-annihilation. The marriage contract to reproduce the family within domestic confines is as transparently fictional here as was the 1817 treaty to end the slave trade, an agreement which should have forced the reproduction of a labor force at home. Beyond a metaphoric relationship between broken conjugal contracts and violated treaties, we see that Havana's moralizing magistrate senses a link of cause and effect between social dissolution and slavery. The brutality allowed by new slave imports, and the unproductive privilege it fostered, he said, corroded society's most sacred values, "familial peace and harmony" (282). The family might not be quite so threatened by extramarital affairs, on which the men look with indulgence, were it not for the secrecy imposed by the conflicting code of bourgeois marriage contracts.

It is secrecy that puts Leonardo at risk of incest. He will not be guilty with Adela, because their relationship is clear. But Cecilia's parentage is an unstable secret, festering where privilege (double) crosses modern family ties. Both the narcissism and the secrecy point to the moral contradictions of a slave society that assumes it can be modern. Neither the sugar industrialists—whose personal excesses produce rebellions, suicides, and English meddling—nor the interracial lovers can make a slave society honor bourgeois contracts.

The tragedy is caused by the contraband dealings in production and reproduction. Several centuries of lying, in a system that was evidently more flexible and porous than United States slavery, blurred racial categories more than the elite would acknowledge. Whites and mulattoes either are ignorant of their situation or they would like to ignore it in order to preserve even their most illusory privileges. Having exhausted every possible avoidance strategy (as the New York émigrés exhausted reform and annexation), they eventually give the knowledgeable narrators a hearing. Blacks know and tell, with admirable command, about the overlapping affairs of Cecilia's family and the consequently fading contrast between (supposedly adventurous) exogamy and (apparently redundant) incest.

But the deteriorating distinction between familial and foreign goes unattended too long, and the whites are so stubbornly blank that, after a while, the ignorance looks as forced and unsatisfying as a slave's fate. Why has the narrative been stopping its rhythm with apparently aimless hesitations and tired pretenses of misunderstanding? Villaverde's spectacularly silly narrator was probably no fool, as any coquette would know. Acting dumb is sometimes an incitation to a leading partner who might ask for the next dance. Cecilia missed her chance with Dionisio, and we readers may have missed it too. But the long Cuban struggle gave time enough for the dance scene to repeat. Is it merely frivolous to note that popular musical theater versions of *Cecilia Valdés* build to a grand finale that can turn into a general *rumba*? Then, at last, everyone dances with everyone else, before they go home.[61]

Notes

1. Imeldo Alvarez García, 14–15. In 1855 Villaverde marries Emilia Casanova, who forced their family to leave Cuba for New York, given her outspoken criticism of Spain. Later, he will write *Apuntes biográficos de Emilia Casanova de Villaverde*, about her continuing political work, courage, and intelligence.

2. Cirilo Villaverde, *Cecilia Valdés o la Loma del Angel, novela de costumbres cubanas*, estudio crítico por Raimundo Lazo (Mexico: Editorial Porrúa, 1979), 174. Page references to the novel will be to this edition, in my translation. An English translation of the novel exists, though. *Cecilia Valdés or Angel's Hill: A Novel of Cuban Customs*, translated by Sydney G. Gest (New York: Vantage Press, 1962).

3. *Cecilia Valdés*, 155.

4. See Norman Holland, "Fashioning Cuba."

5. Arnaldo Cruz Maldavé's reminder in a letter of 8 August 1996 where he mentions Vera Kutzinski's mistranslation of *maliciosa* as malicious in *Sugar's Secrets*.

6. Cirilo Villaverde, *Cecilia Valdés* estudio crítico por Raimundo Lazo (Mexico: Editorial Porrúa, 1979), 150. "No entraban el carácter, ni en las ideas de honor y dignidad de D. Cándido, el pedir a su esposa La explicación del misterio, menos a los hijos con quienes pocas veces hablaba, mucho menos a los criados, alguno de los cuales sabía más secretos de familia de lo que convenía a la paz y a la dicha del hogar."

7. I am grateful to Gordon Hutner for pointing out a fascinating comparison with Villaverde's contemporary, Henry James. Significantly, James does not address the racial or ethnic obstacles to communicability, but he does meditate on the ultimate impossibility of "appropriating" another's experience or meaning in his preface to the "Figure in the Carpet."

8. Miguel Barnet, "La Regla de Ocha: The Religious System of Santería," in *Sacred Possessions*, edited by Fernández Olmos and Paravisini-Gebert, 96–123, 111. "*Yemayá* is the model of the universal mother. Her skirts of seven flounces announce the birth of man and of the gods. She is, to explain it in Hellenic fashion, the goddess of universal maternity. Queen of the sea and of salt water, her color is navy blue with something of white, symbolizing the foam of the waves. Her dances are vivacious and undulating like sea waves . . . She is also the goddess of intelligence, of rationality: a harmonious equilibrium of personality seems to characterize her children. She is 'jet black,' the babalochas say, which is why she is compared to the Virgin of Regla, who also looks to the sea, towards the bay. Multiple legends tell of a diligent *Yemayá*, understanding towards her children and conciliatory."

9. Cirilo Villaverde, *Cecilia Valdés*, 239. "Temo mucho, temo todo. Los negros han de mirar primero cómo hablan."

10. Roberto Schwartz, "Ideas Out of Place." Legally, Cuban slaves had some recourse,

since Spanish slavery was based on the combination of Roman law and Christian philosophy of *Siete partidas* of Alfonso X. See Kline, 59. In practice, though, chattel had almost no personal rights, and Manzano complained that a slave was legally a dead body. See also Orlando Patterson, *Slavery and Social Death*.

11. See the literature review by Imeldo Alvarez García in his prologue to Cirilo Villaverde, *Cecilia Valdés*, 5–46. Also, Roberto Friol, "La novela cubana del siglo XIX," 178.

12. Some provocative work in this direction is offered by Pierre Bourdieu, "Reading, Readers, the Literate Literature." See especially Marianna Torgovnick, "The Politics of the 'We'"; I do not object to the "we" voice in and of itself. What I object to is the easy slide from "I" to "we" that takes place almost unconsciously for many users of the first-person plural or its equivalents—and is often the hidden essence of cultural criticism. This slide can make the "we" function not as a device to link writer and reader, or as a particularized group voice, or even the voice of "the culture," but rather as a covert, and sometimes coercive, universal (48–49). I am grateful to Marshall Brown for these suggestions.

13. Cirilo Villaverde, "Prólogo del autor," Cirilo Villaverde, *Cecilia Valdés*, 47–51, 50–51.

14. George Steiner, *After Babel*, 355.

15. For the differences, see for example the Prólogo by Imeldo Alvarez García, Cirilo Villaverde, *Cecilia Valdés*, 2 vols. (Havana: Editorial Letras Cubanas), 5–46. He quotes Domingo del Monte's letter to the editor of *El Correo Nacional* in Madrid: "No extrañe usted que en esos cuadernitos sólo se hable del amor, pues a este estrecho límite está reducida lo que produce la aherrojada prensa habanera" (28). On pages 36–37, he returns to the difference and also quotes José Varona: "Lo que había de ser en la primera intención, mera novela de costumbres, se convirtió, por la inmensidad de la emoción, la riqueza de los recuerdos . . . en exteriorización palpitante de la vida íntima de un grupo humano." See also 28–29. See also Roberto Friol, "La novela cubana del siglo XIX," 178.

16. Cirilo Villaverde, *Cecilia Valdés ó la Loma del Angel: Novela cubana* tomo primero (Habana: Imprenta Literaria, Calle de Cuba, bajo el convento de San Agustín, 1839): "Que se te parece, como un huevo a otro.—No, que a ti.—Tomara yo. A mí mucho menos, ni por cien leguas. Es la misma cara tuya y la de Leonardo.—¿Por qué se me ha de parecer a mí, a ti y a ti, y no a cualquiera otro de la calle? Hai tal tema de averiguar descendencias por la fisonomía?—A Leonardo no, que a papá.—A pará menos que a nadie. Papá tiene los ojos verdosos y ella los tiene negros; papa tiene el pelo rubio, y ella lo tiene como azabache.—Ya se ve que no se parecen en cuanto al color del pelo, y de los ojos, y de . . . pero en cuanto a la espresion—Ademas, aquella nariz, aquella frente . . . Vamos, es escrita.—Muchacha! ¿Parecerse a tu padre? ¡que locura! (esta a mi entender hacia de tripas corazon.) ¿de a donde? ¿en donde encuentras esa semejanza?—Y en estas y en estas otras, como sucede en las polémicas habidas y por haber de literato a literato en nuestros periódicos . . ." (26).

17. See Verena Martínez-Alier, *Marriage, Class and Colour in Nineteenth Century Cuba*. In 1776, the Crown passed a law, *Pragmatica Sanción*, that prohibited "unequal" marriages. This was followed by an 1803 decree that required parental consent to marry for men until the age of twenty-three, for women until age twenty-five. And the *Real Cédula* of 1805 repeated the prohibition against pure-blooded whites marrying blacks or mulattoes.

18. Cirilo Villaverde, *Cecilia Valdés ó la Loma del Angel: Novela cubana* tomo primero (Habana: Imprenta Literaria, Calle de Cuba, bajo el convento de San Agustín, 1839), 245. "Por mi mulata santa, sería yo capaz de abandonar y despreciar todos los tesoros imajinables."

19. Poyo, 96.

20. The first published version is *The Life and Poems of a Cuban Slave* (London, 1840), prepared by Richard Madden. It appeared in Spanish, prepared by José Luciano Franco in 1937; this is the version reproduced in Juan Francisco Manzano, *Obras* (Havana: Instituto Cubano del Libro, 1972). Then Roberto Friol included several unpublished and relatively unknown works in his *Suite para Juan Francisco Manzano* (Havana: Editorial Arte y Literatura, 1977). See also Sylvia Molloy, "From Serf to Self," 36–54, and Antonio Vera-León, "Juan Francisco Manzano: el estilo bárbaro de la nación," *Hispoamérica* XX: 60, diciembre 1991, 3–22.

21. Sonia Labrador-Rodríguez, her field work in Cuba shows reluctance by intellectuals to acknowledge the publications.

22. See Moreno Fraginals on the bourgeois rationality of sugar industrialists. Tittel, etc.

23. Cirilo Villaverde, *Cecilia Valdés*, 2 vols. Prólogo Imeldo Alvarez García (Havana: Editorial Letras Cubanas, 1981) Prólogo: 5–46, 9.

24. Cf. Herbert Kline, *Slavery in the Americas*.

25. I am grateful to Gerald Poyo for this point, and in general for his book, *With All and for the Good of All*, which appreciates Villaverde the politician.

26. See Richard Rosas' brilliant reading.

27. See Julio Ramos, "The Repose of Heroes."

28. Kline, 211–225.

29. See Pedro Deschamps Chapeaux, "Autenticidad de algunos negros y mulatos de *Cecilia Valdés*," in *Acerca de Cirilo Villaverde*, edited by Imeldo Alvarez García (Havana: Editorial Letras Cubanas, 1982), 220–232.

30. Gerald E. Poyo, "*With All, and for the Good of All*," 18.

31. Martí, *Obras completas* I: 249.

32. Poyo, "*With All, and for the Good of All*," 9.

33. Cirilo Villaverde, "El Sr. Saco con respecto a la Revolución de Cuba." *La Verdad* vol. 2; #96 New York, 10 February 1856. "El Sr. Saco aunque al principio de su carrera pública pareció consagrarse a la causa de la libertad e independencia de Cuba, después dedicó toda su atención y sus talentos a la causa de una raza de sus habitantes, los negros, y hoy día solo sirve a los intereses de una clase . . . de unas cuantas familias cubanas" (my translation). I thank Rodrigo Lazo for this reference.

34. Poyo, 9.

35. Poyo, 13.

36. See George Handley's "Reading in the Dark: A Comparative Study of Creole National Imaginings," in *Theories of Colonialism in/of the Americas*, edited by Sylvia Spitta, forthcoming, Duke University Press.

37. Imeldo Alvarez García, "La polémica sostenida con José Antonio Saco le resultó una derrota, porque en ella 'no llevó la mejor parte'. El hecho registra, no obstante, lo que sentía y pensaba *entonces* el novelista sobre la equivocada y funesta corriente política," 13.

38. Martí on Villaverde, article in *Patria*, 30 de octubre de 1894, Alvarez García, 18.

39. Poyo, 68.

40. Martí, *Nuestra América*, 308.

41. See Juan Gelpí's argument for Villaverde's control of characters and readers, "El discurso jerárquico en *Cecilia Valdés*," *Revista Crítica Literaria Latinoamericana*, 34 (1991): 47–61.

42. Poyo, 47.

43. Poyo, 48.

44. See my "Sab c'est moi," in *Foundational Fictions: The National Romances of Latin America*.

45. For a similar observation, see Julio Ramos, "Faceless Tongues: Language and Citizenship in Nineteenth-Century Latin America," 31. But Ramos assumes that Villaverde coordinates light color with mastery, that María de Regla is mulatta for example (though she is black), while he observes that Villaverde's mulattas were more voluptuous than verbal, 33. See also his excellent piece on law and literature: Julio Ramos, "The law is other: literature and the constitution of the juridical subject in nineteenth-century Cuba," *Annals of Scholarship* 10.3–4, 1995. [Orig. "La ley es otra: literatura y constitución de la persona jurídica," *Revista Crítica Literaria Latinoamericana* XX, no. 40, Lima-Berkeley, 305–335.]

46. Villaverde's flair for writing in Cuban, especially in *Excursión a vueltabajo*, is the focus of Antonio Benítez Rojo, "Cirilo Villaverde, Fundador," *Revista Iberoamericana*, nos. 152–153 (July–December, 1990), 769–779.

47. For the threat and anxiety this posed to marriage alliances, see Verena Martínez-Alier, *Marriage, Class and Colour in Nineteenth Century Cuba*.

48. "La procreación de las castas mestizas [es] mil veces mas temible que la primera [raza pura africana], por su conocida osadía y pretenciones de igualarse con la blanca," from "Informe fiscal sobre el fomento de la población blanca en la Isla de Cuba y emancipación progresiva de la esclava presentado a la Superintendencia General Delegada de la Real Hacienda en diciembre de 1844 por el Fiscal de la Misma" (Madrid: Imprenta de J. Martín Alegría, 1845), 33. Quoted from Julio Ramos, "La ley es otra," 98.

49. Gertrudis Gómez de Avellaneda, *Sab*. I develop this reading in "Sab c'est moi," Doris Sommer, *Foundational Fictions*.

50. "¿A qué raza, pues, pertenecía esta muchacha? Difícil es decirlo. Sin embargo, a un ojo conocedor no podía esconderse que sus laboios rojos tenían un borde o filete oscuro, y que la iluminación del rostro terminaba en una especie de penumbra hacia el nacimiento del cabello. Su sangre no era pura y bien podía asegurarse que allá en la tercera o cuarta generación estaba mezclada con la etiópe."

51. Juan Francisco Manzano, *Obras*, 1972, 31. Julio Ramos reports that he could find no explicit law that prohibited slaves from writing. See his "La ley es otra: literatura y constitución de la persona jurídica," *Revista Crítica Literaria Latinoamericana* XX, no. 40, Lima-Berkeley, 305–335, note 98. From the beginning, Virginians were more explicit; and by 1831, reading and writing were unlawful even for free blacks and mulattos. See Kline 119, 246.

52. The author gives the following footnote to Part II, Chapter iii, about a gala evening at the Philharmonic Society: "La relación que sigue la tomamos casi al pie de la letra de un semanario que se publicaba en La Habana en 1830, titulado *La Moda*," 82. The novel as well as those articles were dedicated to Cuban women.

53. Cirilo Villaverde, *Cecilia Valdés ó la Loma del Angel*, 47. The heroine's race is written into her love of dances and drums ("en esto no desmentía la raza").

54. Cirilo Villaverde, *Cecilia Valdés ó la Loma del Angel*, 103. More precisely, this describes the whole Fair at La Loma del Angel, including the dances.

55. Ada Ferrer, "The Silence of Patriots: Racial Discourse and Cuban Nationalism, 1868–1898," paper at "Our America and the Gilded Age: José Martí's Chronicles of Imperial Critique," 20–21. Irvine, 27–28 January 1995.

56. I thank Enrico Mario Santí for this observation.

57. See Rebecca J. Scott, *Slave Emancipation in Cuba*.

58. I thank Jay Kinsbruner for pointing out the incongruity of an "alcalde mayor" in Havana of the 1820s. This was probably a provisional magistrate, not a mayor. See David Turnbull's *Cuba* (republished 1969), 246.

59. See my *Foundational Fictions*.

60. The liberating possibilities of free markets in general are suggested when, for example, the slave María de Regla learns negotiations to everyone's advantage from a street vendor. Villaverde, 267.

61. I am indebted to Antonio Benítez Rojo for his memory of these shows.

CHAPTER 3

PHANTASMATIC BRAZIL

Nella Larsen's *Passing*, American Literary Imagination, and Racial Utopianism

Zita C. Nunes

"It was with secret thrills of a peculiar and inexpressible joy that I, at last, on the third day of last February, accompanied by my wife, sailed from the port of New York for a visit to the South American republics. It was the opening chapter in realization of a golden dream long cherished."[1] Thus began the first in a series of articles written by Robert Abbott, the founder and publisher of the *Chicago Defender*, chronicling his 1923 trip. Abbott's stated goals in this undertaking were many: to see the Negro in a physical environment similar to that of Africa, albeit organized according to "modern society"; to compare the effect of "Latin-European" racial attitudes to those of North America on democratic participation; to uncover the outlines of South America's "future ethnic homogeneity"; and to provide a sense of the economic and social opportunities "for that enlightened and growing group of North American Negroes, who so recently are beginning to look to the South American continent as, after all, the most likely haven for a solution of their individual problems."

That South America, and particularly Brazil, could provide a haven for middle-class professional African Americans was an idea not peculiar to Abbott. This idea found expression in literary texts as well as journalistic ones, and provides a reference point for many "passing" narratives. I will address, in this essay, Nella Larsen's *Passing*.[2] Many scholars have analyzed this novel's exploration of the dynamic described by its title and/or the psychological and sexual conflicts of the two main characters—Clare Kendry and Irene Redfield. I propose to supplement these readings by calling attention to the ways in which South America, as a discursive formation that derives from an African American imaginary of the 1920s presented to us in Larsen's text as well as in the black press of the United States and Brazil, provides an important component in discussions of African American citizenship.

In August of 1928, Nella Larsen completed the manuscript for her second novel. The title, *Nig*, not only recalled the title of her friend and mentor Carl Van Vechten's controversial novel about Harlem, it also foregrounds the character Clare Kendry in its reference to her nickname, "Nig." According to Larsen's biographer, Thadious Davis, the title was deemed too inflammatory for a novel by an "unproven" author, leading the publisher to substitute the title *Passing*, in order to attract interest and attention without giving offense.[3]

The novel opens as Irene Redfield, from whose perspective the story is told, reads a letter from Clare Kendry, a childhood acquaintance. The letter, on foreign paper, "with its almost illegible scrawl seemed almost out of place and alien" (*Passing* 143). The letter initiates Irene's recollection of their encounter two years before, when Clare and Irene met by chance on a Chicago terrace, and sets in motion the intertwining of their lives that provides the plot of *Passing*. In an exchange of confidences, Clare had revealed to Irene that she passes for white always and everywhere, even—if not especially—with her husband, Jack. Raised by her father's white aunts, Clare followed their command that she keep secret that her mother was a "negro girl." Clare explains to Irene: "When the chance came to get away [from the aunts], that omission was of great value to me. When Jack, a schoolboy acquaintance of some people in the neighborhood, turned up from South America with untold gold, there was no one to tell him I was colored—You can guess the rest" (189). They married. Having made his fortune in South America, Jack apparently has no desire to return to the place that would be a fine place, if (as he says), "they ever get the niggers out of it" (203).

John "Jack" Bellew provides this assessment of South America in the course of a conversation that takes place after Clare has introduced him to Gertrude Martin and Irene Redfield, her childhood acquaintances. He has already shocked Irene and Gertrude with the use of his pet name for his wife—Nig—and by the explanation that Clare prompts him to give her guests—each of whom is, in that moment, passing for white, relative to Jack. The explanation relies on Jack's belief in the impossibility of "Nig" to describe his wife. This is clear enough, as is the reason for the ensuing laughter as Clare, Gertrude, Irene, and the reader enjoy the irony of the moment. What perhaps is not so clear is that the nickname provides one link in a signifying chain that joins Clare and Brazil each to the other, with ultimately disastrous consequences for the characters in the novel. The nickname "Nig," so shocking in its immediate context—a drawing room in Chicago—is not at all shocking; it is, in fact, so common—in another context—as to scarcely draw attention to itself: in the very South American context that is the source of Bellew's wealth. Nig is the English translation of the Spanish and Portuguese *negra* or *nega*, a very common term of endearment, frequently, if not necessarily, detached from any direct identification of race (except, as in the case of *Passing*, by contrast) in that it is often used among people who would consider themselves white. In a display of its roots in slavery, this term is often accompanied by the possessive—*mi* or *minha*—my nig.

In addition to the overt irony provided by the fact that Clare sees herself as precisely that which Jack names as an impossibility, there is also the irony of Jack's adoption of this term. The capacity of language to overdetermine and to exceed its speaker undermines Jack's own claim to be immune to racial mixture. In answer to Clare's query as to what difference it could possibly make if he were to discover that she was one or two percent colored, he declares, "Oh, no, Nig, nothing like that with me. I know you're no nigger, so it's all right. You can get as black as you please as far as I'm concerned, since I know you're no nigger. I draw the line at that. No niggers in my family. Never have been and never will be" (*Passing* 201).

As a discursive system in which cultural, linguistic, biological transmission is precisely a process of mixture and contamination, South America speaks Jack as much as he speaks it. The symptom, his adoption of the term "Nig," betrays as much. South America endures in and through him because it contains within itself a realization that national purity/racial purity is an impossibility. That Jack, the character unambiguously white for the novel's other characters as well as for its readers, transmits this point serves to make it all the more effective.

As Jack, Clare's husband, is associated with South America, so too is Irene's husband, Brian. In his case, South America, for the very reason that it disgusts Jack, makes Brian feel, instead, disgust for his own country. Early in their marriage Irene had fought Brian to remain in the United States, but she "knew, had always known, that his dissatisfaction had continued, as had his dislike and disgust for his profession and his country" (*Passing* 218).

Brian's disgust for his profession and his country is unacceptable to Irene, who sees it in terms of its implications for her citizenship. "She would not go to Brazil. She belonged in this land of rising towers. She was an American. She grew from this soil, and would not be uprooted" (*Passing* 267). Brian's desire to move to Brazil derives from his hatred of segregation and racial violence as well as his perception that Brazil, in contrast to the United States, could provide a safe home for African Americans. On an occasion when Irene and Brian disagree about the extent to which they should discuss with their children the realities of racism and racist violence, the long-buried source of the tension that structures their marriage returns to the surface. Brian tells Irene that if she had wanted him to keep secret from their sons the violence that could touch their lives, she should have allowed the family to move to Brazil, where presumably her desire for silence on the subject of racism could be reasonably justified. Brian's resentment and Irene's insistence on figuring Brazil in opposition to their marriage lead her to watch him and think:

> "It isn't fair, it isn't fair." After all these years to still blame her like this. Hadn't his success proved that she'd been right in insisting that he stick to his profession right there in New York? Couldn't he see, even now, that it had been best? Not for her, oh no, not for her—she had never really considered herself—but for him and the boys. Was she never to be free of it, that fear which crouched, always down deep within her, stealing away the sense of security, the feeling of permanence, from the life which she had so admirably arranged for them all, and desired so ardently to have remain as it was? That strange, and to her fantastic, notion of Brian's going off to Brazil, which, though unmentioned, yet lived within him; how it frightened her, and—yes, angered her! (*Passing* 217).

In Irene's first conversation with Clare's husband, Jack asks her about Brian. Irene tells him that her husband is a physician and Jack replies that it must be trying on her nerves, having a husband with lady patients. Irene, however, does not fear lady patients; she fears rather Brian's desire for Brazil/South America: "Brian doesn't care for ladies, especially sick ones. I sometimes wish he did. It's South America that attracts him" (*Passing* 203). Irene fears that Brian will leave her for Brazil and substitute a place—that place—for her, a woman. Later, this initial fear is itself displaced by fear that Brian is having an affair with Clare, the embodiment of the racial politics of Brazil. Brazil, then, comes to stand in not only for a non-racist society, but also as and for a secret, as well as a place-holder for the object of an impossible desire, a utopic desire, and, eventually, as a double for Clare. Irene and Brian never speak about his desire for Brazil and it is only in her extraordinary efforts to produce a "substitution" (this is Irene's word to indicate her sense that she must compensate Brian for remaining in the United States) that Brazil, as a secret desire, comes to be seen: "Were all her efforts, all her labors, to make up to him that one loss, all her silent strivings to prove to him that her way had been best, all her ministrations to him, all her outward sinking of self, to count for nothing" (*Passing* 224). So, one substitution leads to another and Irene cannot, in the end, be sure that the substitution has been complete or even merely sufficient:

> Then why worry? The thing, this discontent which had exploded into words, would surely die, flicker out, at last. True, she had in the past often been tempted to believe that it had died, only to become conscious, in some instinctive subtle way, that she had been merely deceiving herself for a while and that it still lived. But it would die. Of that she was certain. She only had to direct and guide her man, to keep him going in the right direction (*Passing* 218).

Irene ultimately decides that Clare would be a good substitute for Brazil if a relationship with Clare would keep Brian in the United States. If Irene keeps Clare's secret—that she is passing—Brian may pursue the affair and, out of deference to the children, remain at home with Irene in a show of a continuing marriage. That is, the substitution would permit the conservation of her "negro family," which could exist as such only in the United States and not in Brazil. "Now that she had relieved herself of what was almost like a guilty knowledge, admitted that which by some sixth sense she had long known, she could again reach out for plans. Could think again of ways to keep Brian by her side, and in New York. For she would not go to Brazil. She belonged in this land of rising towers. She was an American. She grew from this soil, and would not be uprooted. Not even because of Clare Kendry, or a hundred Clare Kendrys" (*Passing* 267).

Clare is like Brazil—she simultaneously threatens and makes sense of passing in the United States. In Irene's mind, Clare, with her queer and unreadable smiles, becomes a sign of Irene's inability to know and control. This inability insinuates itself into Irene's relationship with her husband, leading Irene to link the two threats—perhaps to her marriage, but certainly to her security as a well-to-do American Negro woman: "Brian again. Unhappy, restless, withdrawn. And she, who had prided herself on knowing his moods, their causes and their remedies, had found it at first unthinkable, and then intolerable, that this, so like and yet so unlike those other spasmodic restlessnesses of his, should be to her incomprehensible and elusive" (*Passing* 246). Irene blames Clare for the introduction of doubt and unwanted desire, further described as an unwanted desire for desire, which threaten her security: "Security. Was it just a word? If not, then was it only by the sacrifice of other things, happiness, love, or some wild ecstasy that she had never known, that it could be obtained? And did too much striving, too much faith in safety and permanence, unfit one for these other things?" (*Passing* 267). Clare, therefore, like Brian's dream of Brazil, must die, directed and guided, perhaps—the narrative leaves open all possibilities—by Irene's hand, to keep Clare, like Brian, going in the right direction.

Clare's death, linked through the image of Irene's direction and guidance, to the death of Brian's dream of moving to Brazil, provides a final instance in which each can and will substitute for the other. In the course of the novel, each becomes a placeholder for the object of an impossible desire, a utopic desire. In the wake of the Great War, the northern migrations, the urban riots, when the failure of northern opportunity to fulfill the promise of the South is becoming apparent, is it possible that Larsen, in conversation with her peers, offers up a phantasmatic Brazil as a south that is beyond the South, not as a counterpart to the north, but as an apotheosis of southernness? This offer is all the more compelling in light of the other alternative to the American north that Larsen had offered in her novel *Quicksand*, published the year before *Passing*. In *Quicksand*, the alternative is the north of the north—Denmark—to which Helga Crane "escapes" before returning to a disastrous life in the southern United States. The South (the south of the United States and the south of America—Brazil) as the space of disaster has its equally complex expression in *Plum Bun*, the 1928 passing novel by Larsen's friend Jessie Redmon Fauset. In Fauset's novel, Angela Murray is introduced to the reader as a young Philadelphia student living with her mother, who like Angela is light enough to pass, and her father and sister, who are not. The issue of who can claim to be American and in what way is presented early in the novel in a conversation that Angela has in school with a fellow student who thinks that Angela is white. Angela's talent lies in her ability to paint portraits, and she is particularly interested in representing (racial) "types":

> Angela took the sketch of Hetty Daniels to school. "What an interesting type!" said Gertrude Quale, the girl next to her. "Such cosmic and tragic unhappiness in that face. What is she, not an American?"

"Oh yes she is. She's an old colored woman who's worked in our family for years and she was born right here in Philadelphia."

"Oh colored! Well, of course I suppose you would call her an American though I never think of darkies as Americans. Colored—yes that accounts for that unhappiness in her face. I suppose they all mind it awfully" (*Plum Bun* 70).

Because she does mind it awfully, Angela moves to New York, changes her name to Angele Mory, and passes for white as an art student. She falls in love with Anthony Cross, who has changed his name from Anthony Cruz, a name that emphasizes his racial, linguistic, and national crossings. Anthony was born in Rio de Janeiro, Brazil, the son of John Hall, who Angela later learns is an African American from Georgia, and the "apparently white" Maria Cruz, whose own father was the color of John Hall. Initially believing Anthony to be a white Brazilian—"probably Portuguese"—Angela imagines him "a member of a race devoid, notoriously devoid of prejudice against black blood" (*Plum Bun* 265); and therefore, when she discovers that Anthony has some secret from his past, a secret that resolves him against returning to Brazil ("No . . . I'm never going back to Brazil. I couldn't."), Angela assumes that it must have to do with "some hot feud, a matter of hot blood and ready knives" (141). The secret, which has everything to do with blood and knives, is correctly placed not in Brazil but in Georgia, where Tony's father had been lynched at the instigation of a white man who had tried to force himself on Maria. After her husband's violent death, Maria renounces any connection with black people and marries a white immigrant from Germany. Anthony, however, retains his mother's name in an Americanized form rather than his father's name, and vows to hate white people. As in *Passing*, *Plum Bun* ultimately comes down on the side of a specifically black community, and for (North) American citizenship that takes in rather than reproduces the foreign. Anthony and Angele marry, after Anthony and Angela reveal themselves to each other as colored.

What Larsen and Fauset address in fiction, some of their contemporaries addressed in journalistic articles. The perception of a South American and specifically a Brazilian racial democracy drew the attention of African American leaders as an inverse of the situation of the United States. In his series of articles entitled "My Trip through South America," Abbott wrote of his desire to see Negroes living without the consciousness of a racial difference "so strangely portent in hindering the natural and wholesome evolution of 12 millions of Negroes within the confines of North American society" (Abbott 56).

In preparing for the journey, Abbott says, "[w]e received prompt cordial service from all save the Brazilian consul. Thus, it was only after pressure was brought to bear did I succeed in getting the consul from Brazil to visa our passports. This, it seems, has been the experience of every American Negro during the last few years who has sought entry into Brazil" (Abbott 58). Even in the face of the refusal of the Brazilian consul to grant a visa, a visa that was ultimately obtained by Abbott's light-skinned, blue-eyed wife, the articles reveal his determined resolve to present Brazil as an ideal, both of racial harmony and of democracy. Describing a perfect political state thoroughly homogeneous in blood as a result of intermarriage, Abbott observes that "Negro people are evident on every hand, enjoying with inconceivable ease the entire facilities of a present day democracy" (Abbott 68). According to Abbott, Brazil's adherence to a strict notion of democracy, understood as racial democracy, distinguished it from the United States, making it a potential home for African Americans from the United States. "The idea will be to open up a practical avenue for commercial enterprise and to create a connection in Brazil for the Negro of the United States who may desire to settle in a new country, under conditions more in harmony with his notion of freedom. Neither exploitation nor colonization is involved in this scheme of practical business" (Abbott 77). Abbott sought to disassociate himself from United States expansionism by focusing on his perception of a greater possibility for African Americans to amass capital in South America. Abbott, nevertheless, reproduces the imperialist discourse. "This is an age of expansion in which the more vigorous and ambitious types of mankind are refusing to think in mere terms of race or nationality, but in terms of the world" (Abbott 80). In so doing, however, he shifts the emphasis from conquering land to conquering markets and from strictly mercantile-colonial relationships to transnational-capitalistic ones. "No one race will again claim and people any one continent. As other men have branched out into new worlds, under flags distant from the flags of their nativity, so must the American Negro, not upon the silly excursion of conquest, but as a practical idealist, determined to win points in the fields and markets of the world by knowledge and industry" (Abbott 78). The view of Abbott's trip and of his speeches was very different from the perspective of the Afro-Brazilian press. Both his perception of Brazil and his proposal to encourage the emigration of black businesspeople were met with suspicion. Abbott's visit was the subject of many articles and editorials in the Afro-Brazilian newspapers of São Paulo, Rio de Janeiro, and Campinas, and provided an occasion for a discussion of black Brazilian citizenship. Two themes predominated: the impact of immigration by United States blacks on race relations in Brazil, and the correction of Abbott's perception of the state of black Brazilians. In an article entitled, "Preto e Branco" ["Black and White"], the author, Abilio Rodrigues, criticized a talk given by Abbott. According to Rodrigues, Abbott had been invited to Brazil to speak about race relations in the United States, but was so impressed by the sight of what appeared to him as black people in responsible positions that he resolved instead to laud the virtues of Brazil. The response was harsh:

> As conferencias do dr. Robert Abbott, o chamado campeão da raça negra norte-americana, redactor proprietario do *"Chicago Defender,"* não resistem, abolutamente, a uma analyse rigorosa, porque têm fundo vasio.[4]

> [The lectures by Dr. Robert Abbott, the so-called champion of the black race in North America, owner and publisher of the *Chicago Defender,* cannot stand up to a rigorous analysis because they are founded on emptiness.]

The journalist, Benedicto Florencio, criticized Abbott for satisfying himself with a superficial impression of the lot of black people. Abbott and his party stayed in luxurious hotels—although forced to leave several because of complaints by guests or management—and did not meet with any representatives of black organizations:

> O notável apostolo da raça negra chegando à nossa Patria, ficou offuscado com o cosmopolitanismo typico do tradicional povo carioca, onde a fusão das raças deixou de ser principio teórico para tornar-se um metodo pratico.[5]

> [The notable apostle of the black race, arriving in our fatherland, was blinded by the cosmopolitanism typical of Rio de Janeiro society, where the fusion of races has ceased to be a theoretical principle and become a practical method.]

According to this journalist, Abbott, in taking appearance for reality and not recognizing the implications of a theoretical principle made practical method, makes a common error that, in its dissemination, distorts the reality of black people in Brazil:

Nota-se em toda carreira de vida, que o preto carece de um esforço triplo para chegar e conseguir uma posição melhor. Não lhe tolera a mediocridade e o seu valor é allegada a cada passo e na vontade de estinguil-o foi o desamparo que lhe coube em partilha, desde ha trinta annos, deu-se-lhe por misericordia a liberdade.[6]

[It is notable that over the course of [his] life, the black has to make three times the effort in order to achieve a better position. Mediocrity is not tolerated from him and his value is challenged at each step and the desire to extinguish him is what he gets instead and his freedom, given thirty years ago out of pity, has resulted in his forsaken lot.]

Abbott's speeches advocating the emigration of middle-class African Americans coincided with debates surrounding Brazil's immigration policies. In an article entitled, "Echos do Projeto Fidelis Reis," the author drew attention to immigration legislation introduced by the statesmen Fidelis Reis and Cincinato Braga, which promised disaster for the "millions" of Brazilians who have "black skins." "A Camara Alta que acaba de votar a Lei que será o opprobrio inexoravel lançado em face de tantos brasileiros, continuará consciente de que cumprio o seu dever"[7] ["And the Congress, which has just voted in a law that will be an inexorable opprobrium thrown into the face of so many Brazilians, will be confident that it has fulfilled its duty"].

The law called for the cessation of immigration of people of color from Africa and Asia and incentives to increase European immigration in order to promote the policy of *embranqueamento*. Not coincidentally, the law had the support of the National Academy of Medicine.[8]

While the journalist indicates that an increase in the number of blacks through immigration would add to the misery in which blacks already live, he states that what is truly dangerous for blacks is the selection of words which Fidelis Reis used to justify his project: "Sim, por toda uma eternidade vae ficar patente que o sangue negro é uma corrupção, que o elemento negro é uma desordem na formação do carácter ethnologico brasileiro" (Reis 1) ["Indeed, for all time it will be clear that black blood is a corruption, that the black element is a disturbance in the formation of the Brazilian ethnological character"].

Comargo worries that in the future all Brazilians and, indeed, all the world will curse:

. . . esse negro que fez o Brasil agrícola com os seus braços, que fez o Brasil intellectual com o sangue das suas esposas as quaes aleitaram com tanto

carinho os grandes vultos que hoje sentem praser em se tornaram os nossos
mais encarniçados inimigos ("Echos" 1).

[. . . this black who made agricultural Brazil with his hands, who made intellectual Brazil with the blood of his wives who breastfed with so much affection those great men of consequence who now take pleasure in becoming
our fiercest enemies.]

Abbott's interpretation of the present situation of black Brazilians may
have been rejected, but the vision of a future where "there is no kind of
race problem in Brazil" (63) due to miscegenation is embraced by many of
the journalists and letter-writers from Brazil and from the United States:
"A vinda dos negros norte-americanos será o golpe de morte para aquella
obra mathematica do desapparecimento gradativo da raça negra no Brasil"[9] ["The coming of black North Americans will be the death blow for
the work of calculation that is the gradual disappearance of the black race
in Brazil"]. Theodore Roosevelt, reflecting on his own visit to Brazil in
1913, thus summarized this ideology: "In Brazil . . . the idea looked forward to is the disappearance of the Negro question through the disappearance of the Negro himself—that is through his gradual absorption into
the white race."[10] Roosevelt's report of his visit was published in the major
African American newspapers and journals and endorsed in articles and
editorials published in the *Philadelphia Tribune*, *The Crusader*, the *Baltimore
Afro-American*, the *Tulsa Star*, and the *Negro World*, among others.

The phrase, "disappearance of the Negro question through the disappearance of the Negro," threads together several of the themes of this
essay. The notion of racial democracy—which depends for its meaning on a
narrative of assimilation in which the "black race" is incorporated into the
white race—forecloses the possibility of a political life of plurality and difference. Its consequences for black citizenship cannot be overstated. The
articles in the Afro-Brazilian press make clear that the putative choice to
participate in the racial democracy necessitates, in fact, for black people,
the remaindering of blackness in the "racial" of racial democracy. Michael
Hanchard has recently posited that, "[i]n Brazil, the absence of racial or
ethnic 'givens' is more profound than in other polities, but this is a matter of degree of instability with regard to racial or ethnic identifications,
rather than the case of one polity containing 'timeless' features of racial in-
equalities and antagonisms, with another polity—in contrast—having no
identifiable patterns of dominance or subordination informed by race."[11]

While Hanchard frames the question in terms of stable and unstable, or givens and degrees, I would frame the question somewhat differently. Blackness, in terms of racial democracy, is the name given to that which exceeds it and makes it visible—it is the remainder that makes the notion of racial democracy possible and sustainable, yet always destined to fail. As a narrative, it also serves to shore up a specifically North American black citizenship.

It is in this context—the United States defined in relation to a phantasmatic Latin America and its corresponding utopian ideal of racial democracy—that we can fully appreciate not only the ambiguity of Irene's role in Clare's death but also the ambiguity of Jack's final words to Clare: "Nig! My God! Nig!" This cry of horror and agony (in which the nickname Nig is used rather than the nigger of the previous sentence in the novel) at the disappearance of Nig/Clare could be read as an ambivalent response to Roosevelt's description of Brazil's approach to eliminating racial discrimination and as a mourning of the loss of an object of a utopian desire. Even the ambiguity of the end—the police declare Clare's death an accident, yet return to examine the window sill—focuses that which must be remaindered in order to sustain the social, racial, and sexual order in which America (North and South) is so invested.

Notes

1. Robert Abbott, "My Trip through South America," *African-American Reflections on Brazil's Racial Paradise*, 55–81, 55.

2. Nella Larsen, *Quicksand and Passing*, ed. Deborah E. McDowell. Subsequent page references to the novels will be to this edition.

3. Thadious Davis, *Nella Larsen, Novelist of the Harlem Renaissance*, 23.

4. "Cartas d'um negro II," *Getulino* 3 Oct. 1923: 10–11, 10.

5. Ibid., 11.

6. "Preto e Branco," *O Kosmos* [São Paulo] 18 abril 1923: 1.

7. T. Comargo, "Echos de Projecto F. Reis Elite" [São Paulo] 20 janeiro 1924: 3.

8. Fidelis Reis, *Pais a organizar.* The document from the Academia Nacional de Medicina is appended in the book.

9. "Cartas dúm negro," *Getulino* 30 setembro 1923: 10.

10. Theodore Roosevelt cited by Thomas E. Skidmore, *Black Into White*, 68.

11. Michael George Hanchard, *Orpheus and Power*, 15.

MÉTISSAGE AND COUNTERDISCOURSE

CHAPTER 4

NARRATING THE AMERICAS

Transcolonial *Métissage* and Maryse Condé's *La Migration des coeurs*

Françoise Lionnet

Je ne sépare pas la pensée théorique de la création romanesque ou artistique. Pour moi ce sont deux faces d'une même dimension. En ce qui concerne l'Europe, je pense qu'on ne perd pas facilement ses habitudes, surtout quand on a conquis le monde, régi le monde, dominé le monde. Mais je pense que tant qu'il n'y aura pas de changement, non seulement dans la conscience mais aussi dans l'imaginaire du peuple européen, quelque chose ne va pas se passer. [. . .]
    La Caraïbe est un archipel de pays qui sont nés de la créolisation . . . et les pays composites ne peuvent pas se lancer dans l'aventure de la racine unique, de la pureté de la race ou de la langue. Ce qui est bien maintenant, c'est que l'Europe s'archipelise. C'est-à-dire qu'au delà de la barrière des nations, on voit apparaître des îles qui sont en relation les unes avec les autres . . . Faire l'unité de l'Europe signifie développer ces îles, au détriment peut-être de la notion de nation et par delà des frontières nationales.

[I do not separate theoretical reflection from artistic or novelistic creation. For me, they are two faces of the same coin. As for Europe, I think that habits are hard to change, especially when you have conquered the world, ruled the world, and dominated the world. But I think that as long as nothing changes in the mind or the imaginary of European peoples, then nothing new will happen. [. . .]
    [The Caribbean is an archipelago born of creolization . . . and such composite countries cannot embrace the adventure of the single root, the purity of the race or of the tongue. What is good now is that Europe too is turning into an archipelago. That is, beyond the

> barrier of the nation, islands are taking shape in relation to one an-
> other . . . To unify Europe means to develop these islands, perhaps
> at the expense of the notion of nation and the concept of national
> borders.]
>
> EDOUARD GLISSANT,
> "L'Europe et les Antilles: Interview," *Mots pluriels*

> Our ultimate success, the test of our humanity . . . comes from merg-
> ing with all that is diverse, unexpected and exuberantly impure.
>
> PATRICIA J. WILLIAMS,
> "Fresh Eggs, Fried Baloney," *The Nation*

I moved to Los Angeles in 1998, and I now live a few blocks from Pico
Boulevard, one of L.A.'s major thoroughfares. Pico Boulevard, I discovered, was named after Pío Pico, the last Mexican governor of California
before Mexico lost the war with the United States in 1846. While visiting the Natural History Museum, I came upon a photograph of Governor
Pico in ceremonial dress, flanked by his wife and two nieces.[1] Their poses,
demeanor, and dress resonate with the nineteenth-century mestizo world
Maryse Condé re-creates in her 1995 book, *La Migration des coeurs*, which
takes place in Cuba, Guadeloupe, and Dominica. Pico was an African-
Mexican; the women around him in the photograph are much lighter-
skinned. The posed portrait exudes an air of genteel respectability. Pico's
proud expression and his frank and determined look convey the disposi-
tion of a man in his prime who has been successful against the odds. He
is conscious of his status and proximity to power, and his larger-than-life
personality quietly appreciates his accomplishments. In Los Angeles, place
names, city streets, and neighborhoods bear traces of the mestizo cultures
that flourished prior to the war with the Yankees in 1846, and that continue to do so today. Angelenos are often not aware of all the racial details
that make up their city's history.[2] But Pico Boulevard is one of the traces
in what I would call a thoroughly *transcolonial* historical circuit connecting
distinct but comparable sites of conflicts in which racial borderlines and
borderlands have constantly been crossed.

    Condé's novel is also such a site. The opening pages are dense with his-
torical, cultural, and fictional information that sets the stage for the development of a complex and multi-layered narrative. Beginning with "the
procession at Epiphany that marked the start of the New Year" (3) in the
Cuban capital, Condé composes an historical vignette about "Excellen-

Figure 1. The Last Mexican Governor of California, Pío de Jesús Pico (1801–1894), and his wife, Señora María Alvarado Pico, in 1852 with their nieces, Señorita María Anita Alvarado (L) and Trinidad Ortega (R). Courtesy, Seaver Center for Western History Research, Natural History Museum, of Los Angeles County.

tissimo José de Cépéro . . . political head and military governor of the
province of Havana and captain general of the island of Cuba" (4). She
evokes the last white Spanish governor of Cuba as he surveys a crowd of
black revelers during the procession. "Above all," as the narrator puts it,
"he hated these crowds of negroes and turned up his nose in disgust at the
smell of sweat and filth lurking under the velvets and silks" (5). This scene
provides a useful counterpoint to the photograph of Governor Pío Pico.
Together, the two historical figures, Pico and Cépéro, define a context for
understanding the tensions in Condé's fictional world, and the pressures
on Razyé, who conceals his own social and political ambitions. José de Cépéro's "disgust," the revulsion or distaste that he expresses, is directly tied
to the not-quite-hidden, the "lurking" nature of blackness beneath "the
velvets and silks." His proximity to black bodies elicits a fear of contamination that is linked to the rhetoric of passing, the ambiguities of racial
mixture, the secrets of illegitimate lineages, and the theoretical paradigms
of early racial science.

In *La Migration des coeurs*, the various characters' lives unfold along the
routes that link diasporic sites of conflicts in the Americas in the late nineteenth century. References to the explosion of the American battleship
Maine (15, 23) allow the reader to situate the beginning of the novel in
1898. This incident, in Havana harbor, sparked the Spanish-American War.
It forms the historical backdrop against which Razyé is poised to return
to colonial Guadeloupe. He has just spent three years as a mercenary in
the Spanish army fighting against insurgents in the mountainous areas of
Cuba, and his story pulls together the complex racial and cultural dynamics of the New World. Condé's pages convey searingly the fears and anxieties that racial proximity engendered in that unstable era, with its charged
atmosphere of hatred and suspicion, its ideologies of degeneration, and the
transcolonial desires and disavowals that miscegenation provoked wherever slave societies enforced secrecy while encouraging proximity.

Condé represents the ideologies of the time, and the political power
struggles that pitted Western nations against each other in the Caribbean,
without apologies. She thus foregrounds the processes of transcolonial hybridization through which the diasporic cultures of the New World have
flourished, despite the historical and discursive pressures against their accomplishments. These cultures have constituted themselves as integral
parts of the early colonial narratives of these regions, and the black Governor Pío Pico held public office at a time when slavery was still legal in
the U.S., as well as in the Spanish and French colonies. As is the case with

Alexandre Dumas' fictional *Georges*, or Chicago's historical Jean-Baptiste du Sable, the Franco-Haitian founder of that city, Pío Pico's place in history makes *explicit* the racial scripts that only "play in the dark," as Toni Morrison would say, in traditional or conventional narratives of the past. As a figure for the transcolonial identities that the narrative of *La Migration des coeurs* also develops, Pico makes plainly visible the blurred subtexts of history and the dark contours of social and political life in different parts of the Americas. He is a visual reminder of the vigorous presence and contributions of black cultures throughout the hemisphere.

In this essay I will use the term "transcolonial." I prefer it to the more commonly used "transnational" or "postcolonial" since my goal is to stress the spatial dimensions at the heart of the history of colonialism. On the one hand, the increasing use of the term "transnational" in literary and cultural studies is not useful within the framework of my study, since one cannot properly speak of the "nation" in relation to the Francophone Caribbean. Furthermore, the idea of the "transnational" suggests the kind of global corporatism that used to be subsumed under the label "multinational." It connotes far-reaching economic tentacles. On the other hand, this crucial spatial dimension is absent from the term "postcolonial." The intellectual history of the last fifty years is synonymous with a series of contested "posts": post-Holocaust, postmodern, post-structuralist, postcolonial, post-historical, post-theoretical, and even postfeminist. We seem to have reached the edge of time as it has been understood up to now. This habit of thought, which stresses various forms of temporality and their dialectical sublation within new formations, still conforms to a nineteenth-century teleological approach. Resorting instead to spatial thinking, to a relational approach that takes the form of networks among sites marked differentially by the imperial project and the colonial will to power, permits a shift in focus and an alteration in perspective. With the dawning of a new millennium, we are at a liminal moment. It encourages the emergence of new paradigms and demands a pluritopic rather than monologic argument about the role of history and memory, both during the early colonial forms of globalization and within contemporary cultural or discursive formations and economic conjunctures.

The increasing regionalization of the world makes historical circuits of colonial strife and influence more discernible today since the fragmentation of hegemonies reveals the multi-layered landscapes over which they have reigned. Shifting material practices, movements of peoples across cultural borders, and changing perspectives are bringing about transformations in the consciousness and the *imaginaire* of all peoples. As Glissant points out, groups that had long been subsumed under national European categories are now being transformed into smaller units, "islands" and "archipelagoes" among which, to echo Patricia Williams, we can begin to perceive the possibility for a more "tolerant, self-effacing extinction" of traditional frontiers and boundaries. New World societies have been a laboratory for the "diverse, unexpected and exuberantly impure" identities that have emerged from colonial history. The Caribbean, like Los Angeles or my own native Mauritius, is fertile terrain for theoretical and creative reflection on our common processes of hybridization, *mestizaje* or *métissage*, and on the resistance to those dynamics, whether they come from so-called conservative or radical camps. Condé's historical fresco contributes richly to this reflection by making visible patterns of transculturation emerging from colonial conflicts. Condé's perspectives, as I argue below, also expose the disavowals and denials that undermine Caribbean identity and feminist solidarity. This novel thus is a useful rejoinder and a sound complement to the excesses of male-identified *créolité* (see Bernabé et al., 1998).

Braiding Narrative Traditions Across Space

Je n'ai aucune idée des appellations théoriques qu'il faudrait donner . . . je m'efforce de faire une littérature qui échappe à toutes les rigidités, tous les canons, tous les interdits, tous les mots d'ordre.

MARYSE CONDÉ,
"Entretien"

Fiction writers are agents of transformation of our cultures' imaginative spaces, and Condé's work has contributed to the fleshing out of new discourses that can successfully fill in the narrative gaps of our cultural memory. Unlike postcolonial theorists who develop useful but abstract concepts such as ambivalence (Bhabha), *double critique* (Khatibi), double consciousness (DuBois and Gilroy), *créolité* (Bernabé, Chamoiseau & Confiant), and counterdiscourse (Terdiman, Tiffin), her stories paint pictures that mirror many facets of the shared histories and geographies of the Americas. Concepts such as those just mentioned acquire currency as tools for examining representation and resistance in literature and culture, and for understanding heterogeneity across time and space. Some of these theorists operate at the intersection of several languages or develop broad arguments for understanding the translation of cultures and languages. But when Helen Tiffin, for example, states that "the rereading and rewriting of the European historical and fictional record are vital and inescapable tasks" (95) of contemporary theory, and then goes on to discuss a "particular counter-discursive post-colonial field" (97) that she calls "canonical counter-discourse," what she has in mind is a monolithic and monolingual English tradition, viz.: "a post-colonial writer takes up a character or characters, or the basic assumptions of a British canonical text, and unveils those assumptions, subverting the text for post-colonial purposes" (97). One of the best-known examples of this practice is Jean Rhys' *Wide Sargasso Sea*, which "writes back" to Charlotte Brontë's *Jane Eyre*.

The empire, however, does not always write back to the expected *destinataire*, and Condé crosses borders and boundaries to find inspiration and to articulate unexpected affiliations. Her novels have consistently been sites of intersections and crossroads of different linguistic systems: *Moi, Tituba, Sorcière Noire de Salem* [*I, Tituba, Black Witch of Salem*] echoes Hawthorne's Hester Prynne and Ann Petry's Tituba; *Traversée de la mangrove* [*Crossing the Mangrove*] is indebted to Faulkner's *As I Lay Dying*. And *La Migration des coeurs* presents itself as a "reading" of *Wuthering Heights*: it is dedicated

> To Emily Brontë
> Who I hope will approve of this interpretation of her masterpiece.
> Honour and respect!

In offering her version of doomed love to the author who inspired it, Condé makes a gesture which is anything but innocent. Her re-writing is an "interpretation" that makes visible both her debts to Brontë and her creative re-appropriation of a theme—miscegenation and incest—which has elicited censure and prohibitions in real life as well as symbolic representation. In Brontë's rendering, Heathcliff is an ambiguous figure whose dubious origins and implicitly mixed racial identity are never probed, but who functions as Catherine's dark double. By displacing the setting of Brontë's novel from the Yorkshire Moors to the Caribbean islands and the temporal frame from the late eighteenth century to the late nineteenth and early twentieth centuries, Condé foregrounds the racial scripts that are barely hinted at in Brontë's tale of guilty passion and narcissistic or "claustrophobic inbreeding" (Bersani 199).

La Migration des coeurs initially seems to fit Tiffin's formulation of "canonical counter-discourse," except that it is a French text that writes back not to a French canonical work but to a British one. On the face of it, Condé appears to be "unveiling the assumptions" of the earlier text, producing a Francophone re-visioning of the transhistorical and transnational theme of romantic and forbidden love. She turns the ambiguous figure of Heathcliff, that "gypsy brat" (29) as Isabella says, or that "little Lascar . . . [that] American or Spanish castaway" (39) as Linton calls him, into a Caribbean métis, black and East Indian "nègre ou *bata-zindien*" (8). She calls him Razyé, the Creole word for the heath where he was found during a cyclone by Gagneur, Cathy's father, whose name is the obvious translation or French equivalent of Earnshaw. Like Brontë's Heathcliff, Razyé has escaped from l'Engoulvent (Windward Heights) after Cathy's wedding. As the maid Nelly Raboteur's *récit* reveals, he fled shortly after overhearing her conversation with Cathy who confessed that Aymeric de Linseuil (Condé's Edgar Linton) had proposed to her and that she would have to marry him because marrying Razyé instead would be "too degrading. It would be like starting to live all over again like our ancestors, the savages in Africa" (13).

To anyone familiar with the narrative of *Wuthering Heights*, it is clear that Condé's *Windward Heights* (the title of the English translation) follows very closely the plot and many of the details set by her predecessor. But unlike Brontë, she fills in the blanks of the hero's life. The three-year hiatus remains mysterious and external to the story in *Wuthering Heights*, whereas the Caribbean novel begins in Cuba, where Razyé spends these years. Having made his fortune, like Heathcliff, he comes back to get his revenge. He is poised to return "home" as he explains to Melchior:

> Je dis "chez moi" pour parler comme tout le monde. Mais je n'ai pas de pays. C'est en Guadeloupe qu'on m'a trouvé nu comme un ver et braillant plus fort qu'un cochon qu'on égorge, en plein milieu des *razyés*. Mon nom vient de là (17).

> [I say "home" to speak like the rest of you. But I have no home. I was found in Guadeloupe as naked as the day I was born, on the barren heath and cliffs—the *razyés*—hence my name (9).][3]

The colorful Creole expression "nu comme un ver et braillant plus fort qu'un cochon qu'on égorge" expresses with wit and raillery his state of dispossession, for that is all we know about Razyé's origins: he is linked to a landscape, defined by space, not time, free from the cultural vestments and baggage that accrue when one is wedded to an idea of "home" that suggests a history, a line of descent, and a legitimate tradition, rather than a temporary dwelling or a practice that remains open to the future because it is not defined by set pedigrees and clear genealogies. Although dates are blurred and the reader needs to scrutinize narrative details to understand the chronology of events, it is possible to put back together the pieces of the temporal puzzle that the author first seems to scramble. In the last chapter of Part I, with the Proustian title of "Le temps retrouvé" (118) ["The Past Recaptured" (115)], we obtain Razyé's own point of view on his exile, as he tells his story to Jean-Hilaire Endomius, whose political program galvanizes him into participating in the fight against the white Creole planters. Razyé's subjectivity and agency are thus underscored in a way that clearly differentiates him from Brontë's Heathcliff.[4]

Razyé's relationship to loss and death are central to this story, as it is for other Condé protagonists. Although he is meant to be a Caribbean Heathcliff, one cannot help but hear in Razyé echoes of another of Condé's fictional characters, Francis Sancher/Francisco Sanchez from her *Crossing the Mangrove*, a personage of ambiguous parentage and dubious origins, a Caribbean Everyman, whose death defines a community. In *La Migration des coeurs*, the title itself suggests an other-worldly voyage or passage. Here, death is mediated both by Brontë's plot and by Condé's use of some aspects of Simone de Beauvoir's *La Cérémonie des adieux*, from which she takes her epigraph, "Sa mort nous sépare. Ma mort ne nous réunira pas." ["Death has separated us. My death will not reunite us."] The epigraph announces the theme of death and eternal separation that runs through this tale of a tormented man consumed with the impossible desire to hold on forever to the woman who is his soul mate, his other self, the now departed Cathy: "Have you seen people live without their soul?" (82); "Can a human being live without his soul?" (99), he asks anxiously. Condé, however, makes her own Beauvoir materialist stance about life after death, and Cathy's voice, addressing the reader and her absent lover from her deathbed, echoes and reinforces the author's position: "You must realize we shall never see each other again, for death is nothing but the night. It is a migration of no return" (91); "I heard that Aymeric wants to bury my body in the little graveyard at L'Engoulvent beside maman. Only a living person could think that such a belated reunion would be of some use . . . Our bones will crumble into dust beside each other" (95). Condé thus allows herself to part company with Brontë's romantic notion of unity in marginality, that is, with the British author's image of "two bodies uniting, in dissolution," as critic Susan Meyer puts it (122). As Heathcliff's and Catherine's corpses lie together at the conclusion of the tale, they are reunited, but in "unquiet slumbers" (Brontë 256) that suggest spectral anguish and phantom torments. The romantic and gothic elements present in Brontë's version have been replaced by Condé's at once more cynical and more hopeful view that the only inescapable border or boundary is not the one between the races, but the one that separates life and death.

I want to stress, then, that *Windward Heights* is not simply a reaction against the misrepresentations that inform an earlier European text; nor is it an attempt to simply fill in the gaps that lace its edges. It is not simply postcolonial counter-discourse, but a way for Condé to borrow from two women writers, from the British and French canon respectively, in order to develop a cross-cultural poetics and to insert her text into a well-demarcated and highly literate tradition. She side-steps the largely masculine realist canon of the nineteenth-century French novel to find inspiration in two precursors, or "foremothers," who allow her to situate herself in relation to "a creative female subculture" (Gilbert and Gubar 51) that spans continents and centuries. *Wuthering Heights* becomes the warp upon which she threads the woof of her own insights and creativity, thus fashioning a truly mixed or *métisse* intertextuality analogous on the level of form to the thematics of biological and cultural crossings which drives the narrative's development.

I have defined the concept of *métissage* elsewhere as the weaving together of different strands of raw materials and threads of various colors into one piece of fabric or text (*Life/Lines* 277). *Métissage* is a model of intertextuality and hybridization in which the warp and woof of the social fabric, the racial elements of a given group, and the traditions of literary history are interwoven, or juxtaposed, and mirror each other. I want to suggest that this understanding of proximity denotes a *transcolonial* epistemology that emerges from the author's practice and produces a new understanding of the multiple strands of literary history in the Caribbean. This is a practice that shuffles binaries, criss-crosses them, and rearranges them in a thoroughly comparative network. It is a model of relatedness and diversity that respects difference and articulates relations of proximity. As with the intertwining threads of a weave, the strength or functionality of the assemblage depends on the relative positioning of each element within the collective grouping. This is *métissage* in its etymological sense: the interweavings of different fibers to create a heterogeneous social or cultural fabric. The result is not the organic fusion or bland blending promoted by assimilationist ideologies of *métissage;* nor is it the tragic doubleness of Manichean positions with their anxieties of influence or phantasmatic otherings. Transcolonial *métissage* exists in tension with multiple epistemological locations and subjective positionalities. It recognizes the role of traditional centers of power—political or economic institutions, the culture industry, the disciplines—and critiques the maps of knowledge they produce.

In *La Migration des coeurs,* Condé redraws the maps of Francophone literatures and cultures by using English narrative sources as well as oral traditions. She echoes Glissant's poetics of relation, what he has called "le Divers" and "le chaos-monde," and upon which he elaborates further in the above epigraph. Condé performs a reversal of the ideologies of filiation and legitimation that consent and descent (Sollors) produce in colonial societies. She borrows Brontë's plot, thematizes the flaws of nationalist and narcissistic identification and the tensions that colonialism exacerbates. But because her narrative technique makes difference *and* proximity the twinned elements of the familial, social, linguistic, and literary conventions that buttress her poetics of juxtaposition, she exemplifies *métissage* and what that creative process brings to light. Here, it is her transcolonial *affiliations,* her braiding of written and oral histories, and the uncharted possibilities that her open-ended structures promise within a geographical area in which European languages and African customs provide writers with multiple ways of situating themselves and their characters in relation to those traditions.

Memory and Oral Traditions Across Time

> They lived amid a commotion of rites.
>
> MICHELLE CLIFF,
> *Abeng*

As previously mentioned, the beginning of the novel is steeped in an atmosphere of carnival and festivity. These scenes are depicted against a background of somber political events during which "blood was flowing in every neighbourhood . . . [and] there was no telling political assassination from a sordid stab in the back" (11). Chaos is everywhere, and Melchior is murdered before Razyé has had the opportunity to learn the secrets of the *babalawo.* Having missed the chance to complete his ritual initiation into Melchior's *santería* religion, and "sensing that Cuba was going to live through even more dangerous times" (13), Razyé decides to leave the Spanish island and return to Guadeloupe.

In a book that is so intensely historical, it may initially seem surprising that Condé gives few specific dates. She makes passing reference to the death of José Martí (i.e., 19 May 1895), and to the abolition of slavery in the Spanish colonies (i.e., 1886), but she does not supply dates. We also find out that Cathy married Aymeric de Linseuil "on 13 April 18—" (47), and in the third part of the novel, she states: "In 19—, at the time when our story takes place, Marie-Galante began to merit the name it has been known by ever since: 'the island that is dying'" (223–224). Irmine de Linseuil, on the other hand, marries Razyé "on 1 January 1900" (106), and the servant Sanjita begins her story with the words: "On 21 December 1867, the *Allahabad* set sail from the port of Calcutta for the island of Guadeloupe with Sashi, my father, aboard" (155). Although there are numerous allusions to cultural (the Epiphany), historical (the abolition of slavery), and political (the explosion of the *Maine*) events, only readers familiar with their importance and function within the popular memory of the Caribbean basin will be able to situate them in historical time. We thus have to ask: what is the difference between the events that are dated and those that are not? Why use specific dates at all or, alternatively, why not give full historical references every time an event that has become part of "world history" is mentioned? In part, this is because Condé is following Brontë's own lead very faithfully: like the Yorkshire author, she is at pains to represent an oral culture, with a dialect of its own, but with a less than meticulous use of a calendar or "almanack" (Brontë) to record and signify the passage of time.

Throughout the narrative, numerous allusions allow the reader to situate the tale in "ces temps de confusion et de malheurs" (13) ["in this age of chaos and calamity" (5)], which continued during unsuccessful struggles for independence in the region. The *vox populi* of those who are outside of recorded history is heard, first at Cathy's wedding in Guadeloupe, then in the embedded stories of characters who are marginal to the main plot, but who address the reader directly. There are fifteen voices who tell their own stories, representing heterogeneous points of view on the history of the islands and the events of the narrative. The voices provide a kind of chorus which marks the passing of the old and the seemingly eternal recurrence of injustice for those who are on the lowest rungs of the social ladder: "It's been almost fifty years since slavery's supposed to be over and yet the blacks only find misery at the bottom of life's bowl. Meanwhile, the white Creoles are still parading around with the same wealth and haven't suffered a bit" (49). Together, these personal tales constitute the collective cultural memory of those who are not literate, and who "re-member" the past in reference to cataclysms such as cyclones and epidemics ("That year, the year 19—, Guadeloupe suffered a terrible calamity. Typhoid fever landed off the boats . . ." [159]). Complex chronologies measure the passage of time in relation to such events. These do not so much provide important clues to the reader as add historical density to the lives of all the characters, the haves and the have-nots, the literate and the uneducated. In the French colonies, slavery was abolished by decree under the Second Republic on 27 April 1848, and the *Code noir*, which had regulated the lives of slaves for some 150 years, was finally repealed. By alluding to this historical fact, Condé situates the narrative inside a universal history linked to Europe's written culture, but she stresses its momentous *lack* of impact on the lives of ordinary peoples who continue to survive in economic hardships. Their narratives are thus set against the grain of recorded history.

The procession at Epiphany, while taking place in Cuba, invokes African traditions and their transformations in the New World. In Cuban *santería*, as in Haitian *vodou*, European and African traditions merge to produce syncretic forms of worship and disquietingly beautiful art forms that blur the line between the sacred and the secular, the aesthetic and the ethnographic (cf. Cosentino). Condé's opening scenes convey all the magic of New World syncretism, its rituals and performances, and its allegiance to Roman Catholic saints as well as African deities. Melchior is named after one of the three Magi, the one considered to be of African origin in the oral tradition of the Mediterranean region. But on this Christian holiday celebrating the arrival of the Three Kings, it is the African deity Chango who is mentioned:

Melchior headed the procession carrying the banner of his god, Chango.
He was dressed in the god's favourite colours, with a red and white striped jacket and red cotton cambric breeches . . . (3).
The cathedral was deserted, save for a few worshippers in the chapel . . . Melchior passed in front of a row of empty confessionals, then stopped at the chapel to Santa Barbara. . . . By a strange twist of collusion, this frail virgin in her white dress and red cape was one of his god's manifestations of power. In fact her image could be seen in every temple dedicated to *santería*, depicted as a young Yoruba girl, her forehead haloed in frizzy hair, her cheekbones scored with scars . . .
A streak of lightning followed by the thunder of Chango flashed through the vividly coloured stained-glass *vitrales*. The interior of the nave gleamed white (6–7).

Melchior is one of several sorcerer-priests, *kimbwazé* or *gadedzafé* (218), like Madhi or Ciléas, whom Razyé consults in his vain efforts to make contact with the afterlife. All of them are wary of the dangerous possibilities of initiating Razyé, who "would be able to get in touch with those *egun* of which he was the very image, and use their powers for his own ends" (9). These *egun* are trickster figures of the *gede* family, known for their contrary behavior, and common in the oral traditions of the Americas (Cosentino). Condé's description of one of the *egun* (or divinities) includes that of the character known as Baron-Samedi, who dresses "in a black frock-coat and tails, black glasses and top hat" (216). Throughout the text, descriptions of Razyé associate him with this powerful trickster as well as real-life political figures. Razyé thus occupies a symbolic space that stretches between Baron-Samedi and Pico, between the supernatural and the historical, between oral traditions and written documents. Furthermore, the Catholic virgin with the African scarifications evokes multiple symbolic systems. She too figures under several designations (Erzulie, Dantò, Fréda) in the pantheon of *vodou* religious syncretism. These images set the stage for the relational patterns and interconnected movements that underlie Condé's use of a multiplicity of narrative perspectives, including those of several female servants (Nelly Raboteur, Lucinda Lucius, mabo Julie, Sanjita, Etiennise, mabo Sandrine, Romaine) whose insights into the lives of their mistresses shed light on the secrets of colonial society.

   To read *Migration* within all of those traditions demands a "comparatist's" approach, one that neither evacuates European thought and culture nor focuses strictly on the canonical and British literary strands visible in the plot of the book. This approach requires a worldview more complex than a "double consciousness," and not just an understanding of rigid oppositionalities. I would call it a feminist reading practice, a strategy for "reading simultaneity" (Smith xv), intersectionality, and interrelations. As Valerie Smith has argued, feminist criticism or practices of reading can best be understood as "a series of overlapping, discontinuous, and multiply interpretable discursive sites" (xviii). Condé's novel is such a site of convergence. The novel forces the revisioning of counter-discursive practices in light of feminist ones, something the trio of *créolistes* from Martinique (Bernabé et al. 1998) have not been able to grasp. Their recent denunciation of feminist discourses has taken the form of pot shots against Condé's narrative style and strategies (1998, 152–154). But their determination to define an exclusive and static territory of *créolité* only succeeds in bypassing the tensions, transcolonial routes, and conflict zones that a figure such as

Figure 2. "Baron La Croix" by André Pierre. *Gede* dons a top hat and dress coat in mauve or black, the undertaker's attire. 1973. Oil on Masonite. 58.5 × 89 cm.

Milwaukee Art Museum. Gift of Richard and Erna Flagg.

Figure 3. Manbo by a large-scale Dantor (Dantò) and child, Port-au-Prince. Photograph, Phyllis Galmebo, June 1993.

Pío Pico now exemplifies for me. It is Glissant's dynamic notion of creolization, as a theory embedded in a practice, as well as the *inclusionary* models put forth by feminists, that best serve the purpose of illuminating the challenges faced by a writer who transgresses linguistic, national, and colonial borderlines and borderlands.

By interweaving influences and traditions and foregrounding the sources of her inspiration, Condé points toward the elegant interrelations that her aesthetic practice makes possible. Whereas the filiation and identity of several characters in her story remain in doubt, the "identity" of her literary text is established from the start by both the dedication and the epigraph that mark her affiliations, advertise her sources, and openly acknowledge her debts to a female literary tradition. By staging an oral Creole culture steeped in a sense of mystery and fatality, haunted by a past whose chronology is obscure and tortured, Condé does not produce the standard postcolonial counter-discourse, but fleshes out lines of female affiliation which link up to form parallel traditions. She rearranges the patterns that define the literary history of the Caribbean by staking a multilingual and feminist space that is also a *trans*colonial one. Her aesthetics are thus at odds with the historical valence of her thematics, since her formal practice successfully deconstructs the debilitating myths of purity and racial superiority that continue to haunt her characters because they have internalized this inaugural colonial ideology.

Repetition, Incest, and Dissymmetry

Our most fundamental national experience is to raise a ruckus over the lines dividing us, while knowing in our hearts that those lines of racial and cultural purity are probably false—that we are all . . . obliged to find a way of carrying on together.

BARBARA KINGSOLVER,
"Lone Star," *The Nation*

I had joined that band of pilgrims uncenturied, unquantified, who, call it art, call it alchemy, call it science, call it god, are driven by a light that will not stay.

JEANETTE WINTERSON,
Gut Symmetries

In her study of race in Victorian women's fiction, Susan Meyer has argued that Emily Brontë's novel is, more than anything, "an extended critique of

British imperialism" (100) that allows the author to explore "the external, untamable energies" (101) that threaten the structure of British civilization. In her analysis of the constraints on women's lives that *Wuthering Heights* underscores, and in which Heathcliff violently participates, Meyer suggests that, while sympathetic to the plight of the second Catherine and Isabella, women whom Heathcliff savagely oppresses, Brontë is more interested in "the transgressive pleasure of imagining a reversal of imperialist power" (124) than in exploring the plight of these female characters and the question of gender oppression. Heathcliff's brutality, she points out, is a racial metaphor that takes on a life of its own as it suggests black violence and rebellion as well as "the possible insurrection of the subject 'dark races.'" This violence foregrounds the reversal of social power that imperialism both fears and is powerless to stop. In this process, Meyer says, *Wuthering Heights* loses much of the feminist vision that the character of the rebellious Catherine, "half savage and hardy, and free" (163), initially embodies, "a surprising phenomenon to encounter in the work of a British woman writer of this period" (124-125). Meyer's argument that Brontë's metaphoric link between race and gender makes the racial fears of Victorian culture more real than its oppression of women suggests that Brontë had an acute understanding of the racial question, even if she does not develop the theme of Heathcliff's racial ambiguity.

In Maryse Condé's appropriation of Brontë, Heathcliff/Razyé's racial identity is never in doubt, his violent temperament is real, and he reflects the paradoxical and contradictory stereotypes of the "dark races" as wild and aggressive untamed animals. But Condé does more: she complicates the scenario by reading the relations of power that affect race and gender as an intricate system in which both race and gender are so completely enmeshed that it is impossible to privilege one at the expense of the other. She thus recuperates the feminist vision lost by Brontë when the latter denounces the racial politics of her culture. Condé's homage to the British writer suggests an understanding of the revolutionary texture of Brontë's vision. That is why I would be inclined to see her novel as complementary to the Victorian text, and not just because it makes race more visible: as Meyer argues, Brontë does make it as visible as possible within the cultural constraints of her time. Condé's novel fleshes out the feminist vision of the Victorian writer by deploying the possibility for a feminist future in which female voices are heard rather than destroyed as Cathy II's diary is destroyed by Razyé II who fears learning the truth about his wife. Condé writes that after Cathy II's death, "without hesitating, he [Razyé II] threw it overboard. For a few minutes, the diary floated on the surface of the water, wings spread like a bird, then it dived into the foam and vanished amidst the swirl of the waves. Whatever Cathy's secrets might have been he would never know their *monstrosities*" (334, my emphasis).

It is this fear of women's voices and of the truths of their lives that Condé subtly exposes. The various narrative perspectives stress the confused genealogies and uncertain filiations of the main characters. Their ill-fated destinies seem to result from their ambiguous if not always illegitimate origins. Victims of the racial ideologies of their time, they see human beings in terms of phenotypical variations from light to dark, superior to inferior, always anxious to hide and deny the darker, African elements of their ancestry. This exclusionary model of descent gives rise to hierarchies of classification and racial stereotyping that many of Condé's characters voice uncritically. Condé makes no authorial intervention into the fictional universe she has created and in which the *doxa* of the time prevails. Thus Nelly declares about Razyé's look that, "You couldn't say he was handsome because of the colour of his skin, his facial features and his big purplish mouth" (23). As for Cathy, she has internalized the schizophrenic or tragic mulatto syndrome: "It's as if there were two Cathys inside of me and there always have been, ever since I was little. One Cathy who's come straight from Africa, vices and all. The other Cathy who is the very image of her white ancestor, pure, dutiful, fond of order and moderation. But this second Cathy is seldom heard, and the first always gets the upper hand" (40). Her children by the blond Aymeric exert a strange fascination on her: "Was it really her who had made these little dribbling darlings with porcelain cheeks?" (60). Aymeric has utopian dreams of peace and harmony: "When would the world be like a garden where every race on earth could walk together in harmony? When would this island cast off its demons?" (86). But he cannot help but be disturbed when Cathy's newborn, Cathy II, "had nothing in common with the rest of the family" (87). The free-indirect discourse used liberally by Condé allows the reader to enter the thought processes of her characters, and for Aymeric, Cathy II is "unlike her brothers, her skin had already darkened, as if she had gone back in time in search of a lost family tree" (87).

This description of the dark child to whom Cathy gives birth before dying can initially be read as the portrait of the true daughter of her dark-skinned mother. Yet, at age fifteen, she does not look like her mother: "Aymeric looked at the features of the pretty face turned toward him. A low, rounded forehead. Black eyes slit like an almond. Full bodied lips. Dark

brown complexion. . . . 'No,' he said with regret. 'You don't take after her'"
(141). Later on, the description of Razyé's daughter by Irmine de Linseuil
suggests an uncanny similarity between the two cousins: "Freda . . . was
a strong little girl who already looked like her papa, dark-skinned as well,
with very black, slit, almond-shaped eyes" (206). Their resemblance, however, is due to features they both share with Razyé, not with de Linseuil.
Given the ambiguities in Cathy's relationship with both her husband Aymeric and her true love Razyé, it is easy to speculate that Cathy II is in fact
Razyé's daughter, and thus Freda's half-sister.

When the grown Cathy II, living in Roseau on the island of Dominica,
falls in love with Premier-Né and becomes pregnant, she worries about
the legacy of this unborn child. As she confides in Ada, the fishwife: "I am
the daughter of tainted blood . . . As for my real papa, Ada, I'm so fright-
ened, I'd rather not know" (326). Premier-Né finally admits to her: "You
know I was his son, the first of his loins . . . I bear his name: Razyé" (315).
He also explains that his father never loved him and preferred "his white-
skinned bastard, that tubercular hypocrite Justin-Marie" who looks like
his aunt Cathy, but corresponds to the stereotype of the weak, effeminate,
and sickly white mulatto.

Cathy II's death in childbirth leaves her daughter orphaned, and history
repeats itself once more, but with a difference, since Razyé II decides that
he will go back home, to "claim his inheritance. Not for himself . . . For
her. For Anthuria" (322). The concluding line of the novel, the sadly ironic,
"[s]uch a lovely child could not be cursed" (348), gestures toward new possibilities embodied in the person of Anthuria. The birth of this child is a
twist that modifies the original plot of *Wuthering Heights*, in which a closed
system "provides [Brontë's] characters with a biological structure of self-
perpetuation," as Leo Bersani has analyzed (198). But in Brontë's nefari-
ously inbred structure, there are no offspring. Condé opens up the closed
system of Brontë's work with the birth of Anthuria, even if this child may
still be the progeny of a secret, hidden, and racially transgressive inbred
structure.

Condé's ironic stance leaves no doubt as to the "fated" nature of Anthuria. Even if the local *doxa* implies that she might be "maudite" (337) or
"cursed" (348) because she is the dark-skinned descendant of two doomed
characters (her grandparents, the first Cathy and Razyé), for the author,
the problem seems to reside in the fact that she is the product of an *incestuous* union between Razyé II and Cathy II, who have no proof that they are
each other's half-brother and half-sister, but soon become consumed by

this very fear.[5] It is the ignorance and secrecy maintained by their families and societies that threaten them and their offspring.

Anthuria's filiation is thus in doubt, as is Heathcliff's or Razyé's, but hers is doubly so, because her mother's own lineage is in doubt: Cathy II may not be the legitimate child of Cathy and Aymeric; rather, she is more likely to be the illegitimate offspring of Cathy and Razyé's doomed love affair. Anthuria thus becomes a final figure for the intermingled and twisted genealogies of the New World, and the inbreeding characteristic of plantation societies in general. Anthuria's malediction, if it is one, is thus rooted in the secret, narcissistic, and incestuous desires of her ancestors rather than in their mixed racial parentage. The cloud of ignorance that haunts the characters reinforces their difference from those who belong to cultures and families in which written records leave proof of lineages. In the oral traditions of plantation societies, on the other hand, it is the secret, and the *imaginaire* it creates, that constitutes the curse against which so many characters in La Migration struggle vainly. Condé refocuses attention on a "universal" taboo, the incest taboo, instead of perpetuating the racial taboos that have been part of the *imaginaire* of Judeo-Christian societies since biblical times, and which are repeated in various forms by all the main characters, when they mimic the dominant discourses of racial superiority.

The closed world of Brontë's novel is interpreted as narcissistic by Bersani, and so it is. Understood in the context of ideologies of miscegenation that argued that mulattos and mixed-bloods produced the degeneration of the species and the infertility of the race, the narcissism present in the British novelist's story can be read as a form of sterile closure. In Condé, the opening out produced by Anthuria's birth does not erase the narcissism at the heart of her family tree, nor does it disculpate her parents, as Razyé II's tormented thoughts and willful refusal to learn the truth pursue him and ruin his life (348). But it does transform the history of literary representations of miscegenation, since the final note of the novel stresses the loveliness of this child who may take history in a new direction, if only her voice is not drowned like that of her own mother. It may then be possible to read the concluding pages of *Windward Heights* as a warning of the author directed at her Caribbean "brothers": women's lives are the key to the history of the Caribbean, and those who ignore them do so at great cost to themselves and their descendants.

Notes

I am indebted to Louise Yelin for sharing her ideas on *Wuthering Heights* and for bringing the work of Susan Meyer to my attention.

Some sections of this essay were first published as "Transnationalism, Postcolonialism or Transcolonialism? Reflections on Los Angeles, Geography, and the Uses of Theory," *Emergences* 10:1 (2000). I thank the editor, Teshome Gabriel, for his support and for granting permission to reprint.

1. The Seaver Center for Western History Research is housed in the Natural History Museum of Los Angeles County. I could comment at length on that single fact. The conflation of anthropology, history, and natural history when it comes to a "pre-Western" past requires a long, separate argument, which cannot be my purpose here.

2. I asked people randomly: students, colleagues, and even native Angelenos who now live elsewhere in the U.S. The only person who knew exactly who Pico was is a UCLA student in one of my classes; she is majoring in anthropology and studying the cultures of the L.A. basin.

3. Quotations from Condé's novel throughout the essay are both from the French original, *La Migration des coeurs*, and Richard Philcox's English translation, *Windward Heights*. The language of the extract will identify the source.

4. For a discussion of the ways in which Condé makes the silences of Brontë's text "speak," see Vinay Swamy's "Traversing the Atlantic." I agree with many of Swamy's formulations, but I see Condé as doing much more than simply filling the blanks of the British author's text. For me, her braiding of traditions amounts to a *feminist* re-visioning of postcolonial theories of counter-discursive practices, as I argue below. Swamy also provides a useful comparison of family genealogies in Brontë's and Condé's novels:

a) Genealogy in *Wuthering Heights*

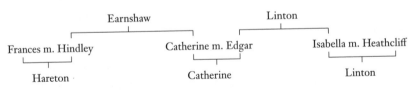

b) Genealogy in *Windward Heights*

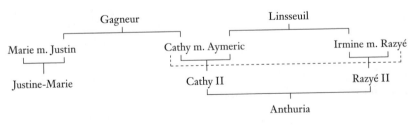

Figure 4. Genealogy in *Wuthering Heights* and *Windward Heights*.

5. For a smart view of these issues, see Swamy. However, he suggests that Anthuria's birth constitutes "an opening-out of the family tree" (ms. p. 11). My reading aims at showing that this is not really the case. The suspicion of incest in Condé's story simply confirms the "narcissistic" aspects of Brontë's text as analyzed by Bersani. But what we have now is repetition with a difference — and an ironic ray of hope about the potentialities embodied in this daughter.

CHAPTER 5

CRÉOLITÉ OR AMBIGUITY?

Michèle Praeger

A cultural, if not political, phenomenon is being acknowledged (or created) by some French Caribbean intellectuals and writers under the name of *créolité*. Let's compare two texts, for instance, one taken from *Un Plat de porc aux bananes vertes* (1967), by Simone and André Schwarz-Bart, and the other from Raphaël Confiant's *La Vierge du Grand Retour* (1996):

> Martinique made up of multiple races engaged in an unremitting hand to hand struggle where sexual weapons are forged with the steel of contempt! . . .
> But Raymoninque would beat these ridiculous acts flat. He could not be placed on any level of this ladder of contempt raised upon the island, like a tower of Babel slowly erected by centuries of oppression and crime. With one word, he would tear out a rung. He would say for instance: the white man despises the Quadroon who despises the Mulatto who despises the "Câpre," who despises the "Zambo," who despises the Negro who despises the Indian who despises the Indian woman who . . . beats her dog, ha ha; and I Ray Raymond Raymoninque I look at you all and I laugh to myself; and if you ask me who is my blood brother, I will tell you that it is the dog! (Schwarz-Bart 127–128).[1]

> When night [le "faire-noir": literally the "make-dark"] enveloped the earth with its usual savagery, the Couli-Indian bowed down, his face on the ground and stopped moving. Dictionneur cautiously got closer do him. He did not dare interrupt his meditation. A sort of affectionate diffidence paralyzed him. He wanted to clasp his hands, embrace him, feel the touch of his beardless cheek sprinkled by a sparse and frizzy beard like a string of pepper corns. He felt that they had become brothers, Dictionneur, the Negro and Manouchy, the Couli-Indian. Not blood brothers but soul brothers, which, he realized now, was the most important. Manouchy finally raised his head, noticed him and started to smile.

"*Ou* . . . You . . . ," uttered Dictionneur.
—Don't say anything! You saw me overcome the kalapani . . .
—The what?
—This malediction which has followed us since our people had to leave their native country, India. Now . . . Now . . . this country, Martinique, this country . . . is my country . . . It is . . . our country . . .
—Yes, it is our country! repeated Dictionneur who took him in his arms.
(*Vierge du Grand Retour* 248).

Something has happened, some things have changed between these two texts.

Where Simone Schwarz-Bart highlights blood, race, sex, violence and scorn, descent into hell, Confiant, in a Camusian type of humanism, joins two men not through kinship of blood but of "soul." While Raymoninque is barking and biting like a cornered dog, Dictionneur and Manoutchy are singing the aria of *créolité*. Where Raymoninque "tears out a rung," Dictionneur wants to touch the Other's cheek; Confiant's text is an illustration of a moment of *créolité*: two men, a Negro and a Couli-Indian, experience an epiphany of *créolité* during a Hindu religious practice. *Créolité* is revealed to them just as God was to Pascal and Claudel. The places are different, a cave and a cathedral, but the moments are similar.

The premise of *Eloge de la créolité* is well known: "Ni Européens, ni Africains, ni Asiatiques nous nous proclamons créoles" (13) ["Neither European, nor African, nor Asian we proclaim ourselves *créoles*"]. We are here in the domain of the linguistic performative, according to Austin, in the "performative present of cultural identification," to borrow Homi Bhabha's expression. Their proclamation is what makes this "nous" *créole*. Furthermore, *créolité* is defined as what "we" are not. And yet, despite any positive pole to counter the triple negativity surrounding its birth, it does come to a dialectical end: the son of a German man and a Haitian woman born in "Peking" will surpass his mother and father, the Germans, the Haitians, and the Chinese in sensitivity, diversity, creativity. He will be, as the authors affirm, "in the state of being-Creole" (53). While, indeed, he could exceptionally be endowed with the positive aspects of his German father, his Haitian mother, and the Pekingese, he could alternatively surpass them in brutality, destruction, senselessness, or he could turn up to be female or worse a homosexual, as eugenicists of the nineteenth century feared.

It would be fruitful at this point of the argument on *créolité* to start reading a short text by Suzanne Césaire, published in the last text of the last issue of *Tropiques* (1945), "Le Grand camouflage"² ["The Great Cover-Up"], where she endows the West Indian man, because of his European and African ancestors, not with an innate wonder for the diversity of the universe and of humanity but with a "double ferocity":

> Here is a West Indian, the great grandson of a colonizer and a black slave. He turns around in circles on his island, spending all the energy needed by the greedy colonizers for whom the blood of others was the natural cost of gold and all the necessary courage of the African warriors who constantly earned their living with their own death (271).

This particular *créole*, exposed and denounced by Suzanne Césaire, as before her by the French Caribbean writers of the review *Légitime Défense*,³ is the "bourgeois de couleur," the accursed mulatto of twentieth century fiction: "He will not accept his Negritude, he cannot whiten himself. Cowardice takes hold of his divided heart and with it the habits of tricks, the taste for schemes" (Césaire 271). I believe, however, that one can read between the lines of her text the implication that every West Indian participates, in varying degrees, in this "double strength" and "double ferocity," feels "cowardice" in his "heart" and also performs a certain amount of "tricks," in order to survive. Suzanne Césaire's view differs from W. E. B. DuBois' notion of "double consciousness," which tears the Negro's soul apart in the sense that these "two warring ideals" team up, albeit for a derisive result: to "turn around in circles" in one's native island. In order to deconstruct the notion of *créolité*, it would be useful to briefly illustrate the concept of modern and postmodern "hybridity," as envisioned by "science" and poetry. In the nineteenth century, biological (and cultural) hybridity was deemed apocalyptic; it signaled the end of a race or of a culture. Thus, in order to "protect" a colonizing race and culture from "extinction," hybridity was declared impossible, and the hybrid (biological or cultural) was doomed to sterility, despite evidence to the contrary. Yet, at the same time, as Robert Young reminds us, and also Raphaël Confiant in *La Vierge du Grand Retour,* le comte de Gobineau claimed, "in a footnote" says Young, that women of mixed race, although "degenerate" and "degraded," were "the most beautiful beings of all" (Young 114; Confiant 130). This ambivalent attitude rooted in anxiety and desire toward the "hybrid" can be highlighted by the example of André Breton who, in a poem, also published in *Tropiques*, "Pour Madame" (who is Madame Césaire), finds that the "chabines rieuses" ["laughing *chabines*"] have "usually lighter hair than complexion" and represent "feminine beauty which has never appeared more striking to [him] than in a face of white cinders and embers" (*Tropiques* No. 3, 41). Feminine beauty, in Breton's own words, is "striking," dangerous and attractive, it is "hysterical," "convulsive," oscillating between life and death, eager to seduce an André Breton. The *chabines* represent for Breton the instantaneousness of the convulsive, which fixes movement without stopping it. The *chabine* is the *Ur* Woman, the original who transforms other women into mere copies of herself. In other words, Breton invented the notion of "convulsive beauty" in France, as a chained man condemned to try and capture the shadow of beauty on the wall of a Platonistic cave, and in Martinique was given the supreme honor and horror of staring Medusa in the face.

Suzanne Césaire, in "Le Grand camouflage," implicitly comments on these two related conceptions of the hybrid, that of Gobineau and that of Breton, when she shows some French Metropolitan civil servants ["fonctionnaires métropolitains"] on a Caribbean beach, ready to fly black to the *Métropole*. These *Métropolitains* do not adapt easily to "our old French possessions," she writes, because the French Caribbeans show them "a delirious image of themselves" ["une image délirante d'eux-mêmes"]. They do not dare recognize themselves in this ambiguous being, the Caribbean man. It is understood, notes Suzanne Césaire sarcastically, that Metropolitan French are not racists. Yet their "colored descendants" ["descendance colorée"] fill them with fear despite "exchanged smiles." They were not expecting this "strange sprouting of their own blood" (270–271) ["étrange bourgeonnement de leur sang"]. "The paranoid threat from the hybrid (Suzanne Césaire's "être ambigu") is finally uncontainable because it breaks down the symmetry and duality of self/other, inside/outside . . . ," suggests Homi Bhabha (176). The Caribbean is half human, half animal; half French, half slave; half Prospero, half Caliban, etc. It is seductive and frightening to the French male bourgeois because it is linked to pleasure and vice if female, to treachery if male. For some Metropolitan French all Martiniquais are *chabins* or *chabines*. It is interesting to note that Raphaël Confiant, a self-described *chabin*, in his "Petit lexique du pays créole," which follows his novel *Ravines du devant-jour*, seems to subscribe, if dialogically, to the Metropolitan view of the *chabins* and the *chabines*. This is his definition of the *chabin*:

> Quality of a Negro endowed with the unheard quality (of which he takes advantage) of turning red with anger or shame because of an influx of white

blood dating from the time of slavery. His eyes, which are often blue or green, shine with suppressed rage and the *chabine*, O golden woman, at the height of orgasm ("coquer" in Creole), nibbles at your ears until they bleed. Often red-headed (and therefore vicious) [Confiant is now referring to the *chabin*] (210–211).

What therefore is a *chabin* in absolute terms? A frightening hybrid or a reassuring *créole*? What is a *chabine*? Is there a *chabin* or a *chabine* essence? At this point, we Metropolitan readers find ourselves truly lost in Confiant's fictional world. We cannot trust definitions as enunciated by a voice mimicking the tone of our dictionaries, hence we can no longer trust our trusted dictionaries. We cannot grasp the complexity of "identity," or we lose our own. "We have entered the age of suspicion," declared the New Novelist Nathalie Sarraute, in the early fifties, about the reader of nineteenth century–like fiction and his or her attitude toward "characters." We postmoderns and postcolonials suspect, as Flaubert did, not only the capacity of language to express but also the locus of its enunciation.

While Breton, in *Martinique charmeuse de serpents*, only seems to notice Aimé Césaire and Martiniquan women and looks at them through his surrealist lenses of (mostly) pleasurable wonder, Suzanne Césaire muses about the stirrings of the French Metropolitan confronted on a beach by male hybrids. Her suppositions are of a biological *and* a political order: they are cultural.

Let's now enter into a discussion with postcolonial critics such as Robert Young, Homi Bhabha and Thomas Spear, with Edouard Glissant and the Caribbean philosopher Jacky Dahomey, in order to highlight the complexities of *créolité* unmentioned by the Creolists. The parameters of biological and linguistic hybridity are now being theorized. Robert Young sees Bakhtin's "linguistic hybridity" as double, as hybrid itself: on the one hand, an unconscious "organic hybridization" mixes and fuses languages and gives birth to other languages, and on the other hand, there is an ironic "intentional hybridization" that is generated by different points of view pitted against each other in a never-ending conflicting structure that retains "a certain elemental energy and openendedness" (20–22). This is Bakhtin's principle of "dialogism," an aesthetic but also social and political operation.

Homi Bhabha sees hybridity not as a conciliatory third term between warring cultures but as a *place* of negotiation, whereas the Creolists see *créolité* as a *moment* of fusion. Hybridity is, to be sure, a double-consciousness, and it is also a site of deceit, where the "hybrid" displays signs of "differentiation" that are translated by the colonizers as effects of "signs of authority" over the colonized (175). Thus, the hybrid, as seen by Bhabha, is the embodiment of a revised Faustian type of contract between the Master culture and the Slave culture. He or she is the living proof that the oppressed have been tricked again. But the mask of hybridity has also helped the colonized dupe the master, but "not quite," only the master who doesn't trust this "delirious image" of himself. If mimicry is repetition with a difference, then the original has been desecrated, copied, deformed; it is the same, but "not quite," according to Bhabha's expression. Hybridity is a highly performative, postcolonial, postmodern place of estrangement, in the sense that it is "estranging" for the "Master" who has come to feel, like Camus' Meursault, like a stranger within his own culture. It is the place of "negotiations" not "negations," according to Bhabha (25), where perhaps all parties can find at least partial satisfactions. As for myself, I believe, contrary to Bhabha's view, that some form of refusal is necessary for any process to "begin," for use of a better verb. It seems to me that the French Caribbeans will never become *créoles*, or even *hybrids*, and that the place of negotiation, at this point of their history, is still to be found for Suzanne Césaire's "êtres ambigus."

Edouard Glissant, of whom Chamoiseau and Confiant claim to be the literary and ideological heirs, expressed doubts about the term *créolité* as early as *Le Discours antillais*,[4] and prefers the term *créolisation*, not as an end in itself, which would lead to the creation of a new "verticality," a settlement, a growing of roots and of a solid trunk with arms extended into the sky, a new model fashioned after an old French myth. Creolization should not strive to become atavistic like *créolité* but should keep its character of decomposition, destructuration, and conflict. Glissant stresses, in *Introduction à une Poétique du Divers*, the terms "circularity" and "spirality" against the "arrow-like projection" ["projection en flèche"] of colonization. Chamoiseau and Confiant are, according to Glissant, creating a "counter-verticality" (19) ("verticality" being also transcendence and universalism). He insists on the unpredictability of Creole culture (16), on a "conversion of the being" ["conversion de l'être" (14)] that the Caribbean has to endure. From the beginning Creolization implies a transformation of the African being, through slavery, oppression, dispossession, and crimes; it is a painful journey. It is an unfair process because the African migrants arrived naked in the Caribbean. Their only possessions were "traces" of traditions, music, language. But this is also part of their strength: from these traces, they created Creole languages and forms of art such as jazz, which can be appreciated by anybody, which are truly universal. Creolization entails a spiritual dimension: simultaneously the recognition of the Other and the recognition of one's own "otherness." What Glissant calls "a spirit of traces" ["la pensée de la trace"] is not so much dogmatic or exclusive as it is a "spirit of roots" ["la pensée de la racine"]. Creolization is happening in the Caribbean, but as African cultures have been devalued within the process, this Creolization also produces a "bitter and intractable residue" ["un résidu amer, incontrôlable" (15)]. This "residue" has to be accounted for, for fear of falling into what the Africanist critic Ama Mazama calls "a complacent *créolité*" ["une créolité béate" (92)]. For Glissant, Creolization represents a series of questions rather than answers. Is true Creolization, that is, many systems of thoughts coming together without destroying each other, really possible? How can one retain a distinct specificity while "creolizing"? (30). It is a question not only of coming together but also of clashing together, that is, of not falling prey to "assimilation," or rather acculturation, according to Glissant. In one of his bleakest fictional moments, Glissant sees Martinique as a museum, the "Museum of the Colony," covered with a glass bubble and filled with gift shops (*Mahagony* 178–180). Glissant is aware of the dual nature of *créolisation*. It entails a "negative" aspect of past enslavement and present "assimilation to French culture" that is unintentional, if not unconscious. It also comprises a "positive" aspect (and here Glissant gives fresh meaning to the adjective) that has always driven the Caribbeans to an "elsewhere which would always be here": Marcus Garvey to the blacks in the United States or Frantz Fanon to Algeria. This "elsewhere-here" drove Lafcadio Hearn and Paul Gauguin away from Martinique to Japan and Oceania, as it was an insurmountable obstacle to their search for more permanent and reliable origins and an unadulterated (or so they thought) purity (25).

Caribbean philosopher Jacky Dahomey, in an article "Habiter la créolité ou le heurt de l'universel" ["Inhabiting *créolité* or the Clash with the Universal"], has called attention to the multiple contradictions that compose the concept of *créolité* and the risks attached to any discourse on the problematics of identity. He addresses in particular the thorny notion of "universality" which Glissant's epigones, as Dahomey calls the Creolists, never cease to deride. While Dahomey recognizes that Glissant has broached the problem in his usual complex way, the authors of *Eloge* have singularly simplified it by equating the Universal with French values. They oppose the universality of the Same and the One (France), to "diversality" without ever specifying what those two notions mean. Dahomey points out that some Antillean intellectuals praise "assimilation" with the culture and politics of the Metropole in the name of universality and therefore put down their own culture, while others denigrate universality to assert the identity of the French Caribbean islands. The latter position (and Dahomey includes also Glissant's reflections on universality) is uncritical of the very notion these writers are attacking. According to him, Glissant and most Antillean intellectuals are deeply marked by a traditionally modern dialectical philosophy of history, culture, and society. When they try to distance themselves from this predicament, they fall back into a "phenomenological conception" without attempting to critically conceptualize history. Their nationalistic aesthetics of identity are bolstered by a Hegelian problematic that they do not question and that they should not necessarily reject. In particular, they do not question their own propensity to attack "French" universalism with the arms of Hegelian universalism. They assume that all human experience can be continually propelled forward through the theorization of an *Aufhebung* (the Hegelian synthesis) without taking into account that certain elements of this experience are not "dialectisable," as shown by Suzanne Césaire. Furthermore, if *francité*[5] and Negritude were but positive or negative moments, and Glissant's *antillanité* their *Aufhebung*, where does that leave *créolité* in the dialectical operation? Should we assume, wonders Dahomey, that there is a fourth moment and that the Creolists are synthesizing *francité*, Negritude, and *antillanité* and are therefore coming closer to the Truth, or are they still in Glissant's "moment"? Will *créolité* also be submitted to the movement of dialectics on its native island or will the movement stop?

Also, the Creolists have not really tackled the question of the Creole being's encounter with modernity, that is, with the "irruption of the individual" (125). The question of this irruption with traditional cultures is a problem faced by all societies of the Third World. For Dahomey, Creolist thinking is flawed inasmuch as the Creolists are running after a lost unity or are trying to recreate one without seeing the dangers inherent in such a position, instead of trying to conceptualize the condition of a modern way of living in the Caribbean [les conditions d'un *habiter moderne*], which would be:

> the elaboration of symbolic forms allowing one to live in a country torn
> between on the one hand, a cultural tradition which is itself tormented by
> its own history and the quest for a common identity and, on the other, the

moral and political obligation of constructing a society ruled by modern notions of nations which require an autonomous individualistic subject, a free citizen (126).

Because "France" allegedly presents her own relative values as "universal," Glissant and the Creolists reject any type of absolute. However, it is impossible to ask for the right to live freely in one's own culture without referring to Human Rights, which transcend any particular culture. A politics of identity can lead to exclusionary practices, and societies are required to take into account these Rights and to enter into a dialogue with "universality" if they want to inhabit an interdependent world.

Moreover, in order to indict the colonialist French Republic, these writers present the Republican ideal as a cause of alienation. But it is in the name of this ideal that people are fighting dictatorships in the Third World. Dahomey vigorously asserts that a democratic regime cannot survive if its citizens accept every element of their own culture. True culture entails a critical examination of one's own culture. This is where freedom comes into play and it can only be absolute, universal. Just like Human Rights, it is neither French nor European. For Dahomey, to be Creole is to accept this encounter with universality and modernity; it is to integrate within one's own *créolité* a critical examination, not just of "Occidental" values, but also of *créolité* itself.

Chamoiseau, Confiant, and Bernabé present a fairly ahistorical view of the French Caribbeans by ignoring the tormented specificity of their "own history" and the contemporary political context of the French Caribbeans who are not "free citizens," as Martinique and Guadeloupe are an integral part of France and nowadays of the European community!

While French and French Caribbean who are observing the Caribbean intellectual scene tend to stress the clashes of male politics and philosophy, Anglo-Saxon critics are haunted by gender and sexuality, and they have pointed out the masculinist and exclusionary characteristics of *créolité*, which further serves to disestablish this notion as elaborated by the Creolists.

Robert Young has noted the fundamental heterosexuality attached to the notion of "hybridity." Whichever model of hybridity is employed, whether *créolité* or *créolisation*, "hybridity as a cultural description will always carry with it an implicit politics of heterosexuality which may be a further reason for contesting its contemporary preeminence," he notes (25–26). Furthermore, within a heterosexist and racist society, the woman is situated "as an agent in any theory of production" as possessing a "tangible place of production, the womb," and silenced, and I may add but not quite "as an agent in any theory of production" (Young quoting Gayatri Spivak 19).

Thomas Spear has pointed out the numerous instances of male sexual prowess in Caribbean fiction written by men, albeit, as he admits, with an "exterior" look on the *discursive* brutal and grotesque heterosexuality present in some Caribbean *texts*. But, as he notes, Glissant himself seems to corroborate this view of male heterosexuality in Caribbean fiction by justifying the "real" sexuality of Caribbean men. This brutal and selfish type of sexuality, which does not take into account feminine "jouissance" and which is allegedly typical of Caribbean men, can be explained, according to Glissant, by the legacy of slavery. The (male) slave had to steal "pleasure," that is, time, from the master and rape the female slave. As far as sexuality is concerned and many other "points," "the Martiniquan, dramatically, *does not have time*" ["Sur ce point comme sur beaucoup d'autres, le Martiniquais, dramatiquement, *n'a pas le temps*"] (Spear 139 and *Discours antillais* 295). One could add that Glissant consciously ignores the "dark continent" of feminine Caribbean sexuality.

James Arnold contests the Creolists' assertion of the transmission of Creolity through the male, albeit castrated *conteur*.[6] "Women and any woman-authored competing tradition are excluded from tradition, are effectively silenced by an exclusively masculine historiography" (32). Thus the contribution of women to the transmission of an oral creole culture is obfuscated. Indeed Chamoiseau and Confiant in *Lettres créoles* see the subversive *conteur* as "the daddy-language of the orality of a nascent culture" (56) ["le papa-langue de l'oralité d'une culture naissante"].

Although in their literary practice the Creolists assign to the Creole language and to "orality" an ambiguous and shifting position, "créolité" asserts itself through the recognition of the Creole language: "No Creole creator, in any domain, can come into being without an intuitive knowledge of the poetics of the Creole language" (*Eloge* 44). Jean Bernabé has shown that the Creole vocabulary "is structured by the lexicon of sexuality" (*Lettres créoles* 94)[7]. The psychoanalyst Jacques André has noticed that in the French Caribbean women tend to use the French language, while men use the Creole language as a way of asserting and displaying an aggressive type of heterosexuality (64–65).

The counter-discourse to oppression and racism has yet to take into account the oppression exerted by men over women, and sexual "deviants" in particular. Creolization will remain a vain notion if it does not entail a true "conversion de l'être," in Glissant's terms in *Introduction à une Poétique du Divers*, that is, a recognition of the plight of the disfranchised descendant of Africans, of the "Nègre-congo," but also a recognition of women's specific condition, a transformation of sexual politics as they are now commonly practiced in the French Caribbean. Questions of sexuality are also the blind spots of Dahomey's criticism of *créolité*, in the name of "absolutes!"

Françoise Lionnet is right to point to the feminine aspect of what she calls *métissage*. Most women, for various historical reasons, are more inclined than their male counterparts to studying the *texture* of daily life. They notice readily its thickness, its many layers, and are less willing than men to totalize or "theorize" the complexities of what cannot be "theorized." Lionnet, in *Postcolonial Representations*, notes about women writers that they point "the way to a new and yet very old concept: humanism," or rather "femihumanism," a nonseparatist feminism committed to bringing about a pluralistic society based on the "rejection of oppression and domination whether globally or locally" (19). For instance, *créolité* as Maryse Condé and Simone Schwarz-Bart understand it is a femihumanism, a recognition of the resemblance all types of oppression share and the particular character of oppression engendered by oppression.

In order to experience what it means to be a French Caribbean, following Suzanne Césaire's footsteps, one has to place oneself at the right height. From too far above, from a plane of the "Pan American Airway System," for example, "you will see" nothing but "the easy love-making of fishes." "Our islands seen from very far above," writes Suzanne Césaire, "take their true dimension of sea shells," born from the sea (268). But this heightened gaze is that of the new conquerors, the tourists: "details" disappear, first the women, then "the cannas," then the "frangipanis and the flamboyants" then the "palm trees in the moon light" and "the sunsets unique in this world," all that make "our islands" special and different. To truly experience the "revelation of the West Indies," one must engage one's own body, walk the islands, climb the "east slope of the Pelée," as Suzanne Césaire did herself fifteen years earlier, "to know" the beauty of Martinique and of the other islands (268). But this beauty is "intolerable," she says (269). When she goes beyond the easy rhetoric of socialism or Negritude, she comes to realize in a moment of "total lucidity" that the French Caribbean islands are a shadow cast upon France's radiant face: "Il faut oser montrer, sur le visage de la France, éclairé de l'implacable lumière des événements la tache antillaise, puisqu'aussi bien, nombre d'entre les Français semblent déterminés à n'y *tolérer* aucune ombre" (269; my emphasis) ["One has to have courage to show, on the face of France, illuminated by the implacable light of events, the Caribbean stain, as a number of French seemed determined not to *tolerate* any shadow which would obscure it"].

What Suzanne Césaire and contemporary critics emphasize is that French Caribbean identity is yet to be born. In their reading, French Caribbeans are still, given their political and economical ties with the Metropole, encroached by a French ideology that forces them into the category of negative *supplément*. As long as the specific history of slavery and its aftermath in the French Caribbean are not exposed, in their political, economic, social, racial, and sexual implications, as non-surpassable, non-dialectic entities, the attempts to come to grips with a Creole identity will find themselves caught within the web of illusions and exoticisms, as perhaps Suzanne Césaire, as a proponent of Negritude, found herself.

Furthermore, reading Suzanne Césaire's sobering remarks along with Homi Bhabha's reflections on identity, one can realize that the Creolists have come to an aporia. Having firmly disestablished the Western tradition of identity by their "repeated negation" of the term ("Neither Europeans, nor African, nor Asian . . ."), they reenter, as Bhabha wrote about how the "missing person" in a poem by Adil Jussawalla had been barred from doing, the same "tradition of representation that conceives identity as the satisfaction of a totalizing, plenitudinous object of vision" and fail to change "the very term of our recognition of the person" (Bhabha 46-47).

Is *créolité*, as enunciated in *Eloge de la créolité*, another form of humanism, as existentialism was proclaimed by Sartre in a vulgarization treatise in 1947? Is it not the effect of an "intentional" state of mind, but not in Bakhtin's seditious use of the adjective as "contesting"? An appeasement, a "containment," a sort of ideological death for the French Caribbeans? Are Bernabé, Chamoiseau, and Confiant, in *Eloge de la créolité*, assembling masks of *créolité* for hybrids to wear?

Notes

1. All translations from the French are mine.
2. *Tropiques* was a review published by Suzanne and Aimé Césaire between 1941 and 1945 while Martinique was occupied by the forces of Vichy.
3. The only issue of *Légitime Défense* was published in 1932 in Paris by a group of Martiniquan students, which included René Ménil and Etienne Léro.
4. *Le Discours antillais* has been translated, but only partially, by J. Michael Dash under

the title, *Caribbean Discourse: Selected Essays*, Caraf Books Ser. Charlottesville: University Press of Virginia, 1989.

5. *Francité*, in this usage, means the realization by the French Caribbean that in order to succeed they have to espouse "French values."

6. James Arnold suggests that the maroon incarnates for the slaves "the ideal figure of the super-male, necessary but inaccessible," while the *conteur* has accepted his fate as a "castrated" Uncle Tom (31).

7. Chamoiseau and Confiant give as a telling example the Creole word *kalzyé* [eyelid], which literally means the eye's foreskin.

INDIGENIZATION, MISCEGENATION, AND NATIONALISM

CHAPTER 6

GENDER AND *MESTIZAJE* IN THE ANDES

Priscilla Archibald

In the Andes the *mestizo* has long been figured as something like an anti-hero. Pertaining to neither indigenous nor *criollo* culture, the *mestizo* has provoked intense mistrust. A symbol of illegitimacy, the *mestizo* is a constant reminder of the terms of the colonial encounter—a reminder that disrupts binary colonial identities. Over the past two decades a reevaluation of the *mestizo* has taken place. There has been a renewed interest in cultural and racial *mestizo* authors such as Guaman Poma and José María Arguedas. These authors have a great deal to teach us about the cultural negotiations masked by official colonial and neocolonial discourse. They undermine essentialized ethnic identities, particularly the centered, prelapsarian indigenous subject, replacing it with the radically historicized *mestizo*. In the Andean region the discourse of *mestizaje* is not a matter of harmony, but rather a deeply unstable, antagonistic hybridity.

There is one important way that the discourse of *mestizaje* that has emerged since the 1980s remains centered. For the most part, theorists of *mestizaje* have neglected the issue of gender. This is highly ironic since in its most literal meaning the *mestizo* is the interracial product of the colonial sexual encounter. As the offspring of the Spanish male and indigenous female, the *mestizo* points to the distinctly gendered dimensions of power that have accompanied colonialism. In this essay I will attempt to decenter the *mestizo* yet further by considering the ways that gender and sexuality have informed issues of ethnicity in the Andean region throughout the twentieth century.

Unless otherwise indicated, all translations from Spanish to English are mine.

Indigenismo: Ethnicity and Nationhood

In the 1920s and 1930s Andean nations were swept by political activity that contested the *criollo* oligarchic hegemony established nearly a century earlier during the wars of independence. In Peru, much of this activity took place during the watershed period of Peruvian history commonly referred to as the *oncenio* (the eleven years). During an eleven-year presidency dating from 1919 to 1930, Augusto B. Leguía attempted to consolidate a new bloc of political and economic power. Leguía sought the support of middle and popular sectors, whose numbers had increased with republican modernizations, but whose political demands were unrecognized by previous civilista governments, the oligarchic political party. Under Leguía important pro-worker legislation was enacted that established an eight-hour work day and a minimum wage as well as commissions to arbitrate labor disputes. He supported educational reform, and an expanding government bureaucracy offered employment to a growing middle class. Self-designated as *viracocha*, Leguía fashioned himself a protector of indigenous populations and created a "Section for Indigenous Affairs" with the goal of incorporating indigenous populations into the nation. The corporate nature of indigenous lifeways was legally recognized and the tradition of obligatory free indigenous labor outlawed. Responding to perpetual unrest in the Andes, Leguía also named a committee to investigate hacienda encroachments of indigenous land.

Much of the anti-oligarchic activity that took place during the 1920s through the 1940s assumed the form of *Indigenismo. Indigenista* writers sought to revindicate Andean culture and expose indigenous exploitation within the republic. By reconfiguring the issues of ethnicity and nationhood in an inextricable and central fashion, *Indigenismo* created the context for later political interventions. In this way, *Indigenismo* is an originary discourse, inaugurating the democratic and "cross-cultural" premises which continue to frame nationalist thought. Despite this historic significance, *Indigenismo* is generally avoided. When critics find it necessary to refer to *Indigenismo* they often do so with a very descriptive language: it is romantic, essentializing, and above all inauthentic. This judgmental posture is a curious exception to today's revisionist atmosphere, where attention to issues like the production of gendered identities in a text or the way a work is situated historically has replaced a purely aesthetic evaluation. Reducing *Indigenismo* to a true or false question of authenticity remains squarely within the logic that it purportedly rejected and entirely disregards the conditions that continue to make *Indigenismo*'s "inauthenticity" inevitable.

No book more radically transformed political and social debate than *Siete ensayos de interpretación de la realidad peruana* [*Seven Interpretive Essays on Peruvian Reality*], José Carlos Mariátegui's Marxist analysis of Peruvian society published in 1928. It focuses on the role of indigenous populations within the republic and in this way marks an important step toward the development of a Third World socialism. Although at the time that Mariátegui wrote, indigenous populations constituted four-fifths of the Peruvian population and their exploitation within the *criollo* republic had become notorious, they were by no means the established concern of thinkers who identified with revolutionary aims. The plight of indigenous populations was generally left to the liberal humanists. Many believed that indigenous rebellions were undertaken to preserve traditional lifeways, and therefore were frequently characterized as reactionary rather than revolutionary. Mariátegui asserts that not only the ineffective but the reactionary character of humanist perspectives obscured as racial, juridical, or educational a problem he believed was fundamentally economic. Mariátegui argued that indigenous exploitation and disenfranchisement was inextricable from the system of land ownership known as *gamonalismo*. The *gamonal*, a landowner whose ties to the modern, liberal government in Lima consolidated his feudal-like authority over his indigenous work force, was a product of republican transformations. According to Mariátegui, as long as *gamonalismo* provided the basis of oligarchic hegemony, all legislative or educational reforms on behalf of indigenous communities were mere rhetorical flourish.

The intensified exploitation that accompanied the organization of the Peruvian export economy provoked continuous indigenous rebellion. When Mariátegui returned from Europe in the early 1920s, indigenous unrest was rampant, particularly in the southern Andes. Like most coastal Peruvians, Mariátegui knew little about Andean society. He made his first and only trip to the Andes in 1923. Yet indigenous rebellions made a lasting impression, deeply influencing the form of his social critique. With the exception of passages that speculate about indigenous communities as primitive forms of communism, Mariátegui's essays are decidedly unromantic. Indigenous struggles were as yet only potentially revolutionary since, Mariátegui claimed, indigenous populations lacked political consciousness and organization on a national level. Mariátegui anticipates the eventuality of indigenous politicization but does not assume that it will necessarily entail a process of proletarianization (Mariátegui 1928: 49–71). The implication that the Peruvian popular/revolutionary subject would be distinct from the European proletariat was a stunningly open-minded attitude at a time when European Marxists were ever more dogmatically constructing the proletariat as what Ernesto Laclau and Chantal Mouffe call the "transcendental revolutionary subject" (Laclau and Mouffe 1985). Although Mariátegui's Socialist Party maintained an affiliation with the Third International, his vision of a uniquely Peruvian socialism centered on indigenous participation was a source of considerable and unresolved antagonism with European Marxists (Poole and Rénique 1992:106).

One of the most important forums for *indigenista* writers was the magazine *Amauta*, founded by Mariátegui in 1926. *Amauta*—a Quechua word meaning "wise man"—was dedicated to the task of "peruvianizing Peru." This seemed to entail thematizing indigenous issues in central and very visible ways. Much of the writing included in the magazine, however, had no direct relation to *Indigenismo*. Producers of elite and definitively Western poetry are found on *Amauta*'s pages. Articles on international figures like Rosa Luxembourg and Charlie Chaplin appear in every issue, and more often than not Mariátegui's column, "Defensa del marxismo" ["Defense of Marxism"], deals with debates taking place on the European continent. While Mariátegui's ideological vision contributes an important note of consistency, when reading *Amauta* one is struck by the nearly incongruous nature of the articles. Writers whose projects seem to share little common ground are joined together on its pages. Regionalist authors are followed by cosmopolitan avant-garde poets, just as nostalgic *indigenistas* share pages with political authors with a modernizing agenda. This variety underscores *Amauta's* indigenous theme. Notwithstanding a genuine concern for the plight of indigenous populations, this theme performed a unifying role in the absence of a common vision or social project. It unified disparate actors more in the way of an icon than by designating a particular interpretive attitude. *Amauta* was tremendously successful in consolidating a new intellectual class that displaced *criollo* intellectuals and in introducing the themes, actors, and issues of twentieth century nationalism. Antonio Gramsci's description of truly progressive intellectual formations could have been written with Amauta in mind:

> Certain intellectual formations that pertain to the historically progressive
> class, exercise such a power of attraction that . . . they end up by subjugat-

ing the intellectuals of the other social groups . . . [and] create a system of solidarity between all the intellectuals. This phenomenon manifests itself "spontaneously" in the historical periods in which the given social group is really progressive (Gramsci 1971:60).

Perhaps no one represents the new romantic nationalism so emphatically as Luis Valcárcel. His book, *Tempestad en los Andes* [*Tempest in the Andes*], published in 1928, fulfills the stereotype of a messianic *Indigenismo*. The first page announces that "[l]a nueva conciencia ha llegado . . ." ["the new consciousness has arrived . . ."], and what follows reads like a blueprint for a triumphant nationalism. An essentialized indigenous identity is what makes for its redemptive power: "La raza permanece identifica a si misma. No son exteriores atavios, epidermicas reformes, capaces de cambiar su ser. . . . Desgraciadamente para el tirano, las razas no mueren. . . . Rusia? El Peru!" (34) ["The race remains identical to itself. External ornaments, epidermic reforms are not capable of changing its being. . . . Unfortunately for the tyrant, races do not die. . . . Russia? Peru!"]. Valcárcel is also the father of Peruvian anthropology, having founded the Institute of Ethnology at San Marcos University in the early 1950s.

Tempestad en los Andes is a product of the deeply inspired political atmosphere of the 1920s. It is a poetic manifesto that proclaims the triumph of a new indigenous voice as the return of authenticity. *Tempestad de los Andes* is a pastoral, "revolutionary" rather than liberal. Yet unlike its reassuring European cousin, it is a very disquieting read, since *Indigenismo*'s objectification of the Indian is vividly apparent. Perhaps this accounts for the fact that what is probably one of Peru's finest pastoral texts has been quietly left to the annals of history. Many exquisite passages, like the lingering innocence of the following, are intolerably paternalistic:

> Desparramados por la cordillera arriba y abajo de las montañas, en las estribaciones de los Andes, en el regazo de los pequeños valles, cerca a las cumbres venerables, cabe a los rios, a la orilla de los lagos, sobre el cesped siempre verde, debajo de los kiswares vernáculos, en las quiebras de las peñas, oteando el paisaje, alli estan los ayllus. . . . Los ayllus respiran alegria. Los ayllus alientan belleza pura. Son trozos de naturaleza viva. . . . (Valcárcel 1928:5).

> [Scattered up and down throughout the mountain ranges, in the foothills of the Andes, in the lap of small valleys, near venerable peaks, next to the rivers, by the shore of lakes, on its grass forever green, below the native *kis-*

wares, in the cracks of the boulders, watching over the landscape, there are the ayllus. . . . The ayllus breathe happiness. The ayllus breathe pure beauty. They are pieces of living nature.]

Considering Valcárcel's celebration of a "pure" indigenous identity as authenticity, his hostility toward the mestizo should perhaps not seem surprising. Metaphors of *mestizaje* as illness and unnaturalness conform to a specifically pastoral vision of evil: "Poblachos Mestizos . . . como atacadas de lepra . . . se deshacen lentamente . . . Gusanos perdidos en la galerias subcutaneas de este cuerpo en descomposición que es el poblacho mestizo . . . el sol los ahuyenta . . ." (36) ["Mestizo towns . . . as if attacked by leprosy . . . they slowly become undone . . . Worms lost in the subcutaneous galleries of this body in decomposition which is the mestizo town . . . the sun flees from them . . ."].

In the story "El pecado de las madres" ["The Mothers' Sin"], Valcárcel provides a gendered interpretation of this degenerate *mestizaje.* The story deals with the rape of an indigenous woman by her *criollo* employer, which as Mary Louise Pratt remarks is a variant of a recurring motif in Spanish American literature: "One of the oldest and most durable myths of self-definition in Spanish America is that of the sexual appropriation of the indigenous woman by the European invader. . . . Endless repetitions and variants have mythified this figure, simultaneously victim and traitor, as the mother of the American mestizo peoples" (Pratt 1990:59). Valcárcel's interpretation of this mythical figure is unusual, however. Of her two sons, one an Indian and the other a mestizo, the offspring of a rape, the mother clearly prefers the latter: "Ella solo amaba al 'otro,' al hijo impuro, al engendrado por la violencia" (37) ["She only loved the 'other,' the impure son, he that was engendered through violence"]. For Valcárcel her unnatural attachment to her mestizo son represents the subversion of natural order. *Mestizaje* here is synonymous with an even older myth of masculine self-definition—the destabilizing feminine order. Instead of locating the mestizo in the sexual politics of colonialism, Valcárcel blames the indigenous mother for her reaction to her misfortune. This refusal to legitimize the mestizo on the grounds of ethnic impurity is a gesture that constructs national identity upon the binary terms of colonial ideology. If we agree with Angel Rama that *Indigenismo* represents "en realidad al mesticismo . . . un mesticismo que . . . no se atreve a revelar su nombre verdadero" (Rama 1982:141) ["in reality mesticismo . . . a mesticismo which . . . does not dare to reveal its true name"], it is a particularly ironic gesture at that.

If extreme, Valcárcel's misogyny is not inconsistent with the masculin-ist character of *Indigenismo*. In the essay, "Women, Literature and the National Brotherhood," Mary Louise Pratt discusses the distinctly mas-culinist nature that issues of ethnicity assumed once incorporated into nationalist politics:

> As an iconic figure, the amauta radically displaced the traditional icon of the indigenous woman violated by the Spanish conqueror. Given the mas-culinist thrust of nationalist and indigenist imagining of the period, it is hardly surprising that women writers and intellectuals in this period seem not to join in them. For example, the early women collaborators in the Re-vista Amauta, notably Dora Meyer de Zulen, Blanca Luz Brum, Magda Por-tal, and Maria Wiesse, tended to write on contemporary politics, art and everyday life. Their lack of engagement with the "problema del indio" con-trasts, however, with the activism of the previous century, when race was very much a women's issue. In Peru, the torch apparently passed into the hands of men, and into mainstream politics. When the women writers of Amauta did engage with the issues of identity, authenticity, and the indige-nous majority in Peru, their work often contested conventional *indigenista* paradigms and located national problematics along lines other than race (Pratt 1990:59).

The *indigenista* movement that centered around *Amauta* was followed by a series of Andean novels produced during the 1930s and 1940s that con-tinued to adopt masculine authenticity as the norm for national subject-hood. This is certainly the case with the classic *indigenista* novel *El mundo es ancho y ajeno* [*Broad and Alien Is the World*], published in 1941 by Ciro Alegría. Throughout the novel the Indian village's mayor, Rosendo Maqui, continually asks himself, "Es la tierra mejor que la mujer?" ["Which is better, woman or the earth?"], a comparison that leaves "woman" with-out agency, only acted upon like the earth. When women and sexuality are portrayed in *indigenista* novels, it is frequently to delegitimize the *criollo* landowner as a false nationalist. This is evident in the *indigenista* novel *Huasipungo*, by Jorge Icaza (1934). The landowner Don Alfonso's daugh-ter, though unmarried, becomes pregnant. Not only is she perceived as immoral, she is also portrayed as an unnatural mother since her milk dries up and they must look for an Indian wet nurse. This wet nurse is then sexu-ally abused by Don Alfonso as he thinks, "Acaso no estaba acostumbrado desde muchacho a comprobar que todas las indias servicias de las hacien-das eran atropelladas, violadas y desfloradas asi no mas por los patrones? El

era un patron grande, su merce. Era dueño de todo; de la india también"
(58) ["Wasn't he used to seeing, and proving, ever since his boyhood that
all the Indian servant girls were outraged, raped, and deflowered as a matter of course by the patrones? He was a patron grande, su merce! He was
master of everything, of the Indian woman, too" (65)]. The upper class is
further portrayed as sexually depraved when both the landowner and the
priest have their way with the sheriff's wife.

Just how dramatically *Indigenismo* rewrote national identities is evident
by a comparison with civilista writer Ventura García Calderón. Counting
his father and brother among Peruvian presidents, García Calderón had
strong *civilista* credentials. Civilismo was the oligarchic party that dominated Peruvian politics throughout the nineteenth century. In a short story
titled "Amor Indigena" ["Indigenous Love"], García Calderón reenacts
the colonial rape with considerable enthusiasm. Pressured by his fellow
travelers to take advantage of an Indian woman, the narrator's original reluctance gives way to a sense of triumph. It is only then that he compre-
hends "el orgullo de aquellos semidioses de la conquista peruana que roba-
ban mujeres despavoridas . . ." (García Calderón 1923) ["the pride of those
demigods of the Peruvian conquest that robbed terrified women . . ."].
This identification with the colonial father coincides with a particular construction of gender and will later, as *Huasipungo* clearly demonstrates, be
recorded by *Indigenismo* as a form of false nationalism. I am not here suggesting that the conception of gender that accompanies *Indigenismo* is
somehow more enlightened, but rather that it is indicative of an entirely
new nationalist script.

In the rare instances that the essentialized identities of *Indigenismo* are
problematized, gender often figures in a central and disruptive way. One
interesting example is the novel *El chulla Romero y Flores*, written by Ecuadorian Jorge Icaza (Icaza 1958). Icaza complicates the nationalist terms set
forth in his earlier text, *Huasipungo*. The novel's protagonist, Luis Alfonso
Romero y Flores, is the son of an indigenous woman and an aristocratic
criollo whose relationship was socially scandalous because of its public character, transgressing sacred class and ethnic boundaries. Unlike classic *Indigenismo*, which simply inverted the terms of social legitimacy, the novel
explores the possibility of producing new terms of social legitimacy from
a rigidly stratified society. As the epithet *chulla* suggests, indicating a lower
class person's adoption of upper class mannerisms, Romero y Flores remained unreconciled to his indigenous maternal origins. His petty life is
spent trying to convince himself and others of his aristocratic standing

while confronting the perpetual reminders of his actual declassé status. His hypocrisy is underlined by his own refusal to publicly acknowledge his mestiza and divorced lover, Rosario, who gives birth to his son. It is only after the transformative impact of successive tragedies, including the death of Rosario and his own degeneration into a social outcast, that Romero y Flores achieves self-acceptance, which in turn inspires the imagining of an alternative social order:

> "Yo, en cambio . . . — chulla Romero y Flores — transformandome. . . . En mi corazón, en mi sangre, en mis nervios," se dijo el mozo con profundo dolor. Dolor que rompió definitivamente las ataduras que aprisionaban su libertad y que llenó con algo auténtico lo que fue su vida vacía: amar y respetar por igual en el recuerdo a sus fantasmas ancestrales y a Rosario defender a su hijo, interpretar a sus gentes (1958:188).

> ["I, in turn . . . — *chulla* Romero y Flores — transforming myself. . . . In my heart, in my blood, in my nerves," said the man with profound pain. A pain which definitively broke the fetters which imprisoned his freedom and which filled with something authentic that which was his empty life: to love and respect his ancestral ghosts equally in memory and on behalf of Rosario to defend her son, interpret her people.]

Though Rosario's son represents the perpetuation of a masculine model of national subjecthood, Icaza displaces identity politics by locating authenticity in pain. The novel concludes with the suggestion of a new beginning: Romero y Flores' commitment to tell a new national story ("interpretar a sus gentes") that transcends the complex history of engendering colonial identities. One can only speculate about the reasons for the canonization of *Huasipungo*, where whites and Indians are portrayed in absolute polarity, instead of this far more subtle and important work. It suggests, however, that Icaza's complex vision of *mestizaje* has yet to gain acceptance as the national story.

The Bolivian Carlos Medinaceli's novel, *La Chaskañawi*, offers another unique and uniquely gendered vision of the national community (Medinaceli 1947). The novel follows the life of Adolfo Reyes, a law student who has returned from the capital to his provincial hometown, where he falls in love with a mestiza, Claudina. Adolfo's rejection of the *criollo* society to which he belongs is not without difficulties. It involves something close to psychosis. Though in love with Claudina, Adolfo rapes a *criolla* woman, whom he is obliged to marry but then soon abandons. Claudina's cultural flexibility contrasts with Adolfo's confusion. She moves between *criollo* and mestizo worlds with ease and is an expert at simulation and dissimulation and at adopting the cultural language appropriate to a specific milieu. The healthy regionalism represented by Claudina is an alternative to the corrupt cosmopolitan and masculine spheres of politics and law. Like Valcárcel, Medinaceli identifies *mestizaje* as particularly feminine, the difference being that therein lies its redemptive power. Medinaceli's alternative social order is a regionalist feminotopia, and masculinist identity politics are replaced with what resembles the very modern concept of the flexible borderland subject.

Mestizaje and Unreconstructed Masculinism

Since the 1980s the Andean has once again become central to nationalist imagination. Studies ranging across a wide spectrum of disciplines have been devoted to Andean culture and society (Matos 1991:86–93). What distinguishes these studies from the interest in Andean culture that took place earlier in the twentieth century is their embrace of the mestizo. Replacing the prelapsarian homogeneous subject constructed by *Indigenismo*, current interest in the Andean focuses on a profoundly hybrid subject. Instead of the harmony that the word *mestizaje* can sometimes evoke, in this context it designates a highly unstable, or as some would allege even a "psychotic" identity (Matos Mar 90). The mestizo is wedged between the contradictory realities of the Andes and the West. Just as there are multiple ways that these social realities come into contact, there are a myriad of ways of being mestizo.

The social subject that has perhaps been most responsible for directing scholarly attention to the mestizo is the Andean emigrant. Massive Andean emigration to coastal cities, most notably Lima, has exaggerated the complexity of Andean social and political identities. In 1940 Lima's population was slightly more than 500,000. By 1995 Lima was home to 6.5 million people. Nearly half of that population consisted of Andean emigrants living in *barriadas* [shantytowns], or as they are now more optimistically called, *pueblos jovenes* [young towns] (Burt and Espejo 1995:19–25). As Andeans adopt Western customs, and in many instances transform them, making them Andean, acculturation no longer strikes as the inevitable outcome of indigenous contact with the West. Not only do indigenous peoples reinvent what it means to be Andean, but their emigration to coastal cities dramatically transforms those urban spaces. Remarking on this phenomenon, the cultural critics William Rowe and Vivian Schelling note how "in some regions (such as the Andean) the cultures referred to as folkloric have upheld their own alternative ideas of nationhood and have been capable of challenging the official state" (Rowe and Schelling 1991:40).

Although feminist authors such as literary critic Jean Franco, sociologist Cecilia Blondet, or journalist Alma Guillermoprieta have underlined the importance of women in the new mestizo cultures, in general critics have been slow to take up the issue of gender. Anthropologist Ernesto Matos Mar's stimulating book, *Desborde popular y crisis del estado*, is a perfect example of this tendency. Matos Mar comments on the pivotal role that Andean women play in this new urban social reality:

> Ligada al carácter familiar de la organización del trabajo es importante destacar la fuerte participación feminina, explicable por su mayor compatibilidad con la responsabilidad de amas de casa: horarios flexibles, trabajos realizados en el hogar o en lugares donde pueden llevar a los hijos menores como en el comercio ambulatorio (Matos Mar 61).

> [Connected to the familial character of the organization of work it is important to highlight the strong feminine participation, explicable by the greater compatibility of this work with the responsibility of housewives: flexible hours, work which takes place in the home or in places where they can bring along the younger children such as ambulatory businesses.]

Ironically, despite Matos Mar's acknowledgement here of the importance of women, this is the only mention of gender in the entire book. The social subject he investigates—"el hombre multiple" ["the multiple man"]—is profoundly masculine. Matos Mar's vision, or rather his blindness in this instance, is overdetermined by the tradition of *Indigenismo*. It seems that when issues of ethnicity enter nationalist discourse, they are invariably coded as masculine.

José María Arguedas: *Mestizaje* and Sexuality

Increasingly, scholars look toward novelist and anthropologist José María Arguedas for help in addressing the new dimensions of Andean society. The most prominent Andean actor in Arguedas' anthropological work is the mestizo. After attending "El primer congreso internacional de peruanistas" ["The First International Congress of Peruvianists"] in 1952, Arguedas expressed disappointment with its limited focus on *lo indigenista* and *lo hispanista*. Once again the mestizo was left to the margins of Andean history, figuring ambiguously in the shadows of what were designated as the two primary Andean actors. This omission comments on the mestizo's illegitimacy and on the persistence of the strictly binary terms of colonial ideology. As the suspicion that has historically surrounded the mestizo suggests, illegitimacy possesses enormous subversive potential. Rather like underground figures, Arguedas comments that they inspire debate and controversy, but no official study. He remarks on the incongruity of this exclusion in a society where mestizos increasingly represent a majority of the population and are, he believes, its most active protagonists. Arguedas stresses the urgency of this issue with unusual severity. He writes that "el estudio del mestizo es uno de los más importantes de los que la antropología está obligada a emprender en el Perú" (1975:2) ["attention to the mestizo is one of the most important studies that anthropology should undertake"]. This apprehension of the increasingly pivotal social role played by the mestizo is overwhelmingly relevant to contemporary Peru, and certainly counts among Arguedas' most important anthropological contributions.

Arguedas not only promoted the study of mestizos, but his own writing is the product of a profoundly mestizo consciousness. It is this consciousness that has allowed him to give expression to a reality that seems to elude articulation. The historian Nelson Manrique comments on this quality of Arguedas' work:

> Creo que uno de los hechos centrales que han multiplicado la vigencia de Arguedas es que, de alguna manera, sentimos que él expresa problemas fundamentales, que tienen que ver con nuestra propia identidad. Es decir que no habría ese problema si, para entender qué es lo andino, bastara con que nos hiciésemos la introspección. Pero precisamente la imposibilidad de entendernos sólo mirando hacia adentro, hace per cibir que en Arguedas hay un conjunto de elementos que se nos escapan y que son tanto más complejos, porque no es simplemente que Argueas sea la voz de los indígenas. . . . (1991: 57).

[I believe that one of the central factors that has multiplied the relevance of Arguedas is that, in some way, we feel that he expresses fundamental problems which are related to our own identity. That is to say that this problem would not exist if, in order to understand what it means to be Andean, introspection was enough. But precisely the impossibility of understanding ourselves by looking within, makes it clear that in Arguedas there are a group of elements which escape our understanding and which are quite complex because Arguedas is not simply the voice of the Indian. . . .]

Over the past fifteen years or so scholars have begun to reevaluate Arguedas' intellectual production, pointing to its nearly prophetic quality. Arguedas had previously often been categorized as a nostalgic *indigenista* writer. There is one aspect of Arguedas' writing, however, that has received very scant critical attention: his representation of sexuality. This representation is not secondary but rather central to his understanding of *mestizaje*. From the figure of Marcelina in *Los ríos profundos* to the homosexual rapes in *El sexto*, to the series of debased sexual practices detailed in *Amor mundo*, sexuality figures as a central trauma around which narrative activity converges.

Arguedas' most well-known novel, *Los ríos profundos*, tells the story of the maturation of Ernesto, a boy attending a boarding school in the Andes. The school is responsible for the production of good Peruvian citizens. This takes place not only in school lessons, and in the school games between "Chile" and "Peru," reliving and correcting the traumatic defeat of the Peruvians in the War of the Pacific in 1883, but also in the unacknowledged yet tolerated sexual abuse of a demented woman, Marcelina, that occurs every night by the schoolboys. At one point in the novel a group of mestiza women lead a rebellion against the privileged whites for hoarding salt. The leader of that rebellion, doña Felipa, is wearing a yellow shawl. The shawl passes from doña Felipa to the demented woman Marcelina— an event that symbolizes the subversion of the heroic narrative about the mestizas. After her death by the plague, Ernesto refers to Marcelina with the epithet of respect, "doña Marcelina," and feels that he is "casi un heroe" ["almost a hero"]. It is a hideous romance, dating back to the violence and subjugation of the Spanish conquest, and one that according to Arguedas continues to be central to the Andean psyche.

Mario Vargas Llosa comments that Arguedas' narratives display "una fascinación por lo asqueroso" ["a fascination for the disgusting"] (Vargas Llosa 1980:5–28). His comment rings true and addresses a central aspect of Arguedas' writing that many critics, reluctant to relinquish more stabilizing interpretive practices, have often chosen to overlook. Yet it is less as Vargas Llosa intimates, a matter of individual idiosyncrasy, than a confrontation of desire constituted in a violent colonial history. Arguedas addresses the force of ideological fictions, the way they constitute desire and motivate actors. Sexual abuse is a recurring theme in all *indigenista* writing.

Typically, as I have mentioned, it serves as an ideological denunciation of a neo-colonial order, delegitimizing the "false" *criollo* nationalist. In Arguedas' work sexuality plays a far more complex function. At the end of *Los ríos profundos*, as Ernesto is fleeing from the Andean school, he runs across the hut of two sisters:

> La mayor levantó la aguja hacia la luz. . . . Ví entonces el ano de la niña, y su sexo pequeñito, cubierto de bolsas blancas, de granos enormes de piques; las bolsas blancas colgaban como en el trasero de los chanchos, de los más asqueroso y abandonados de ese valle meloso. . . . La hermana mayor empezó a afilar un cuchillo (1958:248).

> [The older one raised the needle to the light. . . . Then I saw that the little girl's anus, her little private parts, were covered with enormous, white, insect-bidden swellings; the white sacs hung down as they did from the rear quarters of the filthiest, most abandoned hogs in that treacly valley. . . . The older sister began to sharpen a knife (1978: 227).]

This is a disorienting scene that compresses the grotesque with the gentleness of a sisterly bond. Sexual debasement takes on an endemic quality and is suggestively conflated with the plague that is spreading across the Andes at the novel's conclusion.

In many, perhaps most, of Arguedas' works, sexuality is a force that disrupts a stable social narrative. It is frequently grotesque or disgusting. Before we limit, as does Vargas Llosa, our understanding of this narrative tendency to a matter of Arguedas' personal idiosyncrasy we should keep in mind that, as cultural critic Laura Kipnis writes, "Disgust has a long and complicated history, the context within which should be placed the increasingly strong tendency of the bourgeoisie to want to remove the distasteful from the sight of society. . . ." (Kipnis 1992:377). Just as the heroic symbol of the yellow shawl is displaced from the mestiza leader to the plague-ridden body of Marcelina, Arguedas it seems cannot sustain high discourse—particularly when dealing with matters of romantic interest. At one point in *Los ríos profundos*, one of Ernesto's fellow students asks him to write a love letter on his behalf to a *criollo* town girl. After writing the letter Ernesto is immediately reminded of those indigenous women who do not read or write, "Jacinta o Justina, Malicacha o Felisa" (Arguedas 1985:84), and that cultural heritage rendered voiceless by print culture.

It is not, however, simply a matter of cultural difference that Arguedas portrays. In his representations of sexuality, gender and ethnic differences overlap in highly complex and conflicting ways. Several of the short stories collected in *Amor Mundo* portray this quite vividly (Arguedas 1967). In "El horno viejo," a boy's relative forces himself on a woman whose husband is out of town. Not only is he committing incest—she is his aunt by marriage—but the man has insisted that the boy, Santiago, accompany him. Though Santiago is only nine years old, the older man tells him that "[h]as de ser hombre esta noche" ["tonight you must be a man"], and instructs him to listen or watch if he wishes. The scene is further complicated by the fact that the woman's two young boys—friends of Santiago—are sleeping in the same room. Counterposed to the central activity is the sound of Santiago whispering prayers. The juxtaposition of defilement and the sacred provides a sense of shock and incongruity that effectively undermines dominant or high (ideal, sacred) discourse.

Kipnis goes on to clarify the subversive character of "lo asqueroso":

> The power of grossness is predicated on its opposition from *and* to high discourses, themselves prophylactic against the debasements of the low (the lower classes, vernacular discourses, low culture, shit . . .). And it is dominant ideology itself that works to enforce and reproduce this opposition— whether in producing class differences, somatic symbols, or culture (376).

This "power of grossness" is evident throughout Arguedas' narratives. Another short story titled "La huerta" tells the story of a demented *chola* (mestiza), Marcelina. Marcelina shows her "parte vergonzosa al chico" ["shameful part to the boy"] and says, "Voy a orinar para tí" ["I am going to urinate for you"]. This is then referred to as "la suciedad sin remedio . . ." ["dirtiness without remedy"] (26). Why should "dirtiness without remedy" provide such a disruptive and even a liberating effect? Mary Douglas' classic study, *Purity and Danger: An Analysis of the Concepts of Pollution and Taboo* (1966), offers some insightful suggestions. Douglas writes that "if uncleanness is matter out of place, we must approach it through order. Uncleanness or dirt is that which must not be included if a pattern is to be maintained" (1966:40). In Arguedas' writings, uncleanness or grossness disrupts the "pattern" of the neocolonial order, belying the violence and conflict underlying its overt code of romantic love. Ethnicity and class are key elements in Arguedas' portraits of a degraded sexual atmosphere. As Sara Castro-Klarén points out, the women that Arguedas portrays are generally from lower classes, invariably of mestizo or indigenous origin and nearly always of lower social standing than their male abusers (Castro-

Klarén 1989). The disruptive power of grossness in Arguedas shares much in common with Bakhtin's utopian category of the carnivalesque.

While *Los ríos profundos* tells the story of the maturation of a young man, it might nevertheless be characterized as an anti-*bildungsroman*. As in most of Arguedas' writing, the traumatic relationship to sexuality and gender trips up the protagonist's accession to subjective unity. This failure to achieve an autonomous subjectivity, however, has a curative function. Subject effects are interrogated in a way that resembles what Julia Kristeva calls "the infinite dissolution of desire" (Kristeva 1987:62). The curative effect of Arguedas' narratives is similar to her description of the psycho-analytic process insofar as it interrogates psychic investments in a way that acknowledges and acquiesces to the subject's constitution in alterity.

There is one notable exception to this tendency in Arguedas' work. In his novel, *Todas las sangres*, the class, ethnic, and gender tensions that pervade his other portraits of Andean culture are greatly diminished. When the traditional *misti* (Andean landowner) Don Bruno leads the Indian masses in revolt against the new bourgeois landowner, Arguedas provides the unlikely event of a reformed *misti*, and a decidedly reactionary version of national authenticity. Plot resolutions of a similar type occur with respect to gender and sexuality. At the beginning of *Todas las sangres* sexuality is deeply problematic. Not only are the issues of class and ethnicity raised by Don Bruno's past relationship with a servant woman, but once again the specter of the deformed or the grotesque is present by virtue of the fact that she is a dwarf. By the novel's conclusion, however, the fundamental threat of sexuality to subjecthood and social coherence is resolved. Don Bruno eventually marries the mulatta woman he had taken as his lover, redeeming past sins and establishing a social model. To use Doris Sommer's terminology, *Todas las sangres* is Arguedas' only novel to offer a foundational fiction (Sommers 1988).

Political realities perhaps best account for this compromise on Arguedas' part. Arguedas wrote *Todas las sangres* in 1963 amidst an atmosphere of social euphoria that accompanied Fernando Belaunde's election as president. For the first time, Peru had a government that promised to be attentive to popular demands. At Belaunde's request, Arguedas assumed the position of the director of the *Casa de la Cultura de Peru*. Yet Belaunde never challenged the privileges of elite sectors in any serious way, nor did he manage to achieve the strategic support necessary to bring about the social changes he promised. The novel's fantasy of historical continuity is perfectly consistent with this tepid populism. In 1965, *Todas las sangres* was the focus of a roundtable discussion (Arguedas 1985). The novel was subjected to vituperative criticism, by sociologists in particular. These sociologists complained about the confusing and anachronistic character of the novel. Ironically, thirty-five years later, if *Todas las sangres* seems flawed it is not because it is confusing but because it is all too tidy. The rich and conflicting ambiguity that pervades Arguedas' other texts is here "cleaned up" and put into order for the sake of a particular nationalist engagement.

"Uncleanness is matter out of place"—Mary Douglas

Andean emigration to Lima has certainly challenged *criollo* social imagination. In the 1950s and 1960s scholars referred to the Andean settlements that ringed the city as "cinturones de miseria" ["poverty belts"]. This emigration was viewed as wholly negative, as a loss of Andean culture on the one hand and as a failure to achieve vital modernization on the other. Nowhere is this particular response to the Andean urban presence more clearly illustrated than in the novel, *Historia de Mayta*, by Mario Vargas Llosa (Vargas Llosa 1984). The novel is set in modern Peru and reads almost like a detective story, attempting to makes sense of a very confusing present by recuperating the past. The narrator undertakes a series of interviews that he hopes will uncover what really happened in the life of a revolutionary twenty-five years earlier. Along the way he comes across many aspects of contemporary Peru, including the Andean urban presence. The narrator comments, "Por momentos, tengo la impresión de no estar en Lima ni en la costa sino en una aldea de los Andes: ojota, polleras, ponchos, chalecos con llamitas bordadas, diálogos en quechua. Viven realament mejor en esta hediondez y en esta mugre que en los caseríos serranos que han abandonado . . . ?" (Vargas Llosa 1984:62–63) ["From time to time I have the impression that I'm not in Lima or even on the coast but in some village in the Andes: sandals, Indian skirts, ponchos, vests with llamas embroidered on them, dialogues in Quechua. Do they really live better in this stink and scum than in the mountain villages they have abandoned . . . ?"]. These Andeans are here clearly out of place and, as the reference to "stink" and "scum" indicates, filth and disorder are inextricably related. Garbage is one of the most prominent themes in *The Real Life of Alejandro Mayta:* "Y recuerdo, entonces, que hace un año comencé a fabular esta historia mencionando, como la termino, las basuras que van invadiendo los barrios de la capital del Perú" (1984:346) ["I remember that a year ago I began to concoct this story the same way I'm ending it, by speaking about the garbage that's invading every neighborhood in the capital of Peru"] (1986:310). Notwithstanding the fact that in contemporary Peru the state fails to fulfill some of the most basic services—such as garbage collection—the attention to filth is not simply literal. It coincides with what José Matos Mar calls "un nuevo mestizaje de predominante colorido andino" (79) ["a new *mestizaje* of a predominantly Andean color"]. Matos Mar describes how this Andean presence has "reducido a los sectores medios y opulentos a una situación de insularidad en sus barrios residenciales" (76) ["reduced the middle and opulent sectors to a situation of insularity in their residential neighborhoods"]. Peppered with words such as "invasión" ["invasion"] and "la captura" ["the capture"], Matos Mar celebrates the subversive character of Andean emigration. Ever the representative of the hegemonic order for Vargas Llosa by contrast these emigrants are simply out of place. Unlike Arguedas, where disorder frequently has a curative effect, for Vargas Llosa it is highly dystopic, disrupting the dominant ideologies with which he views the world.

Given Vargas Llosa's ideological leanings it is not surprising perhaps that he consistently misreads Arguedas. Since Andean culture for Vargas Llosa is "primitive," it follows that a revindication of Andean culture would necessarily be a nostalgic gesture. Arguedas' work, however, stands as a powerful critique of the binary terms of neo-colonial ideology. His final novel, *El zorro de arriba y el zorro de abajo*, deals specifically with the urban reality of modern Peru, so drastically transformed by Andean emigration. It takes place in the coastal town of Chimbote where the population, due to a booming fishmeal industry, grew from four thousand to one hundred thousand almost overnight. The text alternates between the author's suicide diaries and the narration about Chimbote—establishing an irreducible heterogeneity. This heterogeneity is furthered by other aspects of the text, namely the conjunction of coastal and Andean culture. Also, Arguedas' representation of sexuality continues to resist containment by dominant discourses. The narration about Chimbote begins in a brothel. The brothel is a stage for the racial diversity of urban Peru, the place where a new *mestizaje*, as Matos Mar calls it, takes form. Once again the way that *mestizaje* coincides with an underside of sexuality precludes a sense of social and discursive propriety. It is precisely this subversion of propriety that offers social promise. In a letter to anthropologist John Murra, Arguedas comments about his final work and conveys the type of redemptive anarchy he felt the new forces represent: "Si alcanzo a mejorar, podré escribir una narración sobre Chimbote y Supe que será como sorber en

un licor bien fuerte la sustancia del Perú hirviente de estos días, su ebulli-
ción y los materiales quemantes con que el licor está formado" (Arguedas
1990:380) ["If I manage to get better, I will be able to write a text about
Chimbote and Supe that will be like sipping in a very strong liquor the
boiling substance of Peru these days, its bubbling quality and the burning
ingredients with which the liquor is formed"].

CHAPTER 7

RACE MIXTURE AND THE REPRESENTATION OF INDIANS IN THE U.S. AND THE ANDES

Cumandá, Aves sin nido, The Last of the Mohicans, and *Ramona*

Debra J. Rosenthal

In an 1815 issue of the *North American Review,* William Channing lamented "the barrenness of American literature viz. the dependence of Americans on English literature, and their consequent negligence of the exertion of their own intellectual powers" (Channing 314). And in 1821 John Gorham Palfrey wrote, "Whoever in this country first attains the rank of a first rate writer of fiction will lay his scene here. The wide field is ripe for the harvest, and scarce a sickle yet has touched it" (Palfrey 1). To these and other white intellectuals, a newly formed nation implied and necessitated a new national literature, and both men believed that the U.S. had unique natural resources for novelists to draw upon for nascent republican ideas, including the Puritans, dramatic landscape and wilderness, and, most importantly, indigenous populations. Significant to my concerns here is the fact that many early U.S. writers answered Channing's, Palfrey's, and others' nationalistic calls by writing fiction that prominently featured Native Americans. Even more significant is that many early white authors not only portrayed Natives, but represented them in terms of sexual relations with the colonists.[1] Linking a new body politic to the body human, these writers based literary sovereignty on Indian-white interracial mixing. The importance of miscegenation[2] to national literature seems to be a hemispheric theme in the Americas, for many Latin American novels also figure Indian-white mixing. In the Andes region specifically, the authors of the national novels of Ecuador and Peru, Juan León Mera in *Cumandá* (1879) and Clorinda Matto de Turner in *Aves sin nido* (1889), explicitly turn to miscegenation to elucidate national concerns. In Mera's evocation of his country's history and landscape and in Matto's contention that she is "making" Peruvian literature, both authors choose to frame their plots in terms of the anxiety of interracial sexual mixing.

In discussing the ways the Natives are portrayed in white-authored fiction, Latin American literary scholars, particularly of Andean literature, have identified two distinct genres, *Indianismo* and *Indigenismo*, and have developed a vocabulary to discuss them. *Indianismo* and *Indigenismo* describe social as well as literary movements in nineteenth- and twentieth-century Spanish American literature, respectively. *Indianismo*, concerned with the romantic portrayal of passive, uncivilized Natives in an exotic, erotically charged natural setting, is often aligned with nineteenth-century romanticism.[3] *Indigenismo*, associated with twentieth-century realism, can be characterized as a socially progressive movement that exposes white and mestizo exploitation of Indians and advocates their eventual liberation.[4]

With these generic classifications, Latin American scholars have an accepted taxonomy by which to distinguish the various modes of representing indigenous peoples.[5] In marked contrast, scholars of U.S. literature do not have such categories; critical discourse grapples with ways to talk about nineteenth-century writings about Indians.[6] In other words, the many U.S. novels dealing with Indians are not distinguished by the *ways* they represent Natives. Instead, such novels retain their primary classification of romance, frontier novel, sentimental fiction, etc., and are only secondarily referred to as writings about Indians. Captivity narratives constitute a separate genre because they are actual autobiographical accounts, and westerns are differentiated by their emphasis not on Indians, but on masculine adventure, violence, guns, horses, the gold rush, the western landscape, railroads, sheriffs, and saloons. Lucy Maddox suggests that if Indians appear in a work of fiction, then it is usually classified as a romance.[7] The blossoming field of Native American literature in the United States, in which Natives write about themselves is, of course, quite distinct from the appropriation and representation of Natives by whites. The lack of ways to describe differing Anglo-authored representations of Natives suggests that critics of U.S. literature have not found such classification useful. In fact, until the recent critical boom in interest in such novels as *Hobomok* and *Hope Leslie*,[8] scholars of U.S. literature often assumed that few nineteenth-century authors were interested in the political and cultural dynamics of Indian-white relationships, and that the only significant writer was Cooper (Maddox 1994).[9]

Even though critics of nineteenth-century U.S. literature do not have a vocabulary to describe different ways of representing Indians, the period from the 1820s to the 1880s in the United States nonetheless witnessed a shift in the novelistic representation of Native Americans and their sexual relations with whites. For example, Lydia Maria Child in *Hobomok* (1824), James Fenimore Cooper in *The Last of the Mohicans* (1826), Catharine Maria Sedgwick in *Hope Leslie* (1827), and other early writers simultaneously portray the Indians romantically, as "noble savages" to be pitied or feared by whites, and tragically, as a doomed race fated to genocidal disappearance from American society. However, later in the century, writers interpreted the figure of the Indian differently. For example, Helen Hunt Jackson in *Ramona* (1884) protests the continued exploitation of Southern California Indians by the U.S. government. Mark Twain in "Huck Finn and Tom Sawyer Among the Indians" (1886) portrays the Sioux as debased and corrupt rapists.

Because Andean literature has a vocabulary specific to novelistic portrayals of Indians, an examination of *Indianismo* and *Indigenismo* literature, especially when compared to U.S. novels about Indians, can be useful for demonstrating the significance of miscegenation to national literature. My intent in this essay is to familiarize scholars of U.S. literature with the Andean categories of *Indianismo* and *Indigenismo* to demonstrate how, when we speak of comparative literature of the Americas, similar literary concerns (here, white-authored novels about Indians) find various modes of critical discourse. Using Gustavo Pérez Firmat's idea of "appositional" or "cheek-to-cheek" literary comparison (Pérez Firmat 1990), I also wish to suggest that scholars of U.S. literature might glean a new perspective on this body of writing by considering other hemispheric epistemologies.[10] I am not recommending we squeeze U.S. literature into borrowed categories, only that Latin American models of organizing discourses challenge our conception of U.S. literary heritage. After my overview of *Indianismo* and *Indigenismo*, I want to discuss *Cumandá* and *Aves sin nido* as examples and turn to *The Last of the Mohicans* and *Ramona* for comparison. But most important to my argument, and to this collection of essays in general, is the centrality of miscegenation. In all four of the novels I discuss, miscegenation is pivotal for evoking historical and political concerns. I want to argue that in both North and South America, writings about Indians engage miscegenation themes to serve nationalist aims, and it is the portrayal of Indian-white sexual relations that can determine a novel's thematic and political concerns.

Although I have briefly mentioned the categories *Indianismo* and *Indigenismo*, I would like to elaborate a bit in order to then apply this vocabulary to U.S. modes of representing Indians. The romantic, sentimental *Indianismo* literary movement was greatly influenced by French Enlightenment thinkers, who were widely read throughout South America, especially Montaigne's "Des Cannibals" and the writings of Voltaire, Raynal, and Marmontel (particularly *Les Incas*). Rousseau's idea that humanity is inherently good if uncorrupted by civilization, and his cult of the noble savage, led to a literary valorization of nature and Indians in their exotic, "pure" state. Chateaubriand, an influential intermediary between Natives and Western literature, and his *Atalá* (1801), served as a model for all subsequent *Indianista* writing. The German Romantics—Hegel, Schlegel, and Goethe—also influenced views of the Indians. With their emphasis on the return to local color and nature, the German Romantics recognized the appeal of North America's wilderness and savages (Sacoto 24–32). Finally, James Fenimore Cooper also inspired the genre; Mera, for example, acknowledges Cooper in the preface to *Cumandá*.

Indigenismo is associated with realism and socialism, influenced by anticlericalism, scientific positivism, faith in progress, and later buoyed by Marxism (Muñoz 72, 74). Drawing a distinction between the two genres, Cometta Manzoni argues that

> la literatura indianista se ocupa del indio en forma superficial, sin compenetrarse de su problema, sin estudiar su psicología, sin fundirse con su idiosincrasia. La literatura indigenista, en cambio, trata de llegar a la realidad del indio y ponerse en contacto con él. Habla de sus luchas, de su miseria, de su dolor, expone su situación angustiosa; defiende sus derechos; clama por su redención (Cometta Manzoni 20).

> [*Indianista* literature is superficially concerned with the Indian, without penetrating his problems, without studying his psychology, without understanding his idiosyncrasies. *Indigenista* literature, on the other hand, tries to

approach the reality of the Indian and come into contact with him. It deals with his struggles, his misery, his pain; it exposes his anguishing situation, defends his rights, cries out for his vindication.][11]

Indigenista writers, mainly urban-educated and uninformed about the Indian majority (Pratt 61), studied the social, economic, and political conditions of native peoples in an attempt to understand their worldviews and problems. They also looked back to the pre-Columbian world to reinterpret the conquest and national history and thereby destroy the myth of the romantic Indian (Muñoz 102). Overall, *indigenista* novels are revisionary, have a distinct political platform, are sprinkled with bits of local native language, feature recognizable stereotyped characters, and support violent solutions to the Indian problem (Echevarría 290). Evelio Echevarría goes so far as to claim a unique position in world literature for *Indigenismo* as a genre written by whites on behalf of an oppressed minority. He maintains that few abolitionist novels can match the zeal with which *indigenista* novels rally for Indian liberation (Echevarría 289).

The answers to the Indian problem suggested in *indigenista* novels tend to fall into two categories: what Muñoz calls the liberal solution and the socialist solution. The liberal solution to Indian oppression was destruction of Indian culture: recognizing that those who exploited Indians would never favor charitable education and equality, liberals advocated rapid industrialization and modernization, a capitalist system intolerant of native communal, quasi-feudal social and commercial structure. A dictator figure was viewed favorably as capable of carrying out such destruction without affecting middle-class interests or investments (Muñoz 138–139). The socialist solution favored *mestizaje:* interracial mixing with whites so that Indian race and culture loses distinct identity, on the theory that the mestizo would inevitably adopt the dominant white culture and reject Indian identity as inferior. José Carlos Mariátegui rejects this theory with a blistering condemnation: "To expect that the Indian will be emancipated through a steady crossing of the aboriginal race with white immigrants is an anti-sociological naiveté that could only occur to the primitive mentality of an importer of merino sheep" (Mariátegui 23; Mariátegui 1971, 25). Involuntary on the part of Indians, *mestizaje* usually appears in novels as a white man's rape of an Indian woman. But like *Indianismo*, *indigenista* novels were written by whites for the urban reading public, not for the Natives themselves. Nevertheless, while *indigenista* novels glorify Indians' salvation, inevitably the Native is denied a future as an Indian. *Indigenismo* as a genre dwindled around 1960 when novelistic innovations of the so-called boom writers superseded interest in the Indians.

Writing in the genre now known as *Indianismo*, Juan León Mera (1832–1894), penned the pioneering fiction of Ecuador, *Cumandá o un drama entre salvajes* [*Cumandá, or a Drama Among Savages*], published in 1879. In the novel, Mera details the geography and panoramic scenery of his beloved country to create an evocative local color resembling an exotic regionalism. He chose to write about primitive jungle Natives, not the sierra Natives of his adulthood (Franco 86), and set the novel seventy years back in time to 1808, twenty-two years before Ecuador achieved independence. Like Lydia Maria Child, James Fenimore Cooper, Catharine Maria Sedgwick, and Helen Hunt Jackson in the U.S., Mera situates his story in a mythic, simple past as if to plumb the depths of national history to find room for his reinterpretation of it. By setting their novels back in time, these authors evaded the reality of contemporary Indians' unfavorable conditions. Like some North American authors, Mera projects onto his Indian characters an aura of mysticism and stereotyped uncivilized exoticism.[12]

However, the idyllic, remote setting of *Cumandá* might have another political purpose besides allowing Mera to recast history in his own image: the distant corner of Ecuador housing the inhabitants of the novel may be the border territory constantly in dispute with Peru. Situating a national novel in contested land suggests reappropriating and reclaiming that land as part of one's history and national identity. Rather than disengaging from contemporary politics, such a move on Mera's part would place him in dialogue with political struggle and give *Cumandá* an added nationalist agenda.

Mera considered himself a lifelong supporter of Ecuador's native population, both as a writer and as a governmental worker. He studied the local Quechua language and incorporated Indian themes into his poetry, fiction, and criticism. While *Cumandá* acknowledges interracial attraction and idealizes Natives, the novel denies the purity of their unconverted, unbaptized souls and insists that society cannot accommodate a mixed-race marriage that unites white and Indian families. If this sounds a lot like *The Last of the Mohicans*, Mera openly acknowledged his debt to Cooper and Chateaubriand.[13] *Cumandá* parallels *The Last of the Mohicans* in many places, most notably in the cruelty of Magua and Tongana, the numerous episodes of danger and narrow escapes, the flights through the woods, the taking of prisoners, the rescues, and the final scenes where Indian and white together mourn over the body of a woman.

Although critics reviewed *Cumandá* favorably, few scholars extensively address one of the novel's central concerns: interracial mixing.[14] Most essays address Mera's treatment of nature, romance, characterization, and incest. Recapitulating the foundational myth of the conqueror Cortés claiming the princess la Malinche, *Cumandá* is obsessed with race and lineage, particularly in the descriptions of the eponymous heroine's skin, remarkably white for an Indian. Mera writes that in Cumandá, "predomina en su limpia tez la palida blancura del marfil" (Mera 54) ["Her clean skin strongly featured the pale whiteness of ivory"]. Mera no doubt had in mind here Cooper's descriptions of Alice Munro's whiteness as well as of Cora Munro's darker skin in *The Last of the Mohicans.* Cooper casts Cora's skin as "not brown, but it rather appeared charged with the color of the rich blood, that seemed ready to burst its bounds" (Cooper 19). The description of the rich-colored skin, along with Cora's dark eyes and hair, immediately alerts the reader to a stereotyped racial taint. Leslie Fiedler calls this miscegenation plot the secret theme of the novel (Fiedler 205), but it hardly seems secret since Cooper emphasizes its centrality and prominence by placing the revelation of Cora's mulatto background in Chapter 16 in a novel with 33 chapters. Cooper reveals Cora's racial identity in the exact center of the novel, which thereby serves as a fulcrum for the novel's action. *Cumandá* similarly demonstrates an obsession with race in its lament that the heroine's only fault is her resemblance to the hated whites, in the forbidden interracial romance between Cumandá and the missionary's son Carlos, and in the fatal ending, where the Indian and her white lover discover they are brother and sister. Cumandá is fully white after all; kidnapped in an Indian raid as an infant and presumed dead by her family, she grew up in the household of chief Tongana as his daughter.

Cumandá's essential whiteness makes her loveable, but her exotic charm attracts the missionary's son (Sommer 247). In his figuring miscegenation as a white man's desire for a seemingly Indian woman, Mera reverses Cooper's Indian man/white woman equation. Cora and Cumandá are both marked by sexual otherness, which makes them attractive to a man of a different race. Cooper casts Magua's lust for Cora as repulsive and degrading, while Carlos and Cumandá share a chaste and ennobling love, yet both North and South American authors demonstrate a failure of the literary imagination to accommodate race mixture in the early history of their countries. Like Cooper, Mera may be suggesting that racial affinity inheres as a powerful determinant in sexual attraction, and hence that miscegenation is unnatural. Cooper hints that Alice attracts Duncan and that Cora attracts Magua because of racial affinity; that is, Duncan prefers Alice over her sister because he is drawn to her unmixed whiteness. Similarly, Magua "senses" that Cora's mixed heritage removes her from sexual circulation among white society; her already mixed blood invites further mixture. Following his predecessor, Mera ascribes his hero and heroine's mutual attraction to their ability to "detect" their shared whiteness and shared parentage, in both a filial and racial sense. By choosing Cumandá, Carlos instinctively chooses whiteness, thereby signaling that miscegenation is not as natural as racial homogeneity and that, like the case of Magua and Cora, thoughts of transgressing the color line, even if unconsummated, meet with death. Further, Carlos' recognition in Cumandá of an inherently good, sympathetic, and Christian soul makes it obvious to the reader that she is somehow more white than Native. As I will show, this ability to "detect" race surfaces also in *Ramona*, where the discovery of the heroine's Indian ancestry accounts for her attraction to the Indian Alessandro.

The anxiety of racial integration in the novel proves unwarranted, for, after a series of unlikely events, the lovers find out that they are brother and sister. The anxiety of violating a blood taboo nonetheless still exists in *Cumandá*, but in a different form. More than the dread of miscegenation, the prohibition against incest keeps the would-be lovers apart. To dissuade readers from concluding the worst, the novel insists that Carlos and Cumandá's love has been purely chaste and fraternal. For example, Carlos claims that they maintain such a pure affection for each other that their love could only have been ordained by angels. By sanitizing their love, Mera deflects the incestuous tensions (Sommer 218). The incest plot provides a convenient reason why the lovers cannot marry, and obviates forcing Mera or the readers to make a moral decision about the interracial romance. Incest, often a novelistic device to produce dread or show corruption, here rescues Mera from imagining miscegenation, and produces a pseudo-happy ending: father, brother, and sister are reunited, but Cumandá subsequently is killed and Carlos dies of grief. As we will see, Clorinda Matto de Turner opted for the same resolution in *Aves sin nido:* the narrative unease with miscegenation is quelled by a convenient incest plot that obviates an authorial moral or political stance.

Doris Sommer finds a significant overlap between nationalistic histories and love stories. She seeks to address "*why* eroticism and nationalism become figures for each other in modernizing fiction" and then "*how* the rhetorical relationship between heterosexual passion and hegemonic states functions as a mutual allegory, as if each discourse were grounded in the allegedly stable other" (Sommer 31). Miscegenation stands as a powerful unifying force, and the prohibition against it often strengthens the erotic interest in Latin American novels. Referring to the theories that intermarriage elevates Latin America's Indians, Sommer suggests "[m]iscegenation was the road to racial perdition in Europe, but it was the way of redemption in Latin America, a way of annihilating difference and constructing a deeply horizontal, fraternal dream of national identity" (Sommer 39). When the romance becomes thwarted, she argues, readers long for a political order in which such a love is possible. In *Cumandá* the romance fails; there are no erotic politics that portend racial integration or national consolidation. The love between Cumandá and Carlos does not offer society redemption by the novel's conclusion, only sorrow at their deaths. Whether miscegenation is prohibitive or redemptive, Mera does not imagine it occurring within the pages of his novel, thus offering a critique of a racist society.

Cooper, the literary grandfather of *Cumandá*, did not concern himself with discrimination against the Indians in his Leatherstocking series. Miscegenation in *The Last of the Mohicans* proves undesirable and Cora and Uncas die to preserve a legacy of unmixed whiteness for those who will dominate the U.S. Departing from Cooper's vision, Mera welcomes Carlos' longing for the Indian maiden, but, in creating an incest plot, offers a twist. According to Mera's schema, it is ultimately not racism that prevents Carlos from uniting his white heritage with Cumandá's Indian family, but incest. Imagine how different *The Last of the Mohicans* would be if Cora and Uncas were kept apart not by racial prejudice but by incest—say, for example, if Uncas was the result of Major Munro's dalliance with Uncas' mother. *The Last of the Mohicans* and *Cumandá* discursively engage political concerns about the role of Indian-white sexual alliances in an industrializing society, thus signaling rhetorically the centrality of miscegenation to national identity.

If Cooper and Mera use the fear of miscegenation and its repression to imagine nationhood, they portray Indians exotically and erotically and in no way do their novels contain elements of social realism or progressive reform associated with the *indigenista* movement. In great contrast, Clorinda Matto de Turner (1852–1909), one of the leading literary figures of nineteenth-century Peru, derives her literary and cultural status from the biting social commentary in *Aves sin nido* [*Birds Without a Nest*], due to its place in the evolution of Peru's literary history.[15] *Aves sin nido* has some generic elements aligning it with nineteenth-century romanticism, yet its portrayal of Indians' miserable living conditions and its critique of clerical abuse suggest a twentieth-century realist political sensibility. *Aves sin nido* tells the story of life in Kíllac, a fictional town in the Peruvian Andes, and the abusive "trinidad embrutecedora" ["brutalizing trinity"] of the judge, the governor, and the priest, who exploit the Indians. The novel details numerous unfair and manipulative ways in which the whites cheat the Indians and keep them in dire poverty. When the *cacique* threatens the Indians Marcela and Juan Yupanqui, Marcela turns in desperation to the rich white Lucía Marín who takes pity on Marcela and gives her money to pay off her crushing debt. The corrupt governor and his cohorts try to kill the Maríns to prevent their assisting the Indians; Marcela and Juan are killed defending their benefactors. While dying, Marcela reveals to Lucía a secret about the birth of her daughter, Margarita. Readers are not privy to the secret until the end of the novel. Lucía and her husband Fernando take in the Indian couple's two girls and raise them as their own. Manuel, the governor's son, falls in love with the Indian Margarita, but Lucía and Fernando try to prevent Margarita from loving the son of her parents' killer. Manuel alleviates the Maríns' concern by telling them that the governor really is not his father. When the Maríns agree to the marriage, Manuel announces that his real father is the bishop don Pedro Mirando y Clara, who had raped his mother. Lucía tragically reveals Marcela's dying secret: Margarita's true father is the same bishop Mirando y Clara, who also raped Marcela. Manuel and Margarita, siblings, share the same father. Like *Cumandá*, the thwarted miscegenous love critiques a racist society while at the same time restoring family ties.

Matto had a lifelong interest in Indians' affairs and considered herself an activist and supporter of their cause. In her preface to *Aves sin nido* she writes, "Amo con amor de ternura a la raza indígena" ["I love the indigenous race with tenderness"], and that she wrote the novel with "la idea de mejorar la condición de los pueblos chicos del Perú" ["the idea of improving the condition of the small towns of Peru"] (Matto de Turner, "Proemio" 37–38), the same reason Helen Hunt Jackson gives for writing *Ramona* (Banning, 201–202). Matto charges the act of writing with the zeal of nationalism: she claims that her purpose in authoring the novel is

recordando que en el país existen hermanos que sufren, explotados en la noche de la ignorancia, martirizados en esas tinieblas que piden luz; señalando puntos de no escasa importancia para los progresos nacionales; y *ha-ciendo* a la vez, literatura peruana (Matto de Turner, "Proemio" 38).

[remembering that in this country many brothers suffer, exploited in the night of ignorance, martyred in the shadows that cry out for light; marking points of not little importance for national progress; and at the same time, *making* Peruvian literature.]

Matto sees her craft as "making" Peruvian literature by writing about the downtrodden Indians. That is, representing and speaking for the Indians embodies the essence of the national literary heritage. Matto's campaign to awaken public consciousness cannot be separated from literary genre because, as a realist genre, *Indigenismo* uses verisimilitude to probe and criticize Indian existence in Peru.

As in *Cumandá*, the incest plot overwhelms the miscegenation plot. But *Aves sin nido* differs remarkably because at no point in the novel does the interracial love affair present conflict. Whereas both Cumandá's and Carlos' parents discouraged the mixed romance, neither the Maríns nor Manuel's mother protest Margarita's Indian bloodline. As representatives of society, the Maríns and Manuel's mother demonstrate the willingness of the general populace to accept race mixture, and its failure stands as a critique of systemic discrimination and clerical abuse. Although Matto's voice does not comment either way on the lovers' racial suitability, it is clear that the foiled romance here serves as a nascent reform movement. Following Sommer, readers of *Aves sin nido* mark with tears and sympathy their sorrow at the lovers' frustration, and are thereby sensitized and inspired to long for national unity and consolidation. Linking the body human with the body politic, the failure of erotic incorporation instigates the desire for partisan incorporation.

On the surface, Manuel and Margarita face a problem similar to that confronting two other couples: Cumandá and Carlos, and Judith and Bon in William Faulkner's *Absalom, Absalom!* — sexual tension between siblings of different races. Perhaps Peter Brooks best articulates the novelistic tension between the dual anxieties of miscegenation and incest. Arguing that Faulkner structures his novel around these twin genealogical anxieties, Brooks labels incest "that which overassimilates, denies difference, creates too much sameness," whereas miscegenation he defines as the "mixture of blood, the very trace of difference: that which overdifferentiates, creates too much difference" (Brooks 308). Judith and Bon cannot marry because they are half-siblings and because Bon is part black, yet for Sutpen, the miscegenation is more abhorrent than the incest. One drop of black blood confounds his design for genealogical purity far more than incest. But Brooks' pairing miscegenation with difference may be misleading. The narrative anxiety of miscegenation reflects fears that races may not be inherently different—interracial attraction presumes the humanity and sameness of the Other. Miscegenous desire levels difference and hierarchy, and instead assimilates. In *Cumandá* and *Aves sin nido*, interracial love creates and acknowledges correspondence and compatibility between the races. Likewise, since incestuous unions are feared for their potential to produce recessive deformities, incest can create too much difference and is thus prohibited.

The novelistic tension in *Cumandá* pulls in the seemingly opposite directions of miscegenation and incest, but here the antipodal taboos of too much sameness and too much difference collapse, and prove to be one and the same. As with Faulkner's novel, the love interest in *Cumandá* cannot sustain the numerous paradoxes, and becomes impossible. But in Matto's schema, no anxiety derives from miscegenation; all the tension comes from the possibility of incest. Again, as with *Cumandá*, the incest plot complicates authorial intention. Whereas Cooper, Child, and Sedgwick unambiguously portrayed frustrated miscegenous desire and reasons for racial segregation, Matto does not have to account for a viable cross-racial relationship. Although Manuel and Margarita desire each other, the reader does not have to formulate a moral judgment about their possible union. The reader can mourn the lovers' separation but celebrate restored family ties. *Aves sin nido* would be bolder had Matto depicted a consummated interracial marriage, yet she stopped short and instead chose to condemn discrimination without anticipating a brighter future.

While *The Last of the Mohicans* seems in many ways to correspond to the Andean *Indianista* genre, as illustrated by Cooper's heir Mera, Helen Hunt Jackson's *Ramona* (1884) has much in common with the *indigenista* movement. Written well after Native Americans were pushed west, *Ramona* critiques social and cultural prejudice against racial amalgamation, and shows the abuse that Indians, especially Indian women, received at the hands of whites. Jackson assumes the inevitability of U.S. government encroachment and puts Indian-white miscegenation to political use to suggest the ways women's bodies and interracial sex come to be powerful narratological devices that perform the cultural work of influencing readers' emotions and prejudices. Miscegenation themes articulate a struggle for control over two territories: the territory of the (white) female body, and

the geographical territory of America. Following Amy Kaplan's observation that "the woman of mixed race preserves the forgotten history of the
nation's westward expansion" (Kaplan 261), Indians, Mexicans, and whites
clash over Ramona's body in a battle to determine the future of the nation.
    In an 1883 letter, Jackson wrote, "I am going to write a novel, in which
will be set forth some Indian experiences in a way to move people's hearts.
. . . People will read a novel when they will not read serious books" (Banning 200). Jackson considered *Ramona* a sugar pill, hoping that the reader
"would have swallowed a big dose of information on the Indian question
without knowing it" (Mathes 77). Jackson modeled *Ramona* after *Uncle
Tom's Cabin:* "If I can do one-hundredth part for the Indians as Mrs. Stowe
did for the Negroes, I will be thankful" (Banning 201–202).
    Despite its popular success, *Ramona* did not do for the Indians what
Uncle Tom's Cabin did for slaves. Alessandro's character also was partly responsible for the romantic reception of the novel. Not an average Indian,
as Uncle Tom supposedly represented a typical slave, Alessandro instead
acted like a high-born Mexican with a Christian sensibility. Even Ramona
hardly considered him an Indian. Moreover, the ending of the novel casts
the work in a romantic light that undermines Jackson's political intent.
Had Ramona lived and died in misery and squalor, then perhaps the novel
would have dramatized the injustices more powerfully (Mathes 84). With
the happy resolution, the reader rejoices in Ramona's good fortune and
second marriage. The tragedy of Alessandro becomes relegated to the forgotten past.
    Furthermore, Jackson refrained from also making Ramona, the cen-
tral figure of the novel, fully Indian. Jackson's conception of the trajectory of U. S. history and her understanding of her audience mandated that
Ramona be of mixed blood, and that she be forced to think about race
when deciding to marry. Unlike Mary Conant in *Hobomok* and Faith Leslie
in *Hope Leslie*, white heroines who exemplify the radical solution—marriage to Indians—to "the Indian problem," Ramona cannot represent an
unmixed white heroine who uses her whiteness to challenge contemporary
racial convictions. She grows up belonging to the Mexican part of Jackson's
tripartite division of race. The characters reflect a clear hierarchy of race,
with white at the top and Indian the lowest. Throughout the novel Jackson
works against this order by portraying the white settlers, other than Aunt
Ri and her family, as depraved and unrepentant, and Mexicans and Indians as respectable and heroic. But as we will see, Jackson still casts a vote
against the Indians in favor of the aristocratic Mexicans who, by virtue of
their education and wealth, are virtually white. With Ramona's mysterious

natal circumstances, miscegenation announces itself early as a central concern of the novel. Ramona herself does not know the secret of her parentage, and the narrating voice informs the reader well before Ramona finds out. Ramona's father was Scottish and her mother was Native American, but her father, shamed by his baby's Indian ancestry, abducts her and entrusts her to his Mexican former love. Born of an Indian and an Anglo, yet raised as a Mexican, Ramona represents a fleshly racial democracy, embodying the conjunction of three competing races.

The indeterminacy of the heroine's blood forces her to circulate among the competing races to determine the future of the nation. By marrying Alessandro first and then her adopted brother Felipe and having children with both, Ramona passes on a mixed-race legacy to her Indian and Mexican children. The closure of Ramona's marriage to Felipe and their move to Mexico distracts readers from the very injustices Jackson is trying to portray. The novel concludes by linking Indian disappearance to women's bodies, for Alessandro is remembered in the mind of his widow and in the body of his mixed-race daughter, named after Ramona. Like little Hobomok, the two Ramonas become so assimilated that they never come to know their mother's Indian identity (Gutiérrez-Jones 63). The bodies of Ramona, mother and daughter, fleshly witnesses to Native existence, disappear in the westward push of an expanding United States.

For all their differences, these nineteenth-century novels of the Americas share a common theme: the inevitable disappearance of the Indians.[16] The myth of the Vanishing American became a well-established political and literary theme in the U.S., where government policy and nineteenth-century novelistic representation were mutually constitutive because each echoed and further entrenched the other's assumptions that the native population would recede, forfeiting the land to whites from coast to coast. Between 1789 and 1820, one hundred novels were published in the U.S. (Davidson viii); in the following ten-year period of 1824–1834, forty novels about Indian disappearance alone appeared, establishing what Brian Dippie terms the "cult" of the Vanishing American (Dippie 21).[17] When cast in historical terms, this myth makes disappearance seem a natural stage in the march of progress. The widespread acceptance of the myth made it easier to blame the Indians for their own disappearance. Since the Indians were disappearing and dying from disease and war, U.S. government officials thought it best to remove the Natives to some distant place where they would be safe and thereby saved (Dippie 71). Thus, the U.S. removal policies became noble rescue missions.

The myth of the Vanishing American acquires a different valence in the context of miscegenation, because disappearance is an easy and credible reason for an interracial relationship to end. Disappearance becomes a narratological device, a *deus ex machina* for allowing authors to extricate themselves believably from controversial or difficult plots. Since nineteenth-century sensibility would not look favorably upon an enduring racially exogenous relationship, writers could create mixed-race ties as long as they ended and, hence, were not condoned. Readers at that time, familiar with the myth of the Vanishing American, readily accepted plots that dissolved interracial romance by having the Indian simply vanish. If miscegenation creates a narrative situation, disappearance resolves it by shaping a satisfactory closure. The authors discussed all portray Indians who, one way or another, disappear.

Again, while I am not suggesting that we force U.S. white-authored novels about Indians into Andean categories, I think it is instructive to subject U.S. novels to the pressures of Latin American genres in an effort to understand literary production in a hemispheric context. As scholars look north and south rather than across the Atlantic for cross-cultural influences and literary communality, interracial mixing figures as a significant thematic concern, and one that I suggest is foundational in thinking about representation, politics, and national identity.

Notes

For their generous and incisive help in formulating and writing this essay, I would like to thank Priscilla Archibald, Martha Cutter, Michael J. Davey, Monika Kaup, Maryclaire Moroney, Carolyn Sorisio, Glenn Starkman, and Brenda Wirkus.

1. For example, see James Wallis Eastburn and Robert Sands' *Yamoyden, A Tale of the Wars of King Philip: in Six Cantos* (1820), Lydia Maria Child's *Hobomok* (1824), *Narrative of the Life of Mrs. Mary Jemison*, edited by James Everett Seaver (1824), Catharine Maria Sedgwick's *Hope Leslie* (1827), George Washington Custis' *Pocahontas; or, The Settlers of Virginia* (1827), and John Augustus Stone's *Metamora; or, The Last of the Wampanoags* (1829).

2. I recognize that this term is extremely problematic, especially when "miscegenation" is not the word used by Latin American writers or U.S. writers before 1864 (when the word was hatefully coined to incite racial unrest between blacks and whites). While "*mestizaje*" is more appropriate when speaking about Latin America, for the thematic purposes of this section of the collection, the word "miscegenation" will refer to a negative view of interracial mixing between whites and Natives. For further critical discussion of terminology, see the Introduction to this volume.

3. Example of *Indianista* novels include José Martiniano de Alencar's *O Guaraní* (Brazil, 1857) and his *Iracema* (1865), Manuel de Jesús Galván's *Enriquillo* (Dominican Republic, 1879), Juan León Mera's *Cumandá* (Ecuador, 1879), and Juan Zorilla de San Martín's *Tabaré* (Uruguay, 1886).

4. Examples of *indigenista* novels include Clorinda Matto de Turner's *Aves sin nido* (Peru, 1889), Alcides Arguedas' *Raza de bronce* (Bolivia, 1919), Jorge Icaza's *Huasipungo* (Ecuador, 1934), Ciro Alegría's *El mundo es ancho y ajeno* (Peru, 1941), and possibly José María Arguedas' *Yawar fiesta* (Peru, 1940).

5. See Peter J. Gold, "Indianismo and Indigenismo," *Romance Notes* 14:3 (Spring 1973), 460–464; Fernando Rosemberg, "Dos actitudes literarias: Indianismo e Indigenismo," *Revista Interamericana de Bibliografía: Inter-American Review of Bibliography* 36:1 (1986), 5; and Julio Rodríguez-Luis, *Hermenéutica y praxis del Indigenismo: la novela indigenista de Clorinda Matto a José María Arguedas* (Mexico City: Fondo de Cultura Económica, 1980). Concha Meléndez is one of the few critics who do not differentiate between the two genres. She labels as *Indianista* any novel encompassing an Indian theme, whether romantic or concerned with social vindication, and considers the Argentinian poems *Santos Vega* by Hilario Ascasubi, and *Martín Fierro* (1872) by José Hernández to be *literatura anti-Indianista*. See her *La novela Indianista en Hispanoamérica* (Río Piedras: Universidad de Puerto Rico, 1961), 13.

6. Critics who struggle to describe the representation of Indians include Roy Harvey Pearce in *The Savages of America: A Study of the Indian and the Idea of Civilization* (Baltimore: Johns Hopkins University Press, 1965), where Pearce discusses novels by the way they represent Indians' nobility or ignobility. Richard Slotkin, in *Regeneration Through Violence: The Mythology of the American Frontier, 1600–1860* (Middletown, CT: Wesleyan University Press, 1973), relies on such terms as the Indian war narrative, the captivity, religious (missionary) literature, travel literature, and hero narratives. Reginald Horsman, *Race and Manifest Destiny: The Origins of American Racial Anglo-Saxonism* (Cambridge: Harvard University Press, 1981), Robert Berkhofer, *The White Man's Indian* (New York: Vintage, 1978), do not discuss categories at all. Interestingly, and significant to my essay, is that none of the critics analyzes the political vindication of Indians in a category such as *Indigenismo* and none discusses the ways miscegenation might influence the representation of the Native. For an overview of critical discussion about Indians, see Cheryl Walker, *Indian Nation: Native American Literature and Nineteenth-Century Nationalisms* (Durham: Duke University Press, 1997), especially pages 29–40.

7. Perhaps one fact that accounts for such varied representation of Natives is geography. For example, nineteenth-century East coast representations of Indians differed greatly from West coast portrayals. Indians were not a visible presence in the East, and their outsider status prompted eastern writers to assume that they would not survive long. Urban blacks lived in much closer proximity, and their presumed permanence in American society motivated writers to represent them, rather than Indians, in fiction. As exceptions to this generalization, Maddox points to Emerson's and Thoreau's resistance to the Removal Act (Lucy Maddox, private telephone conversation, April 13, 1994). Twain would perhaps be another exception to Maddox's claim. Robert S. Levine connects these concerns to the rise of urban reform movements from 1830–1860 in "Fiction and Reform" in Emory Elliott, ed., *The Columbia History of the American Novel* (New York: Columbia University Press, 1991), 147–148.

8. For example, see Carolyn Karcher, *The First Woman in the Republic: A Cultural Biography of Lydia Maria Child* (Durham: Duke University Press, 1994) and *A Lydia Maria Child Reader* (Durham: Duke University Press, 1997); Dana Nelson, "Sympathy as Strategy in Sedgwick's *Hope Leslie*" in *The Culture of Sentiment: Race, Gender, and Sentimentality in Nineteenth-Century America*, ed. Shirley Samuels (New York: Oxford University Press, 1992); Christopher Castiglia, *Bound and Determined: Captivity, Culture Crossing, and White Womanhood from Mary*

Rowlandson to Patty Hearst (Chicago: University of Chicago Press, 1996); and Shirley Samuels, *Romances of the Republic: Women, the Family, and Violence in the Literature of the Early American Nation* (New York: Oxford University Press, 1996).

9. Maddox cogently argues that novels featuring Indians are more numerous than has been recognized, and that this fiction participated discursively in the process of nation-building. In other words, scholars of U.S. literature have paid too little attention to a theme that occupied many nineteenth-century writers, an oversight Maddox redresses in her book. Questions of Indians' role in the emerging United States were so pervasive that it was difficult for a nineteenth-century writer to evade the issue—many novels engaged Indian themes, however inadvertently. While arguing that critics have had a literary blind spot—that they have been incapable of recognizing a substantial body of writings about Indians—Maddox does not differentiate between different types of representation of Natives: she construes all novels as socially and ideologically similar. Further, Maddox is more interested in the political and cultural representation of the Indian figure than in the representation of Indian-white sexual mixing.

10. Cynthia Steele mistakenly argues for a parallel between writings about Indians in the United States and Spanish America: "*Indigenista* fiction, that is, fiction treating the conflicts between Native American and dominant, nation-building societies, reached its apogee in the United States during the Age of Jackson (1820–1860), as it did in Mexico after the revolution (1920–1960)." Steele ignores the differences between *Indianismo* and *Indigenismo*, and brands all U.S. novels with Indian themes *indigenista*, thus invoking, but not acknowledging, a substantial bibliography and critical debate on generic distinctions. By defining as *indigenista* any novel that addresses conflict between Natives and whites, she ignores the different political ideologies behind the various traditions. For example, Cooper's vision was very much complicit with U.S. government Indian removal policy, while much Mexican and South American *indigenista* fiction advocated integrating the Indian into the dominant culture. By comparing nineteenth-century United States romances with the realist, activist *indigenista* novels of the twentieth century, Steele occludes the important activist dimension of *indigenista* novels, and imbues romantic U.S. novels with a social critique that they do not have. She specifically labels Cooper's *The Deerslayer* (1841) and R. M. Bird's *Nick of the Woods* (1837) as *indigenista*, inviting comparison to South American novels that advocate Indian vindication and consolidation into society, agendas that could not be more antithetical to Cooper and Bird. See Cynthia Steele, "The Fiction of National Formation: The *Indigenista* Novels of James Fenimore Cooper and Rosario Castellanos," in Bell Gale Chevigny and Gari Laguardia, *Reinventing the Americas: Comparative Studies of Literature of the United States and Spanish America* (New York: Cambridge University Press, 1986), 60. See also her "Ideology and the *Indigenista* Novel in the 19th-Century United States and in 20th-Century Mexico," in *Proceedings of the Xth Congress of the International Comparative Literature Association 1982*, Vol. 3 (New York: Garland Press, 1985).

11. This and subsequent translations, unless otherwise indicated, are mine. Similarly, Luis Alberto Sánchez asserts that *Indianismo* "utiliza el indio americano como un motivo decorativo. El *Indigenismo*, como una bandera de protesta. Aquél se deleita en los aspectos folklóricos, dentro de un concepto esteticista o sentimental; éste se llena de indignación y convoca a la rebeldía en nombre de la justicia" ["*Indianismo* uses the American Indian as a decorative object. *Indigenismo*, as a banner of protest. The former takes pleasure in the folkloric aspects, within an aesthetic or sentimental framework; the latter is full of indignation and calls for

rebellion in the name of justice"]. See his *Historia comparada de las literaturas americanas. Tomo 3: Del naturalismo al postmodernismo* (Buenos Aires: Editorial Losada, 1974), 28.

12. Mera, Child, Cooper, Sedgwick, and Jackson demonstrate an ethnographic voyeuristic interest in portraying Natives in their own environment, as if to preserve and safeguard them from colonialism. Lee Clark Mitchell argues that this sense of urgency to record a threatened wilderness was particularly American and defined works by U.S. writers: "In Africa, South America, and Australia, landscapes and native peoples suffered at the hands of invaders in ways strikingly similar to those in America. For reasons connected with settlement patterns, however, the invaders' perceptions of their own impact were never as conflicted. In South America, the Spanish and Portuguese clung to the coast; Africa saw only transient explorers, except in the south, where Natives nevertheless outnumbered colonists; in Australia, conversely, the aborigenes were few, and settlements remained coastal" (*Witnesses to a Vanishing America: The Nineteenth-Century Response* [Princeton: Princeton University Press, 1981], 21). Coastal settlements with fewer major pushes to conquer the interior meant invaders and Natives had less mutual exposure, and hence less conflict over the role of miscegenation in nation-building.

13. "Bien se que insignes escritores, como Chateaubriand y Cooper, han desenvuelto las escenas de sus novels entre salvaje hordas y a la somgbra de las selvas de America, que han pintando con inimitable pincel" (Al Excmo Señor Director," *Cumandá*, 40) ["I well know that distinguished writers such as Chateaubriand and Cooper have set the scenes in their novels among bands of savages and the shadows of the American jungles, which they have painted with inimitable brushstrokes"].

14. For example, see Galo Rene Pérez, *Pensamiento y Literatura del Ecuador* (Quito: Editorial Casa de la Cultura Ecuatoriana, 1972), Augusto Arias, *Panorama de la Literatura Ecuatoriana* (Quito: Editorial Casa de la Cultura Ecuatoriana, 1971), or Thomas O. Bente, *"Cumandá y Tabaré: Dos cumbres del Indianismo romántico hispanoamericano," Revista Interamericana de bibliografía* 41:1 (1991).

15. For more information on Matto de Turner, see Alberto Tauro, *Clorinda Matto de Turner y la novela indigenista* (Lima: Universidad Nacional Mayor de San Marcos, 1976), Antonio Cornejo Polar's *La novela peruana: Siete Estudios* (Lima: Editorial Horizonte, 1977) and his *La novela indigenista* (Lima: Editorial Lasontay, 1980), Fernando Alegria, *Historia de la novela hispanoamericana* (Mexico: Ediciones de Andres, 1974), and Mario Castro Arenas, *La novela peruana y la evolución social, segundo edición* (Lima: José Godard, 1967).

16. Lee Clark Mitchell connects the disappearance of the Indians with the destruction of the wilderness and frontier to speak of a more inclusive "vanishing America." See his *Witness to a Vanishing America: The Nineteenth-Century Response* (Princeton: Princeton University Press, 1981).

17. For further information on the frontier and the disappearing Indians, see Edwin Fussel, *Frontier: American Literature and the American West* (Princeton: Princeton University Press, 1965), Richard Drinnon, *Facing West: The Metaphysics of Indian-Hating and Empire Building* (Minneapolis: University of Minnesota Press, 1980), and Brian V. Street, *The Savage in Literature: Representations of "Primitive" Society in English Fiction, 1858–1920* (London: Routledge, 1975).

CHAPTER 8

THE SQUATTER, THE DON, AND THE GRANDISSIMES IN OUR AMERICA

Susan Gillman

This essay is a companion piece to my earlier work on "Ramona in Our America," a reading of José Martí's translation—transculturation, really— of Helen Hunt Jackson's *Ramona* from a local "American Indian" novel into a work worthy of Martí's internationalist vision of "mestiza America."[1] Now I'd like to extend that work by asking what difference a Martíean reading might make for other nineteenth-century U.S. fiction addressing questions of race, and, in particular, how Martí's perspective on interracial politics might help to explore the question of why the post-Reconstruction era witnessed the emergence of parallel, but unremarked, vogues for the local color and history of two regions, the Old South and the Southwest. These twin vogues point to a historical conjunction of the "Negro Question" with the "Indian protest movement" led by Jackson, among others, in the late nineteenth century—a conjunction rarely addressed, however, in U.S. discourse, although it is common in some Latin American political and cultural discourses, associated especially with Martíean pan-nationalist imaginings of hemispheric unity, to bring together the causes of the black and the Indian. Hence the Martí connection.

José Martí's Harriet Beecher Stowe provides the critical intercultural connection. Known throughout the nineteenth century primarily as the author of *Uncle Tom's Cabin*, Martí's Stowe is something more. Rather than standing alone, for Martí she is always invoked in the same breath as Helen Hunt Jackson, author of *Ramona*, the 1884 romance of Indian reform, one of five novels Martí translated into Spanish. Martí's Stowe has a twin, then, in Jackson. *Ramona*, Martí says in the introduction to his 1887 translation, speaks out in favor of the Indians as Harriet Beecher Stowe did for the Negroes; *Ramona* is an "otra *Cabaña*," save, he notes, according to the "norteamericanos," the weaknesses of the book by "la Beecher."[2] It was, at the time of *Ramona*'s publication, a comparison common enough for Jackson herself to have made, in her case concluding, though, that she could never match Stowe. "If I could write a story that would do for the Indian a thousandth part what *Uncle Tom's Cabin* did for the negro . . ." but "I do not dare to think I have written a second *Uncle Tom's Cabin*."[3]

For Martí, however, the point of pairing Stowe with Jackson is less to rank the relative merits of the two reformist writers than to bring together the two oppressed groups for which they speak. To this end Martí begins a long article on the Lake Mohonk Indian reform movement in the U.S. (published in the 4 December 1885 *La Nación*) by invoking not only the well-known example of Jackson, as one would expect, but also the abolitionist tradition of Stowe. And it is Stowe who comes first: "In the United States," the opening paragraph asserts, "a woman opened men's hearts to compassion for the Negroes, and nobody did more to set them free than she. Harriet Beecher Stowe was her name, a woman passionately devoted to justice," and her book, a "prolific success," was *Uncle Tom's Cabin* — "a tear that has something to say!" Next, Jackson: "It was also a woman who, with much good sense and sympathy, has worked year after year to alleviate the plight of the Indians. The recently deceased Helen Hunt Jackson, strongminded and with a loving heart, wrote a letter of thanks to President Cleveland for his determination to recognize the Indian's right to manhood and justice."[4] Martí's composite figure of Stowe-and-Jackson links the world-famous North American abolitionist with the nationally prominent spokeswoman for the Indian cause, bringing together what are in the U.S. the distinctly separate reform movements of the Negro and the Indian.

As writer both of the abolitionist novel and the romance of Indian reform, Martí's Stowe-Jackson is greater than the sum of her parts: she becomes an inter-ethnic, international figure capable of speaking to both the limits and possibilities of the multiple racial and national aspirations of Latin America and the Caribbean. This colonial world is "a vast zone," according to Roberto Fernández Retamar's influential essay, "Caliban: Notes Toward a Discussion of Culture in Our America," for which "*mestizaje* is not an accident but rather the essence," and for which Martí's "our mestizo America" is, therefore, "the distinctive sign of our culture — a culture of descendants, both ethnically and culturally speaking, of aborigines, Africans, and Europeans."[5] The challenge of representing affirmatively this mestizo culture is central to Martí's "Our America." His famous essay of that title, known for asserting that "it was imperative to make common cause with the oppressed," devotes equal time to detailing the divisions, national and racial, that threaten and yet must constitute that common cause.

> We were a masquerader in English breeches, Parisian vest, North American jacket, and Spanish cap. The Indian hovered near us in silence, and went off to the hills to baptize his children. The Negro was seen pouring out the songs of his heart at night, alone and unrecognized among the rivers and wild animals. . . . As for us, we were nothing but epaulets and professors' gowns in countries that came into the world wearing hemp sandals and headbands. It would have been the mark of genius to couple the headband and the professors' gown with the founding fathers' generosity and courage, to rescue the Indian, to make a place for the competent Negro, to fit liberty to the body of those who rebelled and conquered for it.[6]

If Martí's new hemispheric, transnational nation, our mestizo America, must not just be but must mark and represent itself, to itself, as a culture of descendants, both ethnically and culturally speaking, of aborigines, Africans, and Europeans, then Martí's Stowe points to the central challenges he faced in mobilizing and representing as a collectivity the descendants of the Africans, aborigines, and Europeans who are the mestizo inhabitants of "Our America."

As a traveling figure, Martí's Stowe points as well toward the possibility of a reoriented, triangulated U.S. history, viewed from the perspective of Spanish America as well as of the British empire. Looking toward the Southwest as well as the Atlantic seaboard, Martí's Stowe also locates a possible intersection between two important fields of geographical and cultural analysis, the Black Atlantic and the Spanish Borderlands, both of which seek to disrupt the provincial focus and nationalist imperative of traditional American historical and literary studies. Paul Gilroy's *Black Atlantic* takes as its unit of study the trajectory of the historic triangular trade, linking Canada, the Caribbean, Africa, Europe, and the U.S. as "geographical and/or figurative points of contact" in a transnational "narrative of involvement." Gilroy's work represents the new reinvigoration of geography in literary and cultural studies, as well as acknowledges the longstanding role of geography within the historiography of slavery, informing such major studies as Philip Curtin's *The Atlantic Slave Trade* (1969) and

The Tropical Atlantic in the Age of the Slave Trade (1991). Similarly, the Spanish Borderlands, a historiographic field that originated in the 1920s with Herbert Bolton's *The Spanish Borderlands: A Chronicle of Old Florida and the Southwest* (1921), defines both a geography—Spain's possessions in the continental U.S., from northern Mexico and California to Louisiana and Florida, from the Gulf of Mexico to the Atlantic—and a figurative contact zone—the Borderland idea is "a place within the 'conventional framework' of U.S. history that yet still transcends national boundaries, as 'the meeting place and fusing place of two streams of European civilization.'"[7] Martí's composite Stowe-Jackson, located within both of these contact zones, points to the possibility of putting them together in order to internationalize the study of "region" and nation in the U.S.

Both Paul Gilroy and David J. Weber (the latter a prominent Spanish-Borderlands historian) stress the need for a dialectic between regional or national histories and the transnational. Models for, or perhaps rough equivalences of, such a dialectic already exist in the form of Martí's hemispheric nationalism, of Fernández Retamar's Calibanic culture that traverses numerous Indian, African, and European communities, and, finally, of Frantz Fanon's well-known formulation that "national consciousness, which is not nationalism, is the only thing that will give us an international dimension." Paul Gilroy's "outer-national, transcultural reconceptualisation" defines a "diasporic, global perspective on the politics of racism" that is derived from his systematic account of the interconnections, rather than the one-way traffic, among Africa, Europe, and the Americas. David J. Weber, calling for a revitalization and expansion of borderlands historiography, notes the apparent contradiction in Bolton's founding definition of the borderland idea as a location both within and transcending national boundaries. This contradiction should be embraced rather than rejected, Weber concludes, if borderlands historiography is ever to contribute to the larger history of the hemisphere and thus fulfill Bolton's original vision of it as resting "on the borders rather than within the field of most other students" (14). Marginal by definition, the borderlands will remain peripheral to the core areas of both U.S. history and Latin American history, Weber argues, unless a broader definition emerges of a "Greater Borderlands," including perhaps the Central American, Caribbean, and Gulf regions (11). Such a Greater Borderlands certainly could be located at the intersection between the Black Atlantic and the traditional Spanish Borderlands.[8]

How might the study of U.S. culture be affected if it were located at this intersection? Most prominently, a black-Indian connection, á la Martí, emerges to address, even to reveal and formulate, the following puzzles and questions in late nineteenth-century American literary history: why did the post-Reconstruction era produce what amounted to a virtual national fad for the Old South and the Southwest, marketed as locations for history and travel? How do the parallel "fantasy heritages" associated with both regions map national history onto transnational geographies?[9] I will discuss these issues first in relation to the transculturated sentimentality of Martí's Stowe, and then in the context of the construction, and celebration, of Southern and Southwestern heritages in the post-Reconstruction novel in the U.S.

Hemispheric Sentimentalities

Associating the so-called "Negro and Indian Questions" in ways virtually unheard of in the U.S. context, where those terms originate, Martí's Stowe —with her twin Jackson—represents his remaking of the North American "woman's" tradition of sentimentalist reform and romantic racialism in the image of "our mestizo America." From the Cuban Gertrudis Gómez de Avellaneda's abolitionist *Sab* (1841) to the Peruvian Clorinda Matto de Turner's pro-*indigenista Aves sin nido* [*Birds Without a Nest*] (1889), women intellectuals aligned themselves, and their national visions, with the racially oppressed. Stowe has always been the first lady dominating this American—hemispheric—feminist tradition, invoked by writers and critics in both Latin and North America since the mid-nineteenth century.[10] It is notable how such broadly pan-American citations of Stowe's novel come largely from the Latin American side; in the U.S. context, as we have seen, Stowe is paired almost exclusively with her domestic ("Indianist") other, Helen Hunt Jackson. Stowe sets the standard for what has been seen by "Americanists" (that is, critics specializing in the field of U.S. literatures) as the exclusively Anglo-American phenomenon of sentimentality.

From the cultural perspective of "Our America," however, this transcultural woman's tradition is so striking that as recently as 1978, in an essay marking the publication of a new Cuban edition of Martí's *Ramona*, Roberto Fernández Retamar urged Cuban readers toward "four estimable novels" that embody, "in our continent," the "struggle against the enslavement of blacks and against the brutal treatment of indigenous Americans," naming sentimentalists Gómez de Avellaneda, Stowe, Jackson, and Matto de Turner.[11] With recent editions of all their work now available, Fernández Retamar says, Cuban readers will have examples of "how four singular

American women from the past century, in differing ways, would denounce the most terrible aspects of the society in which they lived." Their gender is not incidental but central to their critique:

> One cannot stop calling attention to the fact that these novels were all writ-
> ten by women. . . . Shouldn't one conclude that these talented, energetic and
> valiant women—who knew that despite their virtues . . . they would be situ-
> ated in an inferior position to that of scores of mediocre men—were for that
> reason more likely to identify themselves in some way with other human
> beings unjustly ignored, and to express this sentiment above all through the
> indirect path of the imagination? (Fernández Retamar, "On *Ramona*," 700).

Thus, though these novels may be labeled by "some hasty readers today . . . as sickly sweet or sentimental" (*lacrimosas*, literally, tearful), Fernández Retamar argues for "resituating the works in their age." To measure what *Ramona* represented then, we need only look at Martí's introduction to his translation of the novel, specifically where Martí speculates that "Helen Hunt Jackson . . . has perhaps written in *Ramona* our novel" (Martí, "Intro-duction" to *Ramona*, 204). Although Martí's claim is historically sugges-tive, Fernández Retamar concludes, "Today we know it was not so": it was the Peruvian Matto de Turner's 1889 *Aves sin nido* that "approached the theme of the Indian and opened the path to the Hispanoamerican novel," yet still Martí's *Ramona*—"a thought-through work" ["una obra trans-pensada"], "a work that we must consider as also *his*"—"contributed an-other important work to the development of the Hispanoamerican novel" (Retamar, "On *Ramona*," 705; emphasis in original). The genealogy of the Hispanoamerican novel, according to Fernández Retamar, then, must in-clude the hybrid work *Ramona*, written by a North American sentimental-ist and recreated in a translation by a, perhaps *the*, Cuban nationalist.

Given the visibility of Latin American sentimentality, a tradition that Doris Sommer argues is associated with national romances all over Latin America, why would Martí, as Sommer puts it, choose to hide behind North American sentimentality?[12] I would say rather that Martí works *within* a hemispheric tradition of sentimentality in order to work *through* the problematic terms of two Latin American traditions, the discourses of *mestizaje* and *Indigenismo*, both emerging in Martí's time and destined to come to fruition in the 1920s and 1930s as active agents of a new Latin American national self-understanding.[13] The celebration of racial mixture encoded in the term *mestizaje* produced "the new Americans" of Martí's

"our mestizo America," or what would come to be known in its most famous formulation as the "cosmic race" in Mexican philosopher José Vasconcelos' influential work of 1925, *La raza cósmica*.[14] Similarly, although
Indigenismo did not become a full-fledged literary movement until elite
Latin American intellectuals, writing in the 1920s and 1930s, identified
with indigenous traditions and adopted the *"problema del indio"* as the context in which to work out their new sense of national self-identification,
Martí invariably invokes the Indian as trope for our mestizo America, calling for the telling of "the history of America, from the Incas to the present"
(Martí, "Our America," 88). Just as Martí's rhetorical invocation of the
Indian elides the role of the African in our mestizo America, so too, more
broadly, does *mestizaje* assimilate by whitening the peoples of America, and
Indigenismo celebrate a mythic Indianness while destroying actual Indians
and displacing black Africans. A fundamental contradiction thus emerges
between race and *mestizaje* in its nineteenth-century formulations: the call
for a new race of mixed beings is also a call for racelessness, for citizens
defined by national rather than racial membership.

Fernández Retamar alludes to the problems with Latin American racial
discourse in his essay, "Caliban," when he closes a section on Martí's longstanding identification with and "passionate study" of indigenous peoples
by asserting, somewhat defensively, that "naturally, Martí's approach to the
Indian was also applied to the black." "Unfortunately," Fernández Retamar
admits, the two approaches could not be truly equivalent, since in Martí's
day research in American aboriginal cultures, in which Martí was passionately interested, was far more advanced than similar studies in African cultures and their influence on our mestizo America. Fernández Retamar's
conclusion: "In any event, in his treatment of Indian culture and in his
concrete behavior toward the black . . . [Martí] left a very clear outline of
a 'battle plan' in this area" (Fernández Retamar, "Caliban," 20). Notwithstanding Fernández Retamar's insistence, Martí's lifelong problem was to
formulate a battle plan acknowledging colonial oppression of both the ab-
origine and the African, in order to forge the multi-racial alliances, including the European, essential to the very conception of Our America.

This might be called more specifically the "race problem" of Martí's
Cuban nationalism. Martí would have been confronted by the disjunction between the specific history of Cuban revolutionary and national discourse, deeply entwined with the issue of African slavery, and the history
of most of the countries of Our America that were primarily engaged with
the *"problema del indio."* In Cuba, where the Indian population had been

virtually erased (through extermination and assimilation), the national independence movement throughout the nineteenth century periodically identified its cause with that of slave emancipation, producing temporary interracial alliances ranging from the notorious "Conspiracy of La Escalera" in 1842 to the First War of Independence, the Ten Years' War, 1868–1878, in which slaves joined in an anticolonial insurgency that forced the issue of slavery. The process of emancipation in Cuba was, however, in historian Rebecca Scott's words, "prolonged, ambiguous, and complex," a reflection of the shifting, highly unstable relationship between nationalism and race in Cuban politics.[15] The positions most frequently elaborated by Cuban nationalists themselves (among them, Martí), and later taken up, uncritically, by most Cuban historians, were that a vibrant national discourse, positing equality as the basis of unity and struggle against colonial and racial slavery, culminated in the First War of Independence, 1868–1878 (marked by Afro-Cuban overrepresentation in the ranks of the military forces as well as the emergence of a powerful Afro-Cuban leadership), but disappeared by the late 1890s, when Cuba's "race problem" had been substantially eased, replaced by a discourse of "Cubanidad."

The Martí version of this complex unfolding serves simultaneously to advocate interracial alliance and to assert that there are "no races" in Cuba. That is, Martí's revolutionary rhetoric allots equal time to the call for interracial cooperation, the inclusion of blacks in the movement, and to the nearly opposite claim that race is no longer part of the Cuban independence movement. Indeed, he suggests, the question of race is both unnecessary and divisive, because the issue was resolved during the First War of Independence. Martí's no-races argument belongs to the history of the problematic silencing of race as a significant ideological category for the revolution. Yet as Martí demonstrates, the claim that Cuba is race-neutral could be applied racially, to counter the whitening of traditional Latin American nationalist discourses, just as the language of Cuban patriotism allows both the elision of race and a challenge to racism.

The tension between race consciousness and race neutrality in Martí's construction of Cuban nationalism emerges graphically in the contradictory arguments on race, nation, and gender that form the trajectory of three of his best-known essays, from "Madre América" (1889) and "Nuestra América" (1891) to "Mi Raza" (1893). As their titles indicate, the first two essays are devoted to constructing "America," a hemispheric, new world order dominated by mothers and Indians, whereas "Mi Raza" is more narrowly focused on Cuban nationalism and Cuban racism, both associated exclusively with black and white men. The essays, that is, mediate racial and national relations through gender: tracing a trajectory from Indianness to blackness, from mothers to brothers, from Our America to Cuba, the essays also move from arguing for national solidarity through integration of racial differences to calling for a non-racial society made up of "citizens of Cuba."

In such a context, where the projects of Madre America, Nuestra America, and the Cuban patria were so often at odds, what could Martí's *Ramona* offer by way of a solution? Martí's *Ramona*, reconfigured as the sentimental romance of Indian reform of Our America, locates him somewhere between the high sentimentality of white feminists from Stowe to Matto de Turner and the critical adaptations of sentimentality practiced by African American writers from Harriet Jacobs to Pauline Hopkins. Ironically, then, Martí may have been so drawn to *Ramona* because it was "the America which is not ours," in the form of the composite Stowe-Jackson figure, that provided a prototype at once for rescuing the Indian and making a place for the Negro. Still, though, the comments linking the Stowe and Jackson causes, not to mention Stowe and Jackson themselves, are actually few and far between in Martí's writing. So what is at stake in my foregrounding of "Our Stowe-Jackson"?

First, the United States context. Martí's mestiza Stowe-Jackson brings together what are in the U.S. separate reform movements: if abolitionism preceded, and perhaps preempted, the emergence of a viable Indian reform movement, by the 1880s, the increasing presence of the Indian Question—ironically enough, the disappearing Indian—on the national political and cultural agenda must be balanced against what amounts to a nearly opposite movement, supported by the law and medico-scientific thinking, to erase—by legalized segregation or theories of black degeneracy and biological inferiority—the Negro Question from the national consciousness. In contrast, however, Martí's Stowe-Jackson insists on thinking of the two questions as one. Second, exported, or perhaps repatriated (since Gómez de Avellaneda and Matto de Turner are only two of the Latin American women writers working the "Stowe" vein), to Our America, Martí's composite figure breaks out of the various local critical categories and domestic U.S. debates—the sentimental versus the political, the artist versus the propagandist, the abolitionist versus the Indian reformer—that have heretofore isolated her. She thus complicates the nationalist and exceptionalist focus of American Studies, encouraging us to read "our" texts hemispherically.

The Plantation and the Hacienda: Twin Fantasy Heritages?

Two U.S. novelists, designated "regionalists," yet whose combined terrain comprises both the Black Atlantic and the Spanish Borderlands, from Mexico and California in the west to Louisiana and the Caribbean in the east, provide good test cases: María Amparo Ruiz de Burton, best known for her Californio novel, *The Squatter and the Don* (1885), on the decline of the great ranchos and the ascendancy of monopoly capitalism, and George Washington Cable, chronicler of Creole culture in popular works such as *Old Creole Days* (1879) and *The Grandissimes* (1880). Both writers tap the same vogue for regional local-color and work as well in the dominant post-Reconstruction mode of nostalgic historiography and literary national reconciliation. Both exploit the popular sentimental plot of divided and hostile families—stand-ins for the nation—ultimately reconciled through marriages uniting the principal rival factions. Ruiz de Burton inter-marries the children of the "Spano-American" don and the Anglo-American squatter, making "native Californians" into Americans (for the second time, in classic Ruiz de Burton irony, since the 1848 Treaty of Guadelupe Hidalgo had already conferred citizenship on the Californios). And Cable unites the extended Grandissime clan—feuding, like squatter and Don, in part over old French and Spanish land titles disputed by the new government of the United States after the 1803 Louisiana Purchase— of "the little hybrid city of Nouvelle Orleans," headed by Honoré Grandissime and including not only most of the city's high-born white Creoles but also his quadroon half-brother Honoré Grandissime, f.m.c.[16]

As anyone can tell from even these brief descriptions, however, far from nostalgically constructing twin "fantasy heritages" of two regions in the service of national reconciliation (as did, for example, the popular plantation novels and other "romances of reunion"), the two novels adapt that popular historiography to narrate a critical history of nation and empire, intertwined.[17] In their alternative, regional histories, the process of "Americanization" does not finally renew familial and national harmony. Ending his story of institutionalized miscegenation, frustrated interracial love, and legalized violence toward blacks in Louisiana during the era of the Louisiana Purchase, locally known as the Cession of 1803–1804, Cable concludes, ironically in French, that "today almost all the savagery that can justly be charged against Louisiana must—strange to say—be laid at the door of the *Américain*" (Cable 329–330). And with even more biting irony, Ruiz de Burton laments the fallen condition not just of the Californios but of all "free-born Americans," united in their victimization by monopoly power, who cannot look to the government or the law for protection but "must wait and pray for a Redeemer who will emancipate the white slaves of California" (Ruiz de Burton 365, 372). The regions of the South and the Southwest are collapsed together, just as, in Mark Twain's *Pudd'nhead Wilson* (to take another example), the conflicts of the post-Reconstruction era, when the novels were written, are superimposed on earlier moments of racial and national conflict.[18] In addition to these fairly well-known critiques of the national scene, the two novels adapt what Amy Kaplan demonstrates is a circuit among region, nation, and the looming international context of empire.[19] In their palimpsests of different regional and racial histories and chronologies, the two novelists articulate an emerging critical internationalism of the kind best identified with Martí: Burton's critique of capital's hemispheric domination and Cable's utopian vision of potential interracial alliances in the international borderland of Louisiana, at the juncture of old empires (Spain, France) and conquests (Aztec, Inca) with new nations (United States) and revolutions (French, Haitian).

Ruiz de Burton's project in *Squatter* has several contradictory aims. First, to adapt the popular tradition of historical nostalgia for the fantasy heritage of the plantation or the mission into a critical history of the California rancho and, most important, an alternative narrative of the Californios—a Spanish-speaking minority deprived of legal claims to the land, generally despised as "foreigners" or "greasers." As Rosaura Sánchez argues, in reconstructing an oppositional past ("a memory of an imagined territorial community and shared oppression") and future (based not on territorial-nationalism but on ethnic identity) for the Californios as a people, Ruiz de Burton neither takes a naïve antiquarian view of the mission past nor presents the Don as an idealized figure of a pastoral arcadia.[20] Indeed, the very idea of a Californio fantasy heritage is hard to imagine: when would the Golden Age have been? It wasn't either the 1821–1846 Mexican period or the prior Spanish colonial period (1769–1821), for during these times the Californios didn't exist as a people. Not until the 1848 Treaty of Guadalupe Hidalgo did the Californios come into collective being—an origin, the novel insists, in international betrayal by two nations, Mexico and the United States. "I remember," Don Mariano says,

> that when I first read the text of the treaty of Guadalupe Hidalgo, I felt a bitter resentment against my people; against Mexico, the mother country who abandoned us—her children—with so slight a provision of obligatory

stipulations for protection. . . . [But] . . . How could Mexico have foreseen then that when scarcely half a dozen years should have elapsed the trusted conquerors would, "In Congress Assembled," pass laws which were to be retroactive upon the defenseless, helpless, conquered people, in order to despoil them? (Ruiz de Burton 66-67).

With such beginnings as a "conquered people"—to come into being as the conquered—means that no nostalgic fantasy heritage is compatible with the construction of the Californios as a collective identity.

Second of Ruiz de Burton's contradictory aims: this critical history, the alternative narrative of a people with origins in international betrayal, is also a sanitized history. In what I call a "southernizing" strategy, Ruiz de Burton remaps her local, Southwestern novel onto a national, North-South axis, taking the "west" out of the Southwest and replacing the region and its locally specific ethnic populations and conflicts—the Indian/Mexican/Anglo triangle made famous by *Ramona*—with the dominant national narrative of North and South, freedom and slavery, black and white. Through a detailed plot concerning the corrupt politics of the Big Four railroad barons (Leland Stanford, Collis P. Huntington, Charles Crocker, and Mark Hopkins, who controlled California transportation through the Central Pacific Railroad) and their opposition to Colonel Tom Scott's failed Texas Pacific, which would have made San Diego the western terminus of a southern transcontinental railroad, the novel identifies Southern California with the South. In the analogy, the Californios are twinned with white Southerners, both peoples "conquered" by the same "invader," the United States government, and both fallen in a landless, genteel poverty. "The poor South is in pretty much the same fix that we are," says one of the Californios-by-marriage (Ruiz de Burton 297). "I fear," says another,

> that the sad condition of the impoverished South is not going to have the weight which it deserves in the minds of this Congress. . . . Many of our law-givers seemed not to realize the importance, the policy, the humanity of helping the South, and of giving to the Pacific Coast a competing railway, to get California out of the clutches of a grasping monopoly. . . . Congress turns its back and will not hear the wail of the prostrate South, or the impassionate appeals of California. . . . (Ruiz de Burton 216).

Exposing the transcontinental corruption of the railroad monopoly not only joins the west and the south as the nation's two preeminent, victimized regions but also elevates, by nationalizing, the local struggles of a foreign-seeming group variously called "Spanish people," "Spanish natives," and "Spano-Americans."

Moreover, the novel's southernizing strategy locates the Californios primarily in terms of caste, class, and nation rather than race and ethnicity. On a trip "back East," the Alamar girls make sensational entrances in the most rarified New York and Washington social circles; the "southern beauties," touted as "naturally refined and ladylike," provide a powerful counter-argument to those like Mr. Darrell, the squatter of the title, who see the "conquered natives" as "inferior people" (Ruiz de Burton 155, 203, 221). "It is enough to see one of those Alamar ladies," retorts Mary Moreneau Darrell, the squatter's southern wife who brings her "colored servant" Tisha out west with her, "to learn that they are inferior to nobody" (Ruiz de Burton 222). Some might argue that the novel's Southern California–South pairing, like the aristocratic, "Spanish" identification, is just another means to whiten the Californios by dissociating them from their Mexican-Indian roots. Similarly, the novel's championing of the prostrate South may seem reminiscent of Reconstruction judge and novelist Albion Tourgée's famous complaint that the nation's "literature has become not only Southern in type but distinctly Confederate in sympathy."[21] Yet the key to the southern strategy is not the racial valence but rather the aim to secure for the Californios a place on the national scene and agenda. And while the Californios emerge more distinctly as a people aligned by economic and cultural ties to the aristocratic white South, the novel invites the comparison as much to protest their present proletarianization — their decline into a working class of hod carriers — as to laud their breeding.

Through these sometimes competing strategies, the novel constitutes the Californios as a people — and, perhaps, as the Sánchez-Pita introduction suggests and I'll discuss at the end of this essay, even as part of the larger, international collectivity envisioned by Martí's "Our America" (Sánchez-Pita 39–41). All of these aims come together in the compressed irony of the novel's oft-quoted last sentence, leaving the "we" — no longer just Californios but the "American people" — who "must wait and pray for a Redeemer who will emancipate the white slaves of California." The Christian millenarian moment may be, of course, a long time in the coming, and the wait therefore as much a fatal sentence as a prophetic hope. But more historically specific contradictions emerge in the conjunction of "white slaves," which makes Southern Californians into both the black slaves of the Civil War and the conquered whites of Reconstruction. And given the novel's carefully constructed southern context, "Redeemer" is an equally if not more overdetermined term, generating an excess of possible, deeply contradictory historical meanings. "Redemption," as conservative white southerners termed their return to dominance by 1877, the date of the withdrawal of Federal troops from the South, was laden with meaning, including but not limited to the Christian view of salvation.[22] Redemption also spoke the language of restoration: restoration of home rule (control over state governments), of the pre-war black-white partnership with the old master-class still in control, of Old South values. But as would-be restorers of the Old South and self-appointed purveyors of the Old South myth, the Redeemers were a shifty lot, whose constant theme, C. Vann Woodward says, was, ironically, the New South creed: cheap resources, business opportunities, commercial alliances with northern capital, and above all, railroad developments. With an irony that approaches but doesn't quite equal Ruiz de Burton's, Woodward describes the Redeemers of Kentucky: "Even though they might look like Southern colonels, with goatee and moustaches, and speak like Southern orators, retaining these outer trappings of the olden days, the [Redeemer] program of the 'New Departure' was a program of surrender."[23]

Ruiz de Burton even constructs her own such double-dealer in "ex-Senator Guller," a figure based on a California senator of the 1850s but straight out of Redeemer politics: all that the age expected of a Southern colonel of the old school and a tool of the Big Four. In a chapter titled, "A False Friend Sent to Deceive the Southerners" (based on the evidence of letters from Huntington to an associate, Colton, made public in the famous Colton suit against the Big Four, an eight-year trial that ended in 1885, the year *Squatter* was published), Ruiz de Burton exposes in detail how "Mr. Huntington instructed Senator Guller in all the fictions he was to spread in the South."

> He is going about the South making public speeches . . . and using his influence to mislead Southern newspapers and Southern influential men; trying to convince all that the Texas Pacific will do the South great harm [that it was being built for the benefit of Northern interests]. The Southern people and Southern Press have fallen into the trap. They never doubted, never could doubt, the veracity of ex-Senator Guller, who had espoused their cause during the war of the rebellion, and had always held Southern sentiments (Ruiz de Burton 305).

With a false friend like this, the novel suggests in the last chapter, bitterly titled, "Out With the Invader," a friend (the last chapter reiterates) working "under cover," not as the railroad's "agent, but as an anti-subsidy Democrat and a Southern man," how could one hope to tell the Redeemer from the Invader? So to wait for a Redeemer to emancipate the white slaves of California may be to wait far beyond the millennium. Triply ironic, the novel's last sentence is simultaneously a Christian promise and a secular threat, and, as a specific allusion to the "Redemption of the Southern States," a savage critique of United States law and government.

Cable's *Grandissimes* makes Reconstruction politics a far more obvious context for his novel set during the "Cession" of 1803–1804. Almost universally seen as a metaphor for the entire South during Secession and its aftermath — one of the minor Creoles paints a picture he calls "Louisiana rif-using to hanter de h-Union" (Cable 114) — the novel maps all the major Reconstruction landmarks — both characters and issues — onto the history of the Louisiana Purchase. The gang's all here: the intractable Old South Creole, an "un-American citizen," spokesman for white supremacy and against "the Américain invader" and the Yankee governor (a "young simpleton who attempts to cram [English] down the public windpipe in the courts"), his New South Creole counterpart, Honoré Grandissime, successful businessman, close associate of the Yankee governor, and private critic of slavery ("I am *ama-aze* at the length, the blackness of that shadow! . . . It is the *Némésis* w'ich, instead of coming afteh, glides along by the side of this morhal, political, commercial, social mistake! It blanches, my-de'-seh, ow whole civilization!"), and the tragic quadroon Honoré Grandissime, f.m.c., who can neither help his people ("He 'ave no Cause. Dad peop' 'ave no cause") nor consummate his love for the fiery mulatta voodoo priestess, Palmyre Philosophe, in turn married against her will to the enslaved but "untamable" African warrior-prince, Bras Coupé (in his very name, "he made himself a type of all Slavery, turning into flesh and blood the truth that all Slavery is maiming; . . . he seemed to her the gigantic embodiment of her own dark, fierce will. . . . But . . . her heart she could not give him — she did not have it.") (Cable 87, 157, 48, 156, 195, 171, 175; emphasis in the original).

After the division and conflict, just as inevitably come the unions and resolutions: the marriages that finally unite the warring Creole families and the young German-American immigrant with the Grandissime clan, as well as the abrupt departure of the mixed-race couple, not as husband and wife but asexual brother and sister, to France where he drowns himself and she buries herself in exile. On the annual annuity that she continues to receive, via head-of-the-family H. Grandissime, from the rental properties of his dead quadroon brother, the novel cryptically comments, "But that is only a part of the pecuniary loss which this sort of thing costs Louisiana" (Cable 331). All of these plots comprise the novel's well-recognized critique of Creole and, by extension, Southern and "Américain" culture — so clear an indictment, in fact, that the publication of *The Grandissimes* in 1880 initiated the rapid slide in Cable's reputation that culminated in 1885, when his essay, "The Freedman's Case in Equity," proved to be so controversial that the native son permanently left New Orleans and moved to Massachusetts.

But if Cable's position on the domestic politics of Reconstruction was thus well known, the overdetermined ending, with its displaced persons and racial loose ends, cannot be accounted for within the local context of U.S. race relations alone. The novel also traces a less-recognized international circuit of multiple empires, histories of exploration and conquest, slave rebellion and revolution, located within the novel's many inset narratives, at the center of which is the story of the rebellious slave Bras Coupé. Accompanying the official documented U.S. history of Cession, Secession, and Reunion is a repressed, shadow history, a glimpse of a possibility of a transculturated revolutionary tradition that grafts African warrior-customs onto New World slave revolt and the revolution in France, as well as onto Anglo-American law and an international discourse of rights. This meeting-ground between an American future and a Spanish-French imperial past has explicitly interracial origins in a Creole-Indian alliance going back to the "great Toltec mother-race," predating both Spanish and "conquering" Aztec and Inca (Cable 18). Not only do the Creoles proudly claim "Indian blood" through the classic figure of the Indian queen (here named Lufki-Humma), but also the Creole landscape is repeatedly marked by the much-feared names and places of slave rebellion, from the swamps where runaways like Bras Coupé find refuge to the maroon communities of Cuba and elsewhere in the New World, to the most notorious of all, Toussaint L'Ouverture and the black revolution of San Domingo/Haiti (Cable 182, 184, 196).

But without the usual racial terror: Cable contextualizes the history of New World slave revolt by internationalizing it within a discourse of "universal" rights, best enunciated by the German-American immigrant Frowenfeld. "One great general subject of thought now is human rights — universal human rights. The entire literature of the world is becoming

tinctured with contradictions of the dogmas upon which society in this
section is built. . . . What, then, will they do with the world's literature?"
(Cable 143). The human-rights critique extends from the Creole community to include the United States government, which was perceived by
free black Creoles as reneging on the provision of equal citizenship in
the Louisiana Purchase treaty and, instead, of trying to impose their own
racial order on Louisiana.[24] Although Frowenfeld, sometime-spokesman
for Americanization, ultimately rejects "insurrection" in favor of what he
calls "advocacy," by which he means that Honoré f.m.c. could be "a leader
and deliverer of his people" and "speak for them" (Cable 291), the sheer
excess of revolution and revolutionary discourse, at home and abroad, creates a kind of haunting, utopian counter-movement. The images of Bras
Coupé, runaway slave, "declaring his independence" from within the
depths of the swamp and dancing the Calinda in Congo Square ("the black-
est of black men . . . in breeches of 'Indienne'—the stuff used for slave
women's best dresses—his feet in moccasins . . . and a living serpent twined
about his neck," [Cable 190]) outweigh, or at least counter-balance, the debates over insurrection and the story's conclusion with the capture, ham-
stringing, and death of the runaway. If Cable's Bras Coupé is no Black
Jacobin, still his domesticated Toussaint is situated at the meeting-place of
two streams of European civilization, those of colonization and conquest,
and of rights and revolution. The outlines of a transculturated revolutionary tradition, however shadowy and compromised, emerge in the novel's
internationalism, or what historians Arnold Hirsch and Joseph Logsdon
call Cable's "counterpoint between the Franco-African protest tradition
of New Orleans and the tragic racial mind-set of Anglo-America."[25]

    Ruiz de Burton, too, uses local color and a putatively regional mode
to construct her own incipient, hemispheric vision. The novel's extended
critique of the railroad monopoly not only "southernizes" but also inter-
nationalizes the Californios, Southern California, and the U.S., locating
them on a circuit of global capital. More than simply a transcontinental railroad, the Californios envision San Diego as the shipping point for
"commerce between Asia and the Atlantic seaboard, between China and
Europe" (Ruiz de Burton 323); the demise of those hopes is also expressed
through a global analysis (the Big Four chose to "kill San Diego . . . and
build railroads in Guatemala and British America. . . . Towns are crushed
and sacrificed in California to carry prosperity to other countries" [Ruiz
de Burton 370–371]). Accompanying this critique is the possibility (articulated in her letters and first novel *Who Would Have Thought It?*) that Ruiz de

Burton, like Don Mariano, saw the Californios as part of a larger international collectivity or "raza," Spano-Americans, like the race-family-nation of "Nuestra America" that Martí identified as distinct from the America which is not ours.[26]

Both Ruiz de Burton and Cable have thus reshaped the dominant national cultural icons of Americanization at their time, from the romance of reunion to nostalgia for the passing of the Southern, Mission, and Indian (fantasy) pasts, into tools of critical internationalism and types of imagined international communities. Each novel in a different way, then, may be celebrated as a deliberately disjunctive Reconstruction novel for Our America. Finally, to put together the systems of the Black Atlantic and the Spanish Borderlands, as I am urging, may provide a return to Martí as a new intersecting point for American Studies: the two fields of study meet and overlap right at Cuba, strategically located at the outermost edge, geographically and chronologically, of the Spanish Empire and at the dead center of the Black Atlantic.

But this is not the Cuba whose history begins in 1898, a date which, I think it is fair to say, marks for many literary and cultural types the beginning of U.S.-Cuba relations. Rather, this is also the Cuba of the triangular trade, the colonial Cuba, that establishes the whole prehistory of nineteenth-century nationalism and abolitionism, of annexationism versus Africanization, of Cuban slave "conspiracies" versus U.S. slave "revolts," through which we might construct a comparative history of the multiple roles of "race" and "nation" in imagining the Americas. This is also the Cuban prehistory that leads to the Second War of Independence in 1895–1898, the war in which Martí's revolutionary credentials were laid down once and for all, and the war all too often known here in the U.S. by collapsing it within the Spanish-American War. Though no secret to Cuban historians or to those who know Martí well, the recent (and ongoing) Martí revival in U.S. cultural studies would benefit from an awareness that Cuba-U.S. relations began long before the so-called Spanish-American War.

Or as Roberto Fernández Retamar puts it: "ninety-eight" is not only a Spanish date (which gives its name to a complex group of writers and thinkers in that country), but it is also a Latin American date (which should designate a no less complex group of writers, generally known as *modernistas*). It is "'ninety-eight'—the visible presence of North American imperialism in Latin America—already foretold by Martí, which informs the later work of someone like Darío or Rodó" (Fernández Retamar, "Caliban," 10). "Already foretold by Martí": the pre-revolutionary, pre-emancipation Cuba in which Martí came of age, the Cuba that is not ours, will provide us (the us of "American Studies"), at the very least, with a "situational-specific" reading of the Caribbean image in the American mind, and, at the most, with a thoroughgoing Martíean vision of the internationalism of national cultures.[27]

Notes

1. See "Ramona in Our America," in eds. Belnap and Fernández, *José Martí's "Our America,"* 91–111.

2. Introduction to Helen Hunt Jackson, *Ramona: Novela Americana*, in Martí, *Obras Completas*, vol. 24 (Havana: Editorial Nacional de Cuba, 1965), 199–205. Subsequent references will be cited parenthetically in the text. For the translations of the "Introduction" and all of my other quotations from Martí's work that are not collected in the available English-language editions, I am indebted to my graduate research assistant David Luis-Brown, to whom I am immeasurably grateful.

3. Quoted in Valerie Sherer Mathes, *Helen Hunt Jackson and Her Indian Reform Legacy*, 77, 158.

4. José Martí, *Inside the Monster: Writings on the United States and American Imperialism*, 216–217.

5. Roberto Fernández Retamar, "Caliban: Notes Toward a Discussion of Culture in Our America," 4. Subsequent references will be cited parenthetically in the text.

6. José Martí, "Our America," in *Our America: Writings on Latin America and the Struggle for Cuban Independence*, 91. Subsequent references will be cited parenthetically in the text.

7. Paul Gilroy, *The Black Atlantic: Modernity and Double Consciousness;* I take the notion of the trade as a figurative geography from Hortense Spillers, "Introduction: Who Cuts the Border?" in *Comparative American Identities*, 9; David J. Weber, "The Idea of the Spanish Borderlands," in ed., Thomas, *Columbian Consequences, Volume 3: The Spanish Borderlands in Pan-American Perspective*, 13–14.

8. Frantz Fanon, *The Wretched of the Earth*, 247; Gilroy, 17, 120–121; Weber, 14, 11.

9. Carey McWilliams, "The Fantasy Heritage" in *North From Mexico: The Spanish-Speaking People of the U.S.* (1948; 1968).

10. See Jean Franco, *Plotting Women*, 92–93; Mary Louise Pratt, "Women, Literature, and National Brotherhood," in *Women, Culture, and Politics in Latin America*, ed. Bergmann, Greenberg, et al., 48–73.

11. Roberto Fernández Retamar, "On *Ramona* by Helen Hunt Jackson and José Martí," 699–705. Subsequent references will be cited parenthetically in the text.

12. I am indebted to Sommer's published work as well as to her many provocative questions and conversations with me, among which was this critical question about Martí's relationship to sentimentality. See Sommer, *Foundational Fictions: The National Romances of Latin America*. Subsequent references will be cited parenthetically in the text.

13. On adapting to Chicano cultural criticism the psychological concept of "working through," see Carl Gutiérrez-Jones, *Rethinking the Borderlands: Between Chicano Culture and Legal Discourse*, 182, n. 7.

14. José Vasconcelos, *La raza cósmica, misión de la raza iberoamericana.*

15. Rebecca J. Scott initiated this work with *Slave Emancipation in Cuba: The Transition to Free Labor, 1860–1899;* Aline Helg picks up the next chapter after abolition in *Our Rightful Share: The Afro-Cuban Struggle for Equality, 1886–1912;* and, finally, see Ada Ferrer, *Insurgent Cuba: Race, Nation, and Revolution, 1868–1898.*

16. María Amparo Ruiz de Burton, *The Squatter and the Don;* George Washington Cable, *The Grandissimes: A Story of Creole Life,* 11. Subsequent references to both novels will be cited parenthetically in the text.

17. See Nina Silber, *The Romance of Reunion: Northerners and the South, 1865–1900.*

18. On the chronological layering of *Pudd'nhead Wilson,* see Eric J. Sundquist, *To Wake the Nations: Race in the Making of American Literature,* 225–270.

19. See Amy Kaplan, "Region, Nation, Empire," in *The Columbia History of the American Novel.*

20. Sánchez and Pita, Introduction to *The Squatter and the Don,* 21; Sánchez, *Telling Identities: the Californio Testimonios,* 4, 27.

21. Albion Tourgée, "The South as a Field for Fiction," qtd. in C. Vann Woodward, *Origins of the New South, 1877–1913,* 165.

22. Joel Williamson, *The Crucible of Race: Black-White Relations in the American South Since Emancipation,* 51, 82.

23. Woodward, *Origins of the New South, 1877–1913,* 7.

24. See Joseph Logsdon and Caryn Bell, "The Americanization of Black New Orleans, 1850–1900," in eds. Hirsch and Logsdon, *Creole New Orleans: Race and Americanization,* 205.

25. Preface to *Creole New Orleans,* p. xii.

26. Ruiz de Burton, *Who Would Have Thought It?* (1872; rpt. 1995). See Sánchez and Pita, Introduction to *The Squatter and the Don,* 40.

27. See Fredric Jameson, "Foreword" to Roberto Fernández Retamar, *Caliban and Other Essays,* xi–xii, and Fanon, *Wretched of the Earth,* 248.

HYBRID HYBRIDITY

CHAPTER 9

CHICANO ETHNICITY, CULTURAL HYBRIDITY, AND THE MESTIZO VOICE

Rafael Pérez-Torres

> In the beginning and unto the end was and is the lung: divine affla-
> tus, baby's first yowl, shaped air of speech, staccato gusts of laugh-
> ter, exalted airs of song, happy lover's groan, unhappy lover's lament,
> miser's whine, crone's croak, illness' stench, dying whisper, and be-
> yond and beyond the airless, silent void. A sigh isn't just a sigh. We
> inhale the world and breathe out meaning. While we can. While we
> can.
>
> SALMAN RUSHDIE,
> *The Moor's Last Sigh*

In the United States, where ideas of race and identity politics emerge from the fine specificity of the one-drop rule, notions of hybridity, creolization, mongrelization, and *métissage* represent difficult topics of dialogue. Within a Mexican context, by contrast, *mestizaje* — racial mixture — helps form the core of a nationalist discourse. Indeed, Mexican culture since the Revolu-tion has sought staunchly to praise the peasant class, the campesino, the indio, the mixed heritage of the Mexican people — one reason the Zapatista revolt has so taken the Mexican national imagination.

Of course the reality of United States society and culture has always been more creolized than the one-drop rule admits. Simultaneously, *mesti-zaje* in Mexico proves much more complex than that given voice by official discourses valorizing indigenism. It is these multiple registers — simulta-neous praise, celebration, condemnation — with which (Gabriel-like) writ-ers and critics wrestle when asserting the *mestizaje* of Chicano/Chicana ethnic identity. In articulating notions of *mestizaje*, Chicano cultural objects help trace the varied and vexed paths of racial identification. This identification forms a continuous dialogue between United States ethnic, social, and national discourses.

Tracing History

Chicana/o *mestizaje* represents the trace of a historical material process, a violent racial/colonial encounter. In fact, this type of encounter characterizes the socio-cultural dynamics of the Americas since first contact with Europe. Chicano *mestizaje* derives from a complex history involving both a sense of dispossession and empowerment, a simultaneous devaluation and estimation of indigenous ancestry. Needless to say, the formation of a mestizo Chicano consciousness is complicated and elaborate. At the risk of seeming overly simplistic, three historical moments can be said to form critical points in the conceptualization of Chicano cultural and racial *mestizaje*.

The first is the Spanish conquest of the Aztec Empire in 1521 and the subsequent enslavement, genocide, and oppression of indigenous populations. As with so much that is "American," the processes that wrought our mestizo conditions were (and are) forged in the heat and hatred of violence. Yet the sense of rebirth and renewal, the interweaving of tradition and innovation that likewise characterizes *mestizaje* arose (and arises) from these same processes. As such, the relationship between the invader Hernán Cortés and his translator/mistress Malintzín stands as the index of this originary moment of *mestizaje*.[1]

The second event that informs Chicano *mestizaje* is the appropriation of Mexican lands by the United States. While the Treaty of Guadalupe Hidalgo that closed the Mexican-American War in 1848 represents yet again a moment of betrayal, it also marks the beginning of a new subject in history come to be called the Chicano and Chicana.[2] Violence, fraud, manipulation, and intimidation became means in the nineteenth and twentieth centuries by which Mexicans in the new U.S. territories lost much of their land and became a large and largely landless labor pool forced to seek low-paying field and industrial work.

The third event is more clearly ongoing. The current controversies over immigration, employment, and border control in the Southwest are but the latest conflicts informing Chicano *mestizaje*. For a century and a half, the fluid movements between populations in Mexico (and increasingly Central America) and the United States complicate and enrich the dynamics of identity formation in relation to Chicano and mestizo identities. These historical moments would seem to value the notion of indigenous connectivity as the baseline for *mestizaje*. An emphasis on a Mexican context in understanding Chicano *mestizaje* leads to a kind of litmus test for ethnic identity. The somatic manifestation of "Indianness" becomes the marker of one's identity. This explains the emphasis in the famous "Plan Espiritual de Aztlán" on race: "We Declare the independence of our Mestizo Nation. We are a Bronze People with a Bronze Culture" (403).³ Within an essential nationalist discourse, Chicanismo is measured by the color of the skin and the details of physiognomy. Clearly, this position can easily translate into other non-racialized areas: the test of ethnic identity can be tied to one's linguistic skills—fluency with code-switching, bilingualism, slang—one's clothes, one's taste in music, economic condition, place of domicile, nationality, etc. Chicano/a ethnic identity becomes essentialized, premised on meeting quite specific physical or social conditions.

Strategic *Mestizaje*

Outside of racial discourses, *mestizaje* in a cultural context foregrounds the aesthetic and formal hybridity of Chicano artistic formation. A brief overview of Chicano cultural production reveals the reliance upon creolization and border-crossing as both technique and metaphor for aesthetic expression: visual artist Barbara Carrasco paints canvases that simultaneously quote Aztec codices and the Flintstones; pop-rock group Los Lobos records an ironic rumba version of the Disney *Jungle Book* song "I Wanna Be Like You"; poet Evangelina Vigil plays English off Spanish in an explosively expressive form of code-switching ("eres el tipo [you're the type] / de motherfucker / bien chingón [real tough] / who likes to throw the weight around"); rapper Kid Frost busts rhymes that pun crosslingually—"You think you're so cool / I'm gonna call you a culo [asshole]." *Mestizaje* seems central to the creation of Chicano culture. It represents a strategy by which audiences are gathered, fluid subjectivities enacted, political alliances forged, ethnic identities affirmed.

This type of dynamism makes durable *mestizaje* as both cultural strategy and ethnic identification. *Mestizaje* allows for strategic movements among distinct racial or ethnic classes—Indigenous, African, Hispanic, Asian, Caucasian—and strategic reconfigurations of cultural repertoires—

mythic, postmodernist, nativist, Euro-American. These all form registers that resonate with contemporary Chicanismo. Unlike the typically binary notions of identity within a U.S. racial paradigm (choose black or white), a focus on *mestizaje* allows for other forms of ethnic self-identification, other types of cultural creation, other means of social struggle. So for Chicano/a ethnic identity, a reliance on *mestizaje* becomes a way to articulate subjectivity outside dominant paradigms of identity.

Mestizaje within a Chicano/a context thus represents a strategy by which counter-hegemonic identities can be articulated and enacted. Simultaneously, it stands as a condition engendered through historical processes. *Mestizaje* embodies the struggle for power, place, and personhood arising from histories of violence and resistance. As vying social discourses have produced Chicano/a identities and cultural formations, so too have they given rise to a series of different significances ascribed to the mestizo. In tracing these differences, a pattern of appropriation and misrepresentation emerges. The following discussion suggests that in considering the historical and political exigencies of *mestizaje*, the voice of the mestizo emerges as the articulation of an empowered and empowering ethnic identity.

One of the most devastating conceptualizations of the mestizo fits within a pluralist paradigm of benign difference. The 1956 film *Giant* serves as a prime example, enacting the subordination of mestizo/a figures into a postwar racial hierarchy. While the manifest content of the film bespeaks a national vision in which racial difference is subsumed beneath the signifier "America," in actuality a white patriarchy retains its privileged position as sole agent in writing a new American history. Tino Villanueva's 1993 poem, *Scene from the Movie Giant*, responds directly to the voicelessness imposed upon the mestizo by the film and so helps locate some of the liberating qualities enacted by a voicing of *mestizaje*.

Missing from Villanueva's rendering is a sense of the political and social struggles involved in the formation of Chicano identity that serve as the focus of Oscar Acosta's novels, *The Autobiography of a Brown Buffalo* (1972) and *The Revolt of the Cockroach People* (1973). His Chicano nationalist version of *mestizaje* highlights a sense of collectivity and political project implicit in the development of mestizo consciousness. However, in giving voice to a masculinist mestizo discourse, his articulation serves to devalue numerous voices seeking to broaden notions of *mestizaje* beyond a racial/national paradigm.

If Acosta's view of *mestizaje* serves to erase variety in the term mestizo, the work of poststructural critics in their rush to assert the deconstructive qualities of *mestizaje* at times erases the historical material specificity of the term. In response to the potential elisions and illusions involved in conceptualizing *mestizaje* as the apogee of *différance*, a feminist poetics of *mestizaje* can serve to re-embody and rehistoricize the processes of *mestizaje* occluded by an American pluralist, or a masculinist nationalist, or a poststructuralist valorization of an all-too-evasive borderlands. The poetry of Lorna Dee Cervantes helps crystallize the salient issues involved in this poetics of *mestizaje*. Her work reveals *mestizaje* to be a tactical subjectivity, one that presents a mask in order to give voice to a subjectivity both inscribed by and in rejection of dominant systems of power.

In resonance with a key point made by Chela Sandoval, this essay argues that the term mestiza stands not just as a fixed signifier but serves also as "a *tactical subjectivity* with the capacity to recenter depending upon the kinds of oppression to be confronted" (14).[4] The capacity for change through *mestizaje* is one perpetually negotiated given the systems of power—discursive, repressive, militarized, ideological—mestizos contest. The terrain crossed by mestizo and mestiza bodies forms a topos overlaid by strategies of survival and triumph. *Mestizaje* thus becomes a means of weaving together the traces of a historical material legacy with the vision of a potential—and potentially new—subjectivity.

The Subsumed Mestizo

Gayatri Spivak reminds us that in undertaking social transformation, it is imperative to ignore that the starting point is shaky and that the end will be inconclusive. Uncertainty needs to be placed in the margin. Simultaneously, and most importantly, it is the margins, the space of uncertainty, of aporia, that "haunt what we start and get done, as curious guardians" (158).[5] An endless vigilance is necessary as we construct relations with and challenges to the worlds of power around us. Responsibility lies in interrogating the uses to which we put notions like hybridity and *mestizaje*, while a lack of vigilance leads to a return of repression. To forget this critical function of the margin results in a conservative hailing of established practices and "a masquerade of the privileged as the disenfranchised, or their liberator" (159). Clearly, throughout the contested histories of—on the one side—an Anglo-American United States and—on the other—a mestizo Mexico, the privileged feel themselves either disenfranchised from their own sense of well-being due to the presence of the oppressed or called upon to act as the liberators of the oppressed. A reliance on well-scripted roles (rather than on their critical interrogation) leads again and again to a reinscription of asymmetrical relations of power.

This asymmetry most clearly reveals itself through cultural objects produced by an anxiety about inequality. The 1956 film *Giant* represents such a case. Recounting the triumphs and tribulations of the Benedict family—Jordan "Bick" Benedict, the native Texan (played by Rock Hudson), whose fortune comes from the cultivation of cattle on vast Texas grange lands; Leslie, the fey and spoiled Eastern girl (played by Elizabeth Taylor), who valiantly adapts to the tough demands of life in the wild west; and Jett Rink (played by James Dean), parlaying the inheritance of a small plot of land into a vast oil fortune that ruins him due to drink and excess. Bick and Leslie Benedict work through their differences, expand their ranch, raise a family. *Giant* becomes a representation of post-war America as a (notably heterosexual) national giant whose virile West and refined East come together in a productive union of power and change. The film gives voice to a new America, one that struggles with discourses of inclusion and pluralistic liberalism. The film premiere of *Giant* comes, after all, not long after the landmark Supreme Court decision *Brown v. Board of Education.*

A central thematic conflict of the movie revolves around Bick Benedict's behavior toward the Texan Other: Mexicans. As a white man whose ancestors built their fortune on Mexican dispossession, he views Mexicans as inscrutable minions who have their own mysterious ways and generally keep to themselves. (Early in the film, Leslie—earnestly but innocently—reminds a stiff-backed Bick that Texas "stole" its land from Mexico. Despite her faux pas, Bick is indeed taken with the girl.) Though her own childhood home is run by black servants who cook, clean and care for her patrician family, Leslie proves more accepting of the Mexican Other than her husband. A good liberal Easterner, she is ready to lend some kindness to her humble mestizo servants. Indeed, real racial trouble arises only when their eldest son, Jordie, decides to marry a Mexican woman—named, quite imaginatively, Juana. Bick is less than thrilled at the choice his son has made. His daughter Judy, by contrast, elopes with the humble—but white—ranch hand Bob Deitz. Each union produces a son. One is a blonde, blue-eyed toddler. It is, significantly, the other, the dark mestizo baby boy, who is destined to carry on the Benedict name.

The climax of the rather long film occurs in a roadside hamburger joint named Sarge's Place. Bick, Leslie, youngest daughter Lutz, daughter-in-law Juana, and the mestizo grandchild—"little" Jordie Benedict—are on their way back home from attending the unfortunate grand opening of Jett Rink's resort hotel. The hostility toward Juana and little Jordie, whose somatic presence marks them "Mexican," is immediately palpable as the plump blonde waitress first stares at them and then grudgingly serves the Benedicts water. Sarge likewise is unhappy, but he backs down from confronting the Benedicts after insulting Juana and little Jordie, who wants ice cream ("Ice cream?" Sarge asks. "I thought he'd want a tamale").

Things come to a head when an elderly Mexican man and woman with their daughter take a table by the door. This proves too much for Sarge, who unceremoniously attempts to eject the unwelcome customers. The old man futilely holds out to Sarge a wad of dollar bills proving his ability to pay—which is to say, proving his worth. Bick intervenes, suggesting that Sarge should treat these people with more respect, reminding him: "The name Benedict has meant something to people around here for a considerable time." Sarge jerks a thumb at little Jordie and asks, "That little papoose back there, he a Benedict too?" As if for the first time, it dawns on Bick that, indeed, a mestizo child is the bearer of both his own Christian and family name: Jordan Benedict III. When Bick acknowledges his mestizo grandson, Sarge tells him to forget the question. Nevertheless, he proceeds to eject the Mexican family. At this point Bick throws the first punch, stuns Sarge, and assumes his position as liberator of the oppressed.

The fight scene that follows bespeaks a battle of epic proportions. As Richard Meyer observes, Hudson's body in all his movies assumes a great significance. Hudson represents largeness and strength: even his name, taken from the Rock of Gibraltar and the Hudson River, provides an "expansive landscape of the masculine" (260).[6] (This, of course, proves ironic given Hudson's own impossible position as a gay man representing an image of idealized heterosexual masculinity.) In the fight scene, Hudson plays the role of great white father. The low camera angles accentuate the height and vastness of the titanic combatants. The militaristic drum beat of "The Yellow Rose of Texas" playing in the background adds to the sense of epic battle.[7]

Bick loses the fight. The battle is significant, however, as a representation of the battles America has come to wage in relationship to race and a new pluralistic vision of inclusion. As a metaphor for this greater America, Bick is forced to accept a different relationship to racial identity. The catalyst for this epic battle is, after all, Bick's acknowledgment of his grandson. He in a sense offers a patriarchal blessing by finally admitting familial links to "that little papoose." The mestizo body is claimed in the film, admitted into the national family, and simultaneously erased.[8]

Mestizaje cannot provide an empowered subjectivity, cannot offer agency within the epic battle over racial/national redefinitions. The titanic white father must stand up for the Mexicans, represented as they are by an ineffectual old man, helpless youngsters, and sobbing women. It is the white father who must claim his (grand)son, bestow legitimacy, and defend the family name—even if it belongs to a mestizo child he would under other circumstances scorn. The film thus provides an image of the privileged as savior. A benign, pluralistic vision incorporates difference within its own grand discourse of sameness. The subaltern is left voiceless, his inclusion within a discourse of equality ensuring again erasure.

The final scene of Giant underscores the fact of subalternity due to racial difference. Following the fight, domestic calm returns; Bick recovers from his battle wounds; Leslie affirms her love, support, and respect for her man. The two grandparents speak as they watch over the two grandchildren—one racially "pure," one multiracial—and reminisce over the years spent together. The film asserts a form of triumph, a sense of arrival, an affirmation of progress in relation to human rights. As Leslie tells Bick, until that moment when he stood up for the downtrodden and the excluded, she had been thinking that "Jordan and I and all the others behind us have been failures." This moment in which Bick fights for the inclusion and rights of the dispossessed represents for Leslie a culmination of the hundred-year Benedict family history. Yet that inclusion does not prevent Bick from bemoaning the fact "my own grandson don't even look like one of us. I swear, honey, he looks like a little wetback." Though difference in Giant becomes part of a discourse of liberal humanism and pluralistic democracy, difference still marks alterity and inferiority. That is, there is still an "us" who stand at the center of discourse, agent and subject of history, a constituency composed of an "us" that is yet not "them."

Moreover, the discourse of inclusion and equality suggested by the film is belied by the mise en scène of the closing shot. The grandchildren stand side by side in their crib, cousins, fruits of the same family tree. Behind the white child stands a white lamb; behind the brown child stands a brown calf. The dialogue between Bick and Leslie bespeaks equality; the mise en scène underscores difference. While one might be tempted to view this scene as a vision of pastoral peace—a representation of a world where the calf lies down with the lamb—it is difficult not to read its significance in a more sinister light. The closing moments of Giant suggest that different races represent different species, thus evoking one strain of nineteenth-century racial theory. This other species, embodied by the mestizo, is acceptable only insofar as it fits within an overarching authoritative discourse: in this case one of benign pluralism and liberal democracy. Yet the difference implicit in the mestizo body, that which is unvalued and undesirable, is simultaneously maintained and erased in a double movement of acceptance and repugnance. The mestizo ostensibly serves as the guarantor of post-war American equality. Yet the mestizo remains not more than the "little wetback," long an object of repression and racism. Though ostensibly an equal within the family of post-war America, the mestizo is still a horse of a different color.

The Freed Mestizo

The mestizo body functions within a larger discourse that remains deaf to the particularities of how that body gives voice to its experiences. The old Mexican man silently holding his money up to Sarge—attempting to assure his legitimacy as an agent in economic exchange—becomes an image of the voiceless body, an inarticulate symbol within other systems of meaning in which only Sarge and Bick speak. It is this voicelessness in relationship to *mestizaje* that drives Tino Villanueva to respond to the film in his long poem *Scene from the Movie Giant* (1993).

The autobiographical poem examines the effect the film has had on the poet's sense of self and voice. As a sixteen-year-old boy in a darkened movie theater, the poet feels himself in the margin as the fight scene between Bick and Sarge unfolds and "a small dimension of a film . . . became the feature of the whole" (11).[9] His experience of the movie is one of objectification and marginalization embodied by the presence of Juana, the mestiza figure that becomes the scopic object of the plump blonde waitress. More importantly, the waitress' gaze objectifies little Jordie, the "child, half-Anglo, who in Juana's womb / Became all Mexican just the same" (18). Interpellated by the ideology of race, the poet too feels subjected as he remembers himself "[l]ocked into a back-row seat" (12) watching the film. The sense of impotence and silence makes itself sharply felt to the poet who sits "shy of speech, in a stammer / Of light, and breathe a breath not fully breathed . . ." (19). *Mestizaje* becomes a site of disempowerment within the very cultural object—the film *Giant*—that seeks to affirm new racial attitudes in the U.S. Villanueva's poem helps reveal the incongruities of a *mestizaje* that becomes both subject of and subject to discursive inclusion. This incongruity as a position of disempowerment the poet makes clear: "I am on the side / Of Rock Hudson, but carry nothing to the fight" (36).

Empty-handed, the poet comes to find a voice by which to articulate his sense of outrage and silence. The poem becomes a means of a contestation, a site of an empowering counterdiscourse that asserts a hitherto silent voice: "Now I am because I write: I know it in my heart / and know it in the sound iambics of my fist that / mark across the paper with the sun's exacting rays" (50). Through the poet's words and rhythms, the pale flickering light of the movie house becomes transformed into the exacting rays of the sun. The power of Sarge's fist is transformed into the fist of the poet writing his verses. In this assertion of voice, the poet asserts his own sense of subjectivity: "At this moment of being human / (when the teller is the tale being told), / the ash of memory rises that I might speak" (52). Thus the teller and the tale, the writing and the writer, the speaker and his voice emerge as one out of the ashes of memory. A fiery future is created in which a new voice and a new subject arise. The voice, significantly, is mestizo, one that speaks in English as well as Spanish: "O life, this body that speaks, this / repetitious self drawn out from *la vida revivida,* / *vida sacada de cada clamor*" (52).[10] The poem affirms an Other self, one which interweaves formally on a linguistic level the sense of *mestizaje* that it addresses on a thematic level as a site of conflict. This melding envisions *mestizaje* as a means of speaking, an affirmation of voice.

However, a nagging silence persists. What it is that enables the speaker to leap from silent subjected observer to speaking participant in subjectivity remains unspoken. No mention is made how the speaker moves from standing "on the side / Of Rock Hudson, but [carrying] nothing to the fight" (36), to acting as an agent who can extricate his life from battle. The poet seems to arise *sui generis* as a new subject, speaking and making up for what could not be previously spoken. The self that emerges from the poem stands alone, one dissociated from history, seemingly free of those (historico-/politico-) racialized constituencies who sought to intervene against the silencing enacted in *Giant.* The poem does stand as a rejection of dominant forms of thought, does reject the silence imposed upon the disempowered and dispossessed. But there remains absent a very significant material history.

Scene from the Movie Giant seems to be premised on the grandeur of individual achievement, seems to represent a story of personal—not collective—growth. Ironically, the poem offers a vision of the poet rising majestically above adversity as a type of giant finally able to speak. Yet the poet's assertion of an articulate Chicano ethnicity—an assertion manifest clearly in the bilingualism of the poem's closing lines—becomes dissociated from the political and historical engagements of the 1960s and 1970s, which did, indeed, give the mestizo some voice.[11] Historically, the construction of Chicano ethnicity functions both as an agent moving toward political engagement and as a product resulting from political activity. There is a double movement in which ethnicity becomes a subject of and subject to social forces. That is to say, *mestizaje* interpellates new subjects in history. Villanueva's poem obscures this process of identification.

Indian Nations/Emancipations

The work of Oscar "Zeta" Acosta is—in contrast to Villanueva's poem —incessantly concerned with the political processes swirling around the mestizo. Part of his concern centers on the strongly racialized quality of Chicano ethnic identity. Though there is within both Mexican and Chicano nationalist discourses a clear affirmation of the indigenous, one need not search hard to encounter social values that often reject the autochthonous. Acosta's memoir, *The Autobiography of a Brown Buffalo*—which treats his coming of age during and coming to terms with the counterculture of the 1960s, the antiwar movement, and (most centrally) the rise of Chicano nationalism—dwells at length on the devaluation of his indigenous identity. Reminiscing about his childhood in the San Joaquin Valley, Acosta argues for the importance of race within his community: "Everyone in the Valley considers skin color to be of ultimate importance. The tone of one's pigmentation is the fastest and surest way of determining exactly who one is" (86).[12] He goes on to illustrate:

> My mother, for example always referred to my father as *indio* when he'd get drunk [. . .] If our neighbors got drunk at the baptismal parties and danced all night to *norteno* [*sic*] music, they were "acting just like Indians." Once I stuck my tongue in my sister Annie's mouth—I was practicing how to French kiss—and my ma wouldn't let me back in the house until I learned to "quit behaving like an Indian" (86).

As Acosta is taught that promiscuity, licentiousness, drunkenness are Indian traits, he learns to desire those somatic qualities most unlike his. In the fourth grade, for example, he forms a crush on Jane Addison, the blonde,

shy, pigtailed "American" girl with red acne "all over her beautiful face"
(89). His infatuation with Jane Addison arises from a desire for white
bodies that extends to even his grade school teacher, Miss Rollins. She
reads *Robinson Crusoe* to the class while Acosta sits in the front row: "From
this frontline position I could stare as long as I wanted at the long, creamy
legs of the most beautiful teacher I ever had" (89). These desires for Jane
Addison and Miss Rollins (who most appropriately reads the *opus classicus*
of colonization, *Robinson Crusoe*) represent the conflicted colonized condition of the mestizo subject.

From within his desire for creamy thighs, blonde pigtails, blue eyes,
Acosta recognizes his own self: "I grew up a fat, dark Mexican—A Brown
Buffalo" (86). His own mestizo body is a source of torment and disgust,
a site of dissolution and disdain. When the blonde Jane Addison ridicules
Acosta before the entire fourth grade class, he realizes:

> My mother was right. I am nothing but an Indian with sweating body and
> faltering tits that sag at the sight of a young girl's blue eyes. I shall never be
> able to undress in front of a woman's stare. I shall refuse to play basketball
> for fear that some day I might have my jersey ripped from me in front of
> those thousands of pigtailed, blue-eyed girls from America (95).

The mestizo body signifies all that embarrasses the young Acosta and diminishes him before the blonde, blue-eyed American girls he imagines the
source of some pervasive scopic power. Desire for the (white/colonizing/
female) other leads to an identification in which his own (mestizo/colo-
nized/male) body becomes wholly Other. Acosta's desire demarcates a colonized desiring against his self.[13]

Within the various Chicano and Mexicano communities from which
ethnic identities emerge, the devaluation of the indigenous, of the racial
Other, carries with it a potent charge. The struggle against this devaluation
represents one of the sources of Chicano anti-authoritarian contestation.
To a degree, the anti-indigenous trajectory of Mexicano/Chicano practice
is dismissed as so much false consciousness in Acosta's second book, *The
Revolt of the Cockroach People* (1973).

At a central point of the novel, Acosta participates in a three-day fast
protesting the arrest of twenty-one Chicano demonstrators in Los Angeles. During the fast, Acosta is approached by three teenage Chicanas who
crawl into his tent and under his blanket. Soon political solidarity turns to
something else:

I caress a leg and it holds still, waiting for my hand. It is firm and soft and warm. I reach for a soft arm. It comes into mine easily. There is no hesitation. And then a moist lip to my ear [. . .] I reach for a breast. It is small. Wonderfully small and firm. It fits into my palm. A brown pear in my hand. God Almighty! *This* is the revolution (89).[14]

The reclamation of the mestizo (more significantly, *mestiza*) body initiates a simultaneous process of liberation and containment. This is the revolution in that Acosta's exclamations of appreciation for the mestiza body represent a transformation of sexual desire. The mestiza body returns not as a site of repugnance but of longing. At the same time, the reclamation of the mestiza body enacts simple objectification. The narrative itself highlights the dissembled body parts which comprise Acosta's objects of desire: a leg, an arm, a lip, a breast.

Reasserting ties to the mestizo represents not just an objectification of the body, but also a reinscription of impoverished social roles. As the night wears on with the three girls, Acosta's thoughts turn from the revolutionary to the domestic. All he wants to know about these Chicana protesters is whether they can cook and clean. As a result, after the fast, the three join him to set up house in his small apartment on Sixth Street. Acosta remains the revolutionary, fighting the battles for Chicano nationalism, and the three teenagers become Adelitas, cooking for their revolutionary warrior and providing physical solace.

Throughout Acosta's books there is an incessant, anxious assertion of masculinity, misogyny, and homophobia. So if Chicano identity is to be premised on an embrace of the mestiza/o body, some key questions arise. Does the body become a locus for liberation? The embrace of the mestizo self serves as liberation for whom under what circumstances? Does an embrace of the mestizo or mestiza body always embody a gesture of liberation? Which is to say, is it enough to argue that Chicano ethnic identity be premised on an affirmation of racial hybridity?

In Chicano cultural production, the mestizo body stands as a text, a site of ideological contestation. There often occurs an easy elision of the body with culture, the body with political practice, the body with an affirmation of alterity and resistance. As Acosta's narratives reveal, the affirmation of mestizo bodies too easily becomes the whole of the revolution, a revolution where long-rehearsed and repressive social scripts, unexamined, return. *Mestizaje*, on neither a cultural nor a racial level, guarantees contestation. Only a critical and constantly questioning deployment of *mestizaje* as a contestatory strategy can enable a move beyond that represented by Acosta's embrace of the mestiza body.

Resurrection

The limitations of Acosta's actions are not restricted to issues of gender. The mestizo as well as the mestiza body gets subsumed by his adherence to a nationalist discourse. In a rather intricate middle section of his book, Acosta recounts the trials of the Fernandez family whose son, Robert, has been found dead in his Los Angeles County jail cell. The sheriffs claim his death is a suicide; the family claims Robert was murdered. They contact Acosta who in turn persuades the county coroner, Thomas Noguchi (whom some may remember by the sobriquet "Coroner to the Stars") to conduct an inquest into the death.

As the family's representative, Acosta is present at the autopsy of the exhumed body. Wherever discoloration appears, that portion of tissue must be removed for microscopic examination to determine whether trauma had occurred before or after death (the body again a signifier). As the corpse has already begun to decompose, there are a number of discolored sites requiring removal. Acosta acts as supervisor:

> I cannot believe what is happening. I lean over the body and look at the ears. Can they get a notch from the left one
> Slit-slit-slice blut! . . . into a jar.
> [. . .]
> "Would you please try the legs? . . . Those big splotches on the left."
> "How about the chin?"
> "Here, on the left side of the face."
> "What's this on the neck?"
> "Try this little spot here."
> "We're this far into it . . . Get a piece from the stomach there."
> Cut here. Slice there. Here. There. Cut, cut, cut! Slice slice slice! And into a jar. Soon we have a whole row of jars with little pieces of meat (101–102).

The body in disintegration. One narrative—Robert as a mestizo man, as an outlaw, as a member of a caring family—gives way to another—Robert as a series of specimens, as a murder victim, as a subject of oppression. The body as signifier shifts quite dramatically from one context to the next. Consequently, the narrator exclaims: *"There is no face!* [. . .] The face is hanging down the back of the head. The face is a mask. The mouth is where the brain . . . the nose is at the back of the neck. The hair is the ears. The brown nose is hanging where the neck . . ." (103). The elliptical narrative recounts the loss of identity, the disunion of the body so that no body remains, just jars of specimens and dissociated parts hanging in macabre juxtaposition. The disjointed narrative found in this section of the book conjoins with Robert's dissembled body to tell a story of simultaneous destruction and creation.

This section closes with Acosta addressing directly "the cut up brown body of that Chicano boy." He tells the corpse:

Forgive me, Robert, for the sake of the living brown. Forgive me and forgive me and forgive me. I am no worse off than you. For the rest of my born days, I will suffer the knowledge of your death and your second death and your ashes to my ashes, your dust to my dust. . . . Goodbye, *ese*. Viva la Raza! (104).

Acosta imagines a communion with the dead boy where ash melds with ash, dust with dust. The individual body dissolves in order to forge a political body of "the living brown." The mestizo body meets its destruction and simultaneous resurrection, a resurrection enacted in another form. This finally is the great Chicano nationalist dream: to forge socio-political bodies out of overdetermined brown bodies, bodies already situated in so many disempowering positions of subalternity. There is no coming together of that inextricable contradiction suggested by the close of Acosta's text. The narrative imagines resurrection: the mortal finality of "Goodbye, *ese*," juxtaposed with the war cry "Viva la Raza!" The resurrection is purely rhetorical. Acosta seeks to give voice again to the mestizo body—exhumed, deceased, dissembled. This voice can only be heard within the register of a Chicano nationalist discourse. However, beyond death—despite the most fervent wish—there sounds nothing but an airless, silent void.

Difference and *Différance*

The desire to move beyond oppression leads to a type of delusion, an impossible resurrection. Acosta's narrative gives voice to the mestizo body only through pre-established oppositional politics. The mestizo is therefore buried in history, the voice of a resistant but nevertheless contained revolutionary actor. More recent discourses on the mestizo open onto other vistas. The mestizo within a poststructuralist inflected cultural criticism represents an image of alterity and liberation. From this view, the mestizo risks becoming a mark of absolute transformation, a figure of discursive dislocation, a free-floating signifier. In the attempt to uncouple ethnic identity from biological essentialism, the idea of *mestizaje* often gets cut free from its historical and social moorings. *Mestizaje* becomes a radical means of undoing meaning itself; ethnic identity becomes only a means of escaping prescribed identity formations.

The French critic Jean-Luc Nancy, for example, discusses *mestizaje* as a supreme strategy of discursive disruption:

> Singular existences, points of *mestizaje*, identities are made/cut of singularities, places, moments, languages, passions, skins, accents, laws, prayers, cries, steps, bursts. They are in turn the singular events of these compositions and cuts. Like any proper name, *Chicano* does not appropriate any meaning: it exposes an event, a singular sense. As soon as such a name arises—cut—it exposes all of us to it, to the cut of sense that it is, that it makes, far beyond all signifying. "Chicano" breaks into my identity as a "gringo." It cuts into and re-composes it. It makes us all *mestizo* (121).[15]

By thus recasting the mestizo as a perpetually new subject, Nancy, as Norma Alarcón points out, constructs "a reobjectification of the 'new subject,' a reification or a denial of the historical meaning posited by the differential signifier" (131).[16] A mestizo identity ceases being an agent in history and instead becomes pure signifier, endlessly transgressive, ever unstable. Detached from the historically bound discourses which both form and delimit Chicanismo, *mestizaje* emerges as a sign of absolute *différance*.

Neither wholly bound by the repeated drone of prescriptive discourses nor asserting an absolute emancipation, the poetry of Lorna Dee Cervantes offers a different vision of *mestizaje*. *Mestizaje* in her work represents a complicated cultural condition that both explores interstitiality and asserts historical connection. Her work does more, then, than attempt to move toward a borderlands identity. The poetic imagination envisions a self already present. *Mestizaje* becomes something more than a movement away or a movement toward, something other than an interstitial hanging that serves to mark the desire to become but yet represents a not-being. The poetry affirms something that already is, is other but not purely Other. That is, it asserts a self that has a sense of self and a sense of language neither fully foreign nor yet wholly familiar, but also foreign and also familiar.

Cervantes' poem, "Crow," articulates one aspect of this complex vision. The speaker identifies, in a moment of poetic flight, with a crow startled from a field by a rifle shot:

> She started and shot from the pine,
> then brilliantly settled in the west field
> and sunned herself purple.
>
> I saw myself: twig and rasp, dry
> in breath and ammonia smelling.
> Women taught me to clean
>
> and then build my own house.
> Before men came they whispered,
> Know good polished oak.
>
> Learn hammer and Phillips.
> Learn socket and rivet. I ran
> over rocks and gravel they placed
>
> by hand, leaving burly arguments
> to fester the bedrooms. With my best jeans,
> a twenty and a shepherd pup, I ran
>
> flushed and shadowed by no one
> alone I settled stiff in mouth
> with the words women gave me.[17]

The poem asserts a subject self-sufficient and articulate. The speaker identifies with both herself and other, here represented by the crow. Simultaneously, she identifies with both the feminized role of cleaning a house and the masculinized role of making it. Not mute before worlds of exclusion (neither Spanish nor English, neither male nor female), the poetic voice affirms a self that is both articulate and premised on the assertion of women as the givers of speech. (This brings us quite a distance from Acosta's representation of women solely as sexual mates, food makers, and care takers.) The poem presents an affirmation of a hybrid identity within and without pre-established discursive orders.

As this and other poems by Cervantes suggest, the mestizo body is not a hybrid entity holding out the possibility of what is to come. That ambitious prophetic power cannot be claimed by bodies already so overwritten by historical discourses. Instead, the mestizo body offers a vision of cultural development very much unfolding in—and so constrained by—a contradictory and complicated present. It would be unwise to cathect on that body as some locus of social transformation. Yet one stands in danger of doing just that by highlighting the contestatory powers of cultural *mestizaje* as somehow the result of racial hybridity. Instead, the mestizo body becomes a signifier continually discovered and recovered.

Ada Savin, in her analysis of Lorna Dee Cervantes' poetry, argues that Bakhtin's notion of dialogized discourse allows one to explore more fully the "whole field of bi- or interlingual (Chicano) literature" (215).[18] In bilingual Chicano poetry, Savin asserts, "The alternate use of Spanish and English [. . .] is indicative of a process of identity search through a dialogization of the two cultures" (217). Thus the multilingualism of Chicano literature "is necessarily of the existential kind; their poetry acts out the living contact between the cultures in contact and their respective languages" (217). Due to this "contact" between the Mexican and American, Cervantes "is confronted day after day with an ambivalent reality which throws her identity into permanent question. The historico-political context is burdensome, the cultural conflict is painfully alive" (218). The devaluation of the Mexican by the American, the rejection of one by the other creates a sense of loss. As such, Savin suggests, Cervantes' poetry can only mark an endlessly interstitial condition of estrangement from self and other.

The equation of the mestizo body with a cultural *mestizaje* is premised upon a lack: the mestizo is neither Mexican nor American, neither Spanish nor English, neither Indian nor European, neither foreign nor familiar. The diminishment in this model is obvious.

The point that needs emphasis is that the mestizo body stands not as a site of absence. On the contrary, it is a place of over-determination. Too many discourses engage in a contested dialogue seeking to claim the significance and meaning and function of the mestizo. Cervantes' poem, "Refugee Ship," serves as a literary example of this over-determination:

Mama raised me without language.
I'm orphaned from my Spanish name.
The words are foreign, stumbling
on my tongue. I see in the mirror
my reflection: bronzed skin, black hair.[19]

The bronzed body, the dark hair should signal a connection to the mestizo name, the Spanish language. In her analysis of Cervantes' poetry, Savin suggests that the lack of linguistic ability marks an estrangement between the signifier (the mestiza body) and the signified (mestizo culture). Significantly, "Refugee Ship" is the only poem in the collection, *Emplumada*, that Cervantes has translated into Spanish. Thus, while Savin suggests the poem marks a feeling of "overwhelming estrangement from one's essential identity markers; name, physical appearance, and language" (218), the two poems—one written in English, the other translated into Spanish— taken together suggest something else. While not necessarily a manifestation of socio-cultural wholeness and completion, the two poems do represent something more dynamic, more empowered, and more deliberate at work than an essential estrangement. The poems mark the body as a site where linguistic, familial, racial, and cultural vectors cross. These do not serve as essential identity markers. Instead, they form signs—sites of discourse—that charge the mestizo body with a number of meanings.

As the body is an over-determined signifier, the cultural text too needs to be understood as a multi-dimensional system of signification. The double-voiced text does not only undermine, as Savin suggests, "the official authoritative discourse, whether mainstream American or Mexican" (217). That is, it does not simply hang suspended between two worlds to which it does not belong and into which it cannot dissolve. It moves among those worlds. Chicano culture as a form of *mestizaje* does not mark a paradigmatic quest for self-definition: it enacts that self-definition in multiple ways.

The Mestizo Voice

This infinite remolding of the mestizo body—the recasting of the mestizo voice—is perforce delimited. History traces the ways in which discourses about race, ethnicity, sexuality, gender bring together language and power. Both circumscribe the social and physical worlds in which historical subjects move. In this sense, *mestizaje* represents a subjectivity no different from any other.

As the mestizo is given voice, as meaning is ascribed to notions of *mestizaje*, one can trace numerous transformations in the significance of the term. Meaning moves from the racial to the cultural, from the body to the text. In this circulation of significance, patterns emerge that reveal the limitations in the way *mestizaje* has been employed. It can be situated within a pluralist vision of participatory politics, within an androcentric ethnic-nationalist discourse, within a radically disengaged project of post-structural liberation. Each position charges the mestizo body with a different significance. Each also ultimately leaves the mestizo body voiceless.

The mestizo body, transformed and transmogrified, yet speaks. Mestizo bodies signify precisely as they are bound in and bounded by the social and historical conditions in which they act. The mestizo body serves as signifier, but not as fully free-floating, not as endlessly regressive, not as fully transgressive.

The face of the mestizo is a mask, one that appears simultaneously real and unreal. The body of the mestizo is one created and dissolved, one that changes function and significance as it moves through different systems of exchange. The voice of the mestizo speaks another language, a language in creation, a language suspended—yes—between English and Spanish. But the voice of the mestizo also sounds the depths of cultural transformation, tests the limits of social configurations, articulates the formation of culture in transition. It changes register and pitch depending on where and why it speaks, to whom and which systems of power it addresses. The voice of the mestizo sounds that which, finally, speaks an agency otherwise ever silenced.

Notes

1. Within a Mexican nationalist discourse, Malintzín is known as La Malinche, and she represents an image of betrayal. Octavio Paz discusses the sense of violation inherent to Mexican self-identity in *The Labyrinth of Solitude*. He writes: "The *Chingada* is the Mother forcibly opened, violated or deceived. The *hijo de la Chingada* is the offspring of violation, of abduction or deceit. If we compare this expression with the Spanish *hijo de puta* (son of a whore), the difference is immediately obvious. To the Spaniard, dishonor consists in being the son of a woman who voluntarily surrenders herself: a prostitute. To the Mexican it consists in being the fruit of violation" (1950: 79–80). For a discussion of rape as a trope in the articulation of Chicano (and particularly Chicana) cultural identity, see María Herrera-Sobek's "The Politics of Rape: Sexual Transgression in Chicana Fiction," and Norma Alarcón's "Traddutora, Traditora: A Paradigmatic Figure of Chicana Feminism." Mary Louise Pratt discusses the important role Chicana writers have played in reclaiming the figure of La Malinche "as a vital, resonant site through which to respond to androcentric ethno-nationalism and to claim a gendered oppositional identity and history" (861). See "'Yo Soy La Malinche': Chicana Writers and the Poetics of Ethnonationalism."

2. Historian John Chávez asserts that "[w]e can date to 1848 the modern Chicano image of the Southwest as a lost land" (43). See *The Lost Land: The Chicano Image of the Southwest*. From a cultural perspective, Raymund Paredes argues that "[t]he great divide in Chicano history is the year 1848 when the Treaty of Guadalupe Hidalgo ended twenty-one months of

warfare between Mexico and the United States" (36). See "The Evolution of Chicano Literature." Luís Leal and Pepe Barrón note that the period between 1848 and 1910 "was the time during which Chicano literature laid the basis on which it was later to develop" (18). See "Chicano Literature: An Overview," 9–32.

3. "Aztlán" names, according to Aztec legend, the utopian homeland from which the Mexica migrated southward toward the central plateau of Mexico in 820 C.E. It was a term redeployed during the Chicano Movement in order to crystallize in one term the history of dispossession endured by Mexicans, Mexican-Americans, and Chicanos alike. Angie Chabram and Rosa Linda Fregoso critique the elision of Chicanismo with the types of racial essentialism found in Chicano nationalist discourses. These critics rightly reject the essentialism often invoked in the name of Aztlán. See "Chicana/o Cultural Representations: Reframing Alternative Critical Discourses." Rather than abandon Aztlán altogether, Daniel Alarcón argues, one should consider its multidimensional textuality—Aztlán as palimpsest—in order to make of it more than an empty symbol. Agreeing with Chabram and Fregoso that Aztlán as a monolithic narrative requires deconstruction, Alarcón observes that "a fluid, continuously changing narrative or model is needed" (39). See his essay "The Aztec Palimpsest: Toward a New Understanding of Aztlán, Cultural Identity and History."

4. See Chela N. J. Sandoval, "U.S. Third World Feminism: The Theory and Method of Oppositional Consciousness in the Postmodern World."

5. Gayatri Spivak, "Theory in the Margin."

6. Richard Meyer, "Rock Hudson's Body."

7. The song, a top ten hit in its day, celebrates the beauty of a multiracial African-American woman: not the "white" but the "yellow" Rose of Texas. As a cultural text, the music serves to underscore the national political battle being waged over the role of race in a new post-war America.

8. Two other mestizos appear in the movie: the young Mexican Angel, played by Sal Mineo, and Dr. Guerra. Angel proves himself to be the cowboy Bick's own son never wants to be. Unfortunately, he is killed fighting for the United States during World War II. At Angel's funeral, Bick, in a gesture of national reconciliation, carries the flag of Texas to offer Angel's family. Dr. Guerra, at the behest of Leslie, sets up a clinic in the Mexican shantytown where the workers on Bick's ranch live. He serves as the inspiration for Jordie, Jr., to become a doctor. Significantly, once Jordan makes this decision, Dr. Guerra never again appears in the film. In both cases, the mestizo disappears behind a white presence.

9. *Scene from the Movie Giant.* All further citations will be made parenthetically.

10. "O life, this body that speaks, this / repetitive self drawn out from *renewed life / life taken from each battle.*"

11. This is not meant as a critique of Tino Villanueva as a poet, as a subject, or as an agent in the development of Chicanismo. Anyone familiar with the history of Chicano culture will know that Villanueva was one of the first and most valiant writers to articulate Chicano identity through his poetry. His commitment and sincerity cannot be questioned. Rather, the focus here is to sharpen a critique of mestizo agency as manifested within *Scene*.

12. Oscar "Zeta" Acosta, *The Autobiography of a Brown Buffalo.* All further citations will be made parenthetically.

13. Acosta enacts the kind of dysfunctional desire required by colonization. As Homi K. Bhabha asserts in his analysis of Frantz Fanon's writing: "the black man wants the objectifying confrontation with otherness; in the colonial psyche there is an unconscious disavowal of

the negating, splitting moment of desire" (51). See "Interrogating identity: Frantz Fanon and the postcolonial prerogative." See also "Remembering Fanon: Self, Psyche, and the Colonial Position."

14. Oscar "Zeta" Acosta, *The Revolt of the Cockroach People*. All further citations will be made parenthetically.

15. Jean-Luc Nancy, "Cut Throat Sun."

16. Norma Alarcón, "Conjugating Subjects: The Heteroglossia of Essence and Resistance."

17. From *Emplumada*, 19.

18. See Savin, "Bilingualism and Dialogism: Another Reading of Lorna Dee Cervantes's Poetry." All further citations will be made parenthetically.

19. From *Emplumada*, 41.

CHAPTER 10

CONSTITUTING HYBRIDITY AS HYBRID

Métis Canadian and Mexican American Formations

Monika Kaup

North America, like Latin America and the Caribbean, also has produced new peoples of mixed ancestry, i.e., Métis Canadians and Mexican Americans. Yet, as historians Jacqueline Peterson and Jennifer S. H. Brown point out, the existence of mixed-race peoples has been lost in the racial polarization of North America, where "both the historical process of mixing and the resultant peoples themselves have been obscured. Persons of mixed Indian and European ancestry who, for whatever reasons, are not regarded as either Indian or white are referred to, often pejoratively, as 'halfbreeds,' 'breeds,' 'mixed-bloods,' 'Métis,' 'michif,' or 'non-status Indian.' Collectively, they are characterized by an almost universal landlessness and an oppressive poverty, conditions which historically have inhibited political combination or action" (Peterson and Brown 4). In other words, in history, mixed-race peoples have been marginalized as Other like aboriginal peoples, and their economic position is equally impoverished. Similarly, in language, the erasure of cross-racial mixing, or creolization,[1] is as striking: as Françoise Lionnet points out, there is no English equivalent for *métissage* (French) or *mestizaje* (Spanish): "One can translate Métis by 'halfbreed' or 'mixed-blood' but these expressions always carry a negative connotation, precisely because they imply biological abnormality. . . ." "The Anglo-American consciousness," Lionnet continues, "seems unable to accommodate miscegenation positively through language. It is a serious blind spot of the English language . . . another way of making invisible, of negating, the existence" of mixed-race peoples (Lionnet 327–328).

Evidently, this situation has now changed, as North American literary critical and historical discourse has discovered the differential logic of contact and border zones, liminal identity, syncretism, hybridity, transculturation, in-betweenness (and this list of related formula could go on). Given this vogue for plural cultures and border writing,[2] it would seem that the "new peoples" of North America, too, are finally emerging from their long public invisibility. The present euphoria about hybridity and liminality advocates that we reject "bad" ideas such as cultural essentialism, static foundationalism and linearity, binary thinking, roots-oriented identity politics, cultural nationalism, cultural authenticity and purity (here, too, the list remains open). Accept that culture and identity are porous and have neither a unifying center nor an outer limit. Replace conceptual walls with bridges: the forces of contagion and continuity across boundaries are stronger than lines of division. In sum, the poetics of (autonomous) identity must yield to the poetics of relationality. At the level of community, this means that nation-identity is replaced by models of pluralistic communities.[3]

I borrow the term poetics of relation from Martiniquan philosopher Eduoard Glissant's work of the same title, *Poetics of Relation*. One of the foremost theoreticians of hybridity writing in the Americas today, Glissant advocates that cultural diversity, or relation-identity, be viewed as a dynamic process of crossing and continuous formation. Glissant celebrates the unfinished, open-ended, fluid nature of hybrid identity and its mongrel forms of expression. His rejection of boundaries, single origins, and static definitions stands in direct contrast to nation-identity, conventionally associated with permanence, roots, linearity, and territorial boundaries. Root-identity, or nation-identity, as Glissant explains, looks back to the past, while relation-identity anticipates the future. Relationality celebrates the forces of the present, the triumph of processes of becoming over-established and complete "being," what has been formed in the past (*Poetics of Relation* 143–144). If nationalism is thus vulnerable to charges of nostalgia, hybridity is open to charges of utopianism. The utopian element in hybridity inheres in the notion that transnational cultures, which are discontinuous and unstable systems, can survive and are strong enough to neutralize disturbances from outside. Hybridity has a bad memory, because change prevails over permanence and continuity.

The following discussion looks at two texts by mixed-race writers from

North America, Gloria Anzaldúa's *Borderlands/La Frontera: The New Mestiza* (1987) and Maria Campbell's *Halfbreed* (1973). What constructs of hybridity have emerged from the "new peoples" of mixed ancestry—Canadian Métis and Chicano mestizos—who originate in North America, specifically in the North American West? My goal is to show that, for conceptual and historical reasons, hybrid discourse by North American Métis and mestizo writers cannot be "pure" as defined by Glissant—if the reader will excuse this oxymoron. Instead, we find that tropes of Métis and mestizo identity flow back and forth between the poetics of nation and the poetics of relation.

To pursue my question, I will first follow the leads offered by Glissant, taking a look at Caribbean discourse. As is well known, Caribbean culture, more than any other region in the Americas, is defined by cultural syncretism.[4] My purpose in approaching North American mixed-race texts via the Caribbean is to argue the following: it is not helpful to understand hybridity as a style of identity or culture in abstract and universal terms, thus disregarding the specifics of regional setting and origins. Hybridity is rooted in the local, in its place and history, and it is never One. In *Colonial Desire: Hybridity in Theory, Culture and Race*, Robert Young writes, "Hybridity is itself an example of hybridity, of a doubleness that both brings together, fuses, but also maintains separation" (22).[5] Like Young's study, this discussion of Métis Canadian and Mexican American cross-cultural constructs argues that hybridity itself is hybrid. But, because hybridity is a relatively new concept, and perhaps because hybridity by definition stresses relationality over finite identity, it invites abstract reflections on cross-cultural exchanges. A problematic notion, as I hope to show.

Aquatic Borderlands: A Caribbean Grammar of Hybridity

Applying Caribbean theories of hybridity to the borderlands of the North American West directs attention to the dimension of geography. While there is no doubt that Caribbean discourse is far ahead in inventing a positive discourse of hybridity, it is also clear that this is due in part to the distinct features of Caribbean geography. The Caribbean is an aquatic, not a continental culture. Geography and history in the Caribbean have jointly promoted a fluid network of multiple creolizing cultures. In his influential work, *The Repeating Island: The Caribbean and the Postmodern Perspective*, which explores Caribbean culture as a realm of heterogeneous and dynamic cultural exchanges, Cuban theorist Antonio Benítez-Rojo identifies the sea as the natural setting that generates fluid cultures—a fertile "soil" for hybridity, precisely because it is not earth, but water. The culture of the Caribbean, he writes, "is not terrestrial but aquatic, a sinuous culture where time unfolds irregularly. . . . The Caribbean is the natural and indispensable realm of marine currents, of waves, of folds and double-folds, of fluidity and sinuosity" (Benítez-Rojo 11). Benítez-Rojo offers a "thick description" of Caribbean peoples as "peoples of the sea." Water is one of his master tropes through which he decodes the polyrhythmic patterns of Caribbean hybridity.

Similarly, in *Caribbean Discourse*, Edouard Glissant speaks of the Caribbean as "the estuary of the Americas"—the natural confluence of cultures (*Caribbean Discourse* 139). The two epigraphs in Edouard Glissant's *Poetics of Relation* read, "Sea is history (Derek Walcott)" and "The unity is submarine (Edward Kamau Brathwaite)." Like Glissant, Benítez-Rojo charts Caribbean marine geography as the perfect embodiment of deconstruction—a decentered and limitless field of mobile signifiers. In contrast to the centralizing Mediterranean, which is bounded by nations and shores, Benítez-Rojo argues, the Caribbean "has the virtue of having neither a boundary nor a center. Thus the Caribbean flows outward past the limits of its own sea with a vengeance . . ." (*The Repeating Island* 4). Among the confluence of the Anglophone, Francophone, and Hispanophone, including African, Asian, and European cultures, no single constituent "island" dominates the archipelago. The center is empty, occupied by the polymorphous sea, whose marine currents, as both theorists suggest, disseminate and absorb cultural influences to and from places as far away as Africa, Europe, and Asia.

It is easy to see why marine topography lends itself to a grammar of liminality.[6] A large body of water functions more complexly than a vast expanse of land: on the one hand, like land, the sea creates distance, isolating the island territories of the archipelago from each other and the continental mainland. On the other hand, however, it undoes the distance through marine currents and flows, which form underwater bridges and routes across the empty space. Land resists mobility—overland transportation requires roads or rivers; roads first need to be built. Water, by contrast, favors mobility—unlike a landscape, a seascape can be traversed unhindered and in innumerable directions, without requiring the construction of travel infrastructure.

Hybridity and Borderlandscapes? The Continental Setting

While marine geography lends itself naturally to a cultural poetics of relation, mainland borderlands pale in comparison to the grammar of fluidity that an aquatic culture like the Caribbean can offer. Territoriality favors nation-identity, providing natural conditions for drawing boundaries, creating dualisms, establishing domain and ownership of space. Territory is the natural setting for foundational identity, sea, the natural setting for fluid relational identity. The vocabulary of landscape offers terms such as borders (lines of division), frontiers (a more blurred line referring to the edge between two cultures), and borderlands, signifying an intermediate space between cultures, or crossroads of cultures, which, for lack of a better phrase, Gloria Anzaldúa calls a "third country."[7] Yet in fact, in-betweenness, as the Caribbean example shows, is not a "country" at all, but the very negation of the closure and centralized order that defines nations.

This said, how can one create a new vocabulary and morphology of borderlandscapes (notice how language limits the very attempt to phrase the question) that is not based on territory and land? Or perhaps, a borderlands discourse that is sensitive to the "forgetting" of water, as we might say, echoing French feminist philosopher Luce Irigaray, who has responded similarly to foundationalist Western philosophies that draw attention to the repression of fluidity and non-solid elements.[8] Epistemologically, continental theorists of *métissage* and *mestizaje* obviously face an uphill struggle against the dualist and foundationalist grammar of landscape. And, to recall "halfbreed" and "miscegenation," this problem is compounded by the use of English, which offers parallel divisive concepts of mixed-race identity.

Cycles of Conquest: Métis and Mestizo Borderlands in North America

If mainland geography promotes nation-identity rather than relation-identity, what of the historical dimension? The borderlands of the North American West have been formed in a historical process historian Edward Spicer has termed "cycles of conquest." Centuries after Spain and France conquered and colonized aboriginal America, nineteenth-century Anglo America's and Anglo Canada's expansion into the Western half of the continent initiated a new cycle of conquest. In 1867, with Canadian Confederation,[9] and in 1848, with the Treaty of Guadalupe Hidalgo terminating the Mexican American War, national and cultural boundaries were redrawn. Fur trade Canada and the Spanish, later the Mexican, frontier had promoted *mestizaje* and *métissage*, favoring the inclusion of aboriginal peoples into colonial society and the creation of new peoples of mixed ancestry. This social order was destroyed when Anglo European nations annexed western territories. Anglo Canadian and Anglo American frontiers were superimposed on the older Spanish and French settlements and territories.

The cultural meeting-ground fostered under the older French and Spanish colonial regimes collapsed, destroying the flourishing lifeworlds of métis and mestizo peoples. In the memory of the Métis and Mexican peoples in the North American West, a memory that, as we shall see, gets transcribed in the works of Anzaldúa and Campbell, the nineteenth century marks the tragic decline and fall of their worlds. The beginning of Anglo American and Anglo Canadian history in the West coincides with the dispossession and displacement of mixed-race peoples. When the Métis became Canadian citizens and Mexicans became Mexican Americans, they survived, but the price of survival was life on the margins under a new government and in the new era of an agrarian West. The hybrid became Other—what had been developing, for decades and centuries, as a distinct borderlands culture, a third culture neither Indian nor European, was crushed. On the North American continent, relation-identity fell victim to the binary regime of nation-identity.

The nineteenth-century trauma of displacement has permanently affected Chicano and métis discourse in ways that I will discuss in more detail in the remainder of this paper. But, most crucially—and this is the main point of my argument—the memory of marginalization has placed Chicano and métis discourse forever on the line between the poetics of nation and the poetics of relation. Because of what happened in 1848 and 1871, hybrid discourse by North American Métis and mestizo writers cannot be "pure"—if "openness to otherness," according to Cuban critic Gustavo Pérez Firmat,[10] defines the hybrid. According to Glissant in *Caribbean Discourse*, the dimension of time in a cross-cultural poetics is not linear, not defined by stable roots in the past:

> To confront time is, therefore, for us to deny its linear structure. . . . We do not see it stretch into our past (calmly carry us into the future) but implode in us in clumps, transported in fields of oblivion where we must, with difficulty and pain, put it all back together if we wish to make contact with ourselves and express ourselves (*Caribbean Discourse* 145).

Glissant's rigorous assertion that relation-identity must embrace the pain of oblivion to remain open to the creolization, "the unceasing process of transformation" (*Caribbean Discourse* 142), sets a standard of "pure" hybridity that does not translate into the North American continental setting. Rather, Chicano and métis discourse testify strongly to a search for lost time and resist oblivion. To counter conquest and dispossession by a foreign nation, both mixed-race peoples have developed subaltern and resistant nationalisms. A defensive affirmation of legitimacy in the voice of nationalism—through claims to Native origin, territorial rights, nostalgia for a lost past and homeland—generally underwrites present Chicano and Métis texts. Indeed, the relation-identity articulated in Mexican American and Métis Canadian discourse is permanently infected with its Other, nation-identity.

To gather up the strands of the argument as it has developed so far, it is important to keep in mind all three factors—geographical, conceptual, and historical—as they culminate in interrupting the flow of transculturation in North America. The goal is to keep all these dimensions alive and present, and to avoid lapsing into the extremes of historicism or geographic and discursive essentialism. The geographical position, for instance, agrees with the logic of the historical process: without doubt, borderlands cultures situated on a large land mass are more vulnerable to annexation and invasion than hybrid cultures located on islands, as in the Caribbean. In the Caribbean, external domination by foreign metropoles, such as the U.S. or Europe in the nineteenth and twentieth centuries, while strong, rarely amounted to permanent annexation and seamless territorial incorporation by a foreign nation, as was the case in the North American West. Creolization prevailed as the dominant cultural force in the Caribbean, critics Michael Dash and Gustavo Pérez Firmat agree, because of the insularity of Caribbean islands, the extermination of the aboriginal population and settlement by various immigrant peoples.[11] Despite their economic and political dependency, even politically dependent islands like Puerto Rico and Martinique never faced a total threat to cultural autonomy comparable to the mixed-blood peoples on the continent. In ways that confuse the neat divisions between nation-identity and relation-identity suggested by Caribbean theories of hybridity, the survival of bridge cultures in the Caribbean was made possible by the legal sovereignty of many of the small island nations.

Thus, this comparative approach and focus on regional specifics of borderlands and mixed-race peoples in the Americas suggests surprising interdependencies between national autonomy and creolization. Viewed

spatially, islands are the most fertile settings for cultural borderlands because the surrounding sea, unlike land, creates a non-hierarchical relation
between the hybrid self and colonial Other—by placing external forces
at a safe distance.[12] Thus, while hybridity disavows exclusion and insularity as the logic of nation-identity, hybridity may in fact speak the voice
of nation (democratic nationalism, to be precise) in another guise.[13] For
"openness to otherness" assumes that the meeting-ground between cultures is more or less level. Ultimately, hybridity requires cultural freedom,
independence, and territorial integrity: it can only flourish in a third space
maintained intact and distinct from the home bases of contributing cultures—as on an island that keeps absorbing newcomers from elsewhere.
Without this freedom and independence, the logic of conquest destroys
the democratic logic of relation.

Gloria Anzaldúa's Borderlands and "New *Mestiza*"

Gloria Anzaldúa's theory of *mestizaje* in *Borderlands/La Frontera: The New
Mestiza* (1987) counters the classic definition of mestizo Mexico by Octavio
Paz in *Labyrinth of Solitude*. This touches upon a key difference in the history of the mixed-race Mexico and the Canadian Métis. While métis and
mestizo cultures share the experience of nineteenth-century conquest and
dispossession by expanding Anglo European nations, the Métis originated
in the peaceful union of fur traders and Indian tribes. Mestizo Mexico,
on the other hand, looks back to the memory of violent origins. In *Labyrinth of Solitude*, Octavio Paz traced the national consciousness of his mestizo nation to the trauma of *mestizaje*'s violent beginnings. Paz diagnosed
Mexico's neurosis as its "solitude," or its hermetic withdrawal from the
world in fearful reaction to being open and vulnerable to the Other. "The
question of origins," Paz writes, "is the central secret of our anxiety and
anguish" (Paz 80). In "The Sons of La Malinche," Paz discusses the myth
of colonial Mexico's legendary founding figures, the union of Cortés and
La Malinche, of Native woman and conquistador, as an oedipal family romance. La Malinche, the Native mother of the mestizo nation, betrayed
her people by her alliance with Cortés. She is therefore reviled as scapegoat
and traitor by her mestizo children, who, at the same time, fear and reject their Spanish father. Disavowing both biological ancestors, the raped
and abject Native woman and the colonizer-father, Paz's mestizo "sons"
are orphaned by the violence of conquest at the moment of their birth.
    Clearly, Paz' psychological profile of the mixed-blood "sons of La Ma-

linche" follows not the concept of relation-identity, but what hybridity transcends—the binary logic of power, submission, and domination. Paz' figuration of mestizo Mexico clings to nation-identity; his tragic mestizo is obsessed by the past, genealogy, and ancestral roots. Paz' mestizo is unfree—incapable of "openness to otherness," incapable of embracing change, or Glissant's "unceasing process of transformation" (*Caribbean Discourse* 142), failing, in other words, to realize the utopian potential for creolization that his mixed ancestry has given him.

Anzaldúa's book is the most sophisticated attempt by a mixed-race American writer to celebrate *mestizaje* as relation-identity, countering both Paz's closed model of the tragic mestizo and the North American negation of race mixture.[14] *Borderlands/La Frontera: The New Mestiza* is comparable in its comprehensive, manifesto-like nature to Glissant's work. Although Anzaldúa does not engage Paz directly, her work is a feminist response to the male myth of La Malinche, which attacks the scapegoating of women as traitors in the discourse of Mexican nationalism. *Borderlands* is as much about women as it is about *mestizaje;* we cannot separate her poetics of syncretism from her poetics of Chicana feminism. This Chicana praise song of hybridity furnishes further evidence for the notion that hybridity is most helpfully understood through case-by-case detail, rather than in the abstract. Anzaldúa writes as a Mexican American woman, in the voice of the "daughter" of La Malinche: "*Sí, soy hija de la Chingada.* I've always been her daughter" (*B* 17). The "new *mestiza*" accuses Mexican culture of betraying its daughters, "in making us believe that the Indian woman in us is the betrayer" (*B* 22).

In addition, Anzaldúa is an American Chicana who straddles the boundary between two nations, Mexico and the United States, between her ancestral Mexican and present American cultures, "[a]lienated from her mother culture, 'alien' in the dominant culture" (*B* 20)—as she notes, orphaned and marginalized in both countries by American racism and Mexican misogyny. *Borderlands/La Frontera* is pervaded by the sense of being an outcast in her own home and country, and attempting the impossible: to construct an identity and home on hostile territory. This is the meaning of "borderlands" in her work: having no home, and nowhere to live except a "thin edge of / barbwire" (*B* 13). For Anzaldúa,

[t]he U.S.-Mexican border *es una herida abierta* where the Third World grates against the first and bleeds. And before a scab forms it hemorrhages again, the lifeblood of two worlds merging to form a third country—a bor-

der culture. Borders are set up to define the places that are safe and unsafe, to distinguish *us* from *them*. A border is a dividing line, a narrow strip along a steep edge. A borderlands is a vague and undetermined place created by the emotional residue of an unnatural boundary. The prohibited and forbidden are its inhabitants. *Los atravesados* live here: the squint-eyed, the perverse, the queer, the troublesome, the mongrel, the mulatto, the half-breed, the half-dead. . . . (*B* 3).

Anzaldúa's mestiza cross-cultural poetics is also, as Glissant similarly advocates, a mongrel text that blurs genres. Bilingual throughout, *Borderlands* is organized into two parts, essay and poetry. I will focus on the first and last of seven essays, which debate the contending issues of nationalism and hybridity.

The passage just cited is taken from the beginning of Chapter 1, "The Homeland, Aztlán / *El otro México*." This chapter recounts the well-known landmarks of Chicano history: the southward migration of Aztec tribes from their mythic homeland, Aztlán, located in what is now the American Southwest, to central Mexico; the founding of Tenochtitlan and the Aztec empire; the conquest of the Aztecs by Spain; the birth of the mestizo people; the northward migration of mixed-blood peoples to the ancient homeland of their Aztec ancestors, at the side of Spanish conquistadors and colonizers founding New Spain's northern frontier settlements; the annexation of Mexico's northern provinces by the U.S. in 1848. In short, Anzaldúa reaffirms the claims of Chicano nationalism implicit in this historical plot: the borderlands are the Chicano homeland, for mestizo Mexicans have returned to the origin of their Native ancestors. "We have a tradition of migration, a tradition of long walks. Today we are witnessing *la migración de los pueblos mexicanos*, the return odyssey to the historical / mythological Aztlán" (*B* 11). Anzaldúa stresses that twentieth century mass immigration from Mexico to the U.S., especially undocumented immigration, must be understood as part of this centuries-old tradition of migration and *mestizaje*.

Why resort to nationalist claims to homeland and Native roots if the history of mestizo Mexicans is clearly based on its contrary, mobility, migration, and transculturation? The answer to this question takes us back to the legacy of conquest. In the borderlands, as U.S. Western historian Patricia Limerick points out, "The most enduring issue . . . is the question of legitimacy. Is today's Mexican immigrant an illegitimate intruder into territory that was for two and a half centuries a part of Mexico . . . ?" (Limerick 254–255). In her essay on Aztlán, Anzaldúa challenges the authority of American nationalism in the voice of resistant Chicano nationalism. At the same time, in the passage cited above, notice how Anzaldúa wrestles with the concepts of territoriality and nation. We learn that the Chicano homeland, Aztlán, is not a bounded territory at all, but a borderlands, a "third country" where "the lifeblood of two worlds merge[s]," a place located on the very borderline between Mexico and the U.S. Territorial divisions drawn by the U.S. nation are challenged: the U.S.-Mexico line is "an unnatural boundary." Challenging the dualisms of nation-space splitting the historical landscape of mestizo transculturation, Anzaldúa calls the U.S.-Mexico border "an open wound" (*"una herida abierta"*).

In the very same paragraph, and contradicting her own anti-foundationalism, Anzaldúa turns around to locate the Chicano borderlands in a distinct, "third" space. She also wants it to be an island between the nations whose intersection gives it life, projecting (if tentatively) territorial integrity: "A borderlands is a vague and undetermined place" "in a constant state of transition" (*B* 3). Anzaldúa lapses from her dynamic model of *mestizaje* as migrant flux to consolidate the features of solid space: there is a mestizo borderlands which, like a homeland, has "inhabitants." Though illegitimate transgressors according to the dominant territorial order, "*[l]os atravesados* live here"—in this place, even if it is a non-place, a border line. In short, Anzaldúa's mestizos are shadowy citizens-to-be of a utopian mestizo homeland about to declare its independence. Gradually, from the negative position that views the "between" as void, Anzaldúa culls an affirmative language of hybridity and a geography of in-betweenness. But the logic of Anzaldúa's metaphor suggests that the affirmation of mestizo culture, or the closing of the open wound, will entail the ebbing of blood exchanges between the Mexican and U.S. nations and the ceasing of the process of hybridization. When the wound closes, and the "prohibited and forbidden" come home in their patrimony, the pain of displacement and exile ends, but so does the flow of transculturation.

In Chapter 7, "*La conciencia de la mestiza* / Towards a New Consciousness," Anzaldúa's argument turns away from the past, the legacy of conquest, to the future, or the unfolding dynamics of *mestizaje*. As her discourse blends from Chicano history into her visionary manifesto of a "new *mestiza* consciousness," she replaces the figure of the tragic mestizo, nostalgically looking back to a lost homeland, with the figure of a "new *mestiza*," who embraces the utopian potential of her hybrid identity. Anzaldúa writes,

At the confluence of two or more genetic streams . . . this mixture of races, rather than resulting in an inferior being, provides hybrid progeny, a mutable, more malleable species with a rich gene pool. From this racial, ideological, cultural and biological cross-pollination, an "alien" consciousness is presently in the making—a new *mestiza* consciousness, *una conciencia de mujer*. It is a consciousness of the Borderlands (*B* 77).

Rather than taking Paz as her model, Anzaldúa chooses Mexican philosopher José Vasconcelos' concept of *la raza cósmica* as her point of departure, as Vasconcelos' concept of *mestizaje* differs from Paz' in affirming freedom and visionary utopianism.

"Towards a New Consciousness" can be compared to a planner's sketch of an alternative world that shows a decentered and fluid migrant universe marked by the tracks of the new *mestiza*'s travels through it. In trying to replace the grammar of oppositionality with a plural poetics of relation, Anzaldúa uses the imagery of water: "These numerous possibilities leave *la mestiza* floundering in uncharted seas. . . . [S]he is subjected to a swamping of her psychological borders" (*B* 79).[15] It is no accident that images of ships and sea here intrude upon the imagery of land and rootedness. Water imagery promises to displace the territorial logic of duality and exclusion. At the same time, it is fascinating to watch Anzaldúa's argument struggle as it keeps slipping back from the grammar of cultural fusion into the grammar of division, even as she keeps trying to transcend it: "But it is not enough to stand on the opposite river bank, shouting questions, challenging patriarchal, white conventions. . . . At some point, on our way to a new consciousness, we will have to leave the opposite bank, the split between the two mortal combatants somehow healed so that we are on both shores at once. . . ." (78). Trying to say both/and, she keeps having to return to either/or: her efforts to sketch a third identity, "a plural personality" "beyond stance and counterstance" where "nothing is thrust out" (*B* 79), remain in danger of sliding back; evocations of mestiza flux across divisions revert to assertions of their rigidity. Here, the same paradox is at work as in the first chapter: dynamic *mestizaje* cannot be defined in the language of territoriality. Migration across borders and unnatural divisions constitute hybridity proper, but the hybrid remains an outcast, an exile. Indeed, in "Towards a New Consciousness," Anzaldúa affirms the condition of exile, "As a *mestiza* I have no country, my homeland has cast me out" (*B* 80). But how does this celebration of homeless *mestizaje*, Anzaldúa's manifesto of a new hybrid consciousness, translate into everyday borderlands reality outside the realm of the imagination?

Clearly, the continental setting of Anzaldúa's borderlands of culture places discursive limits on her mestiza poetics of relation. Yet within the dominant terms of landscape, Anzaldúa works out all the tropes of freedom and mobility land can offer: her border "land" scape is (to borrow geographer J. B. Jackson's term) an "accessible landscape,"[16] oriented toward systems of transport, such as roads and rivers, rather than toward enclosure, dwelling, and stability. Mostly, the "new *mestiza*" is outside, criss-crossing space, circling around the crossroads of culture, "continually walking out of one culture / and into another" (*B* 77). Always underway to bridge differences, she does not retreat into a sheltered interior, or seek to inhabit any one single identity: "She learns to be Indian in Mexican culture, to be Mexican from an Anglo point of view. She learns to juggle cultures. She has a plural personality . . ." (*B* 79).

Maria Campbell's *Halfbreed*

As noted earlier, métis culture in the Canadian West does not share mestizo Mexico's trauma of violent origins. Since, as we have seen, the Chicana poetics of *mestizaje* emerges in part as a feminist counter to the male-oriented nationalist construction of a tragic mestizo immobilized by the "anxiety of origins," the absence of similar historical and discursive legacies internal to métis culture promises much better conditions for a plural poetics of *métissage* to unfold. Yet this promise has not been fulfilled. The corpus of métis literature today remains much smaller than that of its fellow mixed-race literature south of the border, and it is overwhelmingly oriented toward the memory of dispossession[17] and the poetics of resistant nationalism.

Because many readers will not be as familiar with métis history as with Chicano history, I will briefly review some key facts.[18] Métis origins in the fur trade were peaceful, not violent. Since traders came neither to settle nor to convert or civilize, fur trade society was a true "middle ground" (Richard White). Relations of equality prevailed between Indian tribes and European fur traders, whose survival and economic success depended on the cooperation of Natives. Fur traders would be married to Indian women "in the fashion of the country" during the sojourn in Indian territory.[19] As Sylvia van Kirk points out, "The norm for sexual relationships in fur-trade society was not casual, promiscuous encounters but the development of marital unions which gave rise to distinct family units. . . . In this, the fur-trade society of Western Canada appears to have been exceptional. In most other areas of the world, sexual contact between European men and Native women has usually been illicit in nature and essentially peripheral to the white man's trading or colonizing ventures" (van Kirk 4). Fur trade companies welcomed ties of blood that bound the mixed-blood children of traders to the company's business. The Métis soon became a distinct third culture neither white nor Indian. Métis national consciousness developed, since the late eighteenth century, in response to two challenges: The first was their rivalry, as independent traders, with the trade monopoly of the London-based HBC (Hudson's Bay Company). The second factor was their opposition to the founding of the first Anglo-Scots and Protestant settler colony at Red River in 1812.

Métis origins in a "middle ground" between white and Indian worlds quickly allowed a truly hybrid culture to emerge, a composite of Native and white lifestyles and technologies. The métis lifestyle was semi-nomadic, organized around a (white) military-style annual buffalo hunt that lasted for months, extended over hundreds of miles, and involved hundreds of people. The métis world was a migrant universe, a fair historical realization of Anzaldúa's ideal vision of a cross-cultural geography. One key feature is the "proximity of the homes of Red River Métis to river and road" (Faragher 102), while métis buildings and settlements fuse Native and white architectural influences.[20] The famous "riverine lots" (at odds with the rectangular grid survey of Anglo settlements), connected each métis dwelling to routes of transport—rivers or roads. At the height of their power at Red River around 1850, métis peoples, at eighty percent of the total population, outnumbered whites and Indians. A true intermediate culture, the Métis were at the same time the strongest military force in the region.

When Canada purchased the fur trade territories from the Hudson's Bay Company in 1869, and because the company's ownership and rights to transfer the territory was questionable, the Red River Métis rebelled. Louis Riel declared an independent Métis government, which led to the creation of the province of Manitoba. In 1870, the Red River Rebellion was crushed and the métis leadership exiled. The opening of Manitoba to white settlers pushed the Métis farther northwest, to the Saskatchewan River, where the same conflict over land erupted again fifteen years later, resulting in a second armed uprising. The defeat of the 1885 Northwest Rebellion by the Canadian army culminated in the spectacular trial for high treason and hanging of Louis Riel, whose execution came to symbolize the defeat of the Métis nation and the collapse of their hybrid culture. Landless, non-status native peoples without aboriginal rights,[21] the Métis ended up on "skid row," in the streets. Neither white nor Indian, the Métis

fell into the void between the cultures that had created them. Overrun by
the expanding Canadian nation, the métis borderlands were annihilated,
a conquest that was inevitable given its location on the western fringe of
continental North America.²²

In the remainder of this section, I want to discuss Maria Campbell's
métis autobiography, *Halfbreed* (1973), against the foil of Thomas Flanagan's biography of Riel, *Louis "David" Riel: Prophet of the New World.* Flanagan, whose biography reinterprets the religious dimension of Riel's career,
portrays Riel as a millenarian prophet. Between the 1870 and the 1885 rebellions, the exiled and defeated president of the Métis government of
Manitoba developed supernatural visions, which prophesied the deliver-
ance of the Métis from the threat of cultural destruction, and their emergence as God's "chosen people." Calling himself "Prophet of the New
World," Riel adopted the Hebrew name "David." Though he was institutionalized for insanity in the inter-war period, his "new religion" flourished during the second 1885 uprising. Then, Riel transformed his religious
doctrine into a nationalist doctrine of Native resistance, which inspired the
Métis with hope for the duration of the two-month uprising. Flanagan's
portrait of Riel traces the transformation of hybrid into nation-identity at
the threat of cultural annihilation. Flanagan writes,

> The millenarian prophet or messiah is usually someone who has lived both
> in the world of his own people and in the greater world outside. . . . The
> leader of a modern nativistic movement has often been in close contact with
> white society as a pupil in a mission school or a member of the native mili-
> tary auxiliaries. Perhaps this wider range of experience shakes his trust in
> the fixity of reality and helps him conceive of a radically different world to
> come. . . . In short, the leader has usually been at the cutting edge of cultural
> conflict. . . . This composite portrait applies accurately to Louis Riel. Seven-
> eighths white, he grew up in the settled portion of the Métis community
> that was closest to white ways. His family farmed and did not participate in
> the characteristic Métis activities of the buffalo hunt, bull trains, boat bri-
> gades, or fur trade. He was sent at an early age to Montreal to acquire an
> education and to become the first Métis missionary priest. Abandoning this
> plan, he tried to become part of white society by marrying a white girl and
> pursuing a career as a lawyer. It was only when these intentions were im-
> peded that he returned to the West. After the first Rebellion, Riel wanted a
> career in Canadian politics, an aim that he pursued tenaciously until he was
> exiled in 1875. Even after his unhappy experience in the lunatic asylums of
> Quebec, he considered settling in the white society of the eastern United

States. Not until 1879 did he go to the frontier to share the roving life of the Métis. There his experience and reputation made him their natural leader. Neither wholly white nor wholly Métis, Riel participated in both ways of life. He came to view himself as a human bridge—between native and white, French and English, Catholic and Protestant, British and American, human and divine (Flanagan 201–202).

Flanagan shows that Riel, who embodied the fluid "bridge" identity of his people, becomes someone else, the leader of a nativist nationalism. In the process, the bridge hardens into a defensive wall. The logic of conquest forces the Métis off the middle ground and back to the position of native Other. In the development of a Native-like resistance movement parallel to those of nineteenth-century native peoples, the Métis accepted this refiguration of their former bridge identity.[23]

One reason I have reviewed métis history in detail is to show the correspondence between the cultural poetics of late twentieth-century blueprints of hybridization and the nineteenth-century métis world. Another is to highlight the lack of such blueprints in contemporary métis writing from the Canadian West, the historical métis heartland. Overwhelmingly, contemporary métis literature testifies to the nineteenth-century annihilation of the hybrid métis lifeworld, adopting a poetics of nation rather than a poetics of relation. Rather than the "anxiety of origins," métis writing recalls the anxiety of exile, which dates from a late period in the history of métis culture. The events of 1870 and 1885 have suppressed a legacy of relationality organic to early métis history and imposed its own. To date, métis literature from the Canadian West has yet to develop a full-blown twentieth-century poetics of *métissage* comparable to the poetics of *mestizaje* generated by Mexican American (primarily Chicana) writers.

Among contemporary métis writing, Maria Campbell's *Halfbreed* (1973) is the most sophisticated attempt at reflecting *métissage* in the light of métis marginalization in the twentieth century.[24] To some extent, *Halfbreed* is a hybrid text, as it interweaves autobiography with history, juxtaposing the nineteenth-century past to the twentieth-century present, and relating the individual story of the autobiographer's life to the larger métis community. But historical discourse in *Halfbreed* functions to mark the rupturing of the cultural dynamics of *métissage.*

That is why Campbell's autobiography bears the title "halfbreed," citing the negative English-language label which degrades mixed-race peoples as unnatural "breeds." Today, the term "métis" has become an English-language term that refers to all people of mixed European and aboriginal ancestry.[25] Historically, the terms "métis" and "halfbreed" distinguish between the French- and English-speaking mixedbloods, respectively. Campbell, despite the English surname, personally traces her descent from the French-speaking Métis—the historical Métis, not the historical "halfbreeds." So much more marked is her use of the English term "halfbreed." Indeed, "halfbreed" identifies Maria's social position in the post-conquest period, the name of her colonial identity.

Exile and diaspora set the tone at the beginning of Campbell's narrative: Campbell begins her autobiography with a summary of the nineteenth-century métis past, discussing the 1870 and 1885 uprisings, their defeat, and the death and exile of the two métis leaders, Louis Riel and Gabriel Dumont. Matter-of-factly, Campbell summarizes the final defeat of the Métis as an independent political force: "The history books say that the Halfbreeds were defeated at Batoche in 1884. / Louis Riel was hanged in November of 1885. Charge: high treason. / Gabriel Dumont and a handful of men escaped to Montana" (*HB* 11).

Chapter 2 moves on to the aftermath of the rebellion: "My people fled to Spring River which is fifty miles north-west of Prince Albert. Halfbreed families with names like Chartrand, Isbister, Campbell, Arcand, and Vandal came here after the Riel Rebellion where the men had been actively involved. Riel was gone now and so were their hopes. This new land was covered with small lakes, rocky hills and dense bush. The Halfbreeds who came were self-sufficient trappers and hunters" (*HB* 12). The Métis become refugees living on the margins of Canadian society, outcasts in their former homeland. Campbell's historical briefing sets the stage for the book's proper concern and subject: What happened to the métis people after the defeat of their leadership and their struggle for national independence? How did the métis community survive facing the death of hope, the death of their future? Even though each Métis received individual land title, Campbell tells us,

> [g]radually the homesteads were reclaimed by the authorities and offered to the immigrants. The Halfbreeds then became squatters on their land and were eventually run off by the new owners. One by one they drifted back to the road lines and crown lands where they built cabins and barns and from then on were known as the "Road Allowance people" (*HB* 13).

Campbell's reduction of history to a backdrop to the present bears the mark of a Native writer. As Native writer and critic Thomas King observes, Native writers tend to stay clear of the past, because history has been so completely scripted by the white romance of the vanishing Native.[26] *Half-breed* is concerned with the mundane present of métis survival, not the heroic and tragic nineteenth-century past.

Halfbreed's Native-like historicism that searches in the past only for sources of present identity, eschewing the historical novel and historical settings and limiting the focus to contemporary settings, classifies Campbell's autobiography as an identitarian, non-syncretic text. Maria's life as a contemporary métis woman is scripted by what has been, rather than what might yet unfold. Métis identity is presented in terms of being, not becoming, as already formed, rather than fluid and in process. Campbell spends little time delineating métis as a distinct "third" culture beyond white and Indian. However, we learn that the Métis are "noisy" and more fun-loving than their "dignified" "Indian relatives," rebellious and "quick to fight," while Indians are "passive" (*HB* 26). Maria thinks that métis women are better off than Native women, "Treaty Indian women don't express their opinions, Halfbreed women do. Even though I liked visiting them, I was always glad to get back to the noise and disorder of my own people" (*HB* 27). Significantly, Campbell here refigures a cultural as a gender feature, claiming that métis culture breeds outspoken and strong women. Her motive is easily found: her two main protagonists are both women. Further, in Campbell's autobiography, neither of the two famous métis leaders, Louis Riel or Gabriel Dumont, but a female elder, Maria's great-grandmother Cheechum, plays the role of resistance warrior and mentor. Recall that *Halfbreed* begins with the loss of (male) métis leadership ("Riel was gone now and so were their hopes" [*HB* 12]) only to move on to what comes next. Rather than looking backward, it poses a question about history that we might define as a woman's question: war has killed and defeated our men, but we are still here. How are we to survive? What next? Campbell recalls the métis rebellion not to commemorate a heroic spectacle, but to open the reader's eyes to its aftermath, the other war that follows the armed fighting—the long-term battle for day-to-day survival endured in obscurity as life goes on.

Briefly, Campbell's story covers the period from Maria's birth in 1940 to 1966. Growing up the oldest child in a destitute and large family of eight children, Maria loses her mother at age twelve and takes her place as housekeeper. Despite experiencing racism upon entering Canadian schools and during weekend trading trips the Métis take to white towns, Maria is raised with a strong sense of métis identity. A rich texture of métis folktales and rituals structures her childhood. With the sudden death of her mother, this world breaks apart. Coping with her father's alcoholism, and her mentor Cheechum's departure, Maria battles social workers to keep the family united. Marrying at eighteen, Maria leaves her family to follow her white husband west, eventually ending up alone and with child in the streets of Vancouver. Her subsequent journey leads through prostitution, drugs, institutionalization, another unhappy marriage, and another child. Her recovery occurs through contacts and friendships with Native and métis activists. The turning point in Maria's personal life and the métis community at large coincides with the rise of the Native Movement in the 1960s.

Yet the parallel renaissance in métis collective and Maria's personal life harks back to the past. The revolutionary events of the 1960s are depicted as the fulfillment of the métis destiny of autonomy that only seemed defeated in 1885. This has been Cheechum's message of hope throughout. Métis cultural nationalism of the 1960s redeems the aspirations for which métis rebels had taken up arms a century earlier.[27] The analogy between past and present resistance struggles is established through the link between Maria and her great-grandmother Cheechum:

> My Cheechum never surrendered at Batoche: she only accepted what she considered a dishonorable truce. She waited all her life for a new generation of people who would make this country a better place to live in (*HB* 156).

Maria is the "new Métis," Cheechum her legendary Métis Malinche, as it were — the female founding figure and mentor whose lineage Maria honors as her descendant and disciple. Maria becomes the heroine of the long-anticipated new generation of métis activists and leaders. Cheechum represents the generation of warriors and survivors of 1885; her death, at the legendary age of 104, occurs in 1966 to coincide with the realization of her dream of métis rebirth. Early in *Halfbreed*, we learn that Cheechum "was a niece of Gabriel Dumont and her whole family fought beside Riel and Dumont during the Rebellion," and that she "hated to see the settlers come . . . as they settled on what she believed was our land" (*HB* 15). Neither her son nor her grandson, but her great-granddaughter Maria is pronounced the heir to whom Cheechum passes on her vision; as Cheechum tells Maria, "Now I know that you belong to me. Don't let anyone tell you that anything is impossible . . ." (*HB* 86). Across the distance of four generations, Cheechum and Maria are prophet and disciple, ancestor and heir united by blood and identity, forming a genealogical bond that bridges a void, the century of dispossession between 1885 and 1966.

More evidence for *Halfbreed's* forgetting of the pre-conquest cultural poetics of *métissage* is found in the family genealogy Campbell reconstructs at the beginning. The narrowing of *métissage* to oppositionality can be traced to a precise point in the Campbell family tree. As mentioned earlier, the legendary Cheechum is from a family of militant Métis, related to Gabriel Dumont. Viewed historically, Cheechum is the key link between public métis history and Campbell's family story. More significantly, Cheechum represents the métis generation of crisis, which witnessed the old order of non-hierarchical race relations break down, terminating the free play of *métissage*. As fur trade society is overrun by settlers, one kind of race mixture—the equal union between Native women and fur traders—disappears and another emerges—the hierarchical union of settler and Native. Born in 1862 on the eve of the opening of the Canadian West, Cheechum marries an immigrant from Scotland, Great Grandpa Campbell. At the outbreak of the 1885 rebellion, husband and wife become enemies, as Great Grandpa Campbell sides with the Canadians, while his wife Cheechum passes on the information gathered through her husband to the métis rebels (*HB* 14). Since Maria Campbell traces her métis lineage to Cheechum as ancestor, métis origins are formed under the new colonial order. Campbell's construction of métis origins thus becomes identical with the violent beginnings of *mestizaje* as portrayed by Octavio Paz. The unique fur trade lineage of relation-identity breaks off; Cheechum cannot reproduce the dynamics of *métissage* in her marriage, as she is powerless to force her husband to the middle ground. Accordingly, her children inherit this dualism, rejecting white culture and ancestors and siding with their Native heritage. The bridge as third term between white and Native has collapsed.

Conclusion

In discussing Campbell's *Halfbreed* alongside Anzaldúa's *Borderlands/La Frontera: The New Mestiza* and comparing the métis and mestizo cultures that produced these texts, this essay marks a beginning in drafting a comparative map of hybrid cultures in the Americas. A thorough examination of differences in hybrid cultures and their literatures across the hemisphere, which is yet to be done, would give us deeper insight into the hidden cross-cultural histories and cultural landscapes beneath the dominant map of nations and nation-formation. Just as we understand differences and parallels in nation-formation in the Americas in a transnational hemispheric context today, we need to understand the formation and ar-ticulation of cross-cultural formations in a hemispheric context. A key conclusion of this initial inquiry is the hybrid constitution of hybridity af-firmed by Robert Young, "a doubleness that both brings together, fuses, but also maintains separation" (*Colonial Desire* 22). Hybridity, a poetics of culture as in-between, registers triangular relationships between at least three terms. Consequently, what it is cannot be considered as a unified and autonomous entity abstracted from the local, cultures and nations "be-tween which" it emerges.

Both Campbell's and Anzaldúa's texts testify to the dilemma of hy-brid cultures on the North American continent. "Pure" hybridity requires an in-between space that is both open and closed, an insular setting with porous boundaries, at once open to adjacent (and distant) cultures by chan-nels of transcultural flow and protected from outright territorial absorp-tion. Historically, the nineteenth century terminated the mediated inde-pendence of métis and mestizo cultures in North America. The westward expansion of the U.S. and Canadian nations extinguished the decentral-ized network of small independent borderlands cultures that had existed in the western half of the continent. I have explored the ways in which the memory of this historical trauma of displacement is inscribed in the cross-cultural poetics of contemporary métis and mestizo writers. Resis-tant nationalism, the defensive affirmation of Native origins and claim to an ancestral homeland, intrudes upon their attempt to construct a poetics of relation and cross-cultural flow. Métis and mestizo writers find them-selves in a double bind, because their articulation of a distinct hybrid poet-ics of continuous and dynamic identity formation leads them back to the need to affirm a lost independence and recover a lost past in the voice of nation-identity that is actually the essence of what they oppose.

Finally, comparing Campbell's "new Maria" to Anzaldúa's "new *mes-tiza*" brings out further surprising and significant differences between Mé-tis Canadian and Mexican American hybridity, which sets off *Borderland*'s poetics of relation from *Halfbreed*'s more limited poetics of nation. As I have argued, Anzaldúa's new mestiza consciousness deconstructs the leg-acy of past exclusion and proposes a cultural model beyond dualisms. In her sustained attempt to work out a mestiza poetics of relation, foreground-ing process over origins, and bridging oppositions, Anzaldúa finds herself either celebrating *mestizaje* in exile, with no place to inhabit except the "thin edge of /barbwire" (*B* 13), or looking forward to a homecoming in a utopian mestiza homeland, which entails the ceasing of the centuries-old mestizo tradition of migration and flow. Published in the wake of 1960s cultural nationalism, Campbell's autobiography predates *Borderlands* by more than a decade. *Borderlands* and *Halfbreed* belong to different generations of North American minority literature; as noted, overall, métis writing has not participated in the shift in minority literature from the nationalist poetics of the 1960s to the post-nationalist poetics of the 1980s and beyond. Ultimately, *Halfbreed* constructs a nationalist grammar of identity, proceeding from roots to destiny, based on the logic of resistance and oppositionality. Like *Borderlands/La Frontera*, *Halfbreed* closes with an affirmation of a rebirth of *métissage*, in the figure of Maria as "new métis." Yet Campbell's hopeful prospect of the renewal of métis culture is marred by a deeper forgetting of the hybrid dynamics of cross-cultural identity. Its defining note is the affirmation of métis survival, rather than the recovery of the métis heritage of "openness to otherness" that drove the process of hybridization in fur trade society.

Notes

I would like to thank Robert Mugerauer, Debra Rosenthal, and Chris Bongie for their helpful feedback during my work on this essay.

   1. The term creolization encompasses the French *métissage* and Spanish *mestizaje* as a generic term for mixture between distinct racial and cultural groups. Creolization is frequently used to invoke the radical nature of the intermixing, as in Edouard Glissant, *Poetics of Relation*, 34. Hardly any of the terms referring to race mixture are free of the legacy of racist discourse. This discussion uses the terms hybridity and hybridization, while being aware of the terms' roots in nineteenth-century discourse of race discussed by Robert Young in *Colonial Desire: Hybridity in Theory, Culture and Race*.

   2. Although not perfect synonyms of each other and related to distinct theoretical backgrounds, the terms listed above all invoke a plural logic of difference that opposes binary oppositions. For instance, "transculturation," an anthropological term, stresses the passage from one culture to another (Pérez Firmat, *Life on the Hyphen* 5). "Creole," referring to a person born in the colonies, is originally a linguistic term for contact languages. Similarly, sometimes usage alternates between "hybridity," originally a biological term, which refers to the outcome of such cultural crossings, and "hybridization," to foreground the dynamics of such exchanges. An in-depth terminological discussion is beyond the scope of this paper, which readers can find in many of the sources cited here. In the same way, the list of titles that could be cited to illustrate the vogue for hybridity, border writing, and transnational concepts of culture is impossibly long, so I will name a few landmark books that have been catalysts for other works: Homi Bhabha, *The Location of Culture*; Mary Louise Pratt, *Imperial Eyes: Travel Writing and Transculturation*; Néstor García Canclini, *Hybrid Cultures: Strategies for Entering and Leaving Modernity*; D. Emily Hicks, *Border Writing: The Multidimensional Text*; Paul Gilroy, *The Black Atlantic: Modernity and Double Consciousness*.

3. This shift in critical discourse from national to transnational and plural concepts of community is clearly set forward in Mary Louis Pratt's "Criticism in the Contact Zone: De-centering Community and Nation."

4. On the Caribbean and creolization, see Antonio Benítez-Rojo, *The Repeating Island;* Michael Dash, *The Other America;* Pérez Firmat, *The Cuban Condition;* Chris Bongie, *Islands and Exiles;* Vera Kutzinski, *Sugar's Secrets.* Explaining the historical and geographical reasons for Caribbean hybridity, Dash writes about the need for "exploring concepts of cultural diversity, syncretism, and instability that characterize the island cultures of the Caribbean. Indeed, because they are marked by an extermination of the original population, were subjected to repopulation, and became totally dependent on the metropole because of their plantation economies, the Caribbean archipelago witnessed the extremes of the New World experience, producing . . . [a] cultural crossroads in a more intense way than is possible in a larger land-mass or where the indigenous population manages to survive" (Dash 5). Similarly, in their introduction to the recent collection, *Caribbean Creolization,* the editors write: "The location of the Caribbean archipelago determined that the islands would be at the center of intense economic and cultural exchanges and would serve as a bridge connecting North and South America. As a result of the slave trade and colonial economic exploitation, vast numbers of people from diverse geographic, racial, and cultural origins were forcibly imported to the Caribbean—a region that stands today as a reminder of the disruption and eventual subversion of both the physical origins of these peoples as well as all academic theories of unitary origins" (Butalansky and Sourieau 2).

5. While Young's claim that hybridity itself is hybrid is addressed specifically to Bakhtin's theory of hybridity, it also underwrites the overall argument of his study.

6. Readers interested in Deleuze and Guattari's maritime model of smooth versus striated space should consult *A Thousand Plateaus,* chapter 14, 478–482. Here they argue that the sea, the archetype of smooth spaces, possesses a greater power of deterritorialization than striated space, thus allowing more open, changing relations to fold and unfold.

7. In describing vernacular landscapes, cultural geographers like J. B. Jackson have privileged mainland geography. Traditionally, cultural geography focuses on territory and "sense of place" and offers few leads on conceptualizing fluidity and mobility. While Jackson's work is exceptional for his consistent attempts to describe an "accessible landscape" that does equal justice to the house and the road as components of landscape representing its polar features of territoriality and mobility, it is also marked by linguistic defensiveness when discussing roads. Thus, in *A Sense of Place, a Sense of Time,* Jackson writes that roads are "disturbers of the peace" of small nucleated communities, talking about travelers and migrants as "intruder[s]" in local settlements (Jackson 190, 7). Yet J. B. Jackson's consistent interest in roads as essential ingredients of landscape makes his work a valuable resource for the charting of cross-cultural geographies. See, for instance, the early essay, "A Pair of Ideal Landscapes," which gives equal attention to opposite modes of dwelling and travel (Jackson, *Discovering* 9–56).

8. See Luce Irigaray, *Marine Lover of Friedrich Nietzsche.* Irigaray dramatizes the response of the feminine fluid to the philosopher's solid in the mode of personal dialogue, which gradually unfolds the hidden and repressed morphology of fluidity. Consider, for instance: "Deeper than the solid crust you must now descend to announce the meaning of the earth. . . . And realize that a solid plane is never just a solid plane. That it rests on subterranean and submarine life, on capped fires and winds which yet stir ceaselessly beneath that shell" (20). "The

embrace of earth and air and fire and water, which have never been wed. Forget the knife-cuts, the chalk-line partitions. Forget the appropriations at frontiers . . ." (21). Irigaray's mongrel discourse, part fiction, part theory, is a rich resource that can inspire similar work dismantling the dominion of earth-dwelling over water-mobility in a geography of borderlandscapes.

9. The British North America Act (1967) established Canada as a dominion and cleared the way for Canadian expansion westward, while the defeat of the métis rebellions of 1871 and 1885 consolidated the conquest of the western territories.

10. In *Living on the Hyphen: The Cuban-American Way*, Pérez Firmat explains the Cuban way of blending cultures, which he argues Cuban Americans inherit, by using Ricky Ricardo as one of his examples: "He embodies an openness to otherness, a liking for unlikeness that defines Cuban America as a whole. . . . As Ricky himself stated, to love Lucy is to embrace the unfamiliar in the form of an americana who stands, more generally, for Americana" (Pérez Firmat 12).

11. See Pérez Firmat, "As is well known, Cuban culture lacks the indigenous substratum that is so strong a presence in other parts of Spanish America. Since Cuban culture is composed entirely from exogenous ingredients, in Cuba the indigenous, in the narrow sense of the word, is little more than a poetic commonplace . . ." (Pérez Firmat, *The Cuban Condition* 2). Michael Dash suggests similarly that, "because [cultures of the Caribbean] are marked by an extermination of the original population, were subjected to repopulation, and became totally dependent on the metropole because of their plantation economies, the Caribbean archipelago witnessed the extremes of the New World experience, producing Pérez Firmat's cultural crossroads in a more intense way than is possible in a larger landmass or where the indigenous population is able to survive" (Dash 5).

12. In *Caribbean Discourse*, Glissant offers a parallel comment that in the Caribbean context, "insularity takes on another meaning. Ordinarily, insularity is treated as a form of isolation. . . . However, in the Caribbean each island embodies openness. The dialectic between inside and outside is reflected in the relationship of land and sea" (139).

13. For a recent argument that shows the extent to which Glissant's poetics of relation is haunted by a poetics of nation, see Chris Bongie, *Islands and Exiles*, 126–186.

14. While this is true, Anzaldúa is just one of many Chicana poets, writers, and critics, such as Cherríe Moraga and Carmen Tafolla, who take the myth of La Malinche as a paradigmatic point of departure for a feminist poetics that opposes the victimization of women in Mexican culture (see Pratt, "Criticism in the Contact Zone"; Alarcón; Cypess).

15. See also the following passage from the preface of *Borderlands*, "Living on borders and in margins, keeping intact one's shifting and multiple identity and integrity, is like trying to swim in a new element, an 'alien' element" (*B* preface, n. pag.).

16. See note 7 above.

17. For this phrase, I am indebted to Rolando Romero, taken from the title of his talk at the 1999 MLA convention, "Memory of Dispossession." Clearly, demographics are also a factor to be considered: the métis population is much smaller than the Mexican American population, anticipated to soon become the largest minority population in the U.S.

18. For historical sources on métis history, see Donald Purich's *The Métis*, Joseph Howard, *Strange Empire: Louis Riel and the Métis People*, Peterson and Brown, eds., *The New Peoples: Being and Becoming Métis in North America*, and the sources mentioned in the following note.

19. For a detailed discussion of fur trade relations between Indians and whites, see Sylvia van Kirk, *"Many Tender Ties": Women in Fur-Trade Society, 1670–1870;* Jennifer S. H. Brown,

Strangers in Blood: Fur Trade Company Families in Indian Country; Jacqueline Peterson and Jennifer Brown (eds.), *The New Peoples: Being and Becoming Métis in North America.*

20. See David Burley and Gayel A. Horsfall, "Vernacular Houses and Farmsteads of the Canadian Métis." For cultural geography of the Métis, see Burley and Horsfall; Peterson, "Many Roads to Red River: Métis Genesis in the Great Lakes Region, 1680–1815," Peterson and Brown, eds.; John Mack Faragher, "Americans, Mexicans, Métis: A Community Approach to the Comparative Study of North American Frontiers."

21. Unlike Indians, with whom the Canadian state negotiated treaties, Métis received "scrip," individual land certificates for homesteading. Because of widespread fraud and Métis indifference to farming, almost all scrip titles ended up in white ownership. Until 1982, the Métis did not have official Native status. See Purich, *The Métis,* 106ff.

22. The dramatic tension felt by historians writing about this turning point of 1885 comes through in Joseph Howard's comments: Métis nationhood would have created the first mixed-race nation in North America, an absolute novelty: "If the Métis had won in 1870, their country would have become an organized Native state. Such a state would have vastly changed the history of the West, Canadian and American. When Sitting Bull's Sioux—of the nation that in 1868 had dictated the terms of peace to the United States after a victorious war—when Sitting Bull's Sioux crossed into Canada after massacring Custer's command in 1876, they would have found allies instead of a mere refuge. They might well have returned to Montana rested, re-equipped, and reinforced. The Métis state might have been a nucleus and unifying force which would have united such Native defenders of the West as the Cree and the Blackfeet. Such a Native alliance would at least have postponed for many years the subjugation of the Western Indians, and it might have enabled some of them to establish semi-primitive [*sic*] but independent tribal societies capable of maintaining a finer way of life and developing in a better direction than in the actual outcome they were permitted. The idea of uniting came to both Sitting Bull and the Métis too late, but American and Canadian military authorities had always feared that they might sometime have to deal with it" (Howard 251–252).

23. On two counts, the example of métis history checks any temptation to generalize from Dash and Pérez Firmat's assumption, based on the Caribbean, that the extermination of aboriginal peoples helps the creolization process (see note 11 above). First, it shows that a new people and a cultural middle ground can flourish in the midst of territory dominated by native peoples. Second, we learn that no matter whether Native or mixed, all non-whites were reduced to the position of Other in the opening of the fur trade West to white settlement. The point seems to be that hybrid identity itself is no better guarantee for cultural survival than aboriginal identity, or that it would provide better coping skills at the moment of conquest.

24. Other métis texts are Beatrice Culleton's novel, *In Search of April Raintree* (1983); Lee Maracle's short story collection, *Sojourner's Truth and Other Stories* (1990); Linda Griffiths and Maria Campbell's collaborative, *The Book of Jessica: A Theatrical Transformation* (1989), records a cross-cultural Métis-white dialogue between the authors. Critics have made an argument for hybridity in these works (see Lundgren 1995). Thus, Lundgren discusses cultural syncretism in *Halfbreed*: ". . . Métis identity has always been syncretic. Campbell says that her family members 'were a real mixture of Scottish, French, Cree, English and Irish. We spoke a language completely different from others. We were a combination of everything: hunters, trappers, and ak-ee-top farmers'" (Lundgren 66). I disagree with these findings, for while Campbell indeed stresses her mixed ancestry, the deeper lesson of *Halfbreed* con-

cerns the dissolution of the traditional métis "third culture" after their defeat in 1885 and the renewal of a dualistic and colonial cultural order.

25. See Donald Purich, *The Métis*, 9ff, and Peterson and Brown, "Introduction," Peterson and Brown, eds. The historical English-speaking "halfbreeds" and French-speaking "Métis" originated separately around the rivaling English and French fur trade companies, the London-based Hudson's Bay Company and the Montreal-based Northwest Company.

26. Thomas King comments that "most of us [Native writers] have consciously set our literature in the present, a period that is reasonably free of literary monoliths and which . . . allows us the opportunity to create for ourselves and our respective cultures both a present and a future" (King xii).

27. On nonviolence and armed struggle, see Maria Campbell's comment, "For these past couple of years, I've stopped being the idealistically shiny-eyed young woman I once was. I realize that an armed revolution of Native people will never come about; even if such a thing were possible what would we achieve? We would only end up oppressing someone else" (*HB* 156).

SITES OF MEMORY
IN MIXED-RACE
AUTOBIOGRAPHY

CHAPTER II

LIVING ON THE RIVER

Rolando Hinojosa-Smith

In Texas, as it has for a million years or so, the Río Grande runs down from somewhere in El Paso to its mouth, just south and east of Brownsville, where it dies peacefully enough in Boca Chica as it empties into the Gulf of Mexico. Geologists call it an old river and to prove it, they will point to the countless meanders of the Río Grande as it wends its way to the Gulf. Meanders also produce the drowned portions of the river, which are called *resacas* in the Valley; the word is now an English-language borrowing and known to native Texas Mexicans and Anglos alike. Language borrowings, of course, are part of the daily life of any area where two countries come together, and I will touch on this later. For now, mention must be made on the general Texas Anglo attitude regarding Spanish and Spanish usage by Texas Mexicans in the Valley.

Texas Anglos have long denigrated the language as not being Castilian; what they don't know is that the language *is* Castilian; it differs in pronunciation and borrowings from that of Spain as the Spanish spoken in Argentina also differs from that of Spain. What the majority of them don't know as well is that Spain has many other languages within the Peninsula (Aragonese, Valencian, Galician, and those spoken with greater frequency in the Basque country and Catalonia). The truth of it all is that they don't care to think matters out; to many of them, if the Texas Mexicans speak Spanish, then it must be of an inferior kind, a sort of bastard Spanish, as it were. This is a matter of cultural superiority on the part of too many Texas Anglos and based not on linguistic knowledge but on ignorance and its corollaries: racial bias, prejudice, and discrimination.[1]

Any border presents different faces to non-borderers, and borders also tend to be self-sufficient in some regards; in the Valley, the ordinary citizenry on both banks of the Rio Grande looks askance, in some ways, to the federal capitals of Mexico and the United States. A result is that they focus on their immediate area. Too, the countries present different laws: in the United States, federal laws are set by precedent, while in Mexico, the Napoleonic code and its modifications prevail. And so, as in most border communities, the topographic barriers are jurisdictional but not necessarily cultural. Added to the relative isolation of the area (from, say, roughly 1747 to 1848), there was a forging of a new culture, not necessarily one hundred percent Mexican or one hundred percent American. As is the usual case in most cultures, those aspects of the culture that have proved cumbersome or displeasing have been modified by the borderers. These changes, obviously, cut across the river and across societal lines.

Language, a part of culture, also changed in time, but it's been the Texas Mexican who has remained firm, for the most part, to Spanish while at the same time adopting English, and then modifying both languages as time goes on.

This is not to claim that that part of Texas and Mexico has forged a new language; but it is to say that the original Spanish language brought to the area by the first settlers in 1747 has been maintained and modified, and then enlarged through time by the additions during the nineteenth and twentieth centuries through the printed word and later by radio and television.

The region's Spanish language, then, has kept the fundamental base and syntax, while at the same time reflecting those changes which are part and parcel of any living language. Had the original Valley Spanish remained unchanged from the mid-seventeenth-century version, then we would have with us the vestiges of a dead language, that is, one that did not admit borrowings from other languages, which is primarily what causes a language to wither. As an instance, in contemporary times, Romansch, spoken still in parts of Switzerland, is a European example of a stagnant and about-to-disappear language.

Marriages, and I will not go into marriage customs, often take place by those who cross from one side of the river to the other, and thus relations are sustained legally and by blood. It is not for me to say how strong or how warm and close the kinships are, since this depends on each individual family. I am well aware, of course, of the Mexican American myth that claims family warmth and how Roman Catholicism influences couples not to divorce. To believe either one of those myths is as illusory now as it was in years past.

Divorce among this predominantly Roman Catholic population is not uncommon anymore.

Marriage unions, however, bring us to the interesting points of names. My hometown, Mercedes, Texas (Hidalgo County), in the 1940s had a population of 6,400, and the Hinojosa-Smiths were but one family whose parents carried Spanish and non-Spanish names.

I will not pretend I knew each family of Mexican and Anglo parentage, but the following are ones I do remember living in Mercedes: Baum, Billings, Bowman, Brooks, Carr, Carroll, Closner, Foley, Gavlin, Handy, Heath, Howell, January, Johnson, McGee, McVey, Moody, Parker, Postell, Pue, Rowland, Starcke, Thomas, and Werbiski. There may have been others.

There are several points here, however. The numbers have increased since my time, and I would put this down to the historical inevitabilities of any borderland. Too, intermarriage is not an infrequent phenomenon in most border areas. However, I do not wish to leave the impression that these families either shared similar interests with each other or looked at themselves as different or as special because of the special parentage. For me, attending the same elementary, junior high, and high school with these family members bore this out. The majority, it should be obvious, carried the paternal last names first, while we and others carried the Spanish name first in the Hispanic manner.

The following surnames represent but a few of similar marriages up and down the Valley: Atkinson, Chamberlain, Hatcher, Hon, Hull, Kingsbury, Putegnat, Ramsey, Randolph, Rutledge, Solitaire, Trdla, and Turner. Across the river, a cursory look at the Matamoros and Reynosa, Tamaulipas, telephone directory immediately reveals such names as Brawn, Brockman, Kelly, Schu, and so on.

Was there racial discrimination on the Texas side? The answer is yes, and it is also a complicated *yes*, for one noticed, indeed one couldn't help but notice, that some Texas Anglos also discriminated socially against other Texas Anglos. The same applied (and applies) among Texas Mexicans, particularly those in the professional class who looked (and look) down upon other Texas Mexicans.

Texas Anglos and Texas Mexicans also forged business and law partnerships, and while this was not uncommon, it was also not the norm.

That was then. As matters stand now, the Texas Anglos are a distinct numerical population minority in the Rio Grande Valley.

The student school population ranges anywhere from seventy percent to ninety-five percent Texas Mexican; the administrators and the schoolroom teachers stand at sixty to seventy percent Texas Mexican in the over seventy cities and towns that dot that part of the state, from Brownsville (Cameron County) to Rio Grande City (Starr County). Similar figures go for the athletic coaches and directors of the independent school districts in the area.

Needless to say, the school boards of education range from one hundred percent to seventy-five percent Texas Mexican members.

When it comes to municipal governments, there are four Texas Anglo mayors at present; the city councils are also overwhelmingly Texas Mexican. The same goes for other elected officials, such as county commissioners, county judges, district attorneys, and so on.

In brief, the infrastructure, businesses, and the free professions (e.g., doctors, dentists, attorneys, accountants) are also in the majority. This is something that began to develop after World War II and Korea and the 1960s with the many-sided civil rights movements.

When it comes to financial institutions—banks and savings and loan companies—these were the last to fall, as it were, but they have come into line as far as boards of directorship, ownerships, partnerships, and other bank officials.

Whether one was Texas Anglo or Texas Mexican, no one who was raised during the Depression could envision the current state of affairs. It is not (and is it ever?) peaches and cream in the Rio Grande Valley, for it is usually listed as one of the poorest areas in the United States, as it should be since it's a simple truth. It is as poor, say, as are Vermont, Maine, and New Hampshire, where unemployment, in the year of 1995, stood at twenty percent.

Those states are also border states, although one should not infer that they are poor as a consequence of being border states.

Now, I know it is an article of faith when one writes about Texas Mexicans in the Rio Grande Valley that one must point out racial injustice, discrimination, and prejudice. I think it is meet and just that one do so, but I also think it incumbent on one to repeat that Texas Mexicans also discriminate against their own. For if skin color is often an important determinant in the United States, the color of one's skin is also a matter of importance in the Valley.

The naked truth is that we come in all colors, personalities, characters, weaknesses, strong points, and so on.

In the Valley border area, our general attitude toward African Americans can be briefly stated by mentioning but two epithets directed against them: *mayate* (black beetle) and *tinto* (inky), as well as anti–African American Spanish-language racial jokes and English-language jokes borrowed from the Texas Anglos.

While these may not be strong enough as evidence for some, the shameful (there is no other word) late nineteenth- and early twentieth-century behavior by border Mexican nationals and by Texas Mexicans against African American soldiers stationed in Brownsville should be.

After months of suffering personal indignities against themselves and their wives, the black soldiers protested and defended themselves physically in Matamoros, Tamaulipas, Mexico, and in Brownsville. The newspapers called it a riot (instigated, the papers said, "by the colored troops"), and those not jailed were hunted down. The upshot was that over two dozen of them were dishonorably discharged; President Theodore Roosevelt refused them a plea of clemency, and the sentences stood for over fifty years.

El puente de los negros is what Texas Mexicans call the bridge (*Nigger Bridge* is what Texas Anglos call it) where the black soldiers took refuge when elements of the U.S. Army, along with civilians and county and city officers, gunned some of them down. This took place in Brownsville, Texas, the same Brownsville where a one-room schoolhouse served as the black school for some years after the *Brown vs. Board of Education* decision of 1954.

This is not to say that all Texas Mexicans are racist, but it is to say that we should recognize our faults in racial matters. The same goes for Texas Anglos; not all are racists, obviously, but in my youth, in Mercedes (and in the other Valley towns without exception) racism was a given. So much so that during the Depression, despite money being scarce in the Valley, the Mission board of education built a second high school exclusively for Texas Mexicans. This in a jackleg town of fewer than 12,000 inhabitants.

Changes have occurred since then, of course, and the former chairman of the House Committee of Agriculture is a resident of Mission: the Honorable Eligio (Kika) de la Garza, Democrat from Texas. In passing, to show another part of the changes, the other three congressional representatives for the area from southern San Antonio down to Laredo and then down the river to the Valley and up the coast to Corpus Christi are all Spanish surnamed: González, Ortiz, and Bonilla.

Congressman de la Garza may be typical, in many ways, of the old Valley families: he was born in Mercedes, raised in Mission, and married Lucille Alamía of Edinburg, all three in Hidalgo County.

In my youth, Texas was a one-party state: solid Democrat. Or, as is said in some circles, Yellow-dog Democrat. The term comes from an apocryphal story that a Texan was such a staunch Democrat that he would rather vote for a yellow dog than for a Republican. This, too, has changed since the Republicans now rule the state in Austin and Washington, D.C.

The point, though, is that Texas was solid Democrat, and that goes to prove how much of a "southern" state it was, despite one of the state's strongest myths that it was a western, hence, cowboy state. Hollywood made it a cowboy state, of course, for prior to the Civil War Texas was a slave-holding state and accordingly seceded from the Union. After the war, it underwent Reconstruction; it also instituted the poll tax to prevent blacks from voting, and it provided separate tax-based facilities to separate the races in schools, hospitals, and in public transportation. And, as in any southern state, private transport also provided for separate seating and toilet facilities for non-Anglo Texans. This was not merely a southern custom, this was a state-legislated mandate.

Part of the Valley was, as some other parts of Texas, in sympathy with the Union during the Civil War. Farther up river, Laredo, a part of South Texas but not the Valley, was decidedly on the Confederate side with Captain Santos Benavides taking part in that war as did his opponent, the guerrilla leader and Valleyite Octaviano Zapata, who fought for the Union. Mexican nationals from the border also volunteered and served in the Union army.

In the Valley, many Texas Anglos who sympathized with the South during the Civil War tried the same discriminatory tactics with Texas Mexicans, and met with some success. Southern racial discriminatory practices and influences lasted even during World War II, and cities such as Harlingen and McAllen, to name but two, did not allow Texas Mexicans in the municipal public swimming pools, while at the same time other towns did not discriminate. Since many of the towns were divided either by the railroad tracks (Mercedes, Weslaco, Donna, and others) into Texas Anglo town and Mexican town, other elected officials relied on zoning laws and division of precincts with a predominantly or exclusively Texas Anglo or Texas Mexican population.

Again, one has to point out that this was not universal in the Valley. While I attended North Ward Elementary School, a one hundred percent Texas Mexican school with Anglo teachers, South Ward was predominantly Texas Anglo, but not wholly, since many Texas Mexican families lived on the south side of the railroad tracks and thus were enrolled in South Ward. The early separation came to naught, however, since Mercedes had but one middle school (grades seven to eight) and one high school (grades nine through twelve), which was attended by both groups.

As for the three black youngsters of school age in Mercedes, they were bussed to McAllen, twenty miles away for high school, or to Harlingen, fourteen miles away for the elementary grades.

The Catholic elementary school admitted both Texas Mexican and Texas Anglos, but there was discrimination there as well: one of the Texas German Catholic families saw to it that Anglo and Mexican schoolchildren were to be taught in separate rooms. This took place in the 1920s, and my parents reacted immediately by disenrolling my oldest sister, Clarissa; unfortunately, they were the only parents to do so. Clarissa was then enrolled in North Ward Elementary where the lone Texas Mexican teacher was Miss Mary Ann Villarreal, who taught in the second grade.

There may have been discrimination on the part of our Anglo teachers in middle and high school, and while one was always sensitive to being left out of school functions, we were nevertheless included. There was, though, separation: in the school dances, each group stayed apart.

Dating was something else. In my time, during the 1940s, some Anglo girls dated Mexican boys, although I never knew of Anglo boys who dated Mexican girls. Still, at a recent school reunion, I saw some old Anglo schoolmates who married Mexican women. So, in keeping with border living, the practice of this type of marriage between the two groups continues now as it had in the past.

Post–high school education in the Valley started with two junior colleges in 1927: one for the lower Valley, in Brownsville, and one for the upper Valley, in Edinburg, each with an Anglo higher administration and faculty.

In 1951, Pan American College was established in Edinburg and is now called The University of Texas—Pan American. With its current president, a native Texas Mexican, there has been a substantial increase in the number of Texas Mexicans in both administration and faculty.

Not long after World War II, Brownsville Junior College became Texas Southmost College but remained a two-year school. The institution is now called The University of Texas at Brownsville (it must be pointed out that neither institution calls for the same admission standards as The University of Texas at Austin).

Because of this and residual racism, Texas Anglos in the Valley refer to both institutions as Taco Tech, Tamale College, and Spick University, among other unhappy names, and those who can afford it prefer to send their university-eligible sons and daughters elsewhere.

Despite the pejorative name-calling, repeated personal visits reveal high morale among students and faculty. Most of the student body are first generation college attendees and are typical Valleyites: quite secure as to who they are, and thus have little doubt as to their identity. One reason I adhere to the Mercedes experience is not that it was unique in any way, but because it was my experience, although not too different from the majority of Valley border towns during that time. Even if we didn't experience discrimination firsthand or on a daily basis, racial prejudice was there, and we reminded ourselves that it was there.[2]

What we had, both societies that is, were separate structures. Not necessarily parallel, however. For instance, Mercedes published the *Enterprise* once a week and it was read, predominantly, by the Anglo residents. It was a typical small-town newspaper with notes about book clubs, garden societies, visits from out-of-town relatives, and such typical fare. Unless the War Department sent a telegram to the family (and to the Mercedes *Enterprise* for propaganda purposes in order to unify the citizenry as Americans), few to no Texas Mexican names appeared in the paper. Those that did, did so usually at semester's end when some of us made the scholastic Honor Roll or when some of us graduated from high school. During the school year, Spanish surnames would also appear when some of us participated in athletic events, school plays, or any other extracurricular activity. In the main however, the *Enterprise* was their newspaper, not ours.[3]

And now? The tilt is inescapable, due to the ninety percent Texas Mexican population, the ads for restaurants, garages, car dealerships, and other business establishments are for and by Texas Mexicans. It's a Texas Mexican town; the older Texas Anglo generation still publishes its announcements regarding the book clubs, the garden societies, and so on, and this will go on until they die out. As for their sons and daughters and grandsons and granddaughters, the majority no longer live there. The same, however, is also true for many Texas Mexicans who moved away and whose presence has been replaced by Mexican nationals who, over time, have become American citizens.

Change, as always, is the only constant.

The change in the political landscape has been mentioned, and I will touch on that again: it used to be that when Texas was a one-party state, the Democratic as said, there would be one effective election for the candidates, the primary election. Whoever won that election would win the general election, since it was always Democrats against Democrats with no Republican opponents available.

It worked this way: thirty-inch by forty-inch yellow sample ballots would be printed by the county government. Each ballot would contain the office and the list of people running for office, and these would be posted all over town by the precinct chairpersons. Election judges would then be appointed, and when election time came for the primaries (after the barbecues, the speeches, the usual promises, etc.), the voting would take place. Whoever won the primaries, as just mentioned, was the sure winner for the general elections to be held five months hence. In case of a run-off election, usually the highest two but at times the highest three candidates would hold an election and the winner would then take office after the general elections.

A sweet arrangement for the ins, obviously. Among the only Texas Mexican names one would see would be for the office of constable; this was usually an assured payment for helping the successful sheriff during the campaign.

After World War II, in Mercedes, Rodolfo Garza and Jesús Salinas ran for city commissioner posts. When Texas Mexicans first started running for public office in the 1930s, it was usually countered in this manner: say there were two Texas Mexicans running for one office; in that case, one Texas Anglo would run against them and defeat both, since the Texas Mexican vote would be divided and the Texas Anglos would vote for their candidate.

In the case of Garza and Salinas, however, they ran as a team: that is, each one ran for a different city commissioner's post. They won. As is usual in politics, they began to form alliances with the Anglo officeholders on various issues. In time, that is the way that Mercedes politics were changed when its population increased, and the voting populace became predominantly Texas Mexican. A result is that Texas Mexicans run against each other, as in the old days, but with a difference: the overwhelming Texas Mexican population could now out-vote the Texas Anglo candidate.

That is the way it is now and has been for the last thirty years. Will it continue? The chances are very good that it will: the border is still porous, newer immigrants, legal or not, continue to cross the river, many professional Mexicans live on the American side, their children attend American schools, and become Americanized. This last is gospel: the boys and girls, Mexican citizens still and thus paying tuition to enroll in school, participate in school functions, become cheerleaders, play football, and so on. They are in the process of acculturation and assimilation; their parents may not speak much English, in the way of the older American citizens of Mexican descent who didn't either, but they too, if not assimilated, are acculturating daily.

This is an interesting phenomenon and one not much taken into consideration by many recent Mexican American scholars unfamiliar with the area, its culture, and most of its history.

Has the overwhelming election of Rio Grande Valley Texas Mexican public officials brought Texas Mexicans a step nearer to the kingdom of heaven on earth?

Hardly. Venality is not necessarily a universal Texas Anglo trait nor is honesty a Texas Mexican monopoly.[4]

Nowadays, school boards with a one hundred percent Texas Mexican membership may (and do) hire and fire Texas Mexican superintendents, principals, and teachers, usually without regard to name, race, blood, or culture. They may do it on a whim or on personal enmity or regard, or whatever it pleases the board to call its collective mind. One thing the hired and fired can't do is complain that the action was taken because of racial prejudice.

Such, too, is the case in other spheres, business for one.

In the 1940s, when it was such a triumph in the Valley for a Texas Mexican to work for an Anglo enterprise such as a public utility or as a clerk or secretary for a law firm, it was considered an advancement. It was more likely an economic advancement as well, but it was a legitimate breakthrough, and it was so, and due in great part to being, in the early days, a high school graduate, and later, a college graduate.

Whatever educational weaknesses existed then and exist now, that road has been well traveled by Valley Texas Mexicans. Education did not bring happiness nor was it intended to do so, I don't think. But the older generations knew that education was what they did not have and something, then, that their children would have to have in order to compete. (Tomás Rivera, in his . . . y no se lo tragó la tierra, at times alludes, at other times points, to education as one means of advancement; education with all its travails and disappointments, to be sure, was something, *anything*, that was an improvement and better than the life being led at the time).

For many Valley Texas Mexicans of my generation (I was born in 1929), our first schooling (and this includes Rivera, a native not of the Valley but of the Winter Garden area) was in the form of private schools owned and operated by Mexican men and women, exiled in Texas during one phase or another of the Mexican Revolution. These were our first schools and meant to be followed later by the public schools or, in some cases, by parochial schools. Current events were read about in *La Prensa*, the Spanish-language daily published in San Antonio and delivered by rail all over Texas.

The above, of course, helped to maintain a Hispanic presence in the state; for the Valley, with relatives living just across the river, with our easy access to Argentine, Cuban, Mexican, and Spanish films on the Texas side, and the schools just mentioned, emphasized one's Mexicanness; true, much of the myth came along with it, but Spanish-language newspapers and radio also helped to steep one in Mexican history.

Added to all of this is the long history of Texas Mexicans in the region (since the 1749 settlement by Escandón on both sides of the river after his exploration and surveying of the area during 1747–1748). Furthermore, the area was and remained decidedly rural for a century and a half; this, along with the preceding, afforded one the opportunity to know the area, its history, and our relationship with Mexico and the United States. That the following generations know little of Mexican history is not to be deplored; it's the way of the world and the way of subsequent generations to rely on myths and not on facts. In brief, family histories are pleasant enough, but they mustn't muscle out the historical truths and tragedies faced by Texas Mexicans after 1848.

The majority of our fellow Texans also rely on myths, and this, of course, goes for the newer Anglo Texans, those who have moved there to evade harsh winters and, at times, relocate due to employment opportunities. That they learn to distrust Mexicans or to consider us as lesser beings or as less than reliable is understandable, given that their initial friendships are formed by Texans steeled in myths about us, about the state, and about their own worth. It's laughable to Valley folk when the newer Texans talk about roots, but such an attitude by Texas Mexicans also betrays a certain smugness on our part.

In the end, when everyone dies, nothing is important, really. Marriages, intermarriages, wars, economic deprivation, missed opportunities for understanding or reconciliation, hatred, racial prejudice, and all other matters, which at times unite and at times disunite us, will mean nothing when one dies.

If the Valley has given me anything, and it's given me much, it has given me a clear picture of what it is to die; the Army focused that picture some, but it was the Valley, with its old cemeteries on both sides of the river, that has formed, cemented for the most part, my view of life.

The careful reader will have noticed that I said "cemeteries on both sides of the river" and not "cemeteries on both sides of the border." The border is a term usually employed by non-borderers. And, when we speak in Spanish we always mention "el rio" but not "la frontera." *La frontera,* or the frontier, is used by those who live in inland territory. We—border-ers—usually say "across" or "this side" or "the other side" (*with the river* or *of the river* being the implied phrase).

A border is a defining place, a separateness of citizenship even, but it may, to outsiders, also imply a separate culture. It shouldn't, and it doesn't do so in the Río Grande Valley.

It isn't that we are special; most of the preceding certainly attests that we aren't. What we are, though, is a culture group that was isolated for a century and a half on land that was contested by many sides for a long time until after Reconstruction, and then forced to assimilate and acculturate while, at the same time, being relegated to a nonassimilative and nonaccul-turative status. That last is obviously a contradiction, but such is life, if it's to have any meaning.

After all, a life without contradictions is not a life worth living and en-joying. Some years back, when the majority of voters in California voted English as the official language, the Texas governor, Republican William Clements, made life interesting once again. As soon as the Californians voted to make English their official language, Governor Clements said no such law would be passed in Texas while he was governor. The heroic Texas legislature kept quiet, which is also a contradiction.

That many suffered and will continue to suffer indignities on both sides of the river is a given. But there had to be some happiness along the way in the midst of suffering: love, children, friendships, self-sacrifice, standing up to be counted, and all those things that make life worth living despite our neighbors who live on both sides of the river.

It must be emphasized that many Mexican nationals also discriminated against Mexican Americans; excoriated our language, our way of life, our culture where, in their eyes, our lack of one is a matter of public record.

But it is also a matter of public record that various Mexican govern-ments protested against the ill-treatment of American citizens of Mexican descent who suffered and underwent discrimination and, at times, lynch-ings, at the hands of their fellow American citizens.

We were not alone, then, not altogether, were we?

That Octavio Paz wrote that wrong-headed article on the Zoot-suiter and whatever else the splendid Nobelist wrote about Mexican Americans in general was in part right; he couldn't help it. But that he was wrong much more of the time is certainly the case. One of the things wrong about our attitude toward Paz is that we should recognize that he was enjoying the first amendment rights under this country's constitution, the right to be wrong at the top of one's voice.

What is also wrong is to attack him at this late date; that should have been done then, at that time, and at that place. That it wasn't is now a waste of time to debate. Does anyone really think that he will recant what he believed then? Why should he, anyway? Let's just admit that he was wrong and let it go at that. The point, of course, is not to live in the past; that territory has long been won over and populated by the neurotics among us. It is best to know about the past so that its injustices will not be repeated, that's all. For if they are repeated, then we only have ourselves to blame for allowing those among us who have no voice, no forum, no means for redress, to be treated with anything less than the respect they deserve.

And no, the Valley is not paradise nor was it meant to be. But then, it wasn't meant to be hell either, although it was that for many and for many years. And before anyone goes off the deep end in a rhapsody or in rapture of federal governmental laws, to improve our lot or that of any other group, experience and common sense have demonstrated that laws that are not enforced are but words on paper. And so, the Valley, that jurisdictional barrier, is alive and well with love and betrayal, with undying friendships and undying enmities, with racial and class discrimination, with new American citizens and old ones, and with all the tensions that make life worth living. After all, without tensions and contradictions, life usually means that someone is in constant control, a situation that guarantees unbridled power and which then provides a feeding ground for the scalping of the helpless.

Just recently, a woman friend sent me a definition of a literary critic that, in many ways, defines any critic who is not involved in a higher service for his or her fellow citizens; this is what she wrote: Literary critics are like military observers on a hill watching the carnage below and who, after the battle, come down and slaughter the survivors.

Are we critics or are we participants? In the Valley, there are many critics and few participants, but make no mistake, it has been the participants who have carried the battle on this or on that side of the river.

Notes

1. *Fear* must be added to this list; fear of miscegenation (as if they were of purer blood), and fear of discovery of their own shortcomings of whatever stripe. This last fear, as being less than perfect in the eyes of Mexican Americans, must have presented a heavy burden, al-

though the local weekly newspaper took care not to mention scandals among the Mercedes Texas Anglo society. Still, Mercedes was a small town and secrets are among the last things that people keep in such places.

2. Gender prejudice has to be included since this mental construct appears in most societies, including that of the Mexican American. That Mexican American males may ignore the fact, it must be pointed out that they were not the usual objects of rape, incest, or of other forms of spousal and parental abuse.

3. In Mercedes, as in other Valley towns (among them Brownsville, Weslaco, and Mission), some Mexican Americans owned their own small presses. Through them, part of the culture was preserved by way of *corridos*, broadsides, and the occasional satirical publication, *Calaveras*.

4. In the 1980s, the Texas Anglo District Attorney for a Valley county was removed for malfeasance; and it is not uncommon for former county attorneys, after they leave office, to represent drug smugglers. In the recent case, former sheriff for Hidalgo County, Brígido Marmolejo, was convicted on charges of bribery and other crimes and is now serving time in federal prison. In mid-summer of 1995, a Texas Mexican county judge was also under criminal indictment. And four years before that, a Texas Mexican former member of the U.S. Congress was also convicted of federal crimes.

And no, it isn't a matter of the Anglos going after Texas Mexican officials, given that the vast majority of state and federal judges, and members of the juries, are Texas Mexicans. Perhaps a quote from Saul Alinsky would help. During a successful attempt at organizing the unorganized, he was asked how they would fare once in power. His reply was: "Oh, they'll all probably turn out to be shits."

CHAPTER 12

THE SYLLOGISTIC
MIXEDBLOOD

How Roland Barthes Saved Me
from the *indians*[1]

Louis Owens

Figure 5. Bailey family, Oklahoma, 1913. Family photograph, Louis Owens.

I'm looking at a photograph of my great-grandfather, Nora Miriam Bailey's father who would vanish from her life shortly after the moment of this photo. A very young man with an angular face and intelligent, intent expression, he looks distinctly like some kind of "other," and I have diverse reasons for valuing that discovered otherness in my ancestor. With his extraordinarily narrow, slanted eyes and pronounced cheekbones, in a different context he could be the offspring of a Chinese railroad worker in the American West or anyone from a lean and hungry part of Asia. However, I am seeking quite specifically an *indian* in this photo, a Native American ancestor. Seated as he is in front of a log home with a blanket nailed over the door, surrounded by a vaguely "other"-looking family (except for his mother standing behind him and his daughter before him—both of whom look disappointingly "not-other"), in what I know to be Oklahoma in 1913, just a few years after it ceased being Indian Territory, I *know* that he is, in fact, a Cherokee-Irish mixedblood from whom I am descended. But this is my *ex post facto* reading of the images before me, my discovery of what I bring intact to the photograph, ultimately a small part of what I wish to find there. Did I not bring to the photograph a narrative, a complex of stories set in motion by words my mother wrote on the back of the photograph shortly before her death? I could not place or define these people or this place, though there are indeed clues if, like Nabokov's Kinbote searching for his own pale fire, I bend my implacable detective's gaze closely enough. Like the mad Kinbote, I can read my own image and story into and thus out of the text before me. Roland Barthes: "Those ghostly traces, photographs, supply the token presence of dispersed relatives" (9).

I am disappointed, of course, to find no *indian* in this formal family portrait (taken most likely by an itinerant photographer who had a decent camera, necessary technical knowledge, and no cultural artifacts to secure). This family from whom I am descended wear no recognizably Indian cultural artifacts; nor are they surrounded by any such signifiers. (Though there is possibility in the blanket nailed across the cabin door: what if my great-grandfather had perversely wrapped the blanket around himself for this picture?) The cabin, alas, could be any homesteader's cabin in Sooner country. The nondescript clothing they wear could be any poor frontier family's best clothing. They could, in fact, be any frontier family.

I know I am descended from indigenous peoples on both my mother's and father's sides. I know this because they told me so, as their parents told them, and so on. Mississippi Choctaw on my father's side and Oklahoma Cherokee on my mother's. Only recently did we discover the box of photographs from which I have taken this one of my great-grandfather's family. My mother's grandfather (he was—and remains in the photograph—of mixed indigenous American and European extraction) is even included in the 1910 Indian census for the state of Oklahoma and on the Cherokee tribal rolls. I lay the photograph before me and search for absent origins. Such a search, the *Anishinaabe* writer Gerald Vizenor has informed us all, must seek "a hyperreal simulation and . . . the ironic enactment of a native presence by an absence in a master narrative" (27). Extracted ultimately in the picture, my great-grandfather's image takes on the polysemous character Barthes has identified as the essence of such images. To find the Indian in the photographic cupboard, I must narratively construct him out of his missing presence, for my great-grandfather was Indian but not an Indian. Like most mixedbloods, I assume, I am aware of the irony of such a wistful enactment, and I have seen it in my own children and brothers and sisters and friends, the familiar tortured syllogism: Indians have Indian ancestors. I have Indian ancestors. Therefore, I am an Indian. Unfortunately, in Indian Territory nothing is so simple.

Clue: *He* looks like me when I was also young; but I am now older than my great-grandfather will ever have been. In a mirror, I have much the same eyes and mouth and perhaps something very similar to the vulpine distrust registered in his resistant expression; but Vizenor has warned us that the *"indian* has never been real in the mirror, or a name of presence in the simulations of history" (28). Nonetheless, I felt a kind of tremor of recognition when I saw the picture for the first time a couple of years ago. We had heard of this man, my eight brothers and sisters and I, throughout our lives. John Bailey, the mixedblood Cherokee grandfather who, our aunt told us, guided wagon trains in Indian Territory (this last surely a childishly apocryphal story about the man our aunt never met). But it was not until several years after our mother's death that the box of photographs containing this particular photo surfaced. For the first time we had some kind of hard, objective evidence that John Bailey had existed, as well as a photograph of our long-dead grandmother as a three-year-old standing between her longer-dead father's knees with his probably longer-dead-still mother standing behind him and brothers and sisters around him.

It was as if a ghost had ceased its rattling and moaning to finally show itself for the first time. He is concrete now in this image, a mixedblood ancestor, for as Barthes insists, ". . . in Photography I can never deny that the *thing has been there.* . . . Hence it would be better to say that Photography's inimitable feature (its *noeme*) is that someone has seen the referent

... *in flesh and blood*, or again *in person*" (76, 79). Susan Sontag, anticipating Barthes, explains: "A photograph passes for incontrovertible proof
that a given thing happened. The picture may distort; but there is always a
presumption that something exists, or did exist, which is like what's in the
picture" (5). The key, in Sontag's statement, of course, is the "like." Someone "like" my great-grandfather, with his rakishly tilted hat and amused-
looking but utterly resistant expression, existed and was seen *in flesh and
blood* and *in person* by at least those people around him and behind the other
aperture. Existed and etched himself into the features of my rogue uncle,
my mother's brother dead now for many years, and into my own face and
most likely other portions of my self. Others among the seven adults and
three children in the photograph look on with sullen, uncertain, or indeterminate expressions, but my great-grandfather squints with definite
amusement and perhaps a touch of contempt mingling with curiosity and
a great withholding, his two hands lightly draped upon the shoulders of his
toddler daughter, whose small, pale hands in turn look to be firmly holding to each of his knees. They are oddly interlocked in the photograph, the
child who would be my wild-drinking, rootless, and reckless grandmother
and her cagey-looking father. Oddly, because I know from family stories
that he would vanish from her life almost as soon as the photograph was
taken, abandoning her for reasons no one ever seemed to know (maybe
death, the way his grandson, my uncle Bob, would be murdered young;
maybe mere irresponsibility). What I know is that the fact of absence already haunts this photograph as does a greater mystery for me.

And greater discovery. My grandmother's mother was said by my
mother and aunt to have possibly been named Edith or Emily and to have
been a "full-blooded Cherokee." But there is no written record of her, and
no one really knows her name or anything beyond the originary simulation of full-bloodedness. Thus our great-grandmother would seem to have
joined the legion of invisible Cherokee great-grandmothers in American
lore, that frontier pageant of ghostly Indian princesses who haunt our
metanarrative bloodlines. She vanished, the stories always indicated, as
soon as our grandmother was born and bore no other race in family memory, a storied "fact" I have cited in my own writings. However—and I
am stunned right now by this recognition—a very young, pretty, *Indian-
looking* woman stands behind my great-grandfather in this recently discovered photograph, her posture straight and dignified and, most significantly,
her right hand resting possessively and confidently upon John Bailey's
shoulder. They are linked thus by hands, my infant grandmother, her

father, and this unnamed woman. No one else in the photograph is touch-
ing another; all hands are held to the sides or on knees or together in laps.
Only my grandmother, her father, and this young woman touch one another as though intuiting that this intimate and crucial connection will too
soon be broken. "The eyes and hands of wounded fugitives in photographs
are the sources of stories, the races of native survivance" says Vizenor, "all
the rest is ascribed evidence, surveillance, and the interimage simulations
of dominance" (158). These hands, forming a signifying chain from child
through man to woman, are not Indian but human. *I think she is my great-
grandmother.* She does not look like the other, heavily Irished, family members in the photograph. She is an other "other" in this grouping. Though
no one is alive who can verify the possibility, I believe I have discovered
my great-grandmother, who has stood invisibly in this photograph for all
the months I have perused it, the invisible Native in the *tableau vivant* of
Indianness I have sought to construct, rendered invisible by the narrative
I have brought to this photograph. Told that my grandmother's mother
did not exist, I could not therefore see her image before me. "Whatever
it grants to vision and whatever its manner," Barthes says, "a photograph
is always invisible: it is not it that we see . . . the referent adheres" (6).
In the case of my ancestral photograph, the fiction has appropriated the
referent; looking for traces of an absent origin, I have been blinded to
the purely human image here. But I have found her at this moment. Now
I believe deeply that this young Cherokee woman had being, *in flesh and
blood,* that she flashed *in person* across Indian Territory and Oklahoma for
brief years and vanished abruptly. Studying the diminutive, very attractive
young woman, I doubt that she is the fullblood I have been told she was.
She doesn't look quite *indian* enough, though she looks beautifully Native,
someone I would like to know. Suddenly the photograph opens to a new
narrative, more poignant, humanly resonant. Off to the side, however, I
hear the whispered warning of Barthes, who writes that "essentially the
camera makes everyone a tourist in other people's reality, and eventually
in one's own" (57).

Barthes, scrutinizing a photograph of his mother as a child, tells himself
that "she is going to die." "I shudder," he writes, "*over a catastrophe which
has already occurred.*" A moment before, contemplating his response to a
photograph of Lewis Payne, taken while Payne was waiting to be hanged
for the attempted assassination of U.S. Secretary of State W. H. Seward,
Barthes has written: "The photograph is handsome, as is the boy: that is
the *studium.* But the *punctum* is: he *is going to die.* I read at the same time:

This will be and this has been; I observe with horror an anterior future of which death is the stake" (96). Examining this picture of my grandmother as a toddler standing between the knees of her father and surrounded by, I am now certain, her vanishing mother, her aunts, uncles, and grandmother, I feel the encroachment of an old catastrophe as well: here are roots of uncertainty and disequilibrium. Already I see in the set of my infant grandmother's tilted mouth the defiance and dis-ease that will mark her and the disasters that she will fling at everyone within the range of her helter skelter life. Very shortly after the photograph was taken, the family in the photograph would disappear from my grandmother's life, leaving her to carom between homes until at the brutally early age of thirteen she would herself be a mother who would in turn abandon her own children. This incipient, catastrophic absence of my grandmother's parents and family haunts the photograph.

All of these people are many years dead, but nonetheless Barthes' catastrophe of the photograph as *memento mori* is not my catastrophe. Death leaves very little residue, actually, despite Barthes' long pondering upon his vanished mother. ("Natives mourned the presence, not the absence of the dead," Vizenor has written.) For me, the *punctum* in this photograph of my ancestors is not *he is dead*, or they are dead, but *he is me*—or they are me.[2] Already in the photograph he and they (and therefore this portion of me) are disturbing absences, pricking, bruising, poignant; and I observe an anterior future in which absence, not death, is the stake. What catastrophe occurred to sever the connections represented in these images, what sent my grandmother at such a fragile age spinning off into a solitary and damaging life and erased all memories of the mother from family stories? Is this simply an aspect of the familiar story of deracination and loss that marks mixedblood history?

Heritage, history, and story are the real crucibles of catastrophe. Phenotype is phenomenal. "But more insidious, more penetrating than likeness," writes Barthes, "the Photograph sometimes makes appear what we never see in a real face (or in a face reflected in a mirror): a generic feature, the fragment of oneself or of a relative which comes from some ancestor. In a certain photograph, I have my father's sister's 'look.' The Photograph gives a little truth, on condition that it parcels out the body. But this truth is not that of the individual, who remains irreducible; it is the truth of lineage" (103). "Lineage," Barthes adds, "reveals an identity stronger, more interesting than legal status—more reassuring as well, for the thought of origins soothes us, whereas that of the future disturbs us, agonizes us . . ." (105). I have much of my great-grandfather's look, the angular and rather disturbing face of the photograph that will be passed first to his grandson, my uncle Bob who would be rabbiting across all our lives, disrupting, stealing, laughing, telling wild tales, being taken away to prison again and again, and dying young and violently.

The thought of origins does not soothe all of us. For some, the thought of origins can, in fact, be far more agonizing than the future. If like a Nabokov creation I can make of the past a necessary fiction, I must also acknowledge that the past's residence within language makes it inescapably mere fiction. However, the future that recedes infinitely before me, beyond language, is helpless to challenge my construction of it, to repudiate my reading. Despite my most strenuous efforts within language, I can determine nothing of the inexorably absolute past, of origins; the past, with its endless accretions, renders me inauthentic. As Barthes admonishes, "The Photograph does not call up the past" (82). Who were those people in the photograph? I know that they were mixedbloods in Indian Territory, living in what my family persisted in calling the Cherokee Nation, with Irish and probably other European roots as well. I know this because that is the fiction I have memorized, my history. But as Barthes also points out, quoting Nietzsche, "A labyrinthine man never seeks the truth, but only his Ariadne" (73). Winding into the labyrinth of the Territory, I find no thread of consciousness or knowledge, no Native Ariadne. There are fibers out of which a thread might be woven, bits of family story, old photographs with scribbling on the backs, but no coherent narrative (Barthes: "language is, by nature, fictional"). Despite the elusive promise of my newly found great-grandmother in the photograph, who would make a splendid Ariadne indeed, the remaining fibers prove too fragmentary for weaving, too thin to cohere. In the end is only the maze and the monster of hybrid potential at its center. I remain in the labyrinth, puzzled, hearing the approach of my own footsteps.

We know they are mixedbloods. My mother and aunt and uncle and grandmother spoke of these people and of this place. But these people could be any people anywhere. Barthes, captivated by the way subjects in photographs are dressed, including his mother, declares that "clothing is perishable, it makes a second grave for the loved being" (64). Clothing may indeed be perishable, but costumes are not, as nineteenth-century ethnographic photographers understood when they kept "typical" Indian dress on hand for those Indian subjects who might not possess such essential attire.[3] Costumes stop clocks. Had my ancestors in the Territory been dressed up as Indians, they would have escaped this Barthesian grave—never mind that their Cherokee relatives had for many years already been dressing and living much as European Americans dressed and lived. Fringed leather, beads, feathers, braids—such signifiers would tell me and anyone else exactly who these people were and are—for these signs of Indianness escape mutability, evade death. These people, however, were *Indian* but not *Indians.* I search vainly for signifiers of Indian presence in this photograph: if only this or that could pronounce these people Indians, but the log cabin with blanket nailed over the door, the nondescript poorfolks' clothing, the suspicious posture—none of this says "Indian." I look more closely at the faces. The hair is for the most part dark, a good "Indian" aspect. Some of the faces have the unmistakably "Asian" look to them that people descended from Bering Strait immigrants are supposed to have, most pronouncedly my great-grandfather's face. The complexions appear to be of varying hues, from light to dark. Distressingly, my young grandmother looks rather white, though her father and aunts appear suitably dark. One of the uncles, August Edward Bailey (I know from my mother's writing on the back of the photograph), looks very much like a surly Irishman. Aunt Nora, John Bailey's sister, appears quite Cherokee to me, but perhaps that is wish fulfillment on my part, since Cherokees, too, come in all forms. I do not seek Irish signifiers in this family, for the stories that have defined me from birth in my own hearing have never been Irish, and of course I enter the labyrinth in search of what I already know to be at the center: the monster of my own hybridization. Were our family stories about Irish clans and leprechauns, rather than lightning-struck trees and little people, perhaps I would study these photographs with different desire and less difficulty. If it is true, as Sontag insists, that "to photograph is to appropriate the thing photographed" (4), then it is more true that to gaze upon a photograph is to appropriate into our own originary history the object of the photograph. In studying this photograph of my ancestors, I cannot deny that I am attempting to appropriate a kind of "Indianness" into my own life.

Writing of Ishi, the famed last survivor of the exterminated Yahi people in California, Gerald Vizenor has explained: "The tribes have become the better others, to be sure, and the closer the captured experiences are to the last wild instances in the world, the more valuable are the photographs . . . the last wild man and other tribal people captured in photographs have been resurrected in a nation eager to create a tragic past" (Lippard 66, 71). In exploring my family photo nearly a century old, I cannot avoid the bothersome sense that I, too, am searching for a "better other," clues to "the last wild instances in the world," that I desire to force my long-dead relatives to enact a kind of cultural striptease to accommodate my desire for lineal contact with the original absent other. But I desire and need something the images in the photograph will not divulge. Though I may have found a great-grandmother, Indianness remains hidden away in the recesses that resist my entrance. These figures repudiate me, and I feel a kind of anger or resentment emanating from their images, as if they anticipate my future larceny. "Nevertheless," Sontag says, "the camera's rendering of reality must always hide more than it discloses" (23).

Sontag declares furthermore that "[i]n America, the photographer is not simply a person who records the past but the one who invents it" (67). But nothing is invented in this photograph of my great-grandfather's family, and nothing remains to be appropriated. Resistant images only are recorded, resisting depth, narrativization, invention, appropriation, assimilation. Faced with this photograph, and others in the family box, I realize that the photographer who supposedly invents the past, like a Curtis photographing "real" Indians, actually invents nothing but rather goes in search of what already exists prior to his subjects, has already been invented by the myth-making consciousness of America, to find, recognize, and verify that prior invention (how otherwise could he bear the signifiers of authenticity with him as props?). "Indians" are thus invented, but conversely, by the same process mixedbloods are recorded and erased, having no place in the metanarrative of fixed colonial others. The opaqueness rendered toward the camera, the exclusion of the photographer from the implied life, the resistance of the pose, all of this comes from the fact that mixedbloods *cannot* be known—and they know full well that they cannot be known, that the camera will obscure them except within their own vision. Ours, they seem to say, is a life undefined and beyond your reach; we invent such a life each day, *sui generis*. Robert Young has written about history that "the other is neutralized as a means of encompassing it: ontology amounts to a philosophy of power, as egotism in which the relation with the other is accomplished through its assimilation into the self" (13). Young quotes Hélène Cixous, who, remarking upon what she terms an "annihilating dialectical magic," states, "I saw that the great, noble, 'advanced' countries established themselves by expelling what was 'strange'; excluding it but not dismissing it; enslaving it" (1).

Mixedbloods were and are exempt from such ontology and from this annihilating dialectical magic because they inhabited and still inhabit a boundary zone. This is not the bleeding "open wound" described in Gloria Anzaldúa's *Borderlands*, for no tragic victimage is embraced or celebrated here; though it is, in fact, very much like Anzaldúa's description of the borderland as "a vague and undetermined place created by the emotional residue of an unnatural boundary . . . in a constant state of transition" (3). In a constant state of transition, Cherokee mixedbloods have had a long and honorable place within post-Columbian America, beginning with the first influx of Europeans. A paragraph from Grace Steele Woodward's *The Cherokees* gives us a sense of the early and thorough reality of such miscegenation:

> John Adair, from Ireland, married Mrs. Ge-ho-ga Foster, a full-blood Cherokee of the Deer Clan. George Lowrey married Nannie of the Holly Clan, and their son George (born about 1770) figured prominently in the affairs of the [Cherokee] Nation until his death in 1852. . . . From mixed-blood unions consummated in the Colonial period came future Cherokee leaders, saints, and sinners (85–86).

Today there is an Adair County in Oklahoma, and the list of prominent Cherokee mixedbloods is unending, including such figures as John Ross, one-eighth Cherokee by blood quantum and highly educated but the most prominent of all Cherokee leaders and the most eloquent opponent of Removal in the early nineteenth century; Sequoyah (George Guess), creator of the Cherokee syllabary; John Rollin Ridge, whose father was educated in New England and who in 1854 became the first Native American novelist. Countless mixedbloods made the long and deadly walk to Indian Territory and built their homes and farms there, entering into a new life as resilient and adaptive survivors, the way native peoples of the Americas always have. No countable cultural artifacts or commodities, these people were simply bent on survival in their place and time. As Vizenor has pointed out, before the twentieth century in America, "Natives had practiced medicine, composed music, published histories, novels, and poetry, won national elections, and traveled around the world . . ." (165). But these Natives were not the Indians sought feverishly by archival imagists on the other side of the aperture and therefore not the ones whose images became, as George Steiner has explained about the "past that rules us," imprinted as "symbolic constructs of the past . . . almost in the manner of genetic information, on our sensibility" (3). The very existence of these heroic pragmatists and syncretic survivors was "obscured by the interimage simulations of the *indian*, the antithesis of civilization in photographs and motion pictures" (165).[4] Mixedbloods or fullbloods, Native Americans who shunned the static props desired and proffered by cultural artificers, and insisted on living and surviving in the dynamic moment, were erased by those who manufacture kitschy history for acquisitive colonial power.

Mixedbloods cannot be appropriated because they cannot be defined. By the absoluteness of their irrefutable presence, beyond myth and metaphor, stubbornly obstructing the construction of simulated Indians, they are annoying obstacles to white appropriation. Mixedbloods cannot be neutralized or encompassed or assimilated. In *White Mythologies*, Robert Young quotes Said: "In occupying two places at once . . . the depersonalized, dislocated colonial subject can become an incalculable object, quite literally, difficult to place. The demand of [colonial] authority cannot unify its message nor simply identify its subjects" (143). Young also quotes Homi Bhabha to the effect that "[i]n racial stereotyping 'colonial power produces the colonized as a fixed reality which is at once an "other" and yet entirely knowable and visible'" (143). Mixedbloods are Said's ultimate "incalculable object" or "dislocated colonial subjects"; neither "knowable" nor "visible" in Bhabha's terms, they resist racial stereotyping and fixed realities as they balance within their two sites of Native and Euramerican selves.

"There is a history of darkness in the making of images," the novelist and photographer Wright Morris has pointedly noted. About nineteenth-century photographs of Indians, Morris suggests: "Presented in their full regalia, as if intuiting a final judgement, they faced the photographer as if assembled to be shot" (16). The mixedbloods in our family photographs imitate nothing, nor do they face the camera ready to be shot. They are ambivalent survivors ready to slip away at the first twitch of history's trigger finger. Uncostumed, they defiantly or sullenly or suspiciously regard the camera as a strange diversion to be briefly borne before they get on with their discordant lives, leaving the photographic record of this one moment to flutter on casual winds across generations. They inhabit neither past nor future. They give me nothing.

These photographs taken in Indian Territory are records of invisibility; and it is within the invisible that I locate mixedblood identity. There is no space for mixedbloods within the national fantasy; therefore they remain uninvented.

"Thus the air," says Barthes, "is the luminous shadow which accompanies the body; and if the photograph fails to show this air, then the body moves without a shadow, and once this shadow is severed . . . there remains no more than a sterile body" (110). In Choctaw cosmology a person possesses two shadows, the *shilup* and *shilombish*, two souls as it were. In life and death these two shadows have different responsibilities, different paths.[5] Though Choctaw and Cherokee belief systems are quite different from one another, it strikes me that the generic Native mixedblood resembles this Choctaw figure of two shadows, differences cast by the unitary unnamable coming between perception and light, without which differences there would indeed be only the sterile body. In the photographs, these shadows form something like a palimpsest of soul, paradoxically simultaneous shimmerings over the flat surface. Posing with two shadows, mixedbloods split the history of darkness at the heart of image-making, withholding what the colonial contriver would take. *Indian* but not *Indians*, Irish but not Irishmen.

Few looking at photos of mixedbloods would be likely to say, "But they don't look like Irishmen," but everyone seems obligated to offer an opinion regarding the degree of Indianness represented. Even my wife, who is descended from Declaration of Independence signers (with resultant family mythologies), who has borne twenty-five years of my personal mixedblood musings, and who knows my knotted family history, peruses these ancestral photographs and says, "They don't look very Indian." I hold my tongue, not responding with what I have said at other times to other people: "Do you mean they don't look Navajo or Lakota or Cherokee or Lummi or Yurok or fullblood or halfblood or quarterblood or *what*?" How, in fact, I want to ask, could anyone in a photograph look like an "Indian," something that never existed? The answer is, of course, that these mixedbloods could look "*indian*" only by being what Vizenor has labeled "cultural ritualists": by dressing in costume, posing as the absent other, stopping the clock. Had these mixedblood Cherokee ancestors posed in traditional Plains Indian headdresses and beadwork, everyone would immediately know they were Indian. A Navajo-Laguna friend (a "real" fullblooded Indian) looks at a photograph of one of my great-aunts who happens to be very dark-complexioned, has a pronouncedly large nose, and stares at the camera with sullen suspicion, and he says, "*She* looks like *something*." What he means, of course, is that she is dark like his relatives and therefore looks like what he thinks of as *Indian*. In my experience, my fox-faced great-grandfather, though not nearly as darkly hued as the aunt, looks more "Indian."

How do we combat this essentialist discourse when it comes even from those we love? How do we teach our own children the meaning of "indian-ness" in their own blood when they can only look to these photographs for signs they will not find? Where is the thread that will take us to the heart of this maze and back out to the ordered world where paths ostensibly do not turn back upon themselves and monsters ostensibly do not lurk? "How are we to distinguish between the real and the imitation?" asks Wright Morris (4). I see in these mixedblood ancestors the kind of suspicious yet resolute indeterminacy that I feel in my own life and see in my own face, a kind of native negative capability. The Indian has never been real in the mirror. I tell my children that I am not an Indian in the photographs they preserve.

Notes

1. For this specific use, I have borrowed this form of the word from Gerald Vizenor, who explains that the "indian is the simulation of a logocentric other," without referent. On most occasions I will retain the familiar "Indian." See Vizenor's *Fugitive Poses* for extensive discussion of the term.

2. "A photograph's punctum is that accident which pricks me (but also bruises me, is poignant to me)," Barthes explains (*Camera Lucida*, 27).

3. See Dorothy and Thomas Hoobler, *Photographing the Frontier*, 117.

4. Of his own mixed-blood father, Vizenor writes: "My father was not a cultural ritualist; he never surrendered to shamans, base traditions, or absence as the source of a native sense of presence. He and many others of his generation moved from reservations to cities some sixty years ago during a severe economic depression in the country. Their concern, and with a much richer sense of humor at the time, was survival" (*Fugitive Poses*, 87).

5. This is not a rare belief. Vizenor cites virtually the same belief in doubled spirits among the *Anishinaabe* (*Fugitive Poses*, 94).

CODA

From Exoticism
to Mixed-Blood Humanism

CHAPTER 13

FROM BLOOD TO CULTURE

Miscegenation as Metaphor for the Americas

Earl E. Fitz

A tangled and explosive function of race, sex, power, and identity, miscegenation merits consideration as the supreme metaphor of the entire American experience, North, South, and Central. Although in the Americas we have long tended to interpret it narrowly, as an issue of biology alone, miscegenation may well be more germane to our collective New World experience[1] if considered in its larger cultural context, a perspective that allows us to view it as being profoundly and inextricably linked to the diverse social, economic, and political structures that guide and align our various American cultures.[2] And while racial mixing is by no means unique to the New World (which, as Gordon Brotherston[3] and others have shown, was, of course, an already ancient world to the millions of people who lived here at the time of the Europeans' arrival), its centrality here, and the ongoing political and cultural implications generated by it, make the issue of interracial sexuality of singular importance to any theoretical conceptualization concerning our American cultures, their identities, and their relationships.

This is certainly borne out in the literature of the Americas where, since the beginning, interracial mixing has been a constant, if deeply conflictive, feature. One of the earliest examples of this must surely be the case of the Native American woman known to history as La Malinche. Captured by Cortés in 1520 and used as a concubine and interpreter, La Malinche played a pivotal role in the Spanish conquest of the Aztec empire. A vital force even in today's modern Mexico as a cultural myth,[4] a symbol of oppression and of the exploitation of the weak by the powerful, Malinche lives on, the epitome of the subjugation of the New World by the Old. One prominent critic, the late Emir Rodríguez Monegal, has even argued that the entire body of writing that we think of as Spanish American literature begins with the work of El Inca Garcilaso de la Vega, a seventeenth-century "mestizo" whose father was a Spanish "conquistador" and whose mother was an Incan princess.[5] The conception of "Latin America" as a largely "mestizo" culture has indeed emerged as one of the defining cultural stereotypes of the Americas, one that has been more than tinged with the pernicious traces of racism. As one examines the literature of the New World, however, it becomes clear that racial mixing has, from the beginning, been a central fact not only of the Canadian experience[6] but also of that of the United States as well, where the entwined stories of Captain John Smith, Pocahontas, and John Rolfe have, for example, passed into the realm of cultural mythology.[7]

The inescapable conclusion of a comparative examination of the literature of the Americas on this point is that miscegenation lies, albeit restively, at the heart of the entire American experience. Moreover, when one considers it in terms of cultural interaction rather than exclusively in its more traditional biological context it becomes clear that miscegenation comes close to epitomizing the American experience, to embodying it in all its conflict, violence and idealism. From Eldridge Cleaver's *Soul on Ice* (1968), which advocates that black men rape white women as an act of political terrorism, to Brazilian Jorge Amado's *Tenda dos milagres* (1969), which posits racial mixing not only as being characteristic of Brazil but as the salvation of the human race, the issue of miscegenation speaks to and reflects virtually all aspects of what it has meant to be an American. But, as I will attempt to show in this essay, now, at the beginning of the twenty-first century, the time may have come for us to begin to think of miscegenation more as a cultural issue than as an exclusively racial one. To do so allows us to see not only our past and present more clearly but, more importantly, our future as well, the people and societies that we ought to be. Should this come about, the issue of miscegenation, understood in a larger, more cultural context, might well help us begin at long last to realize what was one of the driving myths that led the Europeans to our shores hundreds of years ago—the vision of the New World as an edenic paradise.

Yet it also seems clear that, as exemplified in works like *The Last of the Mohicans* (1826), *Ramona* (1884), *The Loved and Lost* (1951), *Light in August* (1932), *Absalom, Absalom!* (1936), or *Halfbreed* (1973), we have, particularly in the English-speaking Americas, been too long obsessed with the purely sexual dimension of miscegenation.[8] Now, however, at the turn of the century, writers throughout the Americas are increasingly coming to deal with the issue of racial mixing not as a hopelessly divisive shibboleth but as an undeniable fact of our historical experience, as a definitive and pervasive — if contentious — aspect of our common "American" heritage.[9] As much of our current Hispanic and Native American literature clearly shows, for example, one result of this new, more culturally inclined attitude about miscegenation is a focus on the forging of a new socio-political identity, one at once "mixed" and that deals with the old issue of power (racial and sexual) not as being effectively immutable, as we have long viewed it to be, but as an issue of assimilation and change, one that, as in Ana Castillo's *Sapogonia* (1990), points to the actualization of a society (a fictionalized United States) in which racially mixed people are getting themselves elected to political office. The degree and kind of evolution involved here can be most readily understood by examining the role racial mixing plays in such works as Cleaver's *Soul on Ice* (1968) or V. S. Naipaul's *Guerrillas* (1975), both of which feature the rape of white women by non-whites as an act of political revolution, and its depiction in narratives like Leslie Marmon Silko's *Ceremony* (1977), Castillo's *Sapogonia* (1990), John Updike's *Brazil* (1994), Alix Renaud's *A corps joie* (1985), Helena Parente Cunha's *A mulher no espelho* (1983), Gabriel García Márquez' *Del amor y otros demonios* (1994), Nélida Piñon's *A república dos sonhos* (1984), or Albert French's *Holly* (1995), books which, without minimizing our numerous and seemingly intractable problems of historical conflict, also seem to point to a way out of the violence, loathing, and self-destructiveness that have so long plagued us in regard to this issue. As such, these works typify what we may justifiably consider a new and more culturally honest late twentieth-century response to our old blood-based preoccupation with the issue of miscegenation and its various socio-cultural ramifications.

From Spanish America, where this movement can be traced from the cultural significance of "La Malinche" through *Sab* (1841) and *Cecilia Valdés* (1882), to the twentieth-century work of Vasconcelos, Pietri, Arguedas, and Márquez, to Brazil, where the issue of miscegenation has long been a thematic staple,[10] and from Haiti to Canada and the United States, which, as a culture, has never been comfortable with the issue of racial mixing (a point reaffirmed in Peter Brimelow's *Alien Nation*), this alternative approach to race relations in the Americas has, I believe, entered a new phase of development, one that has moved beyond both a fascination with and a horror of interracial sexual relations and toward a greater, more comprehensive sense of human solidarity, one in which what has happened in the

Americas can, in fact, be read as a trope for the entire human experience. While no one would argue that we have as yet achieved societies that are blind to differences in skin color, I do believe that we are seeing many of our leading contemporary American writers dealing with the issue of inter-racial sex, and the progeny produced by it, in new, more accepting ways, however, that do not fail to confront the stubborn persistence of racism in the Americas and in the world at large. In conceptualizing this theory as it pertains to the Americas, it may be useful to contrast our "Anglo-American" world (the United States and English Canada), which, judging from its history and literature, still has a long way to go toward accepting racial mixing,[11] with the Spanish, Portuguese and French parts of the New World, areas where people of racially mixed heritages have tended to be more easily accepted, albeit all too frequently, as in the case of Canada's métis, relegated into inferior or second-class socio-economic positions. Keeping this historical perspective in mind, then, we will, in this essay, be-ginning with a recent French Canadian novel, examine several works from throughout the Americas that exemplify this new, more culturally aware approach to the theme of miscegenation.

Tapping into the tradition of the immigrant novel, Dany Laferrière, a 1978 arrival in Montréal from the strife of his native Haiti, has, in *Comment faire l'amour avec un nègre sans se fatiguer* (1985; *How to Make Love to a Negro*, 1987), written a bitingly comic novel that is at once a satire of black/white sexual relations and also a sardonic critique of the problems of cultural assimilation faced by a newcomer to a society hitherto alien and even closed to him. The story of a young black man recently arrived in Montréal, *How to Make Love to a Negro* uses sex as a marker of various aspects of the prevailing social and political code. As the narrator says, at one point, "I'm here to fuck the daughter of these haughty diplomats who once whacked us with their sticks. I wasn't there at the time of course, but what do you want, history hasn't been good to us, but we can always use it as an aphrodisiac" (Laferrière 76). Thus, deliberately utilizing the older term, "nègre," (negro, or as the novel's translator, David Homel, believes, even nigger) instead of the more fashionable "noir," or "black," Laferrière succeeds, as all skillful satirists do, in discomfiting both his white audience and his black one. A short, compact work, *How to Make Love to a Negro* flaunts its sexual explicitness and, moreover, does so in a way that plays off against each other certain key stereotypes about black men and white women. One of these, and perhaps the most decisive myth of all, is that of the black man's vaunted sexuality and its supposedly irresistible attractiveness to white women. What is unique about Laferrière's novel, however, is that he employs this culturally explosive myth in order to debunk it and, in doing so, to open the door, so to speak, for another, less prejudicial and less stereotypical sense of being and identity to emerge from his pages, one which, the reader feels, could liberate not only blacks but whites (and especially white women) as well.

By shifting the paradigm of sexual politics to be employed in this novel so as to undercut its ostensible focus only on the sexuality of the black man vis-à-vis the white woman, the narrator notes how the very fickle "Great Mandala" sex machine "of the Western World" has changed, how it now prefers "yellow," the Japanese, whereas a bit earlier it had preferred "red," that is, Native Americans:

> ... Yellow is coming on strong. The Japanese are clean, they don't take up much space and they know the Kama Sutra like the back of their Nikons. The sight of one of those yellow dolls (4 feet 10, 110 pounds), as portable as a make-up case, on the arm of a long, tall girl is enough to make you cry the blues. I hear the Japs are as good at disco as Negroes are at jazz (Laferrière 18).

But, as the narrator ruefully notes, "It wasn't always that way. God didn't used to be yellow—the traitor! During the seventies, America got off on Red. White girls practically moved onto Indian reservations to earn their sexual BAs" (Laferrière 18). Continuing to play up the sexual aphrodisiac of interracial sexual relations, the narrator goes on wryly to declare that, "Naturally, a great number of Redskins came running from a great number of tribes, attracted by the scent of young, white squaw. A young Iroquois had his pride, but a free fuck is better than a bottle of rotgut. White girls were doing it Huron-style. A Cheyenne screw was the hottest thing around" (Laferrière 18).

However, as befits the image of the Great Mandala, one group always benefits from another's decline, and so we are not surprised to learn that just when life was returning to normal, with "Western Civilization" having survived the titillating red scare, and "just as girls were about to succumb to boredom with the pallid, pale, faded Ivy League boys, the violent, potent, incendiary Black Panthers burst upon the campus scene" (Laferrière 18). Bringing the text up to its present time, but subtly allowing the reader to view the narrator's utilization of black sexual prowess from a satiric perspective, this crucial moment also allows Laferrière to concentrate more

freely on the explosive complexities inherent in interracial sexual relations and on the individual and cultural identities involved: "Put black vengeance and white guilt together in the same bed and you had a night to
remember!" (Laferrière 18). At this juncture in the text's development (and
perhaps best understood more as a problem of how an individual human
being can come to possess a satisfying personal identity than as a lurid and
militant exposé of black/white sexual adventures), the narrator utters what
the reader might take as the narrative's most revealing statement: "The
world has grown rotten with ideologies" (Laferrière 39).

    This decisive scene, in which we gain access to the more serious issue
being dealt with here (the problem of individuation in cultures that demand total conformity to rigid, self-serving systems of belief), prepares
the reader for the novel's perhaps otherwise unexpected conclusion, in
which the author/narrator reflects, in an interview for the radio show,
"Noir sur Blanc"/"Black on White," on the problems faced by individual
human beings who, in a world structured around conflictive points of view
(but most especially those relating to the issues of race, sexuality, power,
and gender), seek their own truths, their own lives. It is in the novel's conclusion, then, that the reader comes to consider the possibility that *How
to Make Love to a Negro* is less about interracial sex per se than it is about
how to avoid living in an ideological straitjacket. Having thus established
the primacy of the writer and of art over the dehumanizing constraints of
doctrinaire politics, the narrator is free to bring the narrative to its logical end, which he proceeds to do in the very short final segment entitled,
appropriately enough, "You're Not Born Black, You Get That Way."

    Another recent "American" novel, *Moi, Tituba, Sorcière de Salem* (1986;
I, Tituba, Black Witch of Salem, 1992), by the Guadeloupean writer Maryse
Condé, deals with much the same theme as *How to Make Love to a Negro*
but does so in a distinctly different fashion. Although both novels concern
themselves with the place of sexuality in the context of race relations and,
to a degree, the prevailing power structures that inscribe them, the Caribbean novel, rich in postmodern irony, does so in a way that advances a col-
lectivist, or cultural, ethic more overtly than the French Canadian novel,
which, with its own ironically self-conscious author/narrator, stresses the
primacy of the individual over the collective. Additionally, one feels that
while *How to Make Love to a Negro* most certainly establishes itself as a
comic novel, albeit a caustic one, *I, Tituba, Black Witch of Salem*, though re-
plete with numerous parodic elements of its own, tends, at times, to come
across as a diatribe, one directed at "white men" and their societies.

Indeed, this latter theme, the damage wrought upon millions of innocent people by the exploitative social, economic, and political systems erected and put into operation by "white men," constitutes the heart of Condé's text, and if its rather constant reiteration may, for some, detract from its artistry, there can be no doubt concerning its cultural significance. The perniciousness of "white men" (a thematic ground for several of the works considered here) is, indeed, established as a motif at the very outset of the novel when the narrator, explaining her background, declares:

> Abena, my mother, was raped by an English sailor on the deck of *Christ the King* one day in the year 16** while the ship was sailing for Barbados. I was born from this act of aggression. From this act of hatred and contempt (Condé 3).

The theme of miscegenation thus appears, as a function of sexuality as well as culture, early on in *I, Tituba, Black Witch of Salem* as a metaphor of the entire "American" experience, one characterized by various forms of rape and exploitation, an issue also elaborated by Octavio Paz in his discussion of "La Chingada." Imbued with a bitter irony (in that the means of conveyance for this rape, physically, culturally, and ethically, is a ship known as "Christ the King"), this powerful and disturbing initial scene is then intensified, eight pages later, with the brutal murder of Abena, the narrator's mother, who, in this second rape scene, is portrayed as fighting back against her attacker (who, of course, will ultimately emerge victorious):

> Turning her head in my direction, my mother screamed: "The cutlass! Give me the cutlass!"
> I obeyed as quickly as I could, holding the enormous blade in my tiny hands. My mother struck two blows. The white linen shirt slowly turned scarlet.
> They hanged my mother.
> I watched her body swing from the lower branches of a silk-cotton tree. She had committed a crime for which there is no pardon. She had struck a white man (Condé 8).

The significance of this deed, which, as a symbolic act of resistance and self-defense, will be replayed in various forms throughout the novel, is then underscored, with a more specific focus on the aggressor, eleven pages later when we read:

My mother had been raped by a white man. She had been hanged because of a white man. I had seen his tongue quiver out of his mouth, his penis turgid and violet. My adoptive father had committed suicide because of a white man. Despite all that, I was considering living among white men again, in their midst, under their domination (Condé 19).

The reason the narrator is considering this option is that she is irresistibly attracted to another slave, one John Indian, for whom the narrator is so "sick" with love that she will ultimately give up her hard-won freedom in Barbados to join him—as a slave—in Salem, Massachusetts, where his master ultimately sells him. Tituba, the novel's narrator and main character, is thus a slave twice over: to slavery as a socio-political and economic institution and, ironically, to love, where the enslavement is self-induced.

Becoming one of the novel's most interesting characters, if not necessarily one of its most likable, John Indian, like Tituba, is also the offspring of a miscegenous union, though in his case it is between "one of the last remaining Arawak Indians that the English couldn't budge" and "a Nago woman he used to visit in the evenings. . . ." (Condé 13). A more significant difference, the reader feels, lies in the motive behind the original coupling; while Tituba's procreation was via rape, an act of violence and aggression, John Indian's was, seemingly, not, although whether their union was the result of pure sexual attraction (a recognition and venting of which constitutes one of Tituba's most essential qualities as a character) or of "love" remains indeterminate.

The lone exception to this pattern of white violence and exploitation, and a man whose relationship with Tituba is the only one able to transcend the purely sexual and, attaining a level of human solidarity and integration, to come to symbolize the kind of complete cultural affirmation and renewal that the issue of miscegenation can also stand for, is Benjamin Cohen d'Azevedo, a Portuguese Jew whose beloved but deceased wife, Abigail, is instrumental in bringing her husband and Tituba together. Appreciable both as yet another act of female solidarity (one woman helping another woman find happiness) and as an act of human solidarity (human beings helping each other), the magical relationship between Abigail, Benjamin, and Tituba successfully merges both sexual and cultural union. As Tituba sums it up:

. . . I had four months of peace, dare I say happiness, with Benjamin Cohen d'Azevedo.

> At night he would murmur: "Our God knows neither race nor color. You can become one of us if you like and can pray with us." I interrupted him with a laugh. "Your God even accepts witches?" He kissed my hands. "Tituba, you are my beloved witch!" (Condé 131).

In its exploitation of female sexuality in the context of race relations, power structures, and gender issues, *I, Tituba, Black Witch of Salem*, a novel featuring a black woman as protagonist (a woman, moreover, as sexually aggressive as the male narrator of Laferrière's novel), is more directly political than *How to Make Love to a Negro*, a novel that featured a black man. Condé's novel only indirectly argues for the acceptance of a more racially mixed America. Rather, as its episodes make clear (and most especially its rape episodes), America is already racially mixed, much more than people think,[12] and to imagine it otherwise is simply to ignore the historical record. Driven, then, by a very pungent "sexual politics," *I, Tituba, Black Witch of Salem* vividly demonstrates the extent to which our New World, "our America," as Martí would put it,[13] was from the beginning a profoundly mixed amalgam of not only races but of histories and cultures as well. And because Condé chooses to end her novel with a power struggle between the maroons and the planters, a struggle in which some of the maroons (those seeking freedom and equality) are betrayed by other maroons (those who have conspired with the planters), she seemingly implies that the future of America rests not on issues of race but on issues of economic and political parity, that is, on issues more culturally based than anything else, the integration of hitherto conflictive and different cultures thus becoming the decisive goal. It is from this new conception of miscegenation that the rebirth of the Americas, like the rebirth of Tituba herself (accomplished through the birth of her daughter, Samantha), depends; the New World, still a utopian vision (female this time?) remains ours to make.

A writer who takes a more jaundiced view of many of these issues is V. S. Naipaul, whose 1975 novel, *Guerrillas*, paints a grim picture of a "half-made" culture ensnared in the throes of an inevitable disintegration. Set in a nameless but prototypical Caribbean island nation, *Guerrillas* is, as Stephen Schiff argues,[14] a richly detailed but corrosive portrayal of "the violence and degradation that have resulted, in Naipaul's view, from the sudden mingling of First and Third World populations in the postwar era." No small part of *Guerrillas*' powerful effect derives from the contrast it establishes between the popularized image so often promoted in regard to the Caribbean, a warm, happy place with endless, sun-splashed beaches full of smiling, pleasure-seeking people of means, and the region's bloody and violent historical past, a place of slaughter, slavery, and indentured servitude as vile as any on our planet. History, in fact, plays a key role in the development of *Guerrillas'* plot structure and may, indeed, be said to constitute a crucial element in understanding Naipaul's vision of the Caribbean experience. Part of that experience, the failure of both reform and revolution, parallels what happens in *I, Tituba, Black Witch of Salem* with respect to the failed revolution of the maroons; in both cases, the revolution was doomed from the outset, though for Naipaul the real reason seems to be the inability of a postcolonial culture to govern itself in the absence of its colonial authority, with its welter of power structures and imposed modes of dependency. *Guerrillas* thus emerges, finally, as a portrayal of a self-absorbing culture, one crippled by its colonial servitude and fatally unprepared to assume a self-governing postcolonial status.

Based on an article entitled "The Killings in Trinidad" that Naipaul had once written about the activities of a would-be revolutionary who called himself Michael X (Schiff 68), *Guerrillas* focuses primarily on three characters: Peter Roche, a white South African who has been exiled for his "revolutionary" activities and who has come to this island as a kind of public relations official for a company that, in earlier times, had dealt in the slave trade; Jimmy Ahmed, a half-breed revolutionary leader fatally caught between the illusions of power bestowed upon him during his sojourn in England and the political realities of his island nation; and finally Jane, a white Englishwoman whose role in the novel as a link between the colonial and the postcolonial mentality goes far beyond the manifestation of sexual fantasies that is commonly attributed to her.

But although it is all but uncommented on in the critical studies devoted to Naipaul, there is another crucial element at work in this despairing assessment of what some readers refer to as Naipaul's overly harsh presentation of the postcolonial world. I am referring to his similar condemnation of the world occupied by the "winners," by the former colonial powers, the most important of which for *Guerrillas* is England, the country of escape for Jane, a young woman who forms a crucial part of the violent, unstable triangle involving sex and politics that drives the narrative. Arguably the most intriguing character in the entire novel, and the one who most fully expresses what we may take as Naipaul's own view of the colonial/postcolonial miasma, Jane, whose "privileged" though otiose life as a London bourgeoise has allowed her to dabble in men and political movements that she finds exciting, has come, along with her lover, a now exiled former hero of the South African resistance, to "help" this archetypal Caribbean island "find itself." In a long section devoted to Jane's character, however, the reader learns that far from being the paragon of stability, worthiness, and virtue in a world (read postcolonial world) that has lost its way, her London, the very heart and soul of the British empire and all it represents, has itself fallen prey to decay and decadence; the "centre" has not held, to paraphrase Yeats, and there is nothing in Naipaul's text to suggest that this is exclusively the fault of Her Majesty's nameless Caribbean island, which itself is about to explode in a fury of flame, violence, and self-degradation. Rather, the text suggests, the greater problem is, simply, what Laferrière termed the "Great Mandala" of change, the endless repercussions of which are to be found in history, which, for Naipaul as for Condé and others, we ignore only at great peril.

Although many of Naipaul's critics have castigated him for portraying so-called "Third World" cultures in an overly negative light, a text like *Guerrillas* clearly implies that a similar demise has overtaken the old citadels of colonial power. With Jane once again serving as the bellwether of this often overlooked aspect of Naipaul's worldview, the reader learns, of Jane, that "[s]he would return to London; that society which she had given up, and whose destruction she thought she had awaited, continued. She would be safe in London, but she would be safe in the midst of decay" (Naipaul 57). Although Jane's "casual nihilism" (Naipaul 108) may well stem from what she clearly perceives to be her "privileged" situation, one that permits her simply to abandon a place or situation when it ceases to be entertaining for her, she nevertheless understands only too well that "[s]he lived in the midst of change, repetitive and sterile; it did not disguise the fact of the greater impermanence. But she was privileged: she told herself that once a day" (Naipaul 57). But while Jane liked to believe that "[s]ecurity was the basis of her privilege" (Naipaul 57), the reader, following her development as a character in this novel, slowly comes to realize that this belief is without foundation, that it is an illusion. This explains why although "she saw, with a satiric eye, the people around her as accumulators, concerned about dead rituals and dead forms, unmindful of the approaching catastrophe" (Naipaul 57), she also sensed that, save for embracing her illusions, she was powerless to do anything about it, to alter, as it were, the course of history. Thus does her "casual nihilism" turn out to be both "her knowledge of her own security and her vision of decay, of a world running down" (Naipaul 57), a world in which, as we see in *Guerrillas*, "she moved from one crisis to another" (Naipaul 58).[15]

The intertwining of sex and politics in *Guerrillas*, however, eventually becomes violent and punitive, this being in sharp contrast to what occurs in *How to Make Love to a Negro* and *I, Tituba, Black Witch of Salem*, where, although both definitely possess a sharp political dimension, it emerges as an at least potentially positive form of human expression, one capable of liberating and unifying us rather than eternally dividing and humiliating us. The great difference between *Guerrillas* and these two novels, then, on the issue of interracial sexuality and its socio-political or cultural significance, is that Naipaul's work shows us a very dark and pessimistic side, one, however, in which interracial sex is less the problem than is the cultural, psychological, and political dismissal of one person by another. In *Guerrillas*, this conflict is powerfully played out between two carefully orchestrated scenes of sexual-cum-political violence,[16] the second of which, Ahmed's sodomizing of Jane against her will, symbolizes his attempt to strike back at a system he feels has long exploited him (Naipaul 274).

The ethos projected by *Guerrillas* in regard to miscegenation is thus of a very different kind than we have in *How to Make Love to a Negro* and *I, Tituba, Black Witch of Salem;* more violent and perverse, it amounts to a dark and singularly pessimistic vision of certain New World cultural enclaves, lost and confused and essentially abandoned in the wake of the postcolonial experience. Yet to keep things in perspective, it is also important to remember that *Guerrillas*, unlike the Laferrière and Condé novels, does not make interracial sex per se the focal point of the text. Rather, it serves Naipaul as a biological barometer of the particular cultural, or socio-political, pathology that is his primary theme. Moreover, Jimmy Ahmed's racial ancestry, which the text of *Guerrillas* leads us to understand less in terms of racism, or issues of racial superiority or inferiority, than in terms of the much more important questions of class, power, sexual orientation, and opportunity that infuse it, allows Naipaul to link the colonialism/postcolonialism issue to biology, specifically to sex, to sexual politics of a particularly debasing level. Thus, while *How to Make Love to a Negro* has the sharp sting of satire and while *I, Tituba, Black Witch of Salem*, though more historically conscious and with its own ideological axe to grind, is relieved by its parodic dimension, *Guerrillas* offers up a vision of the breakdown of an American culture, one highly diversified along racial lines, that is unrelentingly grim in nature. As such, it serves as a disturbing reminder to us of what can happen when the American dream is perverted and allowed to fail.

A more optimistic novel and one that, in a way similar to yet different from *Guerrillas*, uses interracial sexuality to make a particular point about the larger contexts of race relations in the contemporary United States, is Ana Castillo's 1990 work, *Sapogonia*. Heavily informed, in a way reminiscent of Condé's *I, Tituba, Black Witch of Salem*, with a powerful feminist spirit, *Sapogonia* relates the story of Máximo Madrigal, an artist and expatriate of a mythical, though prototypically Latin American, land known as "Sapogonia," and Pastora Aké, a similarly artistic woman of mixed racial heritage whose development in this novel charts the evolution of the "Chicano"/"Chicana" movement in the United States from marginalized invisibility to the halls of political power. And although a heavy sexuality pervades the novel, it is neither as pointedly satirical as it is in *How to Make Love to a Negro* nor as violent and humiliating as it is in *I, Tituba, Black Witch of Salem* or *Guerrillas*. Indeed, the primary thrust of *Sapogonia* is in the direction of cultural assimilation, of the problems and possibilities inherent in the process by which a dominant culture accepts and absorbs— and, as García Márquez has pointed out,[17] is changed by—other, hitherto denigrated cultures, in this case the various Hispanic cultures that exist in the United States.[18] The cautious optimism that this text guardedly exudes, then—and this in contrast to the bleak and despairing situation depicted in *Guerrillas*—is that dominant cultures can adapt; if they are not already too sick, if their best institutions are not hopelessly perverted, they can accommodate change and even benefit from it. In a way that recalls the tactic so successfully employed by Jorge Amado in *Tent of Miracles*, Castillo thus utilizes interracial sexuality in order to demonstrate the beauty and strength of miscegenous progeny and to illustrate the invigorating influence they will have on the future of the larger society around them, a society the prevailing economic structures of which will, however, remain largely intact and unchanged, this being a crucial issue that the author touches on only in passing, as we shall see.

"Sapogonia," the reader learns in the prologue, "is a distinct place in the Americas where all mestizos reside, regardless of nationality, individual racial composition, or legal residential status—or, perhaps, because of all of these" (Castillo 1). ". . . Besieged by a history of slavery, genocide, immigration, and civil up-risings" (Castillo 1), the "Sapogón" or "Sapogona" may "acquire the mannerisms and the idioms of the North American with the intent of assimilation" (Castillo 2), although they are "not identified by modern boundaries. Throughout the Americas, Sapogones, those who are wholly or in part descended from the indigenous peoples of what was erroneously named 'The New World,' continue to populate, breed, and therefore dominate the lands of their ancestors" (Castillo 2). And as the text of *Sapogonia* suggests, because the socio-political power structures of the United States do accommodate change (if not a loss of political and economic control), they effectively "decree" that "the Sapogón pueblo finds itself continuously divided and reunited with the certainty of the northern winds that sweep across its continents to leave evershifting results" (Castillo 2). By building her novel around the political challenge represented by our increasingly organized Spanish-speaking communities and by the tormented love affair between Madrigal and Pastora Aké, Castillo is therefore able to expound on the various ramifications—racial, psychological, and political—of this continuous division and reunification of the "Sapogón pueblo," which the reader takes to be Hispanic culture in general in its historically troubled but fast-changing relationship with the prevailing white male power structure of the United States.[19]

But as *Sapogonia* makes clear, this challenge, for all its political machinations, is deeply rooted in questions of racial appearance and categorization, a conundrum-like issue for politicians and civil rights groups alike (Schiff). This point is made manifest in *Sapogonia* in the wedding scene involving Perla, a mestiza and intimate friend of Pastora, and her white, upper-middle-class fiancé, Bob, a symbol, for Pastora, "of men's indispensability in women's lives" (Castillo 231). The wedding, "a small conservative affair, upholding what white, suburban, middle-America considered good taste" (Castillo 228), was followed by a reception at the country club, "of which Perla's new husband was a member and whose grandfather had been a co-founder" (Castillo 228). Attending but circulating through the party alone, Pastora notices that Perla's twin boys (by a previous relationship), with their "frizzy hair" and their "cherrywood skin" (Castillo 230), were not present while her youngest sister, "who was fair with green eyes" and who "bore no superficial resemblance to the mestizo blood from which she descended" (Castillo 229), was, and happily. Perla, on whose "hand the color of a peeled almond" a "stunning band of diamonds" (Castillo 229) had been placed (as if to imply that while her perhaps sexually based presence there was worth buying, that of her children was not), sees Bob, her husband, as occupying the roles of "guide, mentor, and sole companion," as demanding of her not only a sexual fidelity but an "emotional and intellectual dependency" as well, one in which "[h]e held the power of the Great White Father" (Castillo 230). Learning that the twin boys, having gotten into trouble at school, had been sent to a private school on the East Coast,

Pastora interprets this information as a sign of racial strife, racism being a problem that members of Bob's community choose not to acknowledge in themselves. As the text expresses it, "The boys with their Caribbean looks in a school of Aryan-type children in a community such as the one where Perla now lived—Pastora understood what trouble they had been having" (Castillo 230).

But the wedding, itself a symbol of unification, takes place, though not without strife, as does the other signal event of the novel, the campaign and election of "a Latino named Alan García" (Castillo 266) as mayor of Chicago. With his lover, a caricaturesque character known as Maritza Marín-Levy, exemplifying the problem of how, or on what basis, a person becomes identified as "Hispanic" (an issue the Schiff article discusses in detail), Alan García and his election as mayor of one of the most important cities in the United States come to symbolize an even greater level of unification, however, one that goes beyond the personal to attain the public, and that, with great symbolic value, actually seizes the reins of political power. As such, García's election, and all it means in its various contexts, comes to be a focal point for the second half of the novel.

But while the marriage of Perla and Bob represents one form of miscegenous union, a highly personalized and sexualized one, and while the election of Alan García to the office of mayor of Chicago represents another more public, more politically oriented variation on this theme, there is another scene in *Sapogonia*, one coming late in the novel, that can be taken as the epitome of the problem that both Bob and Perla, and Alan García, face—indeed, that all cultural subgroups and all individuals face: How far should one go in conforming to the demands of the dominant culture? At what point, as Gustavo Pérez Firmat asks in *Life on the Hyphen: the Cuban-American Way*, does cultural assimilation become cultural submersion, the loss of one's culture, one's identity, to the dominant, corporative one? Disgusted and depressed at what had just occurred at a meeting she had attended in which Hispanics were fighting with other Hispanics over questions of dubious value, Pastora decides to drop by for a visit with one of her old friends and comrade in arms, a black woman and jazz singer named Yvonne Harris. Having abandoned the poorly run South Side clubs that, according to conventional thinking, constituted her racial, geographic, and economic birthright to sing in the more lucrative North Side white clubs, Harris, her life and career having fallen on hard times, concludes that "[t]hey're all the same everywhere. Only the faces are a different color. I'm thinking of moving back to the South Side . . . I'd much rather be dealing with my own people if there is no financial benefit for me to be dealing with white folks" (Castillo 318–319). But Pastora, while agreeing with her friend that she, too, misses her people, also declares, in a startling statement that both expresses the disdain we feel for the narrow self-interest and philistinism that drive so many of our political and economic institutions and that acknowledges the all but irresistible power these institutions, and the principles of ideological marketing and consumerism that drive them, exert on our lives and on the decisions we make:

> I miss my people, too . . . but I'll be damned if I can understand why they're so determined lately [one thinks of both the wedding and the election] to emulate the values of the white people in this city who created the problems we have to begin with! (Castillo 319).

It is Pastora's next comment, however, that delivers what is not only the coup de grace to this line of thought but that also calls into question much of what *Sapogonia* has been about, the price that must be paid, personally and collectively, in order to gain entrance into another cultural system, one that, because of its very nature, demands both winners and losers:

> Someone is always going to have to be on top and someone is always going to end up at the bottom according to this system! (Castillo 319).

Perhaps in order for the reader to better consider the various implications of this complex subject, Pastora, having raised the great ethical question of the novel, drops the entire issue at this point, saying only, in regard to the conduct and racial consciousness of Alan García, "He doesn't act white . . . He acts like a politician—which, in this country, is a white game" (Castillo 320).

Even more direct in its avowal of cultural miscegenation as human civilization's most viable path of development is Leslie Marmon Silko's *Ceremony*, a 1977 novel that itself can be understood as being an agent of the healing ceremony that, as the text suggests, we traumatized human beings so desperately need. Intensely poetic, structurally and stylistically, and in effect a written version of a more ancient oral tradition,[20] *Ceremony* lends itself to interpretations as a "thesis novel," a narrative that advances a particular argument. If one reads *Ceremony* from this critical perspective, the thesis would seem to be that, as human beings, we need to bridge the cultural gaps that separate and alienate us, yet we must learn to do so, recalling the dilemma of cultural assimilation implied in *Sapogonia*, without homogenizing everyone into total conformity; we must, in other words, seek if not harmony then at least a state of tolerance, one born of a recognition of our human similarities as well as an acceptance of our differences, those that are biological and, perhaps most important of all, those that are historical. And since our recognition and interpretation of these similarities and differences are functions of language, it gradually becomes clear why Silko's narrative, following a fundamental Native American attitude about the sacredness of language and its symbiotic relationship to reality,[21] stresses the life-giving vitality of words, which are, of course, the raw material of the very healing ceremonies that the text, *Ceremony*, deals with. With the reader's role being analogous to that of the listener in the oral tradition, a member of a cultural community whose responsibility it is to put into action the principles of conduct presented by the shaman, singer, or author, *Ceremony* seems to call for a reading that would lead us to seek a human solidarity that, by facing up to the lies, crimes, and injustices that we have visited upon each other, would allow us to then transcend our violent past and achieve a state of mutual cooperation, one based, ultimately, on a realization that while each of us is "different," and that while all communities, no matter how homogeneous they might like to pretend to be, are "different," we can learn not to savage each other over these differences.

It is this philosophical underpinning, I believe, that requires *Ceremony*'s main character, Tayo, to be of a mixed racial heritage. The illicit offspring of a sordid and depressing encounter between his mother, an Indian woman, and a white man, Tayo, like Jimmy Ahmed, is a half-caste, a pariah who is hung up between two worlds, neither of which he can fully claim as his own and neither of which will fully claim him. A symbolic character, whose healing forms the heart of the narrative, Tayo's story is, in a sense, every American's story, one in which the oppressor is inescapably bound to the oppressed. "I'm a half-breed," Tayo says, "I'll be the first to say it. I'll speak for both sides" (Silko 42). The problem, as Tayo's story illustrates, is that the two sides do not wish to talk, preferring, instead, to continue on with the mutual loathing and exploitation that have so long characterized their relationship that they are felt to be the natural state of affairs.

Tayo begins his recovery, which the reader understands as our recovery, the recuperation of our basic humanity, by confronting, as Condé's novel did, the injustices perpetrated by white culture on other, non-white cultures, in this case Native American peoples. Referring to his own experiences and those of his wartime comrades, and to the feeling of legitimacy that being in the army had given them, Tayo, now back on the reservation and enduring once again the disdain and discrimination of a racist society, knows that his people "blamed themselves just like they blamed themselves for losing the land the white people took. They never thought to blame white people for any of it; they wanted white people for their friends" (Silko 43), the latter thought echoing a similar sentiment in *Sapogonia*. Cruelly tormented by his archenemy, Emo, another Native American veteran of World War II but one who not only learned the arts of killing by the army but who learned to like killing, Tayo is told, "You drink like an Indian, and you're crazy like one too—but you aren't shit, white trash. You love Japs the way your mother loved to screw white men" (Silko 63). This knowledge, of what he feels is the shame of his own birthright, is a burden that Tayo is made to bear throughout the novel, and he is able to cast it off only when his healing ceremony is complete and he has learned the ways of peaceful coexistence, one part of which is everyone's need for white culture to recognize and accept responsibility for the injustices it has committed against Native American peoples. Until this takes place, the need for cultural healing that informs this novel, a great deal of the responsibility for which rests with the reader, who, more likely than not, is a member of white culture, cannot be realized. The reader's role in *Ceremony* thus takes on a significant cultural dimension, one that emphasizes our need to accept cultures different from our own. As the character Betonie, an old medicine man, says to Tayo, making a point that distinguishes *Ceremony* from *I, Tituba, Black Witch of Salem*, "Nothing is that simple, . . . you don't write off all the white people, just like you don't trust all the Indians" (Silko 128). Old Betonie goes on to explain to Tayo that it is "the witchery," that propensity we human beings have that leads us to do violence and evil, that is our great enemy, not our racial differences: "That is the trickery of the witchcraft. . . . They want us to believe all evil resides with white people. Then we will look no further to see what is really happening" (Silko 132). Then, as if to denounce the entire concept of segregation and isolation, "They want us to separate ourselves from white people, to be ignorant and helpless as we watch our own destruction. . . . I tell you we can deal with white people, with their machines and beliefs" (Silko 132).

As Tayo learns, part of his cure is to confront "the lie," the belief that people who are "different" are inherently inferior beings and not worthy of respect, and reject it: "The lie. He cut into the wire as if cutting away at the lie inside himself. The liars had fooled everyone, white people and

Indians alike" (Silko 191). Yet while the text continues to stress how both sides of this issue, the Indians as well as the whites, have been damaged by "the lie" or racism and bigotry, Tayo also realizes that the dominant culture bears certain special responsibilities that, "[i]f the white people never looked beyond the lie, to see that theirs was a nation built on stolen land, then they would never be able to understand how they had been used by the witchery," with the result, ineluctably, that anger and hatred "would finally destroy the world; the starving against the fat, the colored against the white" (Silko 191). The crucial problem here is the human capacity for malevolence, which, as Tayo comes to understand, binds us together in our need to resist this weakness that we all have:

> The destroyers had tricked the white people as completely as they had fooled the Indians, and now only a few people understood how the filthy deception worked; only a few people knew that the lie was destroying the white people faster than it was destroying Indian people (Silko 204).

This same theme, that whites and Indians must learn to coexist peacefully, as human beings inhabiting our planet together rather than as racially distinct and segregated groups, reaches its apex near the conclusion of the novel, when Tayo's restoration to wholeness is brought to completion:

> . . . He had arrived at the point of convergence where the fate of all living things, and even the earth, had been laid . . . the lines of cultures and worlds were drawn in flat dark lines on fine light sand, converging in the middle of witchery's final ceremonial sand painting (Silko 246).

From this moment on, both Tayo and the reader realize, "human beings were one clan again, united by the fate the destroyers planned for all of them, for all living things" (Silko 246). When Tayo, in the novel's crisis moment, resists the temptation to kill his enemy, Emo, he defeats the "witchery" of the "destroyers" and, in so doing, allows the novel to come to its natural conclusion, which is achieved by a poetic or song-like structure in the form of a textual totem pole that reminds the reader that although the "witchery" has been defeated here, it is always there waiting for its next opportunity, and so we must always be prepared to resist it with our humanizing and integrative ceremonies, which grow stronger as we learn from and respect one another, as we practice, in short, cultural miscegenation.

A more comic version of these same issues comes from Thomas King's *Green Grass, Running Water*, a 1994 English Canadian novel that views the problems associated with cultural mixing from the perspective of the minority involved, in this case that of the Native Americans. *Green Grass, Running Water* concerns itself chiefly with two main characters, Lionel Red Dog, a Blackfoot Indian who works in an electronics store selling stereos and televisions, and his uncle Eli, who left the reservation to make a life for himself as a literature professor at the University of Toronto. The problem that connects these two characters is the possibility that, in living out their very different lives, each may have "gone white," and, in so doing, forfeited their original identities as Native Americans. Their anxieties at this prospect reveal the novel's more serious subject, the possibility that the process of living itself involves both the loss and the gain of not merely a single identity but of multiple identities; the problem, as the novel suggests in its later stages, is: How do we accommodate all these changes, with ourselves and with the people around us? This subject is broached early in the text when Norma, Eli's sister, says to Lionel: "Eli went to university, just like you. Only he graduated. With a Ph.D. . . . Your uncle wanted to be a white man. . . . As if they were something special. As if there weren't enough of them in the world already" (King 30).

As the novel progresses, the reader learns that Eli has "come back home" to the reservation after having retired from his teaching post at the University of Toronto. What is not so clear, to the reader and to Eli himself, is why; what is it that has brought him back to a reality that, as we see in his relationship with his white wife, Karen, and her desire to return with Eli to celebrate the annual Sun Dance, is problematic for him. As the Indian who left the reservation and succeeded in the white man's world, Eli's condition—his sense of identity—is crucial to the novel's development, particularly with respect to the case of Lionel, the forty-year-old Indian who has not really left the reservation and who, trapped in a dead-end job, struggles with his own demons. Of Eli, however, the text tells us the following:

> Eli sat down and waited for the coffee to brew and looked about the house at what he had become. Ph.D. in literature. Professor emeritus from the University of Toronto. A book on William Shakespeare. Another on Francis Bacon. Teacher of the Year. Twice.
> Indian.
> In the end, he had become what he has always been. An Indian. . . . An Indian back on the reserve (King 219).

Returning with Karen to participate in a Sun Dance and to reconnect with his family and his neglected, if not rejected, cultural past, Eli is drawn into an ultimately futile struggle to prevent a dam from being built on reservation property, a dam that would necessitate the destruction of his mother's house, which Eli, as if making a symbolic last stand, elects to move into. Although Lionel's story is largely comic, dealing, in part, with an Indian's midlife crisis, Eli's exudes a more somber tone, as befits a man caught between two cultures, two modes of existence, neither of which has been entirely satisfactory for him. Having "surrounded himself" in his mother's cabin "with space and silence" and imagining himself a kind of "Indian Thoreau," Eli contemplates what his life has been; "What," he asks himself, "had he wanted to be?" (King 238). Eli's Thomas Wolfe–like predicament is that of "[t]he Indian who couldn't go home," which was a

> common enough theme in novels and movies. Indian leaves the traditional world of the reserve, goes to the city, and is destroyed. Indian leaves the traditional world of the reserve, is exposed to white culture, and becomes trapped between two worlds. Indian leaves the traditional world of the reserve, gets an education, and is shunned by his tribe. . . . The Indian who couldn't go home (King 239).

But, literally and figuratively, Eli can go home; the tension results from his inner sense of identity, of who and what he is, of what he has become versus what he feels he must be in order to reenter the "traditional world of the reserve," which, as he comes to discover, is itself slowly changing, a condition deemed by the protagonist of *Ceremony* to be absolutely vital to the continued existence and viability of Native American culture. Nevertheless, for Eli, the "successful" Indian, "[i]t had been hard leaving the reserve and his mother and his sisters, and by the time he got to Toronto, it was all he could do to keep from turning around and going back. But he didn't go back that first year, knowing if he did, he would stay" (King 239). But as Eli discovers, each year he stayed away from the reserve it was "easier" to do so because "[e]ach year laid more space between who he had become and who he had been" (King 239). Finally, when "he could no longer measure the distance in miles" (King 239), Eli came to realize the basic conflict at the heart of cultural miscegenation: while it was one thing to enter into another culture and steep oneself in its value systems and codes of conduct, it was another thing to deal with the doubt and uncertainty caused by the displacement of one's original culture; cultures, one concludes, mix less felicitously than blood, yet mix they must.

Reminding us that the problems connected with cultural transference are not a one-way street, and that they are not the exclusive province of only certain cultural groups, and stressing that the problem of cultural identity goes hand in hand with the larger issue of personal identity and being, Thomas King's *Green Grass, Running Water* is a funny, humane book.

A contemporary novel that casts these same issues in a mold that is at once more sexual and more cultural is Nélida Piñon's brilliant family saga, *A república dos sonhos* (1984; *The Republic of Dreams*, 1989), which deals epically with the formation, racially, culturally, and psychologically, of modern Brazil, arguably the least understood of all the American republics. Possessed of a literature that has long made the racial composition of its people a central theme,[22] the Brazil conjured up by Piñon (who is herself a descendant of a family that emigrated to Brazil) is a mysterious, seductive, and deeply sensual realm, a place more of the imagination, of dreams, than of physical realities. Running through this vast yet compelling narrative are two central impulses, the sexual and the cultural, both of which, indivisibly linked, are central to the novel's projection of Brazil as a "republic of dreams," a virtually mythic creation that, perhaps more than any other single American culture, here epitomizes the full extent to which miscegenation has come to symbolize the entire New World experience. Employed throughout the text, in fact, as a synonym for America, the term "Brazil" comes quickly, for Piñon, to be a place defined by a volatile "mixture of black, white, and native races, perpetrated . . . with boundless frenzy . . ." (Piñon 57).

The author constantly stresses the sexual impulse of Brazil's racial formation, and especially its interracial aspects, its profound and vital yet problematic African heritage. As Breta, the granddaughter of the family patriarch observes, "The Africa that had borne us and cradled us . . . we were ashamed of. But who were we after all, an arrogant, mongrel people, to suppose we had the right to choose a land, to mark off areas of exile, and settle masters and slaves in them?" (Piñon 115). Presented relentlessly as a turbulent "mixture of white, black, and indigenous" (Piñon 123) human beings struggling to create themselves as a nation, Brazilians emerge in Piñon's novel as "a people descended from an incalculable mixture of races" (Piñon 196) and as giving life and identity to a place increasingly defined racially, especially for outsiders, in terms of "blacks and half-breeds," yet one that, in the myth-making view of the pilgrims drawn to it, "was establishing itself as the perfect paradise" (Piñon 352). This heavily

Africanized conception of Brazil as a land and a people deeply enmeshed in the wrenchingly difficult process of self-creation reaches its apogee late in the novel when we are told that, for Madruga, the head of the clan:

> At first sight Brazil seemed to him to be an immense iron pot into which there were being thrown black beans, scraps of pork, poverty, lust, fearlessness, red-hot pepper, and bits of magic come from Africa and the Iberian peninsula (Piñon 509).

When his friend, Venâncil, suggests that perhaps someday they will become something, Madruga declares that "we'll be Brazilians!" (Piñon 509), the true possessors of the republic of dreams.

Not content with only one approach to the issue of how the modern nation of Brazil came to form itself, Piñon merges her more overtly political orientation with one that is decisively sexual in nature. Developed in terms of his relationship with the iron-willed entrepreneur, Madruga, Venâncio, the interpreter of the dream that is Brazil, has a vision of his new land that defies even his ability to capture it in words, the latter struggle becoming what might be considered a significant subtext of the novel. As the reader learns, in reference to Venâncio and his embryonic but sexually driven conception of Brazil:

> [His] . . . confused vision brought him only a handful of blacks, Indians, whites, all lying in a heap together on the ground and around the table. Obsessed with making a country and sex at the same time. Their sole motive, moreover, for repeatedly discussing politics, even as they fucked. And speaking of genitalia as they created legal institutions to rule their social life. . . . They were striving to conceive a nation (Piñon 169).

This same sexually grounded sense of political and cultural identity is extended throughout the remainder of the novel and developed as a crucial corollary to the first, more exclusively political thrust of the novel. Referred to by the European father of Madruga's wife as a country made up of a "motley . . . human contingent," Brazil is portrayed by Piñon as a distinctly new social and political entity, one which had been circulating through it "the blood of Indians, Iberians, Moors, blacks, pirating Englishmen and Frenchmen" (Piñon 259). Thus conceptualized, Brazil, like Castillo's mythical "Sapogonia," slowly takes shape for the reader as a culture indelibly defined by its deeply interracial heritage. The crucial question, however, as posed in the text, is whether such a profoundly mixed culture could ever "succeed in constituting itself as a nation, despite this human ferment, whose origins and passions were lost in the night of time?" (Piñon 259). The answer, as posited, especially by Madruga's wife, Eulália, who, speaking for all Brazilians to come, declares that:

> We were all foreigners in Brazil. . . . We formed . . . a contingent . . . with the aim of reaching Brazil and shaping it, of changing its profile, of enriching it with the blood, the culture, and the weakness inherent in us all. . . . Brazil was all of us. Lost, melancholy souls. Together, we would be the failures and the aspirations of this nation (Piñon 361).

Unique in all the Americas because of the sheer number of its texts that deal overtly with the issues of both biological and cultural miscegenation, Brazilian literature is also unique because of the distinctly positive position it has historically taken toward the formation of a racially mixed society. From José de Alencar's *Iracema* (1865) to Nélida Piñon's *The Republic of Dreams* (1984), the writers of Brazil have long expounded on this issue; they have long done so, moreover, in a way that, on this point, makes Brazil the prototypical American culture.

To conclude this survey of miscegenation as it is being redefined in the literature of the Americas, it is interesting to turn to a recent novel by John Updike, a prominent North American novelist long known for his interest in Latin American literature. Published in 1994, the novel in question, *Brazil*, is structured around the legend of Tristan and Isolde and influenced by a number of Brazilian authors, including Machado de Assis, Clarice Lispector, Jorge Amado, and Nélida Piñon.[23] In Mr. Updike's retelling of this venerable legend, Tristan and Isolde emerge as non-exclusive lovers whose highly eroticized relationship flowers in the lush and sensuous New World, which itself comes to life as a more than slightly flawed late twentieth-century version of the edenic earthly paradise. Ironic, wryly humorous, and magical in tone, *Brazil* chronicles the highly stylized, allegorical, and not infrequently parodic (mis)adventures of Tristão Raposo, a young black man reared in the criminal ethos of Rio's "favelas," or slums, and Isabel Leme, a young upper-class white girl bored with life. As if in a fable, Tristão and Isabel engage in a passionately sexual love affair, get married (against the wishes of his slatternly mother and her vacuous father), plunge, mythically, back through time into Brazil's vast hinterland, experience a primordially magical transformation, and then return, having changed places (in terms of racial and sex/power roles), to Rio, where

Tristão, now a successful middle-aged white businessman, is murdered by young toughs very much like his earlier self and on the very beach—the famous Copacabana—where the narrative had begun.

The novel's plot turns on the magical moment when, deep in the Amazon jungle, Isabel, having solicited an Indian shaman, determines to alter her color—to transform herself from a white woman into a black woman—while at the same time changing her black husband/lover into a white man. The effect of this startling metamorphosis is ironic on two counts; first, because it involves much more than a change of skin color, Isabel, now a living part of Brazil's slavery-ridden past, becomes much more aggressive and "masculine" than her now white (formerly black) mate, who is suddenly presented as somewhat less virile than before, and second (and more poignantly), because in undertaking this sacrifice, Isabel both saves and loses not only herself but, ultimately, Tristão as well. Thus, there are really two inversions involved: one involving color, the other power (an issue here closely linked to gender). As the narrative voice describes Isabel's newfound condition, "There was something sardonic in her sexuality now, something jaded by the experience of black female generations" (Updike 203). This point is then carried further, coming, finally, to speak not only to the love between Isabel and Tristão but to race relations in general and the impact they have on all human relations:

> From her dead white mother Isabel had inherited mostly an empty flirtatiousness, and perhaps a fear of childbirth. Now a different inheritance had descended, and a strength not merely passive; black, she found in herself a store of reckless anger, and became, when darkness enclosed the rustling straw pallet she and Tristão shared, something of a bully, a rough tease (Updike 203).

Merging sex and politics is a way that recalls Laferrière's *How to Make Love to a Negro;* this line of development culminates, then, in the following realization by Isabel: "Being a white woman fucked by a black man is more delicious, she had sadly to conclude, than a black woman being fucked by a white man" (Updike 204). While before he had been in control and "on top," "... now," benefiting from the inversion, "it was she who dominated and demanded ... she was the cock and he the hen" (Updike 204–205). Moreover, in *Brazil,* Tristão is characterized largely in terms of his monstrous "yam," or penis, which is the body part of John Indian that most catches the attention of Condé's narrator in *I, Tituba, Black Witch of*

Salem and which also symbolizes the sexual potency of the black narrator of *How to Make Love to a Negro*. In *Brazil*, however, the signifying power of Tristão's penis diminishes (in inverse proportion to a rise in Isabel's potency, her special brand of "jouissance" one might say) following the transformation that she, we remember, has effected:

> His yam was satisfying but no longer, quite, alarming; perhaps it was a new juiciness in herself that diminished, not exactly its size, but its elemental essence, its lovable brute being (Updike 203–204).

Beyond the issue of black/white sexual relations, however, *Brazil* also develops the related issue of female solidarity. And, reminiscent of *I, Tituba, Black Witch of Salem*, Updike's novel features a love affair between women of different races, in this case both white, pre-transformation Isabel, and her black counterpart and an Indian woman, Ianopamoko. Although Condé does not make her novel's lesbian component more than an implicit presence (122 et al.), Updike does, devoting, indeed, several of the novel's most interesting pages to it and culminating, as in the case of the change of skin color, in a declaration of being and identity that possesses distinctly political, psychological, and sexual overtones. Referring to Ianopamoko as "... the only friend I ever had,"[24] Isabel (now black) says to the now white Tristão:

> You were never a friend, you were only a man. A man can never be a woman's friend, not really. She taught me what love was. You, you taught me what it was to be a slave (Updike 199).

Thus implying, as the novels of Condé, Laferrière, and Castillo do, that the world of power (including the enslaving power of love, an issue much worked by Condé) is the world of white men, Updike's *Brazil* concludes sadly, not only with the murder of the now bourgeois Tristão, but with the possibility that the still black Isabel will, now that Tristão, the great, all-consuming love of her life is gone, allow herself to be led back into the otiose middle-class lifestyle she had earlier fled, that, to paraphrase an old Brazilian saw, she will allow money to whiten her again:

> The knife at Tristão's back had felt dull, like a stick or a knuckle, but it slipped through his coat and skin as easily as a razor, painlessly in the first instant, then with a burning that rapidly swelled, into an insult too severe

to bear . . . the boys . . . all striking to express their solidarity, slashed and stabbed at the crouching white man, as a lesson to all such white men who think they still can own the world (Updike 255).

Realizing, as she pressed the dead Tristão's head to her bosom, that he had become nothing more than another piece of litter on the beach and that no lifesaving miracle would be forthcoming, Isabel, her eyes shut, seems about to undergo yet another transformation, one that would restore her to her former status as a bored bourgeoisie (the same condition, ironically, in which her husband had just died): "The spirit is strong, but blind matter is stronger. Having absorbed this desolating truth, the dark-eyed widow staggered to her feet, tightened her robe about her nakedness, and let her uncle lead her home" (Updike 260).

Although the issue of miscegenation has, in the Americas, long been an issue understood almost exclusively in terms of sex and blood, now, at the unfolding of the twenty-first century, we are seeing more and more works of literature that present it in a very different way, one that shows miscegenation to be more of a cultural issue—more of a social reality that has long been a living part of who and what we really are—than a merely biological issue, albeit one that has long both titillated and terrified us. The issue of miscegenation remains a difficult one for many Americans, but perhaps most particularly so for the people of the United States, where, as recently as 1949, thirty states specifically prohibited marriage between blacks and whites. Although the Supreme Court struck down this prohibition in 1967, seventeen states, according to Earl Ofari Hutchinson,[25] declared interracial marriage a felony offense, while twelve states maintained anti-miscegenation laws well into the 1970s. Yet as the literature of the Americas clearly shows, racial mixing has been a central feature of New World reality since the beginning, and perhaps even earlier, if one accepts the theory that the first "Americans," the original "Native Americans," were Asiatic nomads, crossing the Bering land bridge in pursuit of animals some twenty-five to thirty thousand years ago. From Bigger Thomas, of Richard Wright's *Native Son*, to Pedro Archanjo, of Jorge Amado's *Tent of Miracles*, and from Leslie Marmon Silko's Tayo to Mexico's "La Malinche," the women and men of the Americas have for a long time been creating, peacefully and not so peacefully, a new race of people, a "raza cósmica" (as Vasconcelos put it) that now, in the first years of the twenty-first century, demands that we recognize the ubiquitous presence of mixing as a normal, legitimate, and fully empowered part of our multifaceted American reality. As these and numerous other texts make dramatically clear, it is time that we do so, for in the contemporary literature of the Americas the theme of miscegenation has moved from being defined as an issue of lurid and exploitative sexuality to one that speaks to all aspects of our diverse American cultures. In short, it defines who we really are.

Notes

1. I use the term "New World" in its traditional historical context, that is, to distinguish between the "Old World," or Europe, and the several new cultures that would arise out of the violent conflict between the forces of the "Old World" and those of the indigenous peoples who populated the lands now known as the Americas.

2. For an example of how the issue of "multiculturalism" is, at the beginning of the twenty-first century, still a divisive issue in the United States, see Richard Bernstein's *Dictatorship of Virtue*. A conservative diatribe against what the author loosely describes (and despises) as "multiculturalism," a term never clearly defined, *Dictatorship of Virtue* clearly illustrates the degree to which cultural diversity—to say nothing of biological diversity—inspires fear and loathing in a large segment of "American" (understood by Mr. Bernstein to mean only the United States) culture. For other perspectives on the issue, see Shirlee Taylor Haizlip, *The Sweeter the Juice* (1994), Lise Funderberg, *Black, White, Other: Biracial Americans Talk About Race and Identity*, and Michael Lind, *The Next American Nation: The New Nationalism and the Fourth American Revolution*. For a summary statement of miscegenation as it has developed thematically in the literature of the Americas, see Earl Fitz, "The Theme of Miscegenation," in *Rediscovering the New World*, 70–94.

3. See, for example, *American Indian Prose and Poetry*, Margot Astrov, ed.; Dennis Tedlock, *The Spoken Word and the Work of Interpretation; Smoothing the Ground: Essays on Native American Oral Literature*, Brian Swann, ed.; and Gordon Brotherston, *The Book of the Fourth World: Reading the Native Americas through their Literatures*.

4. See Octavio Paz, *El laberinto de la soledad* (1950).

5. See Emir Rodríguez Monegal and Thomas Colchie, eds., *The Borzoi Anthology of Latin American Literature*, vol. I, 67. A similar pattern emerged in Brazil, where Diego Álvarez Correia, also known as "Caramuru," married an Indian woman, Paraguaçu, and took her to Portugal; and in the United States, where the planter, John Rolfe, married Pocahontas and took her to England. A son, Thomas, was born to them.

6. For an interesting discussion of the issue of race as it relates to Canadian literature, of both English and French expression, see Ronald Sutherland, "The Body-Odour of Race." Especially informative are Sutherland's comments on Susanna Moodie and Lionel Groulx, particularly those in regard to the latter's *L'Appel de la race* (1922). See also Terrence Craig, *Racial Attitudes in English-Canadian Fiction, 1905–1980*, and *Miscegenation Blues: Voices of Mixed Race Women*, Carol Camper, ed. For an interesting discussion of the "Métis" in Canada, see Wallace Stegner, "Half World: The Métis," in *Wolf Willow*, 56–57.

7. While the possibly apocryphal story of how Pocahontas saved the life of John Smith is certainly the better known of the two, the well-documented account of John Rolfe's marriage to Pocahontas (in 1614) is much more interesting. The couple had a child, Thomas, who, educated in England, became prominent in seventeenth-century Virginia affairs.

8. See, for example, Samuel Putnam, *Marvelous Journey*, 7–18. Putnam makes the provocative argument that the Portuguese, with their history of racial interaction with other cultures and peoples, were more tolerant of racial mixing than the English.

9. In addition to Spike Lee's film, *Jungle Fever*, one could cite such books as Lynn Lauber's *21 Sugar Street*, Mira Noir's *Mississippi Masala*, Aimee Liu's *Face*, Barbara Chase-Riboud's *The President's Daughter*, Dagoberto Gilb's *The Last Known Residence of Mickey Acuña*, Gregory Howard Williams' *Life on the Color Line: The True Story of a White Boy Who Discovered He Was Black*, Peter Bowen's *Coyote Wind*, Ilan Stavans' *The Hispanic Condition*, Sharon Creech's *Walk Two Moons*, and Albert French's *Holly*. Other, more established, works that deal with this subject include Joy Kogawa's *Obasan*, Louise Erdrich's *Tracks*, Amy Tan's *The Joy Luck Club* (1989), Greg Sarris' *Grand Avenue* (1994), Alix Renaud's *A corps joie* (1985), Helen Hunt Jackson's *Ramona* (1884), Cassiano Ricardo's *Martim Cererê* (1928), Rudy Wiebe's *The Scorched-Wood People* (1977), Derek Walcott's *Omeros* (1990), José Vasconcelos' *La raza cósmica* (1925), José de Alencar's *O Guaraní* (1857) and *Iracema* (1865), Maria Campbell's *Halfbreed* (1973), Rudolfo Anaya's *Albuquerque* (1992), and Alice Walker's *The Way Forward Is with a Broken Heart* (2000). Although it does not deal with "American" texts exclusively, Werner Sollors' *Neither Black Nor White Yet Both: Thematic Explorations of Interracial Literature* (1997) is also informative in this same context, and David Guterson's recent novel, *Snow Falling on Cedars*, is also notable for its treatment of Japanese and North American interracial relations.

10. A partial list of Brazilian works that, in part or in whole, have dealt with this issue would include *Caramuru* (1781), *Iracema* (1865), *O mulato* (1881), *O Bom-Crioulho* (1895), *Canaã* (1902), *Martim Cererê* (1928), *Casa grande e senzala* (1933), *Tenda dos milagres* (1969), *Maíra* (1978), *A mulher no espelho* (1983), and *A república dos sonhos* (1984).

11. An interesting article dealing with the issue of racial mixing in the United States is Lawrence Wright's "One Drop of Blood." Taking another look at this same topic is *Newsweek*'s cover story for 23 February 1995, "What Color is Black? Science, Politics and Racial Identity," (62–74). Defending the alleged "need" to maintain racial (white) purity in the United States is Peter Brimelow's *Alien Nation: Common Sense About America's Immigration Disaster*. And, in a well-publicized series of events that took place in Wedowee, Alabama, in 1994–1995, the white principal of the local high school prohibited mixed-race couples from attending certain school functions, such as the prom. Violence later ensued.

12. As Shirlee Taylor Haizlip, the author of *The Sweeter the Juice* (1994), notes, ". . . the fastest-growing group of children in this country [the United States] are children of mixed race. . . . So the browning of America is inevitable. Corporations have known it, schools know it. And I think it's just getting out there in the consciousness." An interview with Lynell George, the *Centre Daily Times* newspaper (State College, PA), 5 May 1995, C1.

13. See José Martí, *Nuestra América* (1891).

14. Stephen Schiff, "The Human Exile."

15. This same point is reiterated later in the novel (110).

16. See 83–88 and (the rape/sodomy scene) 272–275.

17. See an interview with García Márquez by Enrique Fernández, "Village Voice," 3 July 1984.

18. I am referring here to the "Chicanos," or Mexican Americans of the southwest, the Cubans in Florida, and the Puerto Ricans in New York. Internal patterns of migration have, of course, changed these geographical locations (with Chicago, to cite the locale of much of *Sapogonia*, becoming a major center of Hispanic activity), as have recent immigration pat-

terns; there is currently, in Queens, New York (in the Corona and Jackson Heights areas), a large and growing Colombian population.

19. Demographers, who are typically stymied when trying to categorize the racial "type" of people known as Latin Americans, do know that, by the turn of the century, the Hispanic population of the United States will constitute the largest minority group in the country, a fact that has far-reaching social and political consequences, which may help explain why it occupies a central place in the novel *Sapogonia*. For more proof of how openly this issue has entered mainstream public thought in the United States, see "What is an American?" *Newsweek*, 10 July 1995: 34–35, et seq.

20. Scott Momaday is said to have described *Ceremony* as a "telling" rather than a conventional novel, or written narration.

21. See, for example, N. Scott Momaday, *The Way to Rainy Mountain* (1969), and Astrov (ed.), *American Indian Prose and Poetry*, 19–52.

22. See note 9.

23. Mr. Updike notes, but does not discuss, these influences in a one-page "Afterword" at the end of the novel.

24. It is interesting to note that this same increase in power over Tristão becomes problematic in terms of Isabel's relationship with her lover, Ianopamoko. We are told, for example, that "Isabel at times grew weary of playing the man with her, though there was an exhilaration in being distinctly the stronger, and in striding ahead, tireless in her new skin, swinging a long light spear the mesa tribesmen had given her in farewell, while Ianopamoko followed behind, carrying their few belongings and rations in a basket down her back" (Updike 192–193).

25. See *The Assassination of the Male Black Image*, Los Angeles: Middle Passage Press, 1994.

WORKS CITED

Introduction

Aaron, Daniel. "The 'Inky Curse': Miscegenation in the White American Literary Imagination." *Social Science Information* 22.2 (1983): 169–190.

Avalos, David and Deborah Small, dir. *Ramona: The Birth of Mis-ce-ge-Nation*. Prod. David Avalos, Deborah Small, William Franco, and Miki Seifert. Videocassette. Speckled Gecko Prod., 1991.

———. "Ramona: The Birth of Mis-ce-ge-Nation: The Video Script." *Discourse* 18.1–2 (Fall-Winter 1995–1996): 23–31.

Bakhtin, M. M. *The Dialogic Imagination: Four Essays*. Edited by Michael Holquist. Translated by Caryl Emerson. Austin: University of Texas Press, 1981.

Balutansky, Kathleen M. and Marie-Agnès Sourieau, eds. *Caribbean Creolization: Reflections on the Cultural Dynamics of Language, Literature, and Identity*. Gainesville: University Press of Florida, 1998.

Belnap, Jeffrey and Raúl Fernández, eds. *José Martí's 'Our America': From National to Hemispheric Cultural Studies*. Durham: Duke University Press, 1998.

Berzon, Judith. *Neither White Nor Black: The Mulatto Character in American Fiction*. New York: New York University Press, 1978.

Bialostosky, Don. "Dialogics as an Art of Literary Discourse." *PMLA* 101 (1986): 788–795.

Dash, Michael. *The Other America: Caribbean Literature in a New World Context*. Charlottesville: University Press of Virginia, 1998.

Echevarría, Roberto González. *The Voice of the Masters: Writing and Authority in Latin American Literature*. Austin: University of Texas Press, 1985.

———. *Myth and Archive: A Theory of Latin American Narrative*. Cambridge: Cambridge University Press, 1990.

———. "Latin American and Comparative Literatures." *Poetics of the Americas: Race, Founding, and Textuality*. Edited by Bainard Cowan and Jefferson Humphries. Baton Rouge: Louisiana State University Press, 1997. 47–62.

Fiedler, Leslie. *The Return of the Vanishing American*. New York: Stein and Day, 1968.

Fitz, Earl E. *Rediscovering the New World: Inter-American Literature in a Comparative Context*. Iowa City: University of Iowa Press, 1991.

Gale Chevigny, Bell and Gari Laguardia, eds. *Reinventing the Americas: Comparative Studies of Literature of the United States and Spanish America*. Cambridge: Cambridge University Press, 1986.

García Canclini, Néstor. *Hybrid Cultures: Strategies for Entering and Leaving Modernity*. Trans-

lated by Christopher L. Chiappari and Silvia L. López. Minneapolis: University of
Minnesota Press, 1995.

Goldie, Terry. *Fear and Temptation: The Image of the Indigene in Canadian, Australian, and New
Zealand Literatures.* Montreal: McGill-Queen's University Press, 1989.

Graham, Richard, ed. *The Idea of Race in Latin America, 1870–1940.* Austin: University of
Texas Press, 1990.

Kosofsky Sedgwick, Eve. "Epistemology of the Closet." *The Lesbian and Gay Studies Reader.*
Edited by Henry Abelove et al., New York: Routledge, 1993. 45–61.

Pérez Firmat, Gustavo, ed. *Do the Americas Have a Common Literature?* Durham: Duke University Press, 1990.

Saldívar, José David. *The Dialectics of Our America: Genealogy, Cultural Critique, and Literary
History.* Durham: Duke University Press, 1991.

Spillers, Hortense J., ed. *Comparative American Identities: Race, Sex, and Nationality in the Modern Text.* New York: Routledge, 1991.

Williamson, Joel. *New People: Miscegenation and Mulattoes in the United States.* London: Macmillan, 1980.

Young, Robert. *Colonial Desire: Hybridity in Theory, Culture and Race.* London: Routledge,
1995.

Zamora, Lois Parkinson. *The Usable Past: The Imagination of History in Recent Fiction of the
Americas.* Cambridge: Cambridge University Press, 1997.

Chapter 1

Anon. "Of Rabbits & Races." *Time,* 1 June 1959, 19.

———. "'Rabbit' Book Burning Urged." *Orlando Sentinel,* 23 May 1959, 3A.

———. "'Rabbits' Wedding' Banned: Black Bunny Marries White." *Atlanta Constitution,*
22 May 1959, 12.

———. "'The Rabbits' Wedding' Should Be Burned." *Birmingham Post-Herald,* 23 May
1959, 1.

———. "The Rabbits' Wedding." *New York Times,* 24 May 1959, IV:2.

———. "White Rabbit Married Black One—Book Banned From Open Shelves." *Birmingham
Post-Herald,* 22 May 1959, 26.

———. *Katzen lassen grüßen: Ein Postkarten-Bilderbuch . . . aus der Sammlung Stefan Moses.*
Hamburg: Rasch und Röhrig, 1989.

Bailey, Thomas Pearce. *Race Orthodoxy in the South.* New York: Neale Publishing Co., 1914.

Balch, Henry. "Hush Puppies." *Orlando Sentinel,* 18 May 1959, 8B.

Bluestein, Gene. "Faulkner and Miscegenation." *Arizona Quarterly* 43.2 (Summer 1987).

Diengott, Nilli. "Thematics: Generating or Theming a Text?" *Orbis Litterarum* 43 (1988):
95–107.

Eliot, T. S., *Selected Poems.* 1928; rpt. London: Faber and Faber, n.d.

Ensey, E.R. et al. "Rabbit Story Called Brazen." (Letters) *Orlando Sentinel,* 25 May 1959, A9.

Grady, Henry W. "In Plain Black and White." *Century* 29.7 (1885): 909–917.

Hurston, Zora Neale. "Court Order Can't Make Races Mix." *The American Legion Magazine*
(June 1951): 14–15, 55–60.

Kaemmerling, Ekkehard, ed. *Ikonographie und Ikonologie: Theorien, Entwicklung, Probleme.*
Köln: DuMont, 1991.

Kelsey, Mason D. Letter. *Orlando Sentinel,* 25 May 1959, A9.

Levy, Rita. "All About Rabbits." (Letter) *Orlando Sentinel*, 25 May 1959, A9.

Mangum, Charles S., Jr. *The Legal Status of the Negro*. Chapel Hill: University of North Carolina Press, 1940.

Mayer, Milton. "The Issue is Miscegenation." In *White Racism: Its History, Pathology, and Practice*. Edited by Barry Schwartz and Robert Disch. New York: Dell, 1970. 207–217.

Merchant, Jane. Letter. *Orlando Sentinel*, 25 May 1959, A9.

Myrdal, Gunnar. *An American Dilemma*. New York: Harper, 1944.

Nathan, Hans. "Dixie." *Encyclopedia of Southern Culture*. Edited by Charles Reagan Wilson and William Ferris. Chapel Hill: University of North Carolina Press, 1989.

Nordell, Rod. "Pictures to Read." *Christian Science Monitor*, 8 May 1958, 15.

Ricks, Christopher, ed. *The Poems of Tennyson*. London: Longmans, 1969.

Shell, Marc. *Children of the Earth: Literature, Politics, and Nationhood*. New York and Oxford: Oxford University Press, 1993.

Sollors, Werner, ed. *The Return of Thematic Criticism*. Cambridge: Harvard University Press, 1993.

———. "Of Mules and Mares in a Land of Difference; or, Quadrupeds All?" *American Quarterly* 42.2 (June 1990): 167–190.

———. *Neither Black Nor White Yet Both: Thematic Explorations of Interracial Literature*. New York: Oxford University Press, 1997.

Thompson, Lloyd A. *Romans and Blacks*. Norman, Oklahoma, and London: University of Oklahoma Press, 1989.

U.S. Supreme Court. *Naim v. Naim* decision (1955), at 197 Va. 80, 87 S.E.2d 749.

Villareal, José Antonio. *Pocho*. Garden City, New York: Doubleday, 1959.

Wilkinson, Doris Y. *Black Male/White Female: Perspectives on Interracial Marriage and Courtship*. Cambridge, Mass.: Schenkman, 1975.

Woods, George A. "Pictures for Fun, Fact and Fancy." *New York Times Book Review*, 8 June 1958, 42.

Chapter 2

Alvarez García, Imeldo. Prologo, Cirilo Villaverde, *Cecilia Valdés*. By Cirilo Villaverde. 2 vols. Havana: Editorial Letras Cubanas, 1981. 5–46.

Bourdieu, Pierre. "Reading, Readers, the Literate Literature." *In Other Words: Essays Towards a Reflexive Sociology*. Translated by Matthew Adamson. Cambridge, UK: Polity Press, 1990. 94–105.

Fernández Olmos, Margarite and Lisabeth Paravisini-Gebert, eds. *Sacred Possessions: Vodou, Santeria, Obeah, and the Caribbean*. New Brunswick: Rutgers University Press, 1997.

Friol, Roberto. "La novela cubana del siglo XIX." *Revista Unión*, diciembre 1968, 178–201.

Holland, Norman. "Fashioning Cuba." In *Nationalisms and Sexualities*. Edited by Andrew Parker, Mary Russo, Doris Sommer, and Patricia Yaeger. London, New York: Routledge, 1992. 147–156.

Kline, Herbert. *Slavery in the Americas: A Comparative Study of Virginia and Cuba*. Chicago: University of Chicago Press, 1967.

Martínez-Alier, Verena. *Marriage, Class and Color in Nineteenth Century Cuba: A Study of Racial Attitudes and Sexual Values in a Slave Society*. New York: Cambridge University Press, 1974.

Molloy, Sylvia. "From Serf to Self: The Autobiography of Juan Francisco Manzano." In *At*

Face Value: Autobiographical Writing in Spanish America. Cambridge and New York: Cambridge University Press, 1991. 36–54.

Patterson, Orlando. *Slavery and Social Death: A Comparative Study*. Cambridge: Harvard University Press, 1982.

Poyo, Gerald E. *"With All, and for the Good of All": The Emergence of Popular Nationalism in the Cuban Communities of the United States, 1848–1898*. Durham: Duke University Press, 1989.

Ramos, Julio. "Faceless Tongues: Language and Citizenship in Nineteenth-Century Latin America." In *Displacements: Cultural Identities in Question*. Edited by Angelika Bammer. Bloomington: Indiana University Press, 1994.

Schwarz, Roberto. "Ideas Out of Place." In *Misplaced Ideas: Essays on Brazilian Culture*. New York: Verso, 1992.

Scott, Rebecca J. *Slave Emancipation in Cuba: The Transition to Free Labor, 1860–1899*. Princeton: Princeton University Press, 1985.

Sommer, Doris. *Foundational Fictions: The National Romances of Latin America*. Berkeley: University of California Press, 1991.

Steiner, George. *After Babel: Aspects of Language and Translation*. London, New York: Oxford University Press, 1975.

———. *On Difficulty and Other Essays*. Oxford, New York: Oxford University Press, 1978.

Torgovnick, Marianna. "The Politics of the 'We.'" *South Atlantic Quarterly* 91.1 (Winter 1992): 43–63.

Villaverde, Cirilo. *Cecilia Valdés o la Loma del Angel, novela de costumbres cubanas*. Mexico: Editorial Porrúa, 1979.

———. *Cecilia Valdes or Angel's Hill: A Novel of Cuban Customs*. Translated by Sydney G. Gest. New York: Vantage Press, 1962.

Chapter 3

Davis, Thadious. *Nella Larsen, Novelist of the Harlem Renaissance: A Woman's Life Unveiled*. Baton Rouge: Louisiana State University Press, 1994.

Fauset, Jessie Redmon. *Plum Bun: A Novel without a Moral*. Introduction by Deborah McDowell. London, Boston: Pandora Press, 1985.

Hanchard, Michael George. *Orpheus and Power*. Princeton: Princeton University Press, 1994.

Hellwig, David. *African-American Reflections on Brazil's Racial Paradise*. Philadelphia: Temple University Press, 1992.

Larsen, Nella. *Quicksand and Passing*. Edited by Deborah E. McDowell. New Brunswick: Rutgers, 1986.

Reis, Fidelis. *Pais a organizar*. Rio de Janeiro: Coelho Branco, 1931.

Skidmore, Thomas E. *Black Into White*. New York: Oxford University Press, 1974.

Chapter 4

Bernabé, Jean, Patrick Chamoiseau, and Raphaël Confiant. *Eloge de la créolité*. Paris: Gallimard, 1989.

———. Conversation with Lucien Taylor, "Créolité Bites." *Transition* 74 (1998): 124–161.

Bersani, Leo. *A Future for Astyanax: Character and Desire in Literature*. Boston: Little, Brown and Co., 1976.

Brontë, Emily. *Wuthering Heights*. William M. Sale and Richard J. Dunn, eds. New York: Norton, 1989.

Cliff, Michelle. *Abeng*. New York: Crossing Press, 1984.

Condé, Maryse. *La Migration des coeurs*. Paris: Robert Laffont, 1995.

———. *Windward Heights*. Translated by Richard Philcox. London: Faber and Faber, 1998.

———. "Entretien avec Maryse Condé: de l'identité culturelle." Interview with Marie-Agnès Sourieau. *The French Review* 27:6 (May 1999): 1091–1098.

Cosentino, Donald J., ed. *Sacred Arts of Haitian Vodou*. Los Angeles: UCLA Fowler Museum of Cultural History, 1995.

Gilbert, Sandra and Susan Gubar. *The Madwoman in the Attic*. New Haven: Yale University Press, 1979.

Glissant, Edouard. *Le Discours antillais*. Paris: Seuil, 1981.

———. "L'Europe et les Antilles: Interview with Andrea Schwieger Hiepko." *Mots pluriels* 8 (Oct. 1998): 1–7.

Kingsolver, Barbara. "Lone Star." *The Nation* 268.13 (April 5-12, 1999): 36–38.

Lionnet, Françoise. "Métissage, Emancipation, and Female Textuality in Two Francophone Texts." Edited by Bella Brodzki and Celeste Schenck. In *Life/Lines: Theorizing Women's Autobiography*. Ithaca: Cornell University Press, 1988.

Meyer, Susan. *Imperialism at Home: Race and Victorian Women's Fiction*. Ithaca: Cornell University Press, 1997.

Morrison, Toni. *Playing in the Dark*. Cambridge: Harvard University Press, 1992.

Smith, Valerie. *Not Just Race, Not Just Gender*. New York: Routledge, 1998.

Sollors, Werner. *Beyond Ethnicity: Consent and Descent in American Literature*. New York: Oxford University Press, 1986.

Swamy, Vinay. "Traversing the Atlantic: From Brontë to Condé." Forthcoming in *Journal of Caribbean Studies*.

Tiffin, Helen. "Comparative Literature and Postcolonial Counter-Discourse." *Kunapipi* 9:3 (1987) (as cited in Ashcroft, Griffith, and Tiffin, *The Post-Colonial Studies Reader*. New York: Routledge, 1995: 95-98).

Williams, Patricia J. "Fresh Eggs, Fried Baloney." *The Nation* 268:13 (April 5/12, 1999): 10.

Winterson, Jeanette. *Gut Symmetries*. New York: Vintage, 1997.

Chapter 5

André, Jacques. *L'inceste focal dans la famille noire antillaise*. Paris: Presses Universitaires de France, 1987.

Arnold, James. "The gendering of *créolité*: The erotics of colonialism." *Penser la créolité*. Edited by Maryse Condé and Madeleine Cottenet-Hage. Paris: Ed. Karthala, 1995.

Bernabé, Jean, Patrick Chamoiseau, and Raphaël Confiant. *Eloge de la créolité*. Paris: Gallimard/Presses Universitaires Créoles, 1989.

Bhabha, Homi K. *The Location of Culture*. London & New York: Routledge, 1994.

Breton, André. *Martinique charmeuse de serpents*. Paris: Ed. du Sagittaire, 1948.

Césaire, Suzanne. "Le Grand camouflage." *Tropiques* 13-14 (1945): 267–273.

Chamoiseau, Patrick and Raphaël Confiant. *Lettres créoles: Tracées antillaises et continentales de la littérature 1635–1975*. Paris: Hatier, 1991.

Confiant, Raphaël. *Ravines du devant-jour*. Haute Enfance. Paris: Gallimard, 1993.

———. *La Vierge du Grand Retour*. Paris: Grasset, 1996.

Dahomey, Jacky. "Habiter la créolité ou le heurt de l'universel." *Chemins Critiques* 1 (1989): 109–133.

Glissant, Edouard. *Le Discours antillais.* Paris: Ed. du Seuil, 1981.

———. *Introduction à une Poétique du Divers.* Montréal: Presses de l'Université de Montréal, 1994.

———. *Mahagony.* Paris: Ed. du Seuil, 1987.

Lionnet, Françoise. *Postcolonial Representations: Women, Literature, Identity.* Ithaca & London: Cornell University Press, 1995.

Mazama, Ama. "Critique afrocentrique de *l'Eloge de la créolité.*" In *Penser la créolité.* Edited by Maryse Condé and Madeleine Cottenet-Hage. Paris: Ed. Karthala, 1995.

Schwarz-Bart, Simone and André. *Un plat de porc aux bananes vertes.* Paris: Ed. du Seuil, 1967.

Spear, Thomas. "Jouissances carnavalesques: représentations de la sexualité." In *Penser la créolité.* Edited by Maryse Condé and Madeleine Cottenet-Hage. Paris: Ed. Karthala, 1995.

Young, Robert J. C. *Colonial Desire: Hybridity in Theory, Culture and Race.* London & New York: Routledge, 1995.

Chapter 6

Alegría, Ciro. *El mundo es ancho y ajeno.* 1941. Madrid: Alianza Editorial, 1983.

Arguedas, José María. *Amor Mundo.* Montevideo: Arca Editorial, 1967.

———. *Deep Rivers.* Translated by F. H. Barraclough. Austin: University of Texas Press, 1978.

———. *El zorro de arriba y el zorro de abajo.* Ed. by Eve-Marie Fell. Nanterre: Signatarios Acuerdo Archibos, 1990.

———. *Formación de una cultura nacional indoamericana.* 5th ed. México: Sigloveintiuno editores, 1975.

———. *Los ríos profundos.* Madrid: Editorial Planeta-Agostini, 1985.

———. *El sexto.* Lima: Libreria J. Mejía Baca y Tip. Santa Rosa, 1961.

———. *Todas las sangres.* Buenos Aires: Editorial Losada, 1964.

Burt, Jo-Marie and Cesar Espejo. "The Struggles of a Self-Built Community." *NACLA: Report on the Americas* XXVIII (4) (1995): 19–25.

Castro-Klarén, Sara. *Escritura, transgresión y sujeto en la literatura latinoamericana.* Tlahuapan, Puebla: Premia, 1989.

Douglas, Mary. *Purity and Danger: An Analysis of the Concepts of Pollution and Taboo.* London: Routledge, 1966.

García Calderón, Ventura. *La venganza del cóndor.* 1923. Lima: Peisa, 1987.

Gramsci, Antonio. *Selections from the Prison Notebooks.* Edited and translated by Quintin Hoare and Geoffrey Nowell Smith. New York: International Publishers, 1971.

Icaza, Jorge. *El chulla Romero y Flores.* 2nd ed. Buenos Aires: Editorial Losada, 1958.

———. *Huasipungo.* Buenos Aires: Editorial Losada, 1952.

Kipnis, Laura. "(Male) Desire and (Female) Disgust: Reading Hustler." In *Cultural Studies.* Edited by Lawrence Grossberg et al. New York: Routledge, 1992.

Kristeva, Julia. *Tales of Love.* Translated by Leon Roudiez. New York: Columbia University Press, 1987.

Laclau, Ernesto and Chantal Mouffe. *Hegemony and Socialist Strategy: Towards a Radical Democratic Politics.* 4th ed. London: Verso, 1985.

Manrique, Nelson. "Una mirada histórica." In *José María Arguedas veinte años despues: huellas y horizonte 1969–1989*. Lima: UNMSM e IKONO ediciones, 1991.

Mariátegui, José Carlos. *Siete ensayos de interpretación de la realidad peruana*. 1928. Lima: Minerva, 1972.

Matos, Sylvia. "Una decada de cultura andina: de las monografías a la síntesis." *Ciudad y cultura* 27 (1991).

Matos Mar, José. *Desborde popular y crisis del estado: el nuevo rostro del Perú en la decada de 1980*. Lima: CONCYTEC, 1984.

Medinaceli, Carlos. *La Chaskañawi*. 12th ed. La Paz: Editorial "Los Amigos del Libro," 1947.

Poole, Deborah and Gerardo Rémique. *Peru: Time of Fear*. London: Latin American Bureau, 1992.

Pratt, Mary Louise. "Women, Literature and National Brotherhood." In *Women, Culture and Politics in Latin America: Seminar on Feminism in Latin America*. Edited by Emilie Bergmann et al. Berkeley: University of California Press, 1990.

Rama, Angel. *Transculturación narrativa en América Latina*. México: Siglo Veintiuno Editores, 1982.

Rowe, William and Vivian Scheling. *Memory and Modernity; Popular Culture in Latin America*. London: Verso, 1991.

Sommer, Doris. "Irresistible Romance: The Foundational Fictions of Latin America." In *Nation and Narration*. Edited by Homi Bhabha. London: Methuen, 1988.

Valcárcel, Luis E. *Tempestad en los Andes*. 2nd ed. 1928. Lima: Editorial Universo, 1972.

Vargas Llosa, Mario. *Historia de Mayta*. Barcelona: Editorial Seix Barral, 1984.

———. "Literatura y suicidio: El caso Arguedas (*El zorro de arriba y el zorro de abajo*)." Revista Iberoamericana 110–111, (I–VI) (1985): 3.

———. *The Real Life of Alejandro Mayta*. Translated by Alfred Mac Adam. New York: Random House, 1986.

Chapter 7

Banning, Evelyn. *Helen Hunt Jackson*. New York: Vanguard, 1973.

Brooks, Peter. *Reading for the Plot: Design and Intention in Narrative*. New York: Vintage, 1984.

Channing, William. "Essay on American Language and Literature." *North American Review* 1 (September 1815): 314.

Cometta Manzoni, Aída. *El indio en la poesía de América española*. Buenos Aires, 1939.

Cooper, James Fenimore. *The Last of the Mohicans*. New York: Penguin, 1986.

Davidson, Cathy. *Revolution and the Word: The Rise of the Novel in America*. New York: Oxford University Press, 1986.

Dippie, Brian. *Vanishing Americans: White Attitudes and U.S. Indian Policy*. Middletown, CT: Wesleyan University Press, 1982.

Echevarría, Evelio. "La novela indigenista hispanoamericana: definición y bibliografía." *Revista Interamericana de Bibliografía/Inter-American Review of Bibliography* 35:3 (1985).

Fiedler, Leslie. *Love and Death in the American Novel*. New York: Stein and Day, 1982.

Franco, Jean. *An Introduction to Spanish-American Literature*. New York: Cambridge University Press, 1969.

Gutiérrez-Jones, Carl. *Rethinking the Borderlands: Between Chicano Culture and Legal Discourse*. Berkeley: University of California Press, 1995.

Kaplan, Amy. "Nation, Region, and Empire." In *The Columbia History of the American Novel.*
Edited by Emory Elliot. New York: Columbia University Press, 1991.

Maddox, Lucy. Private telephone conversation. 13 April 1994.

———. *Removals: Nineteenth-Century American Literature and the Politics of Indian Affairs.* New York: Oxford University Press, 1991.

Mariátegui, José Carlos. *Siete ensayos de interpretación de la realidad peruana.* Caracas: Biblioteca Ayacucho, 1978.

———. *Seven Interpretive Essays on Peruvian Reality.* Translated by Marjory Urquidi. Austin: University of Texas Press, 1971.

Mathes, Valerie Sherer. *Helen Hunt Jackson and Her Indian Reform Legacy.* Austin: University of Texas Press, 1990.

Matto de Turner, Clorinda. "Proemio." *Aves sin nido.* Buenos Aires: Ediciones Solar, 1968.

Mera, Juan León. *Cumandá o un drama entre salvajes.* Madrid: Espasa-Calpe, 1976.

Muñoz, Braulio. *Sons of the Wind: The Search for Identity in Spanish American Indian Literature.* New Brunswick: Rutgers University Press, 1982.

Palfrey, John Gorham. Review of *Yamoyden. North American Review* 12 (1821).

Pérez Firmat, Gustavo. "Introduction: Cheek to Cheek." In *Do the Americas Have a Common Literature?* Edited by Gustavo Pérez Firmat. Durham: Duke University Press, 1990.

Pratt, Mary Louise. "Women, Literature, and National Brotherhood." Seminar on Feminism and Culture in Latin America, *Women, Culture, and Politics in Latin America.* Berkeley: University of California Press, 1990.

Sacoto, Antonio. *The Indian in the Ecuadorian Novel.* New York: Las Americas Publishing Co., 1967.

Sommer, Doris. *Foundational Fictions: The National Romances of Latin America.* Berkeley: University of California Press, 1991.

Chapter 8

Cable, George Washington. *The Grandissimes: A Story of Creole Life.* New York & London: Penguin, 1988.

Fanon, Frantz. *The Wretched of the Earth.* New York: Grove Press, 1963.

Fernández Retamar, Roberto. "On *Ramona* by Helen Hunt Jackson and Jose Martí." *Mélanges à la Mémoire D'André Joucla-Ruau.* Vol. 2. Provence: Editions de l'Université de Provence, 1978. 699–705.

———. *Caliban and Other Essays.* Translated by Edward Baker. Foreword by Fredric Jameson. Minneapolis: University of Minnesota Press, 1989.

Ferrer, Ada. *Insurgent Cuba: Race, Nation, and Revolution, 1868–1898.* Chapel Hill & London: University of North Carolina Press, 1999.

Franco, Jean. *Plotting Women.* New York: Columbia University Press, 1989.

Gillman, Susan. "Ramona in Our America." In *José Martí's "Our America": From National to Hemispheric Cultural Studies.* Edited by Jeffrey Belnap and Raúl Fernández. Durham & London: Duke University Press, 1998. 91-111.

Gilroy, Paul. *The Black Atlantic: Modernity and Double Consciousness.* Cambridge: Harvard University Press, 1993.

Gutiérrez-Jones, Carl. *Rethinking the Borderlands: Between Chicano Culture and Legal Discourse.* Berkeley: University of California Press, 1995.

Helg, Aline. *Our Rightful Share: The Afro-Cuban Struggle for Equality, 1886–1912.* Chapel Hill: University of North Carolina Press, 1995.

Hirsch, Arnold R. and Joseph Logsdon, eds. *Creole New Orleans: Race and Americanization.* Baton Rouge: Louisiana State University Press, 1992.

Kaplan, Amy. "Region, Nation, Empire." In *The Columbia History of the American Novel.* Edited by Emory Elliott. New York: Columbia University Press, 1991. 240–266.

Martí, José. *Inside the Monster: Writings on the United States and American Imperialism.* Translated by Elinor Randall. Edited by Philip S. Foner. New York and London: Monthly Review Press, 1975.

———. Introduction to Helen Hunt Jackson, *Ramona: Novela Americana.* Translated by José Martí. *Obras completas.* Vol. 24. Havana: Editorial Nacional de Cuba, 1965. 199–205.

———. *Our America: Writings on Latin America and the Struggle for Cuban Independence.* Translated by Elinor Randall. Edited by Philip S. Foner. New York: Monthly Review Press, 1977.

McWilliams, Carey. *North From Mexico: The Spanish-Speaking People of the U.S.* 1948. New York: Praeger, 1968.

Pratt, Mary Louise. "Women, Literature, and National Brotherhood." In *Women, Culture, and Politics in Latin America: Seminar on Feminism and Culture in Latin America.* Edited by Bergmann, Greenberg, et al. 48–73. Berkeley: University of California Press, 1990.

Ruiz de Burton, María Amparo. *The Squatter and the Don.* Edited by Rosaura Sánchez and Beatrice Pita. Houston: Arte Público Press, 1992.

———. *Who Would Have Thought It?* 1872; rpt. Houston: Arte Público Press, 1995.

Sánchez, Rosaura. *Telling Identities: The Californio Testimonios.* Minneapolis: University of Minnesota Press, 1995.

Scott, Rebecca J. *Slave Emancipation in Cuba: The Transition to Free Labor, 1860–1899.* Princeton: Princeton University Press, 1985.

Sherer Mathes, Valerie. *Helen Hunt Jackson and Her Indian Reform Legacy.* Austin: University of Texas Press, 1990.

Silber, Nina. *The Romance of Reunion: Northerners and the South, 1865–1900.* Chapel Hill: University of North Carolina Press, 1993.

Sommer, Doris. *Foundational Fictions: The National Romances of Latin America.* Berkeley: University of California Press, 1991.

Spillers, Hortense, ed. *Comparative American Identities: Race, Sex, and Nationalism in the Modern Text.* New York: Routledge, 1991.

Sundquist, Eric J. *To Wake the Nations: Race in the Making of American Literature.* Cambridge & London: Harvard University Press, 1993.

Thomas, David H., ed. *The Spanish Borderlands in Pan-American Perspective.* Vol. 3 of *Columbian Consequences.* Washington, D.C.: Smithsonian Press, 1991.

Vasconcelos, José. *La raza cósmica, misión de la raza iberoamericana.* Paris: Agencia Mundial de Librería, 1925.

Williamson, Joel. *The Crucible of Race: Black-White Relations in the American South Since Emancipation.* New York: Oxford University Press, 1984.

Woodward, C. Vann. *Origins of the New South, 1877–1913.* Baton Rouge: Louisiana State University Press, 1951.

Chapter 9

Acosta, Oscar. "Zeta." *The Autobiography of a Brown Buffalo.* Introduction by Hunter S. Thompson. New York: Vintage, 1989.

———. *The Revolt of the Cockroach People.* Introduction by Hunter S. Thompson. New York: Vintage, 1987.

Alarcón, Daniel. "The Aztec Palimpsest: Toward a New Understanding of Aztlán, Cultural Identity and History." *Aztlán* 19.2 (1992): 33–68.

Alarcón, Norma. "Conjugating Subjects: The Heteroglossia of Essence and Resistance." Arteaga 125–138.

———. "Traddutora, Traditora: A Paradigmatic Figure of Chicana Feminism." *Cultural Critique* 13 (Fall 1989): 57–87.

Arteaga, Alfred, ed. *An Other Tongue: Nation and Ethnicity in the Linguistic Borderlands.* Durham: Duke University Press, 1994.

Baker, Houston A., Jr., ed. *Three American Literatures.* Introduction by Walter J. Ong. New York: Modern Language Association, 1982.

Bhabha, Homi K. "Interrogating Identity: Frantz Fanon and the Postcolonial Prerogative." In *The Location of Culture.* New York: Routledge, 1994. 40–65.

———. "Remembering Fanon: Self, Psyche, and the Colonial Position." In *Remaking History.* Edited by Barbara Kruger and Phil Mariani. Seattle: Bay Press, 1989. 131–148.

Cervantes, Lorna Dee. *Emplumada.* Pittsburgh: University of Pittsburgh Press, 1981.

Chabram, Angie and Rosa Linda Fregoso. "Chicana/o Cultural Representations: Reframing Alternative Critical Discourses." *Cultural Studies* 4 (October 1990): 203–212.

Chávez, John. *The Lost Land: The Chicano Image of the Southwest.* Albuquerque: University of New Mexico Press, 1991.

Herrera-Sobek, María. "The Politics of Rape: Sexual Transgression in Chicana Fiction." In *Chicana Creativity and Criticism: Charting New Frontiers in American Literature.* Edited by María Herrera-Sobek and Helena María Viramontes, Houston: Arte Público Press, 1988. 171–181.

Leal, Luis and Pepe Barrón. "Chicano Literature: An Overview." Baker, Jr. 9–32.

Meyer, Richard. "Rock Hudson's Body." In *Inside/Out: Lesbian Theories, Gay Theories.* Edited by Diana Fuss. New York: Routledge, 1991. 259–288.

Nancy, Jean-Luc. "Cut Throat Sun." Translated by Lydie Moudileno. Arteaga 113–123.

Paredes, Raymund. "The Evolution of Chicano Literature." Baker, Jr. 33–79.

Paz, Octavio. *The Labyrinth of Solitude.* Translated by Lysander Kemp, Yara Milos, and Rachel Phillips Belash. 1950; New York: Grove Press, 1985.

Pratt, Mary Louise. "'Yo Soy La Malinche': Chicana Writers and the Poetics of Ethnonationalism." *Callaloo* 16.4 (1993): 859–873.

Rushdie, Salman. *The Moor's Last Sigh.* New York: Pantheon Books, 1995.

Sandoval, Chela N. J. "U.S. Third World Feminism: The Theory and Method of Oppositional Consciousness in the Postmodern World." *Genders* 10 (1991): 1–24.

Savin, Ada. "Bilingualism and Dialogism: Another Reading of Lorna Dee Cervantes's Poetry." Arteaga 215–223.

Spivak, Gayatri. "Theory in the Margin." *Consequences of Theory.* Edited by Jonathan Arac and Barbara Johnson. Baltimore: Johns Hopkins University Press, 1991. 154–180.

Villanueva, Tino. *Scene from the Movie Giant.* Willimantic, CT: Curbstone Press, 1993.

Chapter 10

Alarcón, Norma. "Traddutora, Traditora: A Paradigmatic Figure of Chicana Feminism." *Cultural Studies* 13 (Fall 1989): 57–87.

Anzaldúa, Gloria. *Borderlands/La Frontera: The New Mestiza.* San Francisco: aunt lute books, 1987.

Benítez-Rojo, Antonio. *The Repeating Island: The Caribbean and the Postmodern Perspective.* Durham: Duke University Press, 1992.

Bhabha, Homi K. *The Location of Culture.* London: Routledge, 1994.

Bongie, Chris. *Islands and Exiles: The Creole Identities of Post/Colonial Literature.* Stanford: Stanford University Press, 1998.

Brown, Jennifer S. H. *Strangers in Blood: Fur Trade Company Families in Indian Country.* Vancouver: University of British Columbia Press, 1980.

Burley, David V. and Gayel A. Horsfall, eds. "Vernacular Houses and Farmsteads of the Canadian Métis." *Journal of Cultural Geography* 10.1 (Winter 1989): 19–33.

Butalansky, Kathleen M. and Marie-Agnès Sourieau, eds. *Caribbean Creolization: Reflections on the Cultural Dynamics of Language, Literature, and Identity.* Gainesville: University Press of Florida, 1998.

Campbell, Maria. *Halfbreed.* Lincoln: University of Nebraska Press, 1973.

Culleton, Beatrice. *In Search of April Raintree.* Winnipeg: Peguis Publ., 1983.

Cypess, Sandra Messinger. *La Malinche in Mexican Literature: From History to Myth.* Austin: University of Texas Press, 1991.

Dash, Michael. *The Other America: Caribbean Literature in a New World Context.* Charlottesville: University Press of Virginia, 1998.

Deleuze, Gilles and Félix Guattari. *A Thousand Plateaus: Capitalism and Schizophrenia.* Translated by Brian Massumi. Minneapolis: University of Minnesota Press, 1987.

Faragher, John Mack. "Americans, Mexicans, Métis: A Community Approach to the Comparative Study of North American Frontiers." In *Under an Open Sky: Rethinking America's Western Past.* Edited by William Cronon et al. New York: Norton, 1992.

Flanagan, Thomas. *Louis 'David' Riel: 'Prophet of the New World'.* Rev. ed. Toronto: University of Toronto Press, 1996.

García Canclini, Néstor. *Hybrid Cultures: Strategies for Entering and Leaving Modernity.* Translated by Christopher L. Chiappari and Silvia L. López. Minneapolis: University of Minnesota Press, 1995.

Gilroy, Paul. *The Black Atlantic: Modernity and Double Consciousness.* Cambridge: Harvard University Press, 1993.

Glissant, Edouard. *Caribbean Discourse: Selected Essays.* Translated by J. Michael Dash. Charlottesville: University Press of Virginia, 1992.

———. *Poetics of Relation.* Translated by Betsy Wing. Ann Arbor: University of Michigan Press, 1997.

Griffiths, Linda and Maria Campbell. *The Book of Jessica: A Theatrical Transformation.* Toronto: Coach House Press, 1998.

Hicks, D. Emily. *Border Writing: The Multidimensional Text.* Minneapolis: University of Minnesota Press, 1991.

Howard, Joseph. *Strange Empire: Louis Riel and the Métis People.* 1952; Rpt. Toronto: James Lewis and Samuel, 1974.

Irigaray, Luce. *Marine Lover of Friedrich Nietzsche.* New York: Columbia University Press, 1991.

Jackson, J. B. *Discovering the Vernacular Landscape.* New Haven: Yale University Press, 1984.

———. *A Sense of Place, a Sense of Time.* New Haven: Yale University Press, 1994.

King, Thomas. "Introduction." In *All My Relations: An Anthology of Contemporary Canadian Native Fiction.* Edited by Thomas King. Toronto: McClelland and Stewart, 1990.

Kutzinski, Vera M. *Sugar's Secrets: Race and the Erotics of Cuban Nationalism.* Charlottesville: University Press of Virginia, 1993.

Limerick, Patricia Nelson. *The Legacy of Conquest: The Unbroken Past of the American West.* New York: Norton, 1987.

Lionnet, Françoise. "The Politics and Aesthetics of Métissage." In *Women, Autobiography, Theory: A Reader.* Edited by Sidonie Smith and Julia Watson. Madison: University of Wisconsin Press, 1998.

Lundgren, Jodi. "'Being a Half-breed': Discourses of Race and Cultural Syncreticity in the Works of Three Métis Women Writers." *Canadian Literature* 144 (Spring 1995): 62–77.

Maracle, Lee. *Sojourner's Truth and Other Stories.* Vancouver: Press Gang Publ., 1990.

Paz, Octavio. *The Labyrinth of Solitude and Other Writings.* Translated by Lysander Kemp. 1959; rpt. New York: Grove Press, 1985.

Pérez Firmat, Gustavo. *The Cuban Condition: Translation and Identity in Modern Cuban Literature.* Cambridge: Cambridge University Press, 1989.

———. *Life on the Hyphen: The Cuban-American Way.* Austin: University of Texas Press, 1994.

Peterson, Jacqueline and Jennifer S. H. Brown, eds. *The New Peoples: Being and Becoming Métis in North America.* Winnipeg: University of Manitoba Press, 1985.

Pratt, Mary Louise. *Imperial Eyes: Travel Writing and Transculturation.* London: Routledge, 1992.

———. "Criticism in the Contact Zone: Decentering Community and Nation." In *Critical Theory, Cultural Poetics, and Latin American Narrative.* Edited by Stephen Bell et al. Notre Dame: University of Notre Dame Press, 1993. 83–102.

———. "'Yo Soy La Malinche': Chicana Writers and the Poetics of Ethnonationalism." *Callaloo* 16 (1993): 859–873.

Purich, Donald. *The Métis.* Toronto: James Lorimer, 1988.

Romero, Rolando. "Memories of Dispossession." MLA Convention, Chicago, December 1999.

Spicer, Edward. *Cycles of Conquest: The Impact of Spain, Mexico, and the United States on the Indians of the Southwest, 1533–1960.* Tucson: University of Arizona Press, 1962.

Van Kirk, Sylvia. *"Many Tender Ties": Women in Fur-Trade Society, 1670–1870.* Winnipeg: Watson & Dwyer, 1980.

White, Richard. *The Middle Ground: Indians, Empires, and Republics in the Great Lakes Region, 1650–1815.* Cambridge: Cambridge University Press, 1991.

Young, Robert. *Colonial Desire: Hybridity in Theory, Culture and Race.* London: Routledge, 1995.

Chapter 12

Anzaldúa, Gloria. *Borderlands/La Frontera*. San Francisco: aunt lute books, 1987.

Barthes, Roland. *Camera Lucida: Reflections on Photography*. New York: Hill and Wang, 1981.

Hoobler, Dorothy and Thomas. *Photographing the Frontier*. New York: G. P. Putnam's Sons, 1980.

Lippard, Lucy R. *Partial Recall*. New York: The New Press, 1992.

Morris, Wright. *Time Pieces: Photographs, Writing, and Memory*. New York: Aperture Foundation, Inc., 1989.

Owens, Louis. *Mixedblood Messages: Literature, Film, Family, Place*. Norman: University of Oklahoma Press, 1998.

Rabaté, Jean-Michel. *Writing the Image After Roland Barthes*. Philadelphia: University of Pennsylvania Press, 1997.

Sontag, Susan. *On Photography*. New York: Farrar, Straus and Giroux, 1973.

Steiner, George. *In Bluebeard's Castle*. New Haven: Yale University Press, 1971.

Vizenor, Gerald. *Fugitive Poses: Native American Indian Scenes of Absence and Presence*. Lincoln: University of Nebraska Press, 1998.

Woodward, Grace Steele. *The Cherokees*. Norman: University of Oklahoma Press, 1963.

Young, Robert. *White Mythologies: Writing History and the West*. London: Routledge, 1990.

Chapter 13

Astrov, Margot, ed. *American Indian Prose and Poetry*. New York: Capricorn Press, 1962.

Bernstein, Richard. *Dictatorship of Virtue: Multiculturalism and the Battle for America's Future*. New York: Alfred A. Knopf, 1994.

Bowen, Peter. *Coyote Wind*. New York: St. Martin's Press, 1994.

Brimelow, Peter. *Alien Nation: Common Sense About America's Immigration Disaster*. New York: Random House, 1994.

Brotherston, Gordon. *The Book of the Fourth World: Reading the Native Americas through their Literatures*. Cambridge: Cambridge University Press, 1992.

Castillo, Ana. *Sapogonia*. Tempe, AZ: Bilingual Press/Editorial Bilingüe, 1990.

Chase-Riboud, Barbara. *The President's Daughter*. New York: Crown, 1994.

Condé, Maryse. *I, Tituba, Black Witch of Salem*. Translated by Richard Philcox. Charlottesville: University Press of Virginia, 1992.

Craig, Terrence. *Racial Attitudes in English-Canadian Fiction, 1905–1980*. Waterloo, Ontario: Wilfred Laurier University Press, 1987.

Creech, Sharon. *Walk Two Moons*. New York: HarperCollins, 1995.

Erdrich, Louise. *Tracks*. New York: Harper and Row, 1988.

Fitz, Earl E. *Rediscovering the New World: Inter-American Literature in a Comparative Context*. Iowa City: University of Iowa Press, 1991.

French, Albert. *Holly*. New York: Viking, 1995.

Funderberg, Lise. *Black, White, Other: Biracial Americans Talk About Race and Identity*. New York: William Morrow, 1995.

George, Lynell. *Centre Daily Times* newspaper (State College, PA), 5 May 1995.

Gilb, Dagoberto. *The Last Known Residence of Mickey Acuña*. New York: Grove Press, 1994.

Hutchinson, Earl Ofari. *The Assassination of the Male Black Image.* Los Angeles: Middle Passage Press, 1994.

King, Thomas. *Green Grass, Running Water.* New York: Bantam Books, 1994.

Kogawa, Joy. *Obasan.* Toronto: Lester and Orpen Dennys, 1981.

Laferrière, Dany. *How to Make Love to a Negro.* Translated by David Homel. Toronto: Coach House Press, 1987.

Lauber, Lynn. *21 Sugar Street.* New York: W. W. Norton, 1994.

Lind, Michael. *The Next American Nation: The New Nationalism and the Fourth American Revolution.* New York: Free Press, 1995.

Liu, Aimee. *Face.* New York: Warner, 1994.

Monegal, Emir Rodríguez and Thomas Colchie, eds. *The Borzoi Anthology of Latin American Literature.* 2 vols. New York: Alfred A. Knopf, 1984.

Naipaul, V. S. *Guerrillas.* New York: Alfred A. Knopf, 1975.

Piñon, Nélida. *The Republic of Dreams.* Translated by Helen Lane. New York: Alfred A. Knopf, 1989.

Putnam, Samuel. *Marvelous Journey: Four Centuries of Brazilian Literature.* New York: Alfred A. Knopf, 1948.

Rodríguez Monegal, Emir and Thomas Colchie, eds. *The Borzoi Anthology of Latin American Literature.* 2 vols. New York: Alfred A. Knopf, 1984.

Schiff, Stephen. "The Human Exile." *The New Yorker,* 23 May 1994, 60–71.

Silko, Leslie Marmon. *Ceremony.* New York: Viking Press, 1977.

Sollors, Werner. *Neither Black Nor White Yet Both: Thematic Explorations of Interracial Literature.* New York: Oxford University Press, 1997.

Stavans, Ilan. *The Hispanic Condition: Reflections on Culture and Identity in America.* New York: HarperCollins, 1995.

Stegner, Wallace. *Wolf Willow.* New York: Viking Press, 1966.

Sutherland, Ronald. "The Body-Odour of Race." In *Second Image: Comparative Studies in Québec/Canadian Literature.* Toronto: New Press, 1971. 28–59.

Swann, Brian, ed. *Smoothing the Ground: Essays on Native American Oral Literature.* Berkeley: University of California Press, 1983.

Tedlock, Dennis. *The Spoken Word and the Work of Interpretation.* Philadelphia: University of Pennsylvania Press, 1983.

Updike, John. *Brazil.* New York: Alfred A. Knopf, 1994.

Williams, Gregory Howard. *Life on the Color Line: The True Story of a White Boy Who Discovered He Was Black.* New York: Dutton, 1994.

Wright, Lawrence. "One Drop of Blood." *The New Yorker,* 25 July 1994, 45–55.

Contributors

Priscilla Archibald is Assistant Professor of Hispanic Studies at Northwestern University. She has published work on the literature and anthropology of the Andean region and has recently completed a manuscript entitled "Towards an Andean Modernity," which deals with the literary movement *Indigenismo* and the multidisciplinary work of José María Arguedas. Her current work deals with the relationship between lettered and popular culture in contemporary Lima.

Earl E. Fitz is Professor of Portuguese, Spanish, and Comparative Literature at Vanderbilt University, where he is also the Director of the Program in Comparative Literature. Professor Fitz teaches Brazilian literature, Latin American literature, and inter-American literature and is the author of *Rediscovering the New World: Inter-American Literature in a Comparative Context* and *Sexuality and Being in the Poststructuralist Universe of Clarice Lispector.* He is currently working on a comparative history of the development of narrative in the United States and Brazil.

Susan Gillman teaches World Literature and Cultural Studies at the University of California, Santa Cruz. She is the author of *Dark Twins: Imposture and Identity in Mark Twain's America* (University of Chicago Press, 1989), and co-editor of *Mark Twain's Pudd'nhead Wilson: Race, Conflict, and Culture* (Duke University Press, 1990). Her new book, *American Race Melodramas, 1877–1915,* is forthcoming from the University of Chicago Press.

Rolando Hinojosa-Smith is the E. C. Garwood Professor at the University of Texas at Austin. His main work, The Klail City Death Trip Series, has been translated into Chinese, Dutch, French, German, and Italian. Theses have been written on his work in the U.S. and in Germany, Italy, The Netherlands, Spain, and Sweden.

Monika Kaup is Assistant Professor of English at the University of Washington, Seattle. Her publications include essays on Chicano/a literature and inter-American literature in *American Literature* and *Discourse, Mad Intertextuality: Madness in Twentieth-Century Women's Writing* (Trier, Germany, 1993), and *Rewriting North American Borders in Chicano and Chicana Narrative* (Peter Lang, 2001).

Françoise Lionnet is Professor and Chair of French and Francophone studies at UCLA. She is the author of *Autobiographical Voices: Race, Gender, Self-Portraiture* and *Postcolonial Representations: Women, Literature, Identity*, the co-editor of a two-volume special issue of *Yale French Studies* on "Post/Colonial Conditions," and the editor of the forthcoming special issue of *L'Esprit créateur* on "Cities, Modernity, and Cultural Memory." Her essay on "A Politics of the 'We'? Autobiography, Race, and Nation" appeared in *American Literary History* in March 2001.

Zita C. Nunes is Assistant Professor of Literature at the University of Maryland, College Park. She is currently the Invited Fellow at the Society for the Humanities, Cornell University. She is the author of the forthcoming *Resisting Remainders: Racial Democracy in the Americas.*

Louis Owens is Professor of English and Native American Studies at the University of California at Davis. He is the author of numerous books and essays, including fiction, creative nonfiction, and critical studies. Among his most recent publications are *Mixedblood Messages: Literature, Film, Family, Place* (1998); *Dark River: A Novel* (1999); and *I Hear the Train: Invention and Reflection* (2001).

Rafael Pérez-Torres, Associate Professor of English at UCLA, has published articles on postmodernism, multiculturalism, and such contemporary American authors as Toni Morrison, John Rechy, and Luis Rafael Sánchez. In addition to his book *Movements in Chicano Poetry: Against Myths, Against Margins* (Cambridge University Press, 1995), he has published widely in such journals as *Cultural Critique, Aztlán*, and *Genre*. His current project is a book-length study of the relationship between racial mixture and the Chicano cultural imagination. He has chaired the MLA Executive Committee for the Division of Twentieth-Century American Literature and is on the editorial board of the journal *American Literature.*

Michèle Praeger teaches at the University of California at Davis. She has published a book on the New Novelist, Robert Pinget, and articles on twentieth-century French fiction. For the past few years she has been involved with Francophone and post-colonial studies and is writing a study entitled "The Imaginary Caribbean."

Debra J. Rosenthal is Assistant Professor of English at John Carroll University. She co-edited (with David S. Reynolds) *The Serpent in the Cup: Temperance in American Literature* and has completed a manuscript entitled "Imagining Miscegenation: Reading Race Mixture in Nineteenth Century Fictions of the Americas." She is currently editing a new edition of *Uncle Tom's Cabin* (Routledge Press).

Werner Sollors, Dr. phil. Freie Universität Berlin 1975, teaches Afro-American Studies and English at Harvard University. He is the author of *Beyond Ethnicity: Consent and Descent in American Culture* (1986) and *Neither Black Nor White Yet Both: Thematic Explorations of Interracial Literature* (1997) and editor of *Interracialism: Black-White Intermarriage in American History, Literature, and Law* (2000) and the forthcoming *Anthology of Interracial Literature: Black-White Contacts in the Old World and the New* (2002).

Doris Sommer, Professor of Latin American literature at Harvard University, is author of *Foundational Fictions: The National Romances of Latin America* (University of California Press, 1991) and *Proceed with Caution, when engaged by minority writing in the Americas* (Harvard University Press, 1999). She is currently writing on bilingual aesthetics.

Index

Abbott, Robert, 50, 56–60
Acosta, Oscar Zeta, 166, 173–177
African Americans. *See* blacks
Alarcón, Norma, 178
Alegría, Ciro, 109
Americas, literatures and studies of, xi–xiv, 66–70, 122–126, 135, 185–192. *See also* hemispheric American literatures and studies; New World literatures and studies
Andean discourse, xxv, 103–121, 123–126
Anzaldúa, Gloria, 187, 189; *Borderlands/La Frontera*, 192–197, 204–206, 236
Arguedas, José María, 103, 113–115, 120; *Deep Rivers*, 115–119
assimilation, 60, 221–222, 255–261
Avalos, David, xxix n. 5
Avellaneda, Gertrudis Gómez de, 30, 37, 42, 43

Bakhtin, M. M., xx–xxiii, xxvii, 180
Barthes, Roland, 229–230, 231–234, 237–238
Benítez-Rojo, Antonio, 187–188
Bernabé, Jean, xx, 78, 96–97. *See also* Chamoiseau, Patrick; Confiant, Raphaël
Bhabha, Homi K., 91, 92–93
Bialostosky, Don, xx–xxi, xxiii
binaries. *See* dualism
Black Atlantic, xxvi, 140–148, 149, 157
blacks: in Brazil, 56–61, 264–266; in Cuba, 30–36, 77–78, 146–147; in U.S., 6–20, 140, 148, 216–218. *See also* desegregation; racial: mixture; racial: purity; segregation
blood, as metaphor for biology in race mix-

ture, xii, xiv, xvi, xvii, xviii, 10, 129, 135, 243–246. *See also* miscegenation; racial: mixture; racial: purity
borderlands: Mexican and Mexican American, 163–165, 189–192, 213–225; Spanish, xxvi, 142–143, 157
Brazil, 245, 264–269; Afro-Brazilian responses to African American constructs of, 57–61; in the African American imagination, xxiv, 50–57
Brazil (novel by John Updike), 266–269
Breton, André, 90–92
Brontë, Emily. *See Wuthering Heights*
Brooks, Peter, 132–133

Cable, George Washington. *See Grandissimes, The*
Campbell, Maria, 187; *Halfbreed*, 197–206
Canada, 189–192, 197–204, 246–248, 262–264
Caribbean: discourse and writers of, xxiii–xiv, xix–xx, 75–85, 88–99, 187–188, 207 n.4, 208 n.11, 248–254; nineteenth-century history of, 76–77
Castillo, Ana. *See Sapogonia*
Ceremony, 258–261
Cervantes, Lorna Dee, 167, 178–181
Césaire, Suzanne, xx, 89–91, 98–99
Chamoiseau, Patrick, xx, 96–97. *See also* Bernabé, Jean; Confiant, Raphaël
Chicano/a discourse, xxiii, xxvi, 164–182, 192–197, 213–225, 255–258
Child, Lydia Maria, 124, 127, 133–134
colonialism, 189–192. *See also* transcolonial analysis

291